Front Office Management and Operations

Front Office Management and Operations

Linsley T. DeVeau, Ed. D., C.H.A., C.H.A.E., C.H.R.E.
Lynn University

Patricia M. DeVeau, Ed. D., C.H.A.
Lynn University

Nestor de J. Portocarrero, C.P.A.
Florida International University

Marcel Escoffier
Florida International University

Prentice Hall, Upper Saddle River, NJ 07458

Library of Congress Cataloging-in-Publication Data

Front office management and operations / Linsley T. DeVeau . . . [et al.].
　　　p.　　cm.
　　Includes index.
　　ISBN　0-13-334145-3
　　1. Hotel front desk personnel.　2. Hotel management.　I. DeVeau,
Linsley T., (date).
TX911.3.F75F76　1996
647.94'068—dc20　　　　　　　　　　　　　　　　　95-20165
　　　　　　　　　　　　　　　　　　　　　　　　　　　　CIP

Acquisitions editor:　*Robin Baliszewski*
Editorial/production supervision:　*Kim Gueterman*
Cover design:　*Jayne Conte*
Buyer:　*Ed O'Dougherty*

 © 1996 by Prentice-Hall, Inc.
Simon & Schuster/A Viacom Company
Upper Saddle River, New Jersey 07458

Printed in the United States of America
10　9　8　7　6　5　4　3　2　1

ISBN 0-13-334145-3

Prentice-Hall International (UK) Limited, *London*
Prentice-Hall of Australia Pty. Limited, *Sydney*
Prentice-Hall Canada Inc., *Toronto*
Prentice-Hall Hispanoamericana, S.A., *Mexico*
Prentice-Hall of India Private Limited, *New Delhi*
Prentice-Hall of Japan, Inc., *Tokyo*
Simon & Schuster Asia Pte. Ltd., *Singapore*
Editora Prentice-Hall do Brasil, Ltda., *Rio de Janeiro*

This book is dedicated to our families.
You are the ones who made this possible.
God bless you all.

Contents

3   RESERVATIONS SYSTEMS   48

4   ROOM RATES   77

Preface

Front Office Management and Operations explores the operations and procedures involved in managing the front office area of a lodging operation. Although we use *front office* in our title (as do most colleges in their course titles) the book is ideally suited for a rooms division management course as well and can be used at the two year or four year college/university levels.

It is our belief that writing about the technical aspects of the front office is only part of our mission. We have emphasized customer service throughout the book. The chapter on safety and security of guests and employees addresses one of the most pressing problems facing lodging managers today.

Front Office Management and Operations provides in depth coverage of topics such as technology and accounting and budgeting procedures, as well as training programs and reservations systems. In this book we have included an entire chapter on the latest technology in the rooms division. With the increasing utilization of computers in the lodging industry this is an area of great importance. In addition to covering the night audit, we also provide a detailed analysis of budgeting principles and their specific applications in the rooms division. These skills are essential for every front office manager.

ACKNOWLEDGMENTS

The authors extend their most sincere thanks to all the people who have supported this project. Many of these people and organizations are credited in the book. We also wish to thank: Mr. John Parker, Director of Operations, Concord Resort Hotel; Mr. Robert Thrailkill, Executive Assistant Front Office Manager, Fontainbleau Hilton in Miami Beach; Mrs. Marilyn Harmon, Lynn University; Professor Richard Allerdyce, Lynn University; and Ms. Robin Baliszewski, Executive Editor, Prentice Hall.

As with any book, a reader may wish to discuss a specific item in the text. We encourage readers to present all questions to any one of the authors.

Yours in hospitality,

Linsley T. DeVeau, Ed.D.

Front Office Management and Operations

CHAPTER 1

An Introduction to the Lodging Industry

CHAPTER OBJECTIVES

After reading this chapter you will understand:

- The historical origins of the lodging industry.
- What types of ownership exist in the industry.
- How various types of lodging properties are designed to appeal to different markets.
- How a lodging property is organized.
- What types of services are supplied in a typical lodging property.

INTRODUCTION

The lodging industry is an exciting one in which to work. Throughout history, the lodging industry has provided travelers a "home away from home." It has been a stage—not only for many a great politician and performer, but also for the average citizen—a place where a person can have his or her moment in the spotlight. Made up of hotels, motor inns, and inns, the lodging industry has provided, and will continue to provide, services as simple as guest rooms for overnight stays and as complex as wedding receptions, anniversary parties, conventions, extended vacations, and banquets.

THE NATURE OF THE LODGING INDUSTRY

History

The roots of the U.S. lodging industry can, as with many of our customs and institutions, be traced back to England. In the early years of our country's growth, the colonial inns were patterned after the English inns. These early inns were situated in seaport areas. From the beginning, the colonial inns differed from the English inns in that the colonial inns were operated for anyone who could pay the lodging price, and most people at that time could afford the modest cost. This is in contrast to the English inns, which were operated primarily for the aristocracy.

The first building constructed specifically for use as a hotel was built in 1794 in New York City and named the City Hotel. Following its opening, other cities, such as Boston, Baltimore, and Philadelphia, built similar hotels. While these hotels were crude by today's standards, they did represent a departure from the colonial inn, which was always a private house that had been turned into an inn.

The lodging industry as we know it today had its start in Boston in 1829 with the opening of a first-class hotel named the Tremont House. At that time, this was the largest building constructed in the United States, and it made this country the leader in hotel management.

When architect Isaiah Rogers designed the Tremont House, he established himself as the leading expert in hotel architecture. Prior to the Tremont House, the colonial inns were designed with several beds in a few rooms, which amounted to a communal sleeping arrangement among its guests. The Tremont House revolutionized the industry by having private rooms for both single and double occupancy. Other innovations were a lock on each guest room door, a bowl and pitcher in each room, free soap provided for each room, French cuisine in the hotel restaurant, a bell staff to serve the guests, and an "enunciator" that allowed the front desk to communicate with its guests in their rooms. The importance of training in the lodging industry also had its start at the Tremont House, where each employee was carefully selected and trained in the proper techniques of his job and in guest service.

A revolution had also begun in hotel design, and every city in the country wanted a hotel bigger and better than the Tremont House. The nineteenth century saw many new hotels being built around the United States—the Astor House in New York, the Grand Pacific in Chicago, the Planters in St. Louis, and the Place in San Francisco, to name a few. In 1893, one of the oldest and most famous hotels, the original Waldorf Astoria, was built, and it was one of the first to provide a bathroom in each guest room. The current Waldorf Astoria is a more recent building.

As the twentieth century approached, two major changes occurred in society that put an increased demand on the lodging industry—the increasing numbers of commercial travelers and the improving methods of transportation. Ellsworth M. Statler would prove to be the person who accepted these challenges and created a product to satisfy them. In 1908, Statler opened the Buffalo Statler, which has been considered the first "commercial hotel." This is why Statler has been called the father of the modern hotel. Many of the changes that he made in his hotel are commonplace today, but were then considered revolutionary. Some of his creations included the use of fire doors, the placement of the keyhole above the doorknob to make it easier to find in a dark hall, the installation of a switch for the light just inside the door of each room so that the guest could enter a lighted room, the installation of private bathrooms, the provision of circulating ice water in each room, a free morning newspaper, and a full-length mirror in each room. The hotel was marketed as a destination, a fine place to travel to and to stay at rather than just a minimal accommodation for those traveling between destinations. The Buffalo Statler was a huge success and led to the formation of the Statler Hotel Company.

During World War I, the industry experienced relatively slow growth, but the Roaring Twenties saw the development of hotel projects as never before. The Stevens Hotel, now the Conrad Hilton, was built in Chicago and for many years held the distinction of being the world's largest hotel with 3,000 rooms. Such large properties required very exacting systems and procedures. It was during the 1920s that the Uniform System of Accounts for Hotels was devised, a system of record keeping which is with us to this day. A new Waldorf Astoria was started during this time, replacing the original one that was torn down to make way for the Empire State building. This was a period of tremendous growth and excitement in the lodging industry, and every major metropolitan area of the country felt the effects.

However, what was considered by many to be the golden age of the hotel business was soon brought to a screeching halt. The year 1930 brought the Great Depression, and, with it, the worst time the lodging industry had ever seen. It is said that during this period more than 85 percent of the hotels were in receivership or liquidation.

By 1940 the industry was already getting back on its feet and about to enter a period of high occupancy that has not been equaled to this day. The start of World War II created a flow of people around the country that created a demand for lodging accommodations which could not be met. Military personnel, people relocating, business people, and families all on the move at once raised occupancy levels into the 90 percent range. With these high occupancy levels, profits were correspondingly high. Still, while this can be looked back upon as a period of high performance, it was not a time when operation or services reached an equally high level, since there was a lack of trained personnel.

With the end of the 1940s came a downturn in the high occupancy levels that hotels had enjoyed during the war years. But just on the industry's horizon was a man whose dream would revolutionize the U.S. lodging industry far beyond anyone's expectations. This man was Kemmous Wilson, the founder of Holiday Inns. After an unpleasant vacation with his family, due to poor and overpriced lodging accommodations, Wilson decided to embark on a venture in the lodging industry. He felt there was a void that could be filled by the provision of roadside lodgings. Thus in 1952, he opened the first Holiday Inn near Memphis, Tennessee. Some of the features of the Holiday Inns were large guest rooms, two double beds in each room, a restaurant, an on-site swimming pool, free TV, free ice, and in-room telephones. Improved highway systems and automobiles, combined with the American public's desire to travel, caused the rapid growth of Holiday Inns, as well as other hotel chains, such as Travelodge and Ramada Inn.

The 1960s, 1970s, and 1980s have seen innovations and developments that have had lasting effects on the lodging industry. The following, adopted from the *Cornell Quarterly*, May 1985, represents a few of these major events:

1961 • AM/FM radios were installed in luxury suites in existing Sheraton hotels and in all new Sheraton hotel rooms.
   • Marriott opened the $5 million Philadelphia Motor Inn as its fourth property.
   • Hotel referral systems were considered to be in their infancy.

1962 • Swimming pools grow in number—363,000 in use.
   • The American Hotel Association becomes the American Hotel & Motel Association (AH & MA).
   • The world's tallest hotel opens in New York, the Americana with 2,000 rooms. Every guest room has a 19-inch TV, an AM/FM radio, and a miniature bar/refrigerator.

1963 • The American Automobile Association starts its rating system for hotels and motels—two years after Mobil had started its guide.
   • Three new motor hotel chains start: Friendship Inns, Rodeway Inns, and American Motor Inns.

1964 • A concierge service is offered at the Palmer House Towers.
   • A coin-operated bed massage unit is offered in the Fantasy Motel at Disneyland.
   • The wearing of name tags by service personnel gains popularity.

1965 • A plastic kit, containing a shoeshine kit, laundry detergent, cigarettes, a cuticle stick, a sewing kit, and aspirin, is given to guests at the Towne House Motor Inn in Rochester, New York.
   • Holiday Inn installs an IBM computer reservation system, and names it the Holidex.

1966 • Travelodge opens its first franchised property; previously, the 350 lodges were opened under co-owned agreements.

• Caesar's Palace opens in Las Vegas with a mllion dollar opening.

• Walt Disney makes it public that he plans to develop the 50 square miles of land he owns in Florida as Disney World.

1967 • Howard Hughes bought the Desert Inn and the Sands Inn in Las Vegas.

• A new property-to-property reservation system with no charge to the guest is started by Travelodge.

• Suites that can accommodate guests in wheelchairs are available at the Holiday Inn in Jacksonville, Florida.

1968 • Marriott Hotels can now be franchised.

• Sheraton Hotels accepts the Bank Americard (Visa) at its 168 properties.

• The one-thousandth Holiday Inn is opened.

1969 • An executive floor is opened on the fourth floor of the Tutwiler Hotel in Birmingham, Alabama. It includes plush carpeting, floor porter, free coffee, and turndown service.

• Ramada Inns and Quality Motels will accept the Master Charge credit card (MasterCard).

1970 • Funding approval is given for the Las Vegas Convention Center.

• The Albert Pick hotel chain puts color TVs in all of their properties, as other chains follow.

• Travelodge opens its "USA Deck"; it has operators that speak French, Spanish, German, and Japanese to assist foreign travelers in the United States.

1971 • Disney World opens in Orlando, Florida.

• Holiday Inn now has properties in all 50 states.

• John Portman goes down in lodging history for his design of the atrium lobby in the Regency Hyatt House–O'Hare, in Chicago.

• Academy Award–level movies are available in-room at the Gateway Downtowner Motor Inn, Newark, New Jersey.

1972 • Las Vegas sees the MGM built on one of its famous four corners.

• NCR ceases production of the NCR 2000 posting machine.

1973 • Three Marriotts in the Washington, DC, area experiment in setting up nonsmoker floors.

• Sheraton–Anaheim tries in-room movies at no charge to guests.

1974 • Energy conservation becomes a hot topic, and it demonstrates that the lodging industry is doing its best to save energy. Hotel employees are instructed in ways to save energy. Travelodge cuts off heat to unused rooms.

1975 • Little-known Donald J. Trump negotiates with Hyatt for the purchase of the Commodore Hotel.

• People over age 55 who join Days Inn's "September Days" club will get a 10 percent discount at all Days Inns.

• A $7 million liability award is given to a youth who broke his neck diving into a hotel swimming pool.

• Local and regional telephone companies can now sell telephone equipment thanks to the FCC; this takes away AT&T's monopoly.

1976 • Atlantic City is given the go-ahead for casino gambling.

1977 • The Statler and the New York Hilton rent pocket beepers to guests for $5 per day.

• Computers are seen as being needed; however, the quality of service the guests will receive is still in doubt.

1978 • After a year-long study of overbooking in the travel industry, the Federal Trade Commission takes no action.

1979 • A "Direct Response Line" is installed at the Marriott Essex House, enabling guests to have direct contact with management.

• A study conducted by Procter & Gamble finds that guests use convenience, appearance, and price to select a hotel the first visit, but on repeat stays, cleanliness and good service are most important.

• 236 hotels now have Home Box Office (HBO).

• New technology in the telephone department is starting to change the attitude that it has to function at a loss.

1980 • Trusthouse Forte segments its hotels by service level, not location.

1981 • Red Roof Inn starts fully equipping its new inns for handicapped guests.

1982 • Treadway claims to be the oldest lodging chain in the United States while celebrating its seventieth birthday.

• FCC regulations allow hotels to resell long-distance phone calls; call accounting system vendors are prevalent.

1983 • Fire protection information will be listed in AAA tourbooks.

• A concierge is seen as being mandatory for all hotels who wish to offer quality service.

1984 • All-suite hotels will be built by Marriott.

1985 • Computer rentals are available on the thirty-second floor of the Hyatt Regency Chicago.

1986 • The Tax Reform Act of 1986 changes the investment climate and hotel property values decline.

• The industry stagnates, virtually no new hotels are built in the United States for the next six years.

1993 • The hotel industry, having suffered from overbuilding, begins to consolidate.

• New building of hotels in the United States begins.

Lodging Affiliation

During the history of the lodging industry, five types of hotel affiliations (owner-ship arrangements) have emerged. Each of these has been significant in the growth of the industry and its various operations. The five affiliations are owner-operated hotels, owner-managed hotels, independent hotels, franchised hotels, and chain-operated hotels.

Owner-operated hotels are those properties that are able to operate without the assistance of a staff or payroll outside the owner and his family. Today the small bed-and-breakfast inns found throughout the country are examples of the way this type of lodging establishment has been able to survive and even thrive in today's market. These are, perhaps, the lodging facilities most similar to the old inns of the distant past.

Owner-managed hotels function much the same as the owner-operated hotels. The main difference is that the owner-managed hotel hires the necessary number of line and staff employees to operate the day-by-day hotel while at the same time retaining the management of it by the owner. Many famous families have owned and managed hotels over the years. The Catskill resort area of upstate New York has family-run hotels whose names, such as Grossinger's or the Concord, are known throughout the industry. The families impart a uniqueness to their property which hotel chains just cannot duplicate.

Independent hotels operate separately from any chain affiliation. In this type of operation, the owner does not manage the hotel directly but instead hires a professional manager who exercises direct control over staffing the hotel and running it. This type of operation is seen more frequently than the previous two in large hotel operations. Independent hotels, however, have shown a decrease in number in recent years due to the two forms of operations listed below.

Franchised hotels are properties that are owned by investors but whose operation and even design are controlled by a large, nationally recognizable chain. As can be seen in Exhibit 1-1, the dominant force among the largest 25 chains in the United States are the properties that are run by the chain but whose ownership is actually in the hands of private investors. Through franchising, chains have been able to multiply in size without investors involving themselves in an equity position on a hotel project. This means that they can expand and own many hotels without investing much money into the properties. In franchising, the owner of the hotel enters into an agreement with a hotel chain that enables the owner's hotel to use the name of the chain on his hotel. In addition to this brand-name recognition benefit, a franchise agreement will provide advertising and promotional programs to support it. A centralized reservation system with a toll-free number for guests to call is, by far, one of the greatest benefits to a franchisee. On

EXHIBIT 1-1 25 LARGEST LODGING CHAINS IN THE UNITED STATES

Chain	Total Rooms	Total Properties	Managed Properties	Franchised Properties	Independent Properties	Other Status
Holiday Inn	264,579	1,409	142	1,260	0	7
Best Western	166,152	1,835	37	5	1,793	0
Hilton	103,318	286	49	236	0	1
Sheraton	101,297	388	59	327	0	2
Days Inn	89,748	627	48	558	3	18
Ramada	83,243	519	40	455	0	24
Marriott	76,949	169	124	36	0	9
Quality Inn	61,636	475	12	461	0	2
Howard Johnson	54,246	450	124	324	1	1
Motel 6	48,896	433	425	2	3	3
Hyatt	46,967	85	82	3	0	0
Comfort Inn	37,286	410	0	409	1	0
Econo Lodge	31,783	420	0	385	0	35
Super 8	28,637	449	0	428	0	21
Travelodge	27,813	403	1	48	3	351
La Quinta	24,807	195	185	8	0	2
Radisson	23,113	89	29	59	0	1
Embassy Suites	21,577	90	44	38	0	8
Westin Hotel	20,290	33	33	0	0	0
Red Roof Inn	19,627	179	171	0	0	8
Hampton Inn	18,922	151	16	135	0	0
Rodeway Inn	17,733	153	0	120	0	29
Stouffer Hotel	13,265	32	31	0	4	1
Residence Inn	12,941	112	0	20	0	92
Courtyard by Marriott	11,957	82	0	0	0	82

the operations level, a franchise system, because of its size, is able to employ hundreds of experts to act as a resource for the hotels as well as to provide manuals for operating the hotel and training its staff. So that all hotels in the franchise system maintain the quality standards set by the chain, an inspection system is set up to assure that quality exists throughout the chain. Those hotels that do not meet the standards risk being disenfranchised. While franchising offers these many benefits, it is not without cost. In franchising the owner is charged an initial licensing fee of several hundred dollars per room for a minimum of 100 rooms. Charges such as royalty and advertising fees are accessed, based on a percentage of gross revenue per year. The hotel is also charged for each reservation as well as for the equipment and setup of the reservations system. Chains often restrict the usage of in-room materials in that most materials must be logo-bearing items. This use of the logo is, however, an important marketing tool as it means a connection with a brand-name establishment. All chains work hard for brand-name recognition.

Chain-operated hotels are the fifth type of affiliation. There are two different forms of organization under this type. They are chain-owned and operated and those managed by the chain through a management contract. In the first organization, the hotel chain actually owns the property as well as operates it with their management team. The second type, the management contract, gained popularity in the early 1970s and continues to grow today. By contract, management firms agree to manage the hotel for specific financial remuneration, which is spelled out in the contract along with the details of the administrative, the operations, and the marketing services and support that will be provided. This form of management differs from the franchised hotel in that the franchised hotel may be operated by a third-party management firm (a management company with no financial connection to the chain but who sells its service to manage all types of properties).

Market Segmentation

In hotel marketing, *market segmentation* is the process of pursuing a marketing strategy where the total potential market is broken down into homogeneous groups of guests, each of which responds differently to the marketing mix of the hotel. In other words, companies often design products which appeal to specific groups of customers. Naturally this is an expensive process, so marketing segmentation usually takes place only after companies realize that the current product they are offering is not sufficient to continue the growth of their company. This is exactly what has happened in the lodging industry. Hotel chains were building their properties in the most desirable locations and satisfying the demand for the traditional hotel property in these areas (this is known as *marketing through location*). Therefore, in order to expand it was necessary to create new products that would satisfy the lodging demand of a large enough subset of the market who wanted to stay at a specific location, but who might also want a specific type of accommodation.

Financial backing of hotel projects has been increasingly attractive to financial institutions. With this increased availability of funds, chains found themselves in a position to create new products that would satisfy the demands of these subsets of customers. Numerous market segments were exploited. For example, those travelers who were staying at a given location for a longer period of time were being offered apartment-sized multiroom accommodations. Families could stay in rooms with separate kitchen facilities. The vacation traveler who was traveling by car on a limited budget could find good, clean rooms for as little as $6 per night. It seemed as though everyone who had any kind of preference could find a lodging facility that addressed that preference.

Along with this increased segmentation has come a shifting in emphasis in the lodging industry from an operation mentality to a marketing one. With the proliferation of these new segments has come a need to direct the energies of corporate-level as well as operations-level staff to developing and marketing each new segment. To be successful, lodging operators must analyze each homogeneous segment and design the appropriate product for it. However, all of this must be accomplished while providing a high level of hospitable service.

One of the negatives of all this market segmentation comes in trying to clearly define each segment as a separate and distinct product. This is, if not impossible, extremely close to it. The reason for this is that there is such a high degree of overlapping among the various segments. Lodging properties can be broken out into five major property types: economy, limited service, middle market, first-class luxury, and all-suite. Exhibit 1-2 lists each major type and lists the appropriate brand name for each segment.

Lodging properties are still classified by location. The five major locations used are the following: center city, suburban, airport, highway, and resort. While the location of a property may have a great deal to do with the reason people frequent a given area, there has been an influx of most of the different accommodation-related segments into all five of these locations.

Size of a property is also frequently used to classify properties. Classification by size is usually done by three categories: small, medium, and large. The number of rooms in the property is the size determinant. Small hotels generally have less than 125 rooms. Medium hotels generally have between 125 and 500 rooms. Large properties are generally said to be those with more than 500 rooms. But these room numbers are by no means universal. In Hawaii, for example, a small hotel is any property of less than 500 rooms, with the average property being about 1,000 rooms and the large property having 2,000 or more rooms! This contrasts with Miami, which has hotels ranging in size from 20 rooms to about 1,200 rooms.

The type of guest attracted to the property is another way to classify different properties. Two types of guests are commonly referred to in the industry—commercial and vacationer. Commercial means someone traveling on business, while a vacationer is on holiday. Each of these types of travelers can be further broken down into individual or group travelers, and transient or destination travelers. Individuals are people traveling either on their own or as a family. Groups are two or more individual travelers, often taking advantage of group discounts or employing a tour guide. A transient means someone (or some group) that is just passing through on the way to some other destination. A destination is the ultimate travel goal of the individual or group. Hence, two families traveling on a prepackaged tour to Disney World might be transient while traveling (let's say by bus and staying at night in various towns along the way) but become destination travelers once they arrive at Disney World.

The American Hotel and Motel Association in its 1988 lodging industry profile lists seven types of customers in the lodging industry market mix: vacation, 29 percent; business, 22 percent; conference, 19 percent; personal or family

EXHIBIT 1-2 BRAND MARKETING STRATEGIES—BRAND NAMES

Lower	Middle	Upper	Limited-Service	Full-Service	Full-Service	Full-Service	Limited-Service	Full-Service	Extended Stay
Motel 6	Red Roof Inn	Days Inn	Courtyard	Holiday Inn	Mariott	Four Seasons	Comfort Suite	Embassy Suite	Residence Inn
Sleep Inn	Days Inn	Comfort Inn	Clubhouse Inn	Ramada Inn	Hyatt	Park Hyatt	Lexington Suite	Sheraton Suite	Hawthorn Suite
Microtel Inn	Comfort Inn	Travelodge	Park Square Inn	Sheraton	Westin	Exclusive	Amerisuite	Clarion Suite	Quality-Residency
Regal 8	Travelodge	Econo Lodge	Compri	Hilton	Omni	Ritz	Best Suite	Guest Quarters	Woodfin Suite
Sixpence Inn	Econo Lodge	La Quinta	Cresthil	Quality Inn	Registry	Carlton	Imperial Suite	Radisson Suite	Neighborhood Inn
Scottish Inn	Super 8 Motels	Hampton Inn		Radisson	Doubletree		Sterling Suite	Pickett Suite	
Allstar Inn	Knights Inn	Rodeway Inn		Days Hotel	Royce		Manchester Suite	Bristol Suite	
E-Z 8 Motels	Budgetel Inn	Drury Inn		Howard Johnson Lodge	Clarion		Woodfield Suite	Ramada Suite	
Thrift Lodge	Rodeway Inn	Susse Chalet		Park Inn	Crowne Plaza		Bradbury Suite	Hilton Suite	
	Shoney's Inn	Country Hearth Inn			Howard Johnson Plaza Hotel		Luxford Suite	Hyatt Suite	
	Fairfield Inn	Shilo Inn			Hilton		Days Suite	Park Suite	
	Arborgate Inn	Signature Inn			Sheraton		Sunrise Suite	Marriott Suite	
	Best Inns	Cross Country Inn			Forte		Travelodge Suite	Doubletree Suite	
	Luxury Budget	Dillon Inn						Howard Johnson Plaza Suite	
	Red Carpet	Country Hospitality Inn						Raintree Suite	
	Cricket Inn	Lees Inn						Viscount Suite	
	Envoy Inn	Cypress Inn							
	Roadstar Inn	Franklin Inn							
		Luxbury							
		Wellesley Inn							

business, 17 percent; weekend trips, 7 percent; government/military business, 4 percent; and moving jobs or residences, 2 percent.

Four types of lodging operations that deserve special attention are the all-suite, economy, conference center, and resort segments. Although there may be similarities in the types of guests attracted by these operations, each is significant because of its distinctive characteristics. Further explanation is needed.

All-Suite

All-suite hotels make up the fastest growing segment of the lodging industry today. The reasons for this are many but some of the more salient are the following: all-suite hotels fall in the midrange of room rates between economy-oriented and luxury-oriented guests; guests see the all-suite hotel as an excellent value—instead of getting one guest room, in an all-suite, two rooms, a living area, and sleeping room are provided; kitchenettes, which often include a sink, refrigerator, stove, microwave oven, coffee maker, dishes, glasses, and flatware, are also provided. Guests that are attracted to all-suite hotels are 60 percent business travelers, 22 percent leisure travelers, 11 percent conference attendees, and 7 percent other types. Business travelers find the all-suite hotel an excellent place for relocation and extended stays for training, and an ideal room arrangement for meetings and interviews. Families traveling enjoy the convenience of having two separate rooms and a kitchenette that would be unavailable in most hotels. The benefits to the developers of all-suite hotels are many as well: a smaller parcel of land is needed due to the lack of banquet and restaurant facilities in many all-suites. This correspondingly reduces the number of parking spaces needed and the amount of public space that is needed. According to Laventhol & Horwath, all-suites have a higher level of occupancy and a higher median rate of occupancy than all other hotels.

Economy

The economy lodging operation is commonly referred to as a *budget* hotel or motel. In the early years of the budget segment, the rooms were very Spartan in design and the amenities scarce, even to the point of charging an extra day to turn on the in-room television. Today's economy rates are still considerably less, half the rate, than a full-service midrange hotel. In most cases, economy properties still do not have restaurants or lounges, but today's economy properties are far from Spartan in design and in amenities. In fact, many new economy property rooms are superior to the older midrange motor hotels that they share markets with. Cost of construction per room and cost of operations for economy properties are less than midrange motor hotels due to the lack of facilities and the smaller number of employees needed to operate the property. According to Laventhol & Horwath, the market for economy properties on the average is business 58.9 percent; government, 31.5 percent; leisure, 4.9 percent; and conference participants and others, 4.7 percent.

Conference Center

With the increase in meetings taking place today and the demand for more sophisticated facilities for these meetings, the Conference Center segments are increasing. Conference Center operators are trying to make the distinctions known between such centers and hotels that are simply adding "Conference Center" to their name. Exhibit 1-3 lists the seven types of conference centers, their clientele, and their identifying characteristics. Some outstanding traits of a professional conference center that will not be found in a hotel (even one that adds the words "Conference Center" to its name) are a professionally trained staff of conference coordinators, all of the necessary equipment and supplies needed to conduct the many various types of meetings, and the planning of space in the hotel so that meeting attendees are not distracted by groups with a less serious purpose. The International Association of Conference Centers (IACC) is attempting to inform meeting organizers of the importance of these differences when they are planning a meeting.

Resort

Over the years, the resorts of the early 1900s have changed from seasonal to year-round operations. No longer can resort hotels, or any hotel, survive only on a market of leisure travelers. Resorts can be categorized into three types of properties: convention-oriented, area, or recreational. Convention resorts primarily serve meetings and conferences. An area resort is one that attracts guests because of some local attraction. Recreational resorts are chosen for their unique recreational facilities. With the increase emphasis on enlarging their market share, both area and recreational resorts have absorbed the convention-oriented category. Exhibit 1-4 shows that recreational and area resorts receive more than 30 percent of their business from business and conference attendees.

Recreational resorts provide business people attending a conference a place to relax and unwind after a full day of work, which adds to the improvement of the attendees productivity. The close contact with their co-workers away from the workplace can also help business people to improve their relationships with colleagues when they return to the workplace. These benefits have helped to shift convention and business meetings to resort locations.

Some of the factors that contributed to the growth of the resort business were lower travel costs—airfares and fuel costs—and the increase in international terrorism, which slowed down Americans traveling overseas. The increase in the number of two-income families also caused more getaway vacations to resort facilities.

While any of the hotel segments may offer meal plans, resorts are among the few which still do so. There are three ways that people are fed in a hotel. By far, the most common way is the European Plan (or EP). In an EP hotel the guest pays for all meals consumed as a separate charge. That means that the guests can use any of the hotel's dining facilities as often or as infrequently as they wish.

EXHIBIT 1-3   CHARACTERISTICS OF CONFERENCE CENTERS

Type of Center	Clientele	Unique Characteristics
Executive	Specialized meetings for middle-to-upper-level management.	Meetings gravitate toward training and strategy/planning sessions, including board meetings.
		Meetings range from 20 to 300 people.
Corporate	Two Types: (1)Exclusive for parent company and subsidiaries. (2)Priority bookings for in-house use with facilities available for outside organizations.	Training for supervisory and management personnel for parent company. For outside users, meeting purposes are similar to executive centers. Outside organizations increase utilization and offset costs of maintaining centers.
Resort	Group meeting business is primary market.	Meetings for educational as well as training purposes, and incentive or reward programs. Have extensive recreational facilities which can affect meeting outcome. Occupancy generally is influenced by seasonal demand. Fastest-growing segment of conference center industry.
College/University	Adult education programs, academic meetings. Large corporate or entry-level meetings geared toward management training or continuing education.	Many of these centers were developed as a result of the information explosion and declining undergraduate enrollment. Advantageous to have a recognized, talented faculty.
Not-for-profit	Mainly selected groups, to maintain tax advantage status. Center may be for the primary use of parent organization.	Usually offer a full array of facilities as found in other conference center segments.
Nonresidential	Same as executive, college/university, or not-for-profit.	No sleeping accommodations, conferees usually are locals. Located in urban or suburban areas with high concentration of corporate offices nearby. Appeals to users wishing to avoid the high cost of air travel.
Auxiliary	Conferees are a mixture of executive and resort clientele.	An auxiliary conference center is one segment of a larger organization. They are similar in all respects to the other types of centers.

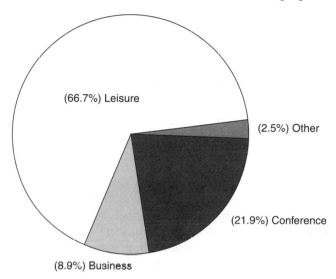

(66.7%) Leisure

(2.5%) Other

(21.9%) Conference

(8.9%) Business

Exhibit 1-4   Sources of Resort Business: Type of Guest Staying at Resorts

They may charge any meals consumed (if they desire) to their account at the front desk. Some resorts (especially those which have been in business for many years) still offer either the American Plan (AP) or the Modified American Plan (MAP). The AP includes all meals in the price of the room. Like a cruise ship, the hotel guest in an AP hotel can eat meals "for free" in the dining areas. By "free" we mean that there is no separate charge for the meals; their cost is factored into the room rate. The MAP hotel allows guests to eat breakfast and dinner or just breakfast in the hotel without incurring an additional charge. (Think of the MAP hotel as being any hotel that offers less than three meals but at least one a day included in the price of the room.) Economy hotels have begun using the MAP program in their advertising when they offer free breakfasts. While no statistics are available concerning the popularity of the three plans, clearly most hotels are on the EP, in that the room rate is strictly for the rental of the room. The next most popular plan is the MAP, with economy hotels and others offering "free" breakfasts, and with many resorts offering breakfast and dinner inclusive in the room rate. The AP is rarely found except in resorts or on cruise ships. The popularity of the AP in those situations is usually because there are no alternative sources of food convenient to the property—try ordering out when you are on a cruise ship!

PHYSICAL COMPONENTS OF A LODGING FACILITY

The Guest Room

No matter what type of property we are talking about, the most important aspects of it in the minds of the guests are the guest rooms and bathrooms. These two items leave an impression on the guests that is far more lasting than the other aspects of the hotel. Guests today demand more from guest rooms than ever before. Prior to a guest's arrival at the hotel, he or she has a preconceived notion as to what the hotel and guest rooms are going to be like. This we can call *expectation.* When the expectation level of the guest is not met, or possibly exceeded, a negative reaction is going to be experienced. Ultimately, this will result in a lack of repeat business for that property and for the chain with which the individual hotel is associated. Decor is an important aspect in satisfying the guest in that the decor of the guest room must follow through consistently with the decor of the public areas of the hotel. Guest room layout varies with the size of the room, but no matter what the size, ease of movement throughout the room is of primary importance when furniture is being arranged.

Furnishing the guest room depends a great deal on the identity of the property's targeted markets. The space limitations of the room and the public safety and fire department regulations must be considered. In addition, consideration for the handicapped traveler must be taken into account. Business and corporate travelers have generated a need for a more upscale type of accommodations, called the executive floor or executive tower. Primary emphasis is placed on a much higher level of service and a lounge area specifically available to these guests. In many instances, a special check-in area and/or concierge area is provided for the guests staying at this level. Usually a lounge is available for use only by these guests, which helps to set this level apart even more and to add an almost clublike atmosphere to the guest's stay. This type of setting is particularly attractive to those conducting business meetings. Surprisingly enough, even though the rates are higher, the occupancy in many of these properties is also higher.

Exhibit 1-5 lists some rather important do's and don'ts for designing guest rooms.

There are a variety of guest rooms available to today's travelers. The following is a list defining the different types, and the more common forms of abbrevations used in the industry to designate each type. Double (D) is a room that has one double bed that can be occupied by one or two guests, single or double occupancy. Double/double (D/D) is a room with two double beds that is usually occupied in one of four ways:

1. When one person is in the room, a D/D is rented under a "single" category when all one-bed rooms are sold out; in this case, the guest is most often charged a rate that corresponds with a one-bed room.
2. Triple—three guests in the room.
3. Quad—four guests in the room.
4. A double/double may be further expanded by adding a roll-away, which is a bed that folds up lengthwise and is easily stored until needed.

Queen (Q) is a room that has one queen-size bed and is capable of accommodating one or two guests. Many hotels are deviating from the traditional double/double and going to a queen/queen layout. The thought here is that two

EXHIBIT 1-5   GUEST-ROOM DESIGN GUIDE

Do's:

✔ Use two lamps or dual-light fixtures at head of bed.

✔ Include two vanities, one in the bathroom and one in the dressing area.

✔ In small rooms, drapery treatments should include a sheer curtain.

✔ Use light palettes and tone-on-tone in small rooms. Also use fewer and smaller patterns.

✔ Include French doors (or sliding doors) and full or false balcony.

✔ Divide deep room with L-shaped desk to create separate work and sleep areas.

✔ Use patterns and color schemes that complement the type of hotel (resort, business, or other).

✔ Create an atmosphere that is consistent with the public areas.

✔ Install adequate lighting in entryway and at vanities.

✔ Use adjustable lighting at bedside and in working or lounge areas.

✔ Protect carpets from mildew with antimicrobial treatment.

Don'ts:

✔ Avoid filling the rooms with too much furniture, especially pieces with no function.

✔ Do not use fluorescent light—it is hard on the eyes and unflattering.

✔ Do not block drapery controls or heating/cooling units with furniture.

✔ Do not use swag lamps.

✔ Avoid placing the bed against the bathroom wall in standard-configuration rooms.

✔ Do not use large or busy patterns in small rooms.

✔ Do not compensate for a large room by using oversized furniture.

queen-size beds are more comfortable and similar to what the guests are accustomed to in their own homes. King (K) is a room that contains one king-size bed. These rooms are less common than the previously mentioned types, but because of the added luxury and the price-value relationships, they are becoming more popular. The important point to be brought out is that a king-size bed and linens are not that much more costly when compared with the additional revenue this type of room can generate.

Mini or junior suites have become very popular, as witnessed by the rapid growth of the all-suite hotels. These rooms have a sitting area and sleeping area all located within the same room. A suite, as mentioned above, is extremely popular with many different market segments for a variety of reasons. Suites provide a living area separate from the sleeping room and are usually found in one- or two-bedroom layouts that closely resemble a one- or two-bedroom apartment. When property food and beverage services are limited (as is the case with the new all-suite, extended-stay properties), a small kitchenette is often provided in the living area, which includes a sink, dishwasher, stove, microwave oven, refrigerator, and various small appliances.

Hotel Amenities

Amenities can be broken down into two main categories—in-room and out-of-room. Items falling in the out-of-room category include a swimming pool, a cocktail lounge, an exercise room, and so forth. The in-room category of amenities have by far received the most attention. This is because guests will pay more for a room when amenities are provided. Exhibit 1-6 shows the change in guest preferences for a room from one week where no amenities were provided to another week when amenities were provided. As can be seen, guests in all categories were happier with their room when amenities were provided.

Procter & Gamble has conducted numerous surveys to determine which amenities are most important to hotel guests. The results of these surveys have shown that guests should be provided two bars of soap—a 2.5 ounce bar of deodorant soap for the shower and a 1.5 ounce bar of nondeodorant soap for the vanity. Shampoo is one of the items guests expect to find in their room, so a shampoo and conditioner combination is quite popular. Another on the list of amenities is mouthwash. Although two out of three people use mouthwash at home, most do not pack it for their trip. This is an especially nice amenity for business travelers. Toothpaste is an item most guests do bring, but it is still an appreciated amenity. Hand and body lotion is well received by female travelers and is one item that may be needed more in some locations of the country or during certain seasons of the year. Shoeshine cloths not only are popular, but also reduce the damage done to guest room towels that would otherwise be used on shoes.

The next logical question to ask is whether the hotel logo, the product's brand name, or both, should appear on the amenity. One argument is that the hotel logo will suffice because it alone connotes a sense of quality and therefore a quality product must be involved. The use of the product brand name alone would seem to be an error from a marketing standpoint, and its use should receive little consideration, if any. The smartest choice would seem to be to use the hotel's logo, include a quality product, and then identify the product by its

EXHIBIT 1-6   CHANGE IN GUEST SATISFACTION WHEN AMENITIES ARE PROVIDED

Type of Hotel	Satisfaction* before amenities were provided	Satisfaction* after amenties were provided	Percent Change
Midpriced hotels	51%	62%	22%
Airport hotels	38%	51%	34%
Downtown luxury hotels	85%	90%	6%
Average	57%	65%	14%

*"Satisfaction" means those guests saying that the room was "excellent" or "very good" when asked to rate the rooms.

brand name as well. This provides an association of quality with quality that can only benefit the hotel. Another reason for including the brand name is that a guest may be allergic to a particular product. It is only fair to the guest that each amenity be identified by its brand name. One amenity that has impressed this text's author over the years is one at the Stouffer's Resort in Orlando, Florida. For a lack of a better term, I have named it "wake-up coffee." When a guest places a wake-up call, the operator asks whether complimentary coffee or tea is desired in the morning, and if so, for how many. The next morning, within ten minutes after the wake-up call, a knock at the door informs the guest that a tray of coffee or tea is waiting.

RATING LODGING FACILITIES

Over the years, two major rating systems have evolved in the lodging industry. The Mobil Travel Guide© utilizes from one to five stars to rank the level and quality of accommodations. Five stars is the highest ranking a property can receive. The American Automobile Association uses the diamond rating system, with five diamonds being the highest a property can receive. These services provide travelers with an independent rating of the facility. Inspectors visit the properties on a regular basis and make sure that the lodging facility meets certain minimum standards (otherwise no stars or diamonds are awarded), and then rank the properties based on the property's meeting or exceeding the standards.

THE STRUCTURE OF THE LODGING ORGANIZATION

Structuring the operation refers to the establishment of an organizational form for the lodging property. The goal of this structuring is to arrange functional areas and people in such a way that work doesn't just happen, but that it gets done as efficiently as possible. While it is not the purpose of this book to teach organizational theory, we are concerned with the organization of a lodging operation as it appears in its organizational chart. An organizational chart gives a schematic summary of a lodging operation structure. Such charts are helpful for understanding an organization's functions and lines of authority. Once developed, the organizational chart should be reviewed at least yearly to ensure that they represent an accurate depiction of the operation's structure. Every lodging operation is going to have its own individual organizational chart, based on the needs of that particular operation. Exhibit 1-7 illustrates an organizational chart for a full-service hotel. This chart lists various job titles under each functional area. Depending on the size of the operation, these titles may represent a person or several people responsible for that work. In a smaller operation, these titles could represent tasks merged together to

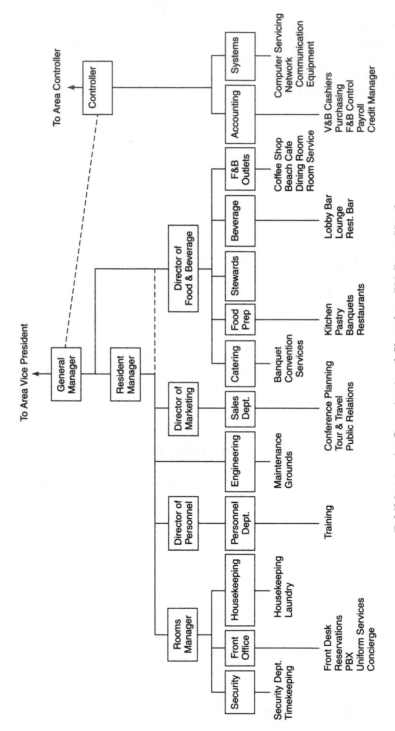

Exhibit 1-7 An Organizational Chart for a 500-Room Hotel

To Area Vice President

To Area Controller

General Manager

Controller

Resident Manager

Rooms Manager

Director of Personnel

Director of Marketing

Director of Food & Beverage

Accounting

Systems

Security
Security Dept.
Timekeeping

Front Office
Front Desk
Reservations
PBX
Uniform Services
Concierge

Housekeeping
Housekeeping
Laundry

Personnel Dept.
Training

Engineering
Maintenance
Grounds

Sales Dept.
Conference Planning
Tour & Travel
Public Relations

Catering
Banquet
Convention
Services

Food Prep
Kitchen
Pastry
Banquets
Restaurants

Stewards

Beverage
Lobby Bar
Lounge
Rest. Bar

F&B Outlets
Coffee Shop
Beach Cafe
Dining Room
Room Service

Accounting
V&B Cashiers
Purchasing
F&B Control
Payroll
Credit Manager

Systems
Computer Servicing
Network
Communication
Equipment

form a single job. For example, in a 100 room hotel, the front desk clerk may be responsible for checking guests in, checking guests out, taking reservations, answering the phone and performing various other tasks. In a 1,000 room hotel, there would be several people assigned the task of checking guests into the hotel.

DEPARTMENTAL FUNCTIONS

The general manager is the person who has the overall responsibility of the success of the operation. Success is measured in terms of the attainment of certain financial goals. Financial goals are set by the ownership, and it is the responsibility of the general manager to achieve these goals while following the broad policies and procedures laid down by the hotel's ownership.

To accomplish the goals, the hotel is broken down into different functional areas called departments. Some of these departments, such as the rooms department that sells guest rooms, and the food and beverage department that operates the restaurants and lounges in the hotel, bring revenue into the hotel. The other category of departments is made up of cost or expense functional areas, such as accounting, personnel, marketing, and engineering, which pay out revenue in various ways.

Another way to look at departmentalization is from a line and staff perspective. *Line* departments are those that carry out the work of the operation, such as housekeeping, which cleans the rooms so they can be rented. An area such as accounting, on the other hand, does not directly involve itself with the product, but provides support to those areas that do. This is an example of a *staff* department, which provides support to the line areas.

In Chapter 2, we will discuss the rooms, which is the focus of this book. It includes the front office, reservations, and uniformed services areas. The other departments of the hotel will be covered here. It has been said that the front office of a hotel is the nerve center of the operation. With this in mind, members of the lodging industry will recognize the importance of the other departments and their interaction with the front office area.

HUMAN RESOURCE MANAGEMENT

In the past, the personnel function or department did little more than take job applications and file insurance forms. In fact, many hotels did not even have a separate department for this, but would let a secretary handle this work. With the growth of government labor laws and regulations, unions, fringe benefits, computerization, and training methods, the personnel area has grown into a needed specialization that can be found in most hotels today. Personnel is a staff function that is there to support the other areas of the hotel. The duties of the personnel department include the following:

1. Recruiting.
2. Interviewing and screening applicants.
3. Verifying and checking references.
4. Recommending applicants to the appropriate departments.
5. Inducting and orienting new employees to the hotel.
6. Developing and conducting training programs.
7. Developing and conducting safety programs.
8. Setting up and administering benefit programs.
9. Dealing with labor unions on all levels, from negotiation to interpreting contracts.
10. Explaining and enforcing labor laws and regulations to ensure compliance.

With the current shortage of labor and high degree of training needed in the front office area, the personnel department is critical to the success of the front office area. Guest relations, computer usage, and telephone skills are a few of the areas in which training is needed. The front office can provide knowledge about a specific job, but it is the personnel department that provides the expertise in creating training programs to prepare workers for that job.

MARKETING AND SALES

Due to the increased building of hotels and the market segmentation mentioned earlier, marketing and sales has become an extremely important department in the hotel business. The director of marketing and sales heads up this department and is responsible for the following areas: group and convention sales, travel agent sales, banquet sales, local sales, public relations, and other functions dealing with the public. Depending upon the size of the hotel, there may be different people in charge of and working in each area. It is the director's responsibility to set policies and coordinate all of these areas. The duties of the marketing and sales area may include planning, setting policies, training for interdepartmental cooperation, budgeting, developing incentive programs, supervising direct mail, and overseeing internal selling. Interdepartmental cooperation and internal selling are critical functions that interface with the front office area. It is critical to the success of any hotel that the marketing and sales area be in constant cooperative communication with the front office reservations area. Only through this positive relationship can occupancy and revenues be maximized.

FOOD AND BEVERAGE

The sale of rooms in a hotel contributes the largest amount of revenue to the operations. Food and beverage sales are next in magnitude. Without an adequate food and beverage department, guest rooms sales would not continue. Guests today require a higher degree of service and quality of product in this area than ever before. Interaction between the food and beverage department and front office area occurs for a variety of reasons: billing of a guest account for food and beverages consumed, passing along guest complaints and compliments about the food and beverage area, and having the front office recommend the hotel's food and beverage outlets to its guests when they ask where to dine. Instead of sending guests outside of the hotel (as many front office employees may unthinkingly do), the hotel's employees can develop the habit of referring guests to food and beverage centers within the organization.

MAINTENANCE AND ENGINEERING

The maintenance of a hotel includes repairing and maintaining equipment, furniture, and fixtures. Some of the more common interactions between the front office and the maintenance department involve unplugging clogged drains and commodes, repairing broken furniture, and replacing broken televisions. A work-order system or maintenance logbook is kept at the front desk and is used to pass along problems, usually registered by guests, to the maintenance area for correction.

Engineering in a hotel includes the running of the electrical, plumbing, steam, air-conditioning, and other mechanical systems. It is the responsibility of the engineering area to see that none of the services these systems provide to the hotel and its guests is interrupted. The most common complaints registered with the front desk have to do with the heating and air-conditioning systems. It is critical that any and all complaints and requests for service receive immediate attention and correction.

ACCOUNTING

The accounting department can be divided into two major areas. First is the area of accounting and auditing. In most cases, this area is unknown to guests. The second area includes the accounting department employees who interact with guests through their work in other departments of the hotel. Restaurant cashiers, who work in the various restaurants of the hotel but are employees of the accounting department, are an example of this type of employee. Later in this book, we will discuss in detail the work of accounting department employees who work in the front office area, such as cashiers and night auditors. These employees play a major role in the functioning of the front office.

LODGING PERFORMANCE RATIOS

Exhibit 1-8 gives a picture of hotel revenue sources by type of service purchased and according to the destination of these revenues for covering the various expenses of the hotel and for returning a profit. As can be seen, the majority of revenues (60.2 percent) comes from guest room rentals, with food sales being the next (23.1 percent). In the area of expenses, payroll and related costs consumes 36 percent of each revenue dollar—more than any other expense item. This is testament to the labor intensiveness of the lodging industry and proof of the

THE U.S. LODGING INDUSTRY DOLLAR

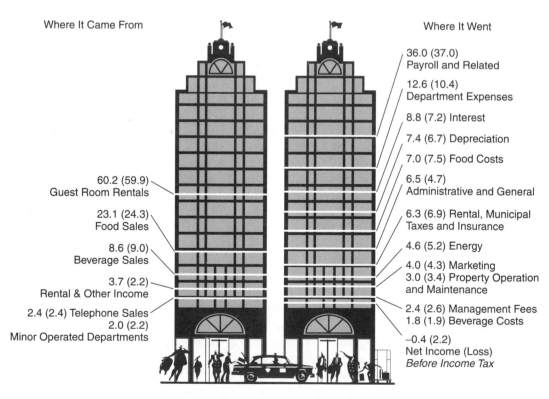

Where It Came From

60.2 (59.9)
Guest Room Rentals

23.1 (24.3)
Food Sales

8.6 (9.0)
Beverage Sales

3.7 (2.2)
Rental & Other Income

2.4 (2.4) Telephone Sales
2.0 (2.2)
Minor Operated Departments

Where It Went

36.0 (37.0)
Payroll and Related

12.6 (10.4)
Department Expenses

8.8 (7.2) Interest

7.4 (6.7) Depreciation

7.0 (7.5) Food Costs

6.5 (4.7)
Administrative and General

6.3 (6.9) Rental, Municipal
Taxes and Insurance

4.6 (5.2) Energy

4.0 (4.3) Marketing
3.0 (3.4) Property Operation
and Maintenance

2.4 (2.6) Management Fees
1.8 (1.9) Beverage Costs

−0.4 (2.2)
Net Income (Loss)
Before Income Tax

Exhibit 1-8   The U.S. Lodging Industry Dollar in 1995 (1984 amounts in parentheses)

need for training programs that will improve employee performance, productivity, and job satisfaction.

In Exhibit 1-9, we see the statistical information gathered by Laventhol & Horwath in their annual report, entitled *U.S. Lodging Industry.* By looking at the data in all the columns, we see that the hotel revenue coming from room sales (26 percent) went to cover departmental expenses. This left a departmental profit of 74 percent in the rooms department. Food and beverage operations had departmental costs of 81.4 percent, leaving 18.6 percent as departmental profit in the food and beverage department.

Taking all of this information as a whole, we can see that the rooms department outperforms the other departments not only in revenue produced, but also in terms of departmental profit.

Before we move along and analyze the rooms department in detail, it would be beneficial for us to go over some terms and ratios that will be used throughout this book.

EXHIBIT 1-9   ROOMS DEPARTMENT
MEDIAN RATIO TO ROOM SALES AND RATIO TO TOTAL SALES

		Size of Property			
	All	Under 150 Rooms	150–299 Rooms	300–600 Rooms	Over 600 Rooms
Revenue					
Room Sales	100.5%	100.0%	100.6%	100.9%	100.7%
Allowances	0.8	0.7	0.9	0.9	0.7
Net Revenue	100.0%	100.0%	100.0%	100.0%	100.0%
Expenses					
Payroll & Related	17.6%	17.3%	17.4%	17.9%	19.1%
Travel Agent Commissions & Reservation Expense	2.2	1.5	2.1	2.7	2.7
Contract Cleaning, Dry Cleaning, Linen & Laundry	2.2	2.2	1.7	2.6	2.9
Operating Supplies	1.9	1.7	2.0	1.9	1.8
All Other Expenses	1.8	2.2	2.0	1.6	1.1
Total Departmental Expenses	26.0	24.8	25.5	28.0	29.1
Net Departmental Income	74.0%	75.3%	74.5%	72.0%	70.9%
Ratio to Total Sales					
Net Revenue	63.4%	73.0%	63.9%	59.7%	59.6%
Payroll & Related Expenses	11.1	12.1	11.0	10.6	11.3
Net Departmental Income	46.6%	54.6%	47.6%	42.7%	43.9%

Source: Courtesy of Laventhol and Horwath

Percentage of Occupancy

The percentage of occupancy is a ratio that is derived by dividing the number of rooms sold by the number of rooms in the hotel:

$$\frac{Rooms\ Sold}{Rooms\ Available} \times 100 = Occupancy\ \%$$

$$\frac{300}{400} \times 100 = 75\%$$

This calculation tells us that 75 percent of the rooms in the hotel were sold. Sometimes the denominator will be replaced with rooms available. For example, if five rooms were out of order, the number in the denominator would be $(400 - 5 = 395)$ or 395 rooms available. However, we feel this compensation should not be made. Management should be judged on its performance in selling rooms. If out-of-order rooms are deducted, the occupancy figure is inflated. A manager wishing to inflate his occupancy percentages might simply declare a set of rooms as being out of order, thus artificially inflating the occupancy percent figures. This can be particularly confusing to the buyer of a hotel. The method by which the percentage of occupancy has been calculated should always be made clear.

Percentage of Double Occupancy

The percentage of double occupancy tells us what percentage of the rooms sold have two guests in them:

$$\frac{Total\ Guests - Rooms\ Occupied}{Rooms\ Occupied} \times 100 = Double\ Occupancy\ \%$$

$$\frac{450 - 300}{300} \times 100 = 50\%$$

In this example, we had 450 guests in the hotel and sold 300 rooms. This gives us a double occupancy of 50 percent which means that half of the rooms sold had two guests in them, and half had one guest.

Number of Guests per Occupied Room

The method for determining the number of guests per occupied room is similar to the method for finding the percentage of double occupancy. It tells us, on the average, how many guests were in each room:

$$\frac{Total\ Guests}{Rooms\ Sold} = Guests\ per\ room$$

$$\frac{450}{300} = 1.5$$

These two ratios, along with the percentage of occupancy figure, provide us with information that is critical when we are ordering food, beverages, and supplies, and when we are scheduling personnel and planning for future financial decisions.

Average Daily Rate

The average daily rate is calculated by dividing the room revenue by the number of rooms sold:

$$\frac{Today's\ Room\ Revenue}{Rooms\ Sold} = Average\ Rate$$

$$\frac{\$20,700}{300} = \$69$$

This is also called the *average daily room rate*. When the average daily room rate is discussed, it is critical to include the percentage of occupancy. In order for a hotel to be financially successful, it must achieve a respectable percentage of occupancy and an adequate average daily room rate.

CONCLUSION

The lodging industry comprises a variety of establishments. All provide one essential service: rooms for rent. The primary source of revenue, regardless of the type of property being examined, is from the rooms department. The rate one can get for a room and the number of people willing to occupy rooms at the posted rate are important indicators of performance. The next chapter examines the rooms department operations in greater detail.

DISCUSSION QUESTIONS

1. Why do you think that the hotel business flourished so well in the United States? Could there be a sociological explanation?
2. Discuss the advantages and disadvantages of each of the five types of hotel affiliation. Which would you prefer? Would the choice be affected by your desire to be an active versus passive owner?
3. We discussed five types of lodging operations. What are they? Do you think the travel market is adequately served by this segmentation? Can you suggest any other way of segmenting the travel market?
4. How is a hotel organized? What is the function of the various departments found in a hotel?
5. If you were designing a hotel, what room design criteria would you use?

STUDY QUESTIONS

1. Name the four types of properties that make up the lodging industry.
2. The U.S. lodging industry can trace its roots back to which of the following?
   a. The ancient resorts of Rome.
   b. The monasteries of Europe with their guest accommodations.
   c. The English inn and its tradition of care for travelers.
   d. It is unique, and has no precedents.
3. The two names that we associate with the founding of the modern hotel during the first half of this century are _____ and _____.
4. Kemous Wilson was famous for which of the following?
   a. For inventing the Wilson tennis racket.
   b. For founding the Holiday Inn hotel chain.
   c. For being a president of the United States.
   d. For drawing the cartoon series "Dennis the Menace."
5. A lodging property that is owned and operated by the same person and is not affiliated with a chain of properties is known as which of the following?
   a. Owner-managed hotel.
   b. Independent hotel.
   c. Franchised hotel.
   d. Chain-operated hotels.
6. How would we classify a hotel in Chicago with 325 rooms that has very low room rates?
   a. Economy, center city, medium hotel.
   b. Limited service, suburban, small hotel.
   c. Economy, resort, large hotel.
   d. Middle market, airport, medium hotel.
7. It is possible for people traveling on vacation to be classified as more than one type of traveler. (True or False)
8. The single most important design aspect of a hotel (in the mind of a guest) is which of the following?
   a. The bedroom and the bathroom.
   b. The restaurant and the pool.
   c. The service and the entertainment.
   d. The location and the price.
9. Generally, guests will pay more for a room that has amenities provided than they ordinarily would for just the basic room. (True or False)
10. The functional area whose task it is to handle the selling of the hotel's rooms to potential guests is which of the following?
    a. The rooms department.
    b. The food and beverage department.
    c. The marketing and sales department.
    d. The human resource management department.

PROBLEMS

1. If you have a 200-room hotel, and 150 rooms are occupied, what is your occupancy percentage?

2. You have 150 guests in-house, and 100 rooms are occupied. What is your percentage of double occupancy?

3. When there are 225 guests in-house and there are 150 rooms occupied, how many guests are there per room?

4. The hotel sold $12,500 in rooms last night and 250 rooms were occupied with paying guests. What was the average daily room rate last night?

CHAPTER 2

Staffing the Rooms Division

CHAPTER OBJECTIVES

After reading this chapter you will understand:

- The importance of the rooms division.
- How the rooms division is organized.
- Who works in the rooms division.
- What each person does in the rooms division.
- Problems encountered by managers of the division.

INTRODUCTION

The rooms division in a hotel is very important to the hotel's overall success in terms of providing quality guest service. This is because this division has a high degree of guest contact. This contact must create the impression of a quality experience for the guest. The rooms division prepares its product—the guest room—for the guest's stay. If the guest room does not meet the guest's expectations, then a lack of quality will be perceived by the guest.

The rooms division consists of housekeeping, reservations, front office, uniformed services, transportation, PBX, and concierge. A synergistic relationship between these divisions is necessary in order to achieve the goal of quality service. This relationship can only come about through a cooperative team effort among the departments.

From the moment a guest makes a reservation, he or she has an image of the level of service that the hotel will provide. A good portion of this impression is based on the manner in which the reservations agent speaks with the guest. If the exchange is a pleasant, friendly, professional, and timely one, a positive image is already created. Upon the guest's arrival at the hotel, another interaction occurs between the guest and the uniformed services personnel, the doorperson and bell staff. A pleasant, sincere greeting and a helpful manner on the employee's part will continue to enhance the positive impression the guest has already formed. Next, the front desk staff has their turn at continuing what, to this point, has been a pleasant experience for the guest. Again, a pleasant and sincere greeting followed by prompt and expedient service is what most guests are expecting. This all comes about by the accurate retrieval of the guest's reservation and the selection of the appropriate guest room to meet the needs of the guest. After this, on his or her way to the room, the guest will be accompanied by a bellperson who will explain the different features and amenities in the guest room. Housekeeping efforts at preparing the guest room for occupancy will be immediately visible to the guest, further confirming the impression the guest has concerning the type of hotel in which he or she has chosen to stay. A clean, orderly room goes a long way in pleasing the guest; it always has and always will be critical to the guest's overall experience. During the guest's stay, he or she will continue to interact with all of these areas and employees. If each and every one of them has been given proper training, every guest should have a pleasant stay at the hotel.

ROOMS DIVISION

The structure of the rooms division will vary from hotel to hotel. These variations can be caused by differences in the size of hotels, the types of service and levels of service provided by different hotels, the geographic location, local work force skill levels, and the organization preferences of management. Exhibit 2-1 displays the rooms division organizational chart for a typical 500-room full-service hotel. The three major subdepartments in this rooms division are security, front office, and housekeeping. These subdepartments come under the control of the rooms division manager.

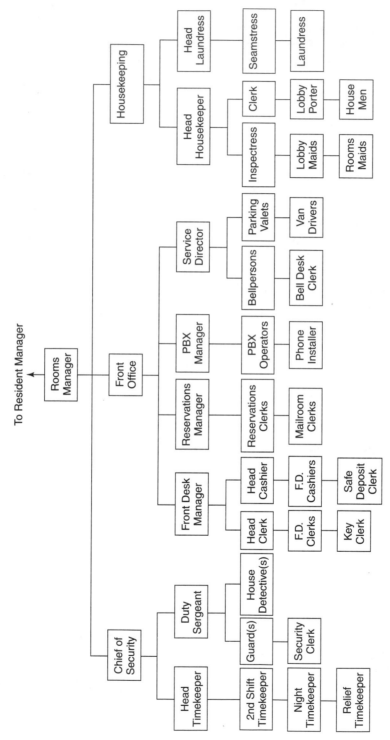

Exhibit 2-1 An Organizational Chart for a Hotel Rooms Division

Rooms Division Manager

A rooms division manager has the following duties:

- Responsible for the supervision of employees engaged in the operation of the front areas of the hotel.
- Coordinates with other departments in the hotel and maintains open communications with them to find better ways to service the guests.
- Maintains responsibility for staffing, purchasing, and budgeting.
- Supervises the rooms division payroll, availability controls, and monthly plans.
- Develops guidelines and standard operating procedures to carry out the policies of the rooms division.
- Creates plans to maximize the average daily rate and percentage of occupancy.
- Handles customer complaints and suggestions.
- Stays up to date with events taking place in the market, in market segments, and in the competition.

The minimum requirements for the position of rooms division manager usually include a college degree and five years of front office experience, with three of those years spent in a supervisory role. Knowledge required includes a complete understanding of hotel operations, specifically those operations involving the front office, uniformed services, housekeeping, and basic accounting procedures.

FRONT OFFICE

The front office department in a hotel typically includes front desk reservations (which includes the functions of registration and check-out), PBX, uniformed services, and concierge. Each of these areas is extremely important in creating a positive experience for the guests of the hotel. Although each of these areas is separate, it is only through a team effort that a hotel can create an environment that will provide the highest level of guest services. The front office manager is responsible for the smooth functioning of the front office functions.

Front Office Manager

It is the basic function of the front office manager to directly supervise the front desk, uniformed services, PBX, and reservation departments on a daily basis and to monitor guest service. He or she also assists the rooms division manager in compiling information for reports in whose production he or she will assist. Other duties of the front office manager include the following:

- Assists in the training and cross-training of front office employees.
- Prepares the daily payroll report, VIP room assignments, and out-of-order rooms report.

- Assists the rooms division manager in the formulation and implementation of front office policies and procedures.
- Prepares the weekly schedule of employees.
- Aids the group coordinator with all group arrivals, either directly or through the delegation of this duty to other staff members.
- Reviews and approves all room moves and room rate changes to ensure they were necessary.
- Handles guest complaints and follows them up to reduce future complaints.
- Assists the rooms division manager in forecasting room availability to ensure that the optimal level of occupancy is attained.
- Is available to work in the front office area where there may be a shortage of staff.
- Maintains the necessary stock of supplies in all front office areas, while controlling costs in these areas.

The front office manager should be the graduate of a four-year hospitality management school. He should have at least two years front office experience that includes front desk and night audit work. In this position, it is imperative that the person possess excellent interpersonal communication skills. These skills are needed to keep all functional areas of the front office communicating effectively and working together as a team. This team's primary concern is to provide the highest level of service possible to every guest of the hotel.

FRONT DESK

The front desk area in a hotel is open 24 hours per day, 7 days per week, 365 days a year. It is the nerve center of a hotel, the place where guests turn to seek information, to get help, and to register most of their complaints. Work flow on the front desk usually has two speeds, fast or slow. When the busy check-in or check-out times occur, the front desk area takes on the challenge of serving every guest as quickly as possible. This is a challenge because just checking in or checking out the guest quickly is not enough. All guests must be dealt with in such a way that they feel as though they have received special treatment. The front desk supervisor is the person who is directly involved in meeting this challenge.

Front Desk Supervisor

It is the front desk supervisor's basic function to directly supervise the front desk procedures that include check-in and check-out. The supervisor supervises and assists the front desk clerks (commonly referred to as *guest service agents*) in their primary functions. The front desk supervisor performs the following duties:

- Trains and cross-trains front desk personnel in the tasks of registration, mail handling, information services, and check-in and check-out procedures.
- Prepares daily and weekly payroll reports for the front desk.
- Completes a reconciliation of housekeeping, out-of-order rooms, and room-status reports.
- Regulates the service given in the front desk and lobby area by requiring additional personnel to work the area when needed.
- Acts as a liaison between the guests and management, particularly with regard to problem-solving activities.
- Is responsible for seeing that daily and hourly computer reports are run and distributed.
- Assigns VIP rooms to ensure guest satisfaction.
- Resolves room discrepancy report through inspection.
- Inspects other guest rooms on a daily basis to see that standards are being met.
- Is responsible for authorizing all rebates, petty cash, and other miscellaneous vouchers prepared by guest service agents.

The front desk supervisor should be proficient in the usage of all front desk equipment such as the computer system and reservations system. A college degree in hospitality management is desirable, with training in computer systems operations. In addition, the front desk supervisor should have two years of front office experience, within which he or she should have learned cashiering, front desk operations, and the night audit. Familiarity with the local area is extremely helpful. A high level of human relations skills is needed to effectively deal with employees and guests.

Guest Service Agent

If there is one employee in a hotel who can and should be singled out as the most important, this person would be the guest service agent. This individual, more than any other employee, represents the hotel to the guest. Through the registration process, the guest service agent provides the first initial contact a guest has with the hotel. After this contact, guests feel that the front desk is the place to call or go when they have a question or problem. An area that needs special attention is the effect that the agent has on the guest's perception of the hotel and the amount of satisfaction the guest will derive from his or her stay. The effect of a pleasant, friendly, helpful agent, as opposed to one that is rude, aloof, and uncaring, can easily be seen.

The basic functions performed by the guest service agent are the registrating process (with related cashier duties) and the assisting of guests with any requests they make. The guest service agent's main concern is, of course, service to the guests. This service can be accomplished by acknowledging the guests' presence even if they cannot be served at once, always calling guests by name, and smiling and looking at the guests when serving them. The guest service agent's duties include the following:

- Handles the guest registration process and adheres to all hotel credit policies in the process.
- Handles guest check-out procedure.
- Issues and controls guest safe-deposit boxes.
- Always answers the front desk phone within three rings or less.
- Maintains the assigned house bank and makes an accurate report of moneys received and paid out.
- Attempts to sellup guest rooms, and informs and sells the guest on all hotel services and facilities.
- Is aware of all daily events in the hotel and local area.
- Is trained in all emergency procedures.
- Handles guest mail and reservations when the reservation department is closed.

The guest service agent should have at least a high school diploma, and fluency in foreign languages is extremely helpful in most hotels. This person must be able to communicate effectively, have a friendly and pleasant personality, and possess great patience. Tolerance is required when one is dealing with guest complaints and answering the same types of questions for different guests all day.

That the front desk area is opened 24 hours per day means that three eight-hour shifts will make up the day's schedule for this area:

7:00 A.M.–3:00 P.M.	1st shift	Day shift
3:00 P.M.–11:00 P.M.	2nd shift	Swing shift
11:00 P.M.–7:00 A.M.	3rd shift	Graveyard shift

These represent the typical schedules and names of the three eight-hour shifts of the front desk. When more than one guest service agent is being scheduled per shift, which is the case in most full-service hotels with over 100 rooms, the beginning times should be staggered. If two agents are working on the day shift for instance, one of them should start at 7:00 A.M. and one at 7:30 A.M. Then, the two agents coming in on the second shift should be scheduled similarly, with one beginning at 3:00 P.M. and the other at 3:30 P.M. This overlapping of the shifts will allow for a smooth changeover and a thorough communication of all necessary information between the shifts. Part-time employees may be utilized for a full eight-hour shift when they fill in on full-time employees' day off. Regardless of whether guest service agents are full- or part-time, they should all receive equal training. *Cross-training*, the preparation of employees to perform in positions other than in their primary jobs, has an unlimited potential for solving labor shortages in the front office area. For example, a reservations agent can be trained as a guest service agent. This will then enable a reservations agent to assist at the front desk during busy periods, breaks, vacations, and so forth. *Job rotation* occurs when employees move around and work in different positions. Rotation of employees to different positions may help to relieve some of the stress with which certain employees are faced. Guest service agents are under much more stress than reservationists, due to the high degree of guest contact they have. By rotating these two jobs, a manager can reinforce cross-training, cause job boredom to be reduced, and provide a "stress break" for the guest service agent.

Night Auditor

One of the most difficult positions to fill at the front desk is that of the night auditor. The reasons for this are many, but one of the more prominent ones is that the hours the employee works are difficult. It is hard for most people to stay awake from 11:00 P.M. to 7:00 A.M., all the while trying to focus their attention on work that requires a great deal of accuracy with numbers. Thus, one of the most important traits a manager should look for in a night auditor candidate is the ability and desire to stay awake and work during this shift.

The basic functions performed by the night auditor include auditing of all daily charges and adjustments posted by the front desk to ensure that the guest ledger is in balance, posting any late charges, posting room and tax charges, and updating the guest ledger. This person also performs the following duties:

- Balances restaurant, beverage, laundry, valet, phone, and all other charges with the cashier reports.
- Balances all allowances and city ledger transfer postings.
- Reviews all postings to the city ledger and credit cards.
- Checks credit limits on individual guest accounts.
- Prepares and balances the daily report for presentation to management.
- Prepares all work for presentation to the accounting department.
- Switches the system over to the next business day.

The night auditor prepares various reports for management. Statistics such as the average room rate, percentage of double occupancy, percentage of occupancy, and other figures are needed daily by management to review the results of operations. Additionally, a report indicating the status of every room is prepared for the housekeeping department. For minimum requirements, a night auditor should have a high school diploma, an ability to work with numbers, and at least one year of front desk experience where an understanding of the guest ledger, trial balance, and hotel cashiering has been gained.

RESERVATIONS

The reservations area is critical to the success of a hotel. It is the area involved in selling rooms to future guests. In this sales capacity, reservations must work very closely with the marketing and sales department.

Reservations Manager

The reservations manager's basic functions are to supervise and oversee all the operations of the reservations area. He or she must assure that all reservations, both group and individual, are recorded and followed up on as necessary. Other duties of this position are to perform the following:

- Making sure proper telephone etiquette is used and correct information is being given to potential guests.
- Being sure that personal service is stressed and that sales techniques are being used appropriately.
- Following up on tentative booking, watching cut-off dates, and monitoring group tour business accounts blocks for productivity.
- Training reservation agents and setting up cross-training programs.
- Reviewing all VIP reservations and working with the rooms division manager and the front office manager on assignments.
- Preparing and distributing to other departments a 10-day and 30-day forecast.
- Handling requests for reservation information and room rates.
- Resolving billing disputes with regard to room rates quoted by the hotel.
- Developing and maintaining a solid working relationship with the central reservations office and travel agents.

A reservations manager should have a high school diploma and some hotel management course work. Two years of reservations experience in a hotel, an ability to sell, and a desire to provide a high degree of service are also necessary.

Reservations Agent

The reservations agent is responsible for taking reservations and for providing future guests with information about the facilities of the hotel. He or she also provides transportation to the hotel and facts about the local area to guests. Work performed by reservations agents includes:

- Giving friendly and courteous service to future guests while involved in telephone sales.
- Answering all reservation phone calls, taking reservations, and dealing with reservation correspondence.
- Dealing with group bookings such as cancellations, changes, and rooming lists.
- Checking to see that all equipment is working properly and that the needed amount of supplies is on hand.
- Conducting telemarketing under the direction of the director of marketing and sales.
- Operating the property management reservation module.

While it is not necessary for a reservations agent to have a college degree, it would be beneficial for promotion and transfer into other areas such as marketing and sales. The reservations agent must be able to communicate by telephone and in person, have a pleasant personality, and possess a high level of patience in dealing with people.

UNIFORMED SERVICES

The uniformed services area is headed up by the bell captain and includes the valet parking personnel, doorpersons, and bell staff. In a large hotel where this area contains numerous employees, this area will be supervised by a person entitled the superintendent of services or director of uniformed services. In smaller hotels, the front office manager will have responsibility for this area.

Valet Parking Attendant

Valet parking attendants are, in many cases, the first and last hotel employees that a nonguest or guest who has driven to the hotel has contact with. This position requires an individual who is physically agile enough to run back and forth from the hotel entrance to the place where cars are parked. When it is busy with arrivals or departures (often due to banquet guests arriving or departing), this job is extremely demanding physically. The basic function of a valet parking attendant is to park and retrieve the cars of the hotel guests and nonguests in a friendly, hospitable, and safe manner. A valet parking attendant must possess an excellent driving record. Due to the large amount of gratuities a person can receive in this job, it should be possible to attract employees who are capable of providing the level of quality service the hotel desires.

Doorperson

The employee who greets the guest and offers the first service of the hotel is the doorperson. The service is assisting the guest into the hotel with his or her luggage and directing the guest to the front desk area. In the case of guests of the hotel who are there only to attend functions being conducted at the hotel, the doorperson will greet the guest in a friendly manner and direct the guest to the function. At check-out time, the doorperson is busy taking the luggage from the bell staff and helping the guests with their departure from the hotel by loading their luggage into their car or by calling a taxi. During their stay, the doorperson is there to assist the guests with directions and by answering questions in a pleasant and helpful fashion. When guests return to the hotel, a warm and pleasant greeting from the doorperson goes a long way in making guests feel important to the hotel.

Bellperson

After the guest checks into the hotel, he or she is turned over to the bellperson who will escort the guest to the guest room. Some terminology used in the bell staff area are the terms "first" and "last." A "first" is what the bellperson is called when he or she is going to be the next one called upon to assist a guest with her luggage. The term "last" is used to describe the bellperson who is at the end of the line waiting "to room" guests. *Rooming* a guest refers to the process a bellperson goes through when escorting a guest to the room. During this rooming process, the bellperson has an opportunity to act as the hotel's sales representative and ambassador of goodwill. While escorting the guest to the room, a bellperson can start up a conversation that will make the guest feel welcome, inform the guest of the hotel facilities, and sell the hotel's food and beverage areas to the guest. Upon arriving at the room and placing the guest's luggage inside the room, the bellperson should explain the workings of the heating and cooling system, the television set, and he or she should answer any questions the guest may have. Bellpersons also act in a security capacity. They are constantly moving throughout the hotel, and should be trained to keep their eyes and ears open for anything unusual. While guests are checking in and being roomed, bell staff can look for light luggage or any other suspicious signs that should be reported to management. The bell staff will perform other duties during a guest's stay such as delivering messages, running errands for the hotel and its guests, and completing other duties as assigned by management.

Concierges

In Europe, the service of concierges has been available for over a century. It is said by the Hilton organization that the Waldorf Astoria had a concierge in its Towers section as early as the late 1930s. Today, most full-service hotels are adding a concierge to their staffs. This person, if not available to all of the hotel guests, can usually be found in a towers section or in many cases on what has been termed the concierge floor of the hotel.

The services of the concierge are many and varied. Anything from making reservations on airlines or at theaters to locating a pharmacy that can fill a guest's prescription. A concierge may arrange for a babysitter. A concierge is there to serve the guest in whatever way necessary. The addition of the concierge function in hotels has taken a lot of the stress off front desk guest service agents, to whom guests have always turned for assistance in the past. Now, hotel guests are learning to look for the concierge with their questions and requests. The concierge can also help out during rush periods at the front desk by taking keys or retrieving mail and messages that guests have waiting for them at the front desk.

PBX

PBX stands for *private branch exchange.* This area is commonly referred to as the *switchboard* and is staffed by switchboard/telephone operators. The switchboard must be kept open 24 hours per day. In small hotels, the night auditor may take on these duties during the third shift. It is important that the phone be answered as quickly as possible (by the third ring), and in a friendly and polite manner.

Most larger hotels have room-to-room dialing by which guests in one room can dial directly to another room. Direct dialing is in use in most lodging properties today. This means that guests can dial local and long-distance phone calls from their guest rooms without going through the hotel or phone company operator. By a large margin, the greatest duty of a switchboard operator is that of transferring calls from outside the hotel to the appropriate guest room. Operators must do this without ever giving out the room number of a hotel guest. If a party calls and asks for the room number of Mr. Smith, the operator should inform the party that he is not permitted to give out room numbers of the hotel guests, but will be happy to connect the calling party to the guest's room. There are two methods used to locate a guest's room number. The first is by using what is called an information rack. This contains slips of paper that have the guest's name and room number on it. These slips are placed in the information rack in alphabetical order. A second method is to have a computer terminal at the switchboard area and to use this to access the guest's room number by a last name search. One of the most important things an operator must do when answering the phone is to speak slowly and clearly enough so that the calling party will know the correct number has been reached. This also reinforces the name of the hotel with the caller. An appropriate greeting should be made as well. Such greetings may range from a simple "Good Morning" to a more involved phrase such as, "Good Morning! It's a beautiful day at the Deveau Hotel. How may I direct your call?" Again, as with most of the employees in the rooms department, the switchboard operators represent the hotel to the callers and hotel guests. Therefore, if the operators are hospitable, a pleasant picture of the hotel is painted for these individuals. Wake-up calls are usually taken by the switchboard operator if a guest-controlled computer system is not in use. It is extremely important that when a wake-up call is requested that proper procedures are followed so that the call will be made at the right time. Taking messages for guests falls into the same category of importance as providing wake-up calls. An inaccurately taken message is going to leave such a poor impression on the guest that the hotel, and quite possibly the entire chain with which it is affiliated, may lose this guest forever.

HOUSEKEEPING DEPARTMENT

Although the housekeeping department has less guest contact than the other rooms division departments, it performs services for the guest that play a large factor in the guest's decision to patronize the hotel. In most cases, guests will decide whether this hotel is going to receive their business in the future based on their impression of the room cleanliness. The major services provided by housekeeping are the cleaning of the guest rooms and the rest of the hotel. The executive housekeeper is the person responsible for all personnel and functions in the department. Areas of the hotel maintained by the housekeeping department include guest rooms, halls and corridors, lobby, public rooms, restaurant, offices, stairways, windows, and shops. Four principle functions of the housekeeping department include cleaning and maintaining the property, training the different employees of the department, selecting and ordering the supplies needed, and performing the clerical work of preparing work schedules and reports requested by management.

In some cases, hotels have found it beneficial to have outside contractors handle some of the cleaning and maintenance work in the hotel. *Contract cleaning,* as it is termed, is the responsibility of the hotel's upper management. Areas under contract cleaning include public rooms, restaurants, offices of the hotel, and, very often, window cleaning. Due to the hazardous nature of the work involved and the special equipment used, window cleaning is an area that requires skilled personnel. The appearance of the guest rooms is extremely important to the satisfaction of the guests. Guests are not very tolerant of poor housekeeping procedures that lead to a poorly made up room.

Maids

There are two different types of maids in a hotel, day maids and night maids. Day maids clean and make up the hotel guest rooms. In some hotels there are also bath maids. Bath maids clean the bathrooms while another maid prepares the sleeping area of the guest room. This is a teamwork program that is being tried to improve productivity and morale. Maids perform the following work:

- Maintaining the inventory of their maid cart, which contains all cleaning supplies, guest room supplies, and linens.
- Removing all linens and towels from check-out rooms and soiled linens and towels from stayover rooms.
- Checking all blankets, pillows, and bedspreads for damage and soiling.
- Emptying all wastebaskets and ashtrays; checking for lighted cigarettes.
- Checking to see if all lights, televisions, radios, phones, clocks, and such are working.
- Reporting any articles left behind by a guest in a check-out room, and removing any room keys left by checked-out guests.
- Reporting to a supervisor any damage to the guest room or any suspicious looking substances or situations.

Housemen

Housemen do deep-cleaning work in the guest rooms as planned by the executive housekeeper. This deep cleaning includes spot washing guest room walls; shampooing; tile cleaning in bathroom; vacuuming drapes, blinds, and couches; turning mattresses; and so forth. On a daily basis, housemen help the maids by removing soiled linen from the maids' carts; by replenishing maids' carts; and, in general, by being available to assist maids with tasks, particularly those that require the lifting of heavy objects.

Inspectors/Floor Housekeepers

Inspectors/floor housekeepers are responsible for assigning rooms to the maids for cleaning, along with the keys or cards needed to gain entry to the guest rooms. After the maids have completed making up the guest room, the floor housekeeper will inspect it to see that all of the work conforms to the set standards, and that guest room supplies have been stocked and located in the proper location. Inspection of guest rooms is also done to locate any damaged items needing repair or replacement, such as lamps, commodes, bathroom fixtures, and furniture.

Executive Housekeeper

The executive housekeeper is responsible for the overall cleanliness of the hotel in his or her assigned areas of responsibility. He or she has these duties:

- Coordinates the work of the maids, housemen, and the floor housekeepers, as well as workers in the linen room and laundry.
- Spot checks the inventory of the laundry, linen room, and supply room.
- Supervises the deep cleaning and remodeling work performed by hotel employees and outside contractors.

- Is responsible for testing all cleaning supplies and linens, and for selecting those for usage in the hotel.
- Prepares purchase orders for submittal to the purchasing department or to vendors.
- Is familiar with all sanitation regulations and ensures that proper procedures are followed in keeping with these regulations.

Executive housekeepers should have a college degree in hotel management and three years of supervisory experience in a housekeeping subdepartment of similar size. Speaking knowledge of a foreign language is mandatory in many parts of the country in order to communicate with many of the housekeeping employees.

SECURITY

With the increase in crime throughout the nation and an increased emphasis on guest safety, the security function in hotels has increased in size and importance. There are three basic methods of handling the staffing of security: contracted security, in-house security, and off-duty police. Contract security companies offer many advantages to hotels. They can provide screened and well-trained security personnel that will be rotated to different companies. This prevents them from becoming too friendly with the employees of the hotel. There is always the chance for employee friendliness with security to lead to illegal collusion with employees or the covering up of misconduct by hotel employees and security. Contract security firms have all of the latest technology and methods at their disposal, which is something an independent operator of a hotel cannot possibly afford to provide. Additionally, the supervisors of the security firm monitor the work performance of the security guards and indicate to management where improvements in its security program need to be made.

In-house security is more difficult for a small hotel than for a large one. With in-house security, the hotel takes on the responsibility of training the security force as well as designing the security program. Due to the depth of specialization security involves today, it is difficult to improve on the services of an outside security firm.

One alternative to an outside security firm is to hire off-duty police officers to work as security guards at a hotel. This option is feasible for the smaller hotel. It provides the hotel with trained law enforcement officers who are able to respond to security and emergency situations much better than most contract security personnel. Also, by hiring off-duty local police officers, the hotel helps to cement its position within the community. Because of police presence, this practice even reduces the chances of criminal activity of ever occurring. Supervision of the security function can be under the director of security in a larger hotel. In a situation where outside contract security or off-duty police are used, the responsibility of supervision will usually rest with the rooms division manager.

LABOR PRODUCTIVITY AND SCHEDULING

With labor costs in the rooms division accounting for more than 50 percent of this division's expenses, a close watch must be kept on them. Many reasons are frequently cited for the lack of ability to control labor costs in the rooms divisions. Some of these reasons are represented in such statements as: "We have a union situation to deal with," "Because of our guest room layout, it takes longer to clean the rooms," and " If we cut back, it will negatively impact the level of service we want to provide our guests."

Whatever the current situation is, the objective of a labor productivity system is to provide the desired level of service to the guest with the least possible cost. In order to do this, hotel management must ask several questions: "What level of service are we striving to deliver to our guests?" "Why are we doing things the way we are?" "Can our methods of operation be changed?" "Is this task really necessary or can we eliminate it?"

Each job must be analyzed based on the job content and the scheduling of the individuals holding these positions. Job content analysis requires an examination of the different methods used to carry out the tasks of the job. It must also be decided whether automation can be used or is being used in the job, and whether any tasks can be combined or eliminated. After this job content analysis has been completed, each position should be simplified and made as efficient as possible, while still providing the level or service originally required.

A review of job scheduling must include an analysis of the customer service demanded, the minimum employee schedules, the maximum employee schedules, and the work demand schedules. Certain types of employees may be scheduled traditionally in such a way that the position becomes a fixed cost because of the fixed schedule. This can happen very often on the front desk and in housekeeping. Demand based on the percentage of occupancy varies and schedules should reflect this. Areas that provide a service should be examined for those periods of time when there is little or no demand for their services. Bell service, valet parking, and the laundry/valet areas are the ones that stand out in the rooms division and deserve special examination for demand and scheduling.

To maximize labor productivity, management must have forecasts of activity prepared for each day, as well as an hour-by-hour forecast. In the rooms division, the activities to be considered are check-ins, check-outs, in-coming phone calls, and the percentage of occupancy. Staffing standards should be prepared for each position; these will be based on a level of activity, such as one maid for every 15 rooms, one bellperson for each 25 arrivals, and one guest service agent for every 40 arrivals.

EXHIBIT 2-2   VOLUME MEASURES USED FOR VARIOUS AREAS IN THE HOTEL

Area	Activity (Volume) Measure
Front Office	Arrivals & departures
Uniformed Services	Arrivals & departures
Housekeeping	Last night's occupied rooms
Telephone	Guests in-house/Telephone-call volume
Laundry	Pounds of material
Garage	Arrivals & departures using automobiles and food and beverage activity

From these staffing standards, a *staffing chart* can be prepared. The staffing chart contains a listing of all the job positions, the different volume of demand ranges from lowest to highest, and the staffing standards for the different positions. These staffing charts help to control the labor costs associated with various positions, seeing that the hours worked will vary with changes in the volume of demand for the work. Exhibit 2-2 displays the departmental areas along with the appropriate volume forecasts that must be considered when preparing a staffing chart.

In a computerized labor productivity/scheduling system, all of the above areas are considered in the written program. These systems can be purchased as a ready-to-run software package or created by management utilizing a spreadsheet software package. When mathematical formulas are developed correctly, all that is necessary to determine the required number of hours to be scheduled for any position is to input the volume of demand forecasted for that particular period of time into the computerized system.

DISCUSSION QUESTIONS

1. Discuss the importance of the rooms division for effective hotel operations. Be sure to include in your discussion both the importance of the rooms division from a guest's point of view and the hotel's point of view.

2a. If you were the general manager of the Imperial Grand Resort (a luxury 500-room hotel located at a world-famous resort), what qualities would you look for in a new rooms division manager?

2b. You have narrowed down your search for a new rooms division manager to the following three candidates, as shown in the following table. Discuss the strengths and weaknesses of each according to the discussion in the text. Who would you choose?

Candidate A	Candidate B	Candidate C
Age: 29	Age: 55	Age: 40
Schooling: college bachelor's degree	Schooling: college master's degree	Schooling: no college degree
Experience: 5 years in the department; 3 years as front office manager.	Experience: 25 years in hotels; 21 years in food and beverage; 4 years in rooms department; 5 years director of food and beverage; 1 year as rooms department manager.	Experience: 20 years in rooms department; 5 years as front office manager; 3 years as rooms department manager

3. Why is it so important that we hire the right kind of person for the rooms department?
4. Are any of the employees in the rooms department likely *never* to have any guest contact?
5. What qualities do you think an employee in the rooms department should possess in order to handle the guests in the best possible way?

STUDY QUESTIONS

1. What are the three major departments in the rooms division?
2. Name the position that is responsible for the overall control of these departments.
3. Which department typically includes the registration of guests, check-in/check-out, and PBX?
4. Which person (or persons) is responsible for handling guest complaints?
5. How many shifts are there at the front desk and what are their usual hours?
6. What are the basic functions of the night auditor?
7. What kind of education and experience are required for the position of reservations manager?
8. Valets, bellpersons, and doorpersons are in which area of the rooms department?
9. In what area of the rooms department might you hear the term "first" or "last"? What do these terms mean?
10. If you were to visit a hotel in America in the 1930s and you found a person occupying the position of "concierge," what hotel were you visiting?
11. What does PBX stand for?

PROBLEM

1. The front desk is open 24 hours a day, 7 days a week. Staffing levels are the following: Day shift, 5 positions; swing shift, 3 positions; night shift, 1 position. If no worker can work more than 40 hours a week (five 8-hour shifts), how many people will you need to work at the front desk?

CHAPTER 3

Reservations Systems

CHAPTER OBJECTIVES

After reading this chapter you will understand:

- Why the reservations system has such an important function within the rooms division.
- What types of different reservations systems are available.
- How a reservations system keeps track of the room inventory.
- How to forecast rooms availability.
- Who makes reservations.
- How a reservation is made.
- Various discounts and alternative room rates policies and their implications concerning profitability.

INTRODUCTION

As we have seen, the proper control of labor and product costs are largely dependent upon an accurate forecast of future levels of occupancy. These future levels of occupancy are accessed through the reservation system of the hotel. A hotel's reservation system is critical to the financial success of the hotel. It is through this system that the majority of requests for rooms will be processed. All hotels must have in place a system that is capable of processing the maximum number of reservation requests possible in the most efficient and effective manner. This must all be accomplished while providing the highest level of guest service the hotel has pledged to give its guests.

A reservation inquiry is usually the first contact a guest is going to have with a hotel, whether it is at the hotel itself or at a distant central reservation office that services the entire hotel chain.

So, as is always the case with guest contact and particularly with this initial one, the reservation is an excellent opportunity for the hotel to put its best foot forward. There are several components to the reservation system: receiving the guest's request, matching the request with accommodations the hotel has available on that particular date or dates, recording the information in the hotel's reservation system, confirming the reservation with the guest immediately after accepting it, updating the reservation and the status of it prior to the guest's arrival, and formulating reservation reports to be used before, during, and after the guest's stay. All of these components must be in place and working at their full potential to guarantee the maximization of the hotel's room revenue. With a hotel's room revenue accounting for over 60 percent of its total revenue, it is not very difficult to see why such importance is attached to the reservation system and why constant attention is paid to its improvement.

Exhibit 3-1 shows that 82.2 percent of all hotel guests make a reservation prior to arriving at the hotel. The majority of reservations (69.5 percent) come from either the guest contacting the hotel directly or by utilizing the reservation system, which may be the central reservation office for the hotel chain. This information further demonstrates the need for a hotel to have an efficient operating reservation system.

CENTRAL RESERVATION OFFICE

In a chain-operated hotel, the central reservation office services the entire chain through one or more reservation centers. A person making a reservation can access the reservation center through a toll-free 800 number that is widely advertised by the chain. If the particular chain involved has more than one reservation center, the caller will be routed to the one closest to the calling location. If no operators are available, the call will be placed in a holding system and routed to the first available operator. The size of the hotel chain will dictate the volume of business received at the center and hence the number of operators needed. Some large hotel chains employ several hundred employees for their reservation centers, which are open 7 days a week and, in some cases, 24 hours a day.

EXHIBIT 3-1   MARKET DATA*

	All Establishments	Size			
		Less Than 150 Rooms	150–299 Rooms	300–600 Rooms	More Than 600 Rooms
Source of Business					
Foreign	8.7%	9.3%	6.3%	9.5%	13.3%
Domestic	91.3	90.7	93.7	90.5	86.7
Total	100.0%	100.0%	100.0%	100.0%	100.0%
Percentage of Repeat Business	41.0	43.7	40.6	34.9	32.6
Composition of Market					
Leisure	66.7%	79.5%	54.5%	58.0%	52.1%
Business and Government	8.9	9.2	15.3	5.6	2.6
Conference Participants	21.9	10.3	28.9	31.3	39.1
Other	2.5	1.0	1.3	5.1	6.2
Total	100.0%	100.0%	100.0%	100.0%	100.0%
Percentage of Guests with Advanced Reservations	82.2%	75.3%	86.5%	88.5%	91.8%
Advanced Reservation Mix					
Direct Inquiry	54.2%	64.3%	48.2%	55.2%	36.5%
Own Reservation System	15.3	11.3	21.4	9.5	16.2
Independent Reservation Systems	2.3	3.4	1.7	0.6	2.2
Travel Agent	13.0	9.6	12.7	17.0	18.4
Tour Operators	7.4	4.7	7.7	11.9	11.6
Hotel Representative	7.1	5.7	7.8	5.0	15.1
Transportation Company	0.7	1.0	0.5	0.8	0.0
Total	100.0%	100.0%	100.0%	100.0%	100.0%

*All amounts are means.

Source: Courtesy of Laventhol and Horwath

When the person making the reservation contacts the reservation center, a four-step process will begin: determining the needs of the caller, determining the availability of the hotel, recording the information about the guest, and confirming the reservation. This is a very simplified, abbreviated version of what occurs. However, even though the system is detailed and complicated, the portion of it that interfaces with the guest must be both simple and informative. All of this must take place as quickly as possible, so that the next caller can be accommodated.

When the caller makes contact with the reservation center, the first information the operator needs to ascertain is the caller's destination and dates of stay. From this information, the operator can determine if the chain has any properties in that location and if they have any vacancies on the dates of stay indicated by the caller. If there is more than one property in that location, the guest is asked for a first choice. Next, the caller must select the type of room or rooms he or she requires. At that point, the operator enters the information and is informed by the system whether that type of accommodation is available on the requested dates. The operator also has information available about the property, such as its location; the facilities available—pool, restaurants, meeting rooms (space), and so forth; its proximity to local attractions and airports, and directions for reaching the hotel by automobile. When the caller makes his choice, the operator will enter the guest's name, address, telephone number, and other information with regard to guaranteeing the reservation. (We will cover this in detail later in the chapter.)

The next step in the process is to print out and mail the guest a confirmation of the reservation. This confirmation contains all of the information about the guest's stay at the hotel and acts as a reminder for the guest to aid in the prevention of no-shows. As a last step in the process, the reservation is sent to the property that the guest has selected. Telecommunications have made this an extremely simple and quick procedure.

PROPERTY-LEVEL RESERVATION SYSTEMS

As we have already seen in Exhibit 3-1, direct inquiry—reservations made directly at the hotel—accounted for more than any other source with 54.2 percent of all reservations being made in this fashion. The procedure for processing a reservation at the property level is very similar to that employed by the central reservation office, except that it occurs on a smaller scale. Where a central reservation center may have a few hundred employees, a small hotel may only have one or two people working in its reservation area, assisted by the front desk staff. However, a large hotel of over 2,000 rooms will employ a dozen or more people in the reservation area. When a guest calls directly to the hotel, more information will be available about specifics of the hotel, its surrounding area, and events taking place in the area. This added benefit may encourage many guests to call the hotel directly.

Many hotels would prefer the guests call directly to the hotel in that this allows the reservationists of the hotel to "sellup." By selling up, we are referring to the process by which the hotel attempts to maximize its revenues by selling the most expensive rooms first. If the guest should object to the price, the reservationist will suggest a less expensive room to fill the guest's needs. This is a process that is not followed in most reservation centers because it requires too much time, and the operators at the reservation centers are more concerned with filling the guest's needs as they are presented to the operator than in negotiating the price. Overall, the property-based reservation area gives the hotel management much more control over the sale of its main revenue producing item—the guest room. Also, when a hotel is affiliated with a chain of hotels, there is a charge for each reservation made through the central reservation center. This charge is either a fixed dollar amount per reservation, a percentage of the revenue generated, or a combination of both.

DETERMINING ROOM AVAILABILITY

The first phase of the reservation process requires the hotel or its reservation center to determine whether or not the type of room the guest is requesting is available on the specified dates. This is a critical phase in the reservation process. If accurate information about future availability is not accessible, one of two very costly errors can occur: either overbooking or underbooking can take place. Overbooking occurs when too many reservations are accepted and there are not a sufficient number of rooms available to meet the demand of that day. This can be, and often is, very damaging to the reputation of the hotel involved. Under-booking, on the other hand, is a situation that occurs when a hotel stops taking reservations for a particular date, and when that day arrives, the hotel does not fill up because of its premature refusal of future business. The financial loss here is one that can never be recaptured, not to mention the business that was turned away and may never attempt to stay at that hotel again.

Determining availability in the hotel business is an ongoing process with an emphasis on forecasting both short-term and long-term availability. Short-term forecasting can be for 10 days in the future or for only an hour ahead. Long-term forecasting with regard to future availability may be concerned with next month or with more than a year ahead. The time frame for which the forecasting is done is really unimportant; the key factor here is that an accurate and reliable technique is used when we are attempting to ascertain the answer to our query—how many rooms do we have available? In addition to forecasting, the determination of future availability of rooms is dependent on a well-designed and operated inventory control system.

INVENTORY SYSTEMS

The number of rooms that are in a hotel represent the total inventory of rooms to be sold each and every day of the year. As reservations are taken for future usage of these rooms, a removal must be made of them from the inventory of saleable rooms on the specified dates of stay. This requires a system of inventory control that will allow for ease of depletion when the rooms are reserved and for quick access to determine the number and types of available rooms on any day in the future. There are a number of different systems used in a nonautomated environment. Some of these are still kept even in an automated hotel, although most experts would say this is an unnecessary duplication of work. Three of the most commonly used reservation inventory control systems are the density chart, wall chart, and reservation book.

Density Control Systems

The density control chart method of reservation inventory control provides a simple yet effective method for tracking the sale of guest rooms. There are two different ways to set up a density control system. It can be set up on a daily basis or on a monthly basis.

When the system is set up on a daily basis, the forms used will be similar to the one in Exhibit 3-2. Here, each day of the year has a separate form. All of these forms are then kept in chronological order, usually in a three ring binder for easy access. As we can see in Exhibit 3-2, the total number of rooms in the hotel is broken down by type and by number of each type. The number of rooms in the hotel with one queen-size bed is 60. Each room is then given a number starting with the number of rooms in this category; in this case 60 is the first number. Then, all the other rooms of this type are listed in descending numerical order until the last room is listed and given the number one. As guests call and make reservations for these rooms, the numbers are then marked off.

Let's run through an example of this to see exactly what happens when a guest calls the hotel directly to make a room reservation. First, the reservationist must find out what dates the guest wants to stay at the hotel and the type of room or rooms that will be required. After securing this information, the reservationist will turn to the page that represents this date of arrival in the daily density control book. If the guest is requesting a three-night stay in a room with one queen-size bed for arrival on September 8th, the reservationist will turn to the page for September 8th. As we can see in Exhibit 3-2, there are 60 rooms in the hotel with queen-size beds. However, the first 10 rooms have been crossed out with an X. This means that there have been 10 reservations taken for arrival on September 8th. The next five rooms have circles around them. This means that a reservation has been made for a guest who will be arriving on a date prior to this, but will be staying over on this date also. Forty-five is the first number on the page for September 8th, under the queen-size bed type room, that is not marked off. This means that there are 45 rooms with a queen-size bed available for sale on this date. Next, because the guest wants to stay for three days, we must turn to the pages in the book for September 9th and 10th. If these two days show rooms under the queen-size bed type of room available, then we can proceed with the reservation process. In the event that there are not queen-size bed rooms available on the 9th or 10th, the reservationist should suggest an alternative type of accommodation that is available. Assuming that there are rooms

EXHIBIT 3-2   DENSITY CONTROL CHART

Date *Sept. 8, 199_*
Queens

☒	☒	☒	☒	☒	☒	☒	☒	☒	☒
㊿	㊾	㊽	㊼	㊻	45	44	43	42	41
40	39	38	37	36	35	34	33	32	31
30	29	28	27	26	25	24	23	22	21
20	19	18	17	16	15	14	13	12	11
10	9	8	7	6	5	4	3	2	1

available on all three days, the reservationist would fill out the reservation form that will be discussed later in this chapter. Following the filling out of the form and confirmation of the reservation, this reservation must be entered in the daily density control book. This is done by turning to the page that represents September 8th and crossing out with an X the next number under the queen-size bed type of room. Then we must turn to the pages for the 9th and 10th and circle the next available numbers under the queen-size bed type room. This indicates that the room will be occupied by a guest who is a stayover on these days. After the reservation has been recorded in the book in this fashion, these rooms are now deleted from the available inventory of rooms to be sold on these days.

The next step in the process is to file the reservation form in such a way that it can easily be retrieved for any future follow-up. Filing the reservations by date of arrival and then in alphabetical order is a very efficient method. A tray filing drawer is set up by month and then by the day and dates of the month. In situations where there are a great many reservations to go through on any one day, they should be broken down into alphabetical order to facilitate easy access of a reservation.

When the density control system is set up on a monthly basis, one form or chart will be utilized for an entire month. Exhibit 3-3 is the form used to represent the rooms available for sale during the month of September. As with the daily control system, each type of room is grouped together. Here we see the days of the month displayed across the top of each room type grouping, directly across from the room type. Vertically along the left side of the form are the numbers of rooms that are in that grouping. In this example, there are ten rooms with king-size beds in them. The numbering of the rooms is the same as in the daily control system, starting with the highest number and going down to one. When

EXHIBIT 3-3

Room Type: Q	SEPTEMBER 199_																														
	1	2	3	4	5	6	7	8	9	10	11	12	13	14	15	16	17	18	19	20	21	22	23	24	25	26	27	28	29	30	31
10																															
9																															
8																															
7																															
6																															
5																															
4																															
3																															
2																															
1																															

a reservation is taken, a check mark can be placed in the column that represents the date of arrival and any additional days for which the guest will be staying. An advantage of the monthly method is that one is not required to be turning pages for each day that the guest stays over, and one can easily determine at a glance the number of rooms available for a month at a time. However, this system does not lend itself well to usage in a hotel with a large number of rooms, simply because of the amount of space the form or chart would take up. Computer systems, which work on the principle of the density control system in that when a reservation is input into the computer a room is removed from the available saleable inventory of rooms, are a viable alternative. Later in this chapter, we will discuss in depth the computerized reservation system and its forms. One point that we have not made so far, and it may be a critical one for a hotel with a large number of stayovers, is that stayovers must be recorded into the density system. This is extremely important when there are a large number of stayovers and the hotel is running at a high level of occupancy. If these stayovers are not entered, the hotel could very well find itself in an overbooked situation.

Wall Chart

The reservation wall chart functions as a density control system. However, it is different enough to be discussed by itself. Originally, the wall chart was designed by Dallett Jones. The chart works much the same as the monthly density control chart explained above. That is, in principle; the main difference arises in the amount of detail that is possible to include on the wall chart. Instead of using the number of rooms in each room type on the left side of the chart (as is the case with the monthly density control), the wall chart uses the exact room numbers for the rooms in the hotel. Also, the rooms are not checked off, but, instead, a piece of colored tape is placed across the days on which the room will be occupied by a particular guest. Then the guest's name is written across the piece of tape. Difficulties can arise with this system with regard to the assignment of guest rooms. When reservations are taken, a specific room is reserved for the guest. If the hotel is experiencing a situation in which many guests change their plans and decide to stay longer than originally indicated, a great deal of changes will have to be made. This is different from a system where particular rooms are not reserved, but rather types of rooms such as those with queen-size or king-size beds.

FORECASTING METHODS

The forecasting of room availability for the future is extremely important in the operational planning of a hotel. The three different types of forecasts we will discuss here are the 10-day forecast, the 3-day forecast, and the daily availability formula. Each of these calculations plays an important role in the day-to-day operation of the hotel. Included here is everything from planning how many staff members to schedule to how to order in the food and beverage area. Later, in Chapter 12, we will discuss forecasting over a longer period of time, such as a month or more, with regard to the budgeting function.

Ten-Day Forecast

The 10-day forecast is prepared by the front office manager. This forecast is then distributed to the other areas in the hotel, such as the food and beverage and the housekeeping areas. Food and beverage will use this forecast in planning the purchasing of items used in this area as well as in scheduling employees to work. Based on the number of rooms reserved and the number of guests coming in, an accurate estimate of the number of meals to be sold over the three-meal periods can be made by the food and beverage manager looking at the trends that have occurred in the past. Exhibit 3-4 is an example of what should be included in a 10-day forecast and how it should be set up for ease of preparation and readability. The 10-day forecast is going to project the number of rooms that will be occupied over each of the next 10 days. This is accomplished by taking the number of rooms occupied last night and adding to this figure the number of reservations that have been taken for this date. Next, the estimated number of check-outs for the day are subtracted from this. Other factors that must be con-

EXHIBIT 3-4

10-Day Forecast											
September 199_	1	2	3	4	5	6	7	8	9	10	
Rms. Occup. Last Night											
+ Today's Reservations											
− Projected Check-outs											
+ Projected Walk-ins											
= Projected Rms. Occup.											

sidered are the estimated number of reservations that will be received after the forecast is completed and the number of walk-ins that are projected for that day. All of the estimates that are made are based on patterns, such as those that have emerged over a period of time or those which are related to the season. In addition to this information, it is important that the other departments be notified of any groups that will be coming in over this same period and any special information that may be known about their needs.

Three-Day Forecast

The 3-day forecast is prepared by the front office manager as an update to the 10-day forecast. Exhibit 3-5 is an example of a 3-day forecast. As is the case with the 10-day forecast, the 3-day forecast is distributed to the other departments for their last minute planning. This is particularly useful in the scheduling of staff. These last minute changes to the schedule can prove to be extremely beneficial to the hotel in the long run. For example, if the occupancy now appears to be higher than originally planned for the time period covered by the schedule, an addition of staff members will aid in providing better customer service, which, in turn, will result in more repeat business. Conversely, if the occupancy now appears to be lower than forecasted, a reduction in the number of staff members will result in substantial savings over the period of a year. Additionally, the 3-day forecast will allow the management of the hotel to make adjustments to the rates, and this may result in a greater number of walk-ins accepting the accommodations offered.

EXHIBIT 3-5

3-Day Forecast				
September 199_	1	2	3	Comments
Rms. Occup. Last Night				
+ Today's Reservations				
− Projected Check-outs				
+ Projected Walk-ins				
= Projected Rms. Occup.				

Daily Availability Formula

The daily availability formula is similar to the 10-day and 3-day forecasts mentioned above. The major difference between the daily availability formula and the other forecasts is the amount of information utilized in the preparation of the daily formula. In the daily availability formula, the following items of information are used in its preparation: number of no-shows, number of cancellations, number of understays, number of overstays, and the number of rooms out-of-order. These items are forecasted for the day in question prior to the beginning of the day's business. A front office manager needs this information to make decisions about the reduction of room rates for walk-ins, to alert his or her employees about the number of rooms that they will be responsible for selling on this day, and to work with the other hotels in the area with regard to referral business. Without this information available first thing in the morning, it may not become apparent until after check-out time how many rooms remain unsold. At this point in the day, many requests for lodging may have been turned away because of an erroneous belief that there would not be any rooms available. Information such as this could cause a reduction in the potential room revenue for the day.

When the daily availability formula is prepared, as it is in the 10-day and 3-day forecast, it appears as follows:

	number of rooms in the hotel
Less:	number of stayovers
Less:	number of reservations
Equals:	number of rooms available

There are a number of shortcomings in this method of preparing the daily availability formula. Missing is the consideration of the number of rooms that will be affected by such factors as were mentioned above. When these variables are taken into consideration, the formula will appear as follows:

	number of rooms in the hotel
Less:	number of stayovers
Less:	number of reservations
Plus:	number of no-shows
Plus:	number of cancellations
Plus:	number of understays
Less:	number of overstays
Less:	number of out-of-order rooms
Equals:	number of rooms available

A number of new factors is taken into consideration in this more expanded formula. Let's take a closer look at each of the elements to see how they are determined and the effect that they have on the availability calculation.

One can calculate the number of stayovers by taking the number of rooms occupied last night and subtracting from it the number of rooms that are known to be checking out, based on information given by the guests.

> number of rooms occupied last night
> Less: number of known check-outs
> Equals: number of stayovers

This stayover figure is, in all probability, incorrect because of two factors: one that has the potential to increase it, and one that decreases the number of stayovers. Overstays are those guests who originally plan to check out on the day in question, but, for whatever reason, their plans change and they extend their stay at the hotel. This change in the length of stay does not come to the attention of the hotel until after the daily availability formula is prepared. This situation is quite common in resort areas where guests change their plans at the last minute. Such overstays can cause a problem between guests in the hotel and reservation arrivals if the hotel is running at 100 percent occupancy. The problem is that the guests in the hotel most often feel they have first right at retaining the room for an extra period of time. However, quite the opposite is true; the guest with the guaranteed reservation has a contract with the hotel to occupy that room. The guest currently occupying the room has the right of occupancy only for the agreed upon period of time as was stipulated at his or her check-in time or as was later changed by mutual agreement between the hotel and the guest. In any case, the hotel should do its best to retain the current guest as well as to give first right to the room to the guest coming in on the guaranteed reservation. If the hotel is unable to retain the guest currently in the hotel, every effort should be made by the hotel to secure accommodations at a hotel close by as well as to provide the necessary transportation to the new hotel and any additional services the hotel feels are needed.

Understays are those guests who alter their plans so as to reduce the number of days of their stay at the hotel. Understays cause quite the opposite problem that overstays cause. In this case, the hotel finds itself with more rooms available than previously expected. The problem is that the hotel does not find out about the premature check-out until the guest actually does check out, which is anytime prior to the stipulated check-out time. In some cases, the front desk may not find out until housekeeping notifies them of the status of the room. This is usually the case when a guest has prepaid for the room and departs without informing the front desk or anyone else in the hotel. Now the hotel finds itself with an extra room available to sell for that evening. Many times the hotel may have been turning away other reservations based on the availability projections made prior to having this new information. If many guests are understaying, then this can cause a real problem in trying to fill up the hotel. Also, if this is occurring often, it is an indication to management that something is in need of attention either in the reservation system or in the operation of the hotel and its services.

The number of reservations is easily discernible from the reservation inventory system that is used in the hotel. For example, if the hotel in question is using the daily density control system, all that is needed is to turn to the page in the book for the day and count the number of rooms that are under reservation. Two factors that affect the rooms available figure, and also have a specific relationship to the number of reservations for the day, are the number of no-shows and the number of cancellations.

No-shows are those people who have made a reservation, but never arrive at the hotel to check in. Many hotels justify overbooking because of the number of no-shows that they experience. Granted, no-shows are a serious problem for the lodging industry; however, with the different types of guaranteed reservations in effect, most hotels have been able to reduce the number of reservations accepted on an overbooking basis. Yet, this figure is still a necessary one in the calculation of rooms available but to a lesser degree of importance than it used to be.

The effect that cancellations have is dependent on the cancellation policy of the hotel. In many hotels, cancellations are required 24 or more hours in advance of the date of arrival. If the reservation is not canceled in time, a guest is responsible for the payment of the room charges, unless it is subsequently sold. In any event, the hotel should make every effort to sell the canceled room even if it is after the stipulated cancellation time. By doing this, the hotel is able to avoid billing the guest for not showing. This can go a long way toward creating good customer relations, but only when the hotel lets the guest who has canceled know what it has done to save them the charge.

These four items just discussed—understays, overstays, no-shows, and cancellations—are calculated as a percentage of the element they affect. The number of understays and overstays are calculated as a percentage of the number of known check-outs for the day. By known check-outs, we mean the number of rooms that have notified the front desk that they will be checking out prior to the preparation of the daily availability formula. No-shows and cancellations are calculated as a percentage of the number of reservations for the day. One arrives at percentages by tracking these factors over a period of time. This is first done by using a form similar to the one in Exhibit 3-6. On this form, information is recorded daily as to the number of stayovers for the day and the related number of understays and overstays, as well as the number of reservations for the day and the corresponding number of no-shows and cancellations. Additionally, a tally is kept for the remaining information on the daily availability formula.

In Exhibit 3-7, some of this information is transcribed to the form that is utilized in preparing a listing of the no-shows, cancellations, understays, and overstays as a percentage of the appropriate element of the daily availability formula. These calculations are made in the following manner:

Understay % = Number of understays ÷ Number of known check-outs × 100%
Overstay % = Number of overstays ÷ Number of known check-outs × 100%
No-show % = Number of no-shows ÷ Number of reservations × 100%
Cancellation % = Number of cancellations ÷ Number of reservations × 100%

EXHIBIT 3-6

Month of September 199_

Day	Date	Stayovers	Understays	Overstays	Number of Resv.	No-shows	Cancellations	Check-outs
Mon.	1							
Tues.	2							
Wed.	3							
Thurs.	4							
Fri.	5							
Sat.	6							
Sun.	7							

EXHIBIT 3-7

Res. History 100 Rms.		No. of Reservations	Early Arrivals		Cancellations		No-shows		Beginning of Day Estimated Departures	Understays		Overstays	
C/O	S/O	#	#	%	#	%	#	%	#	#	%	#	%
100	240	130	2	1.5	6	4.6	3	2.3	100	4	4	5	5

These percentages are then used as a guide in estimating the number of rooms that will fall into the above mentioned categories. This information is extremely useful in helping the hotel plan its reservation strategy. Caution is needed, however, when one is applying these percentages. They will change based upon the individual situation of the hotel. Examples of factors that can change these percentages are types of guests making reservations, seasonality, and competition in the local market.

RESERVATION INITIATION

There are basically four main sources for the initiation of hotel room reservations. These four sources overlap considerably, but it still remains important to discuss them individually at the outset.

Guest

The individual guest is most apt to be making his or her reservation when the trip is specifically related to a personal vacation. In this case, the person making the reservation will be the one occupying the room. Many times this can work to the advantage of the hotel in that all of the information and requests made will not fall prey to a breakdown in the communication process. Additionally, the hotel has an opportunity to sellup the guest to a higher rate room or sell additional services to the guest prior to his or her arrival. Without question, one of the greatest advantages is the personal contact with the guest and the chance that is given the hotel to begin building its relationship with the guest.

Company

Business travelers seldom have time to make their own reservations. So, in these cases, when someone from the company is making the reservation for the traveler, it is extremely important to make sure all of the information is correct. In most cases, if someone from the company makes a mistake, the traveler will still hold the hotel responsible. Getting the name of the person who made the reservation and a phone number for that person may prove to be very helpful.

Travel Agent

Travel agents are extremely important to the lodging industry. In some hotels, the majority of business is booked through travel agents. When dealing with travel agents, one must remember one thing above all else and that is to pay them their commission. Travel agents are working for their clients to place them in the hotel that the client requested or to place the client in a hotel that the agent feels will satisfy the needs of the client. Most hotels pay travel agents a 10 percent commission on the room rate paid by the guest. So, if a guest's reservation is booked by a travel agent for five nights at the rate of $100 per night, the following calculation would determine the amount of commission:

$$\$100 \times 5 \text{ nights} = \$500 \times 10\% = \$50 \text{ in commission.}$$

The reason we emphasize paying travel agents their commissions is that if an agent has a choice between two hotels of equal quality in which to place a client, most probably the agent will place the client in the hotel that pays the commission on time. (Not to mention the fact that the travel agent has earned the commission.) To further promote the hotel's relationship with the travel agent, if a guest's reservation was for five nights as in the above example and the guest should stay six nights, pay the travel agent his commission for the sixth night also. Then, when you pay the commission, let the travel agent know what you have done. It not only shows that you want to be fair in your dealings with the agent, but it also indicates that the guest must have enjoyed your hotel to have stayed an extra night.

Groups

Group reservations come from a variety of different types of businesses, organizations, and associations. With this variety there comes a wide range of backgrounds of experience among the people booking the group business. It is the responsibility of the hotel to understand this disparity in backgrounds and to accommodate the different group representatives.

Two of the more common group reservations are for conventions and tour groups. Both of these can involve different parties making the reservations and corresponding arrangements.

In the case of convention bookings, the reservations will usually be made directly by a representative of the convention group. In the case of a large citywide convention, the arrangements will be through the convention and housing bureau for the city. When the association is working with only one hotel, the meeting planner for the association will request a block of rooms from the hotel. Then, as reservations are made by the members of the association, the hotel will inform the meeting planner of the number of rooms taken from this block of rooms. This list of confirmed reservations should be sent to the meeting planner at regular intervals throughout the process. Additionally, confirmations should be sent to the individual members of the association, as they would with any other type of reservation. If an individual member cancels his reservation, the room should be returned to the group block of rooms and the meeting planner should be informed of this cancellation.

A citywide convention is one in which the group is too large to be housed in one hotel and space is occupied in many of the city's hotels. In this type of convention, one hotel will act as the convention headquarters. This hotel will house the leaders of the convention and host many of the functions associated with the convention. The headquarters hotel is usually the first hotel to fill its block of rooms.

Reservations for a citywide convention are usually handled by the city's convention and housing bureau. Initially, the bureau will contact the various hotels in the city and request from them a commitment for space and rates for the convention. After this is done, the bureau will submit this information to the convention meeting planner. Reservation requests are sent to the bureau, who will deduct these reservations from a hotel's block of rooms and send the request on to the hotel. It is then the responsibility of the hotel to confirm the reservation with the guest. Hotels must remember to inform the bureau of all cancellations so that they can be returned to the block of rooms for that hotel.

Tour group reservations are usually made for the group by a third party, such as a travel agency. With this type of reservation, the hotel must be careful to establish cut-off dates by which the reservations are to be made. After this date, the hotel should not hold any more rooms in the block. If this is not closely monitored, the hotel may end up with unsold rooms on the dates requested. By a specific preestablished date, a rooming list, including the names of the guests occupying rooms and the types of rooms they will occupy, must be sent to the hotel by the tour operator.

Of course, a contract should be made up between the tour operator and the hotel. This contract should include information about the number, types, and rates of the rooms being blocked. Information should also be included about the deposit to be sent and the method of final payment for rooms occupied.

Baggage-in and *baggage-out* are terms used to specify how much the hotel will be paid for each piece of luggage its bell staff carries into the hotel and out again at check-out time. The hotel will then use this money to pay the bell staff and door staff for their work during the high-traffic time of group tours. It ensures that the uniformed services employees will receive a fair gratuity for their work.

RESERVATION CONTACT METHODS

There are various methods used by guests and representatives of guests to make reservations at a hotel. Some of the more common methods are telephone, mail, fax, and contact in person. These methods will be dealt with in this section, as they are used by guests and their representatives to contact the hotel directly as opposed to going through the central reservation office of a hotel chain.

Telephone

When a person calls the hotel's reservation office, he or she should be given the full and undivided attention of the reservationist, who represents the hotel to the guest. The impression created at this point is a lasting one and should demonstrate the hotel's concern for the guest's satisfaction. The following points provide a list of guidelines for the reservationist to be taken into consideration when speaking over the telephone:

1. Act alert—Speak in such a way that will convey to the caller that you are wide awake and ready to help him or her with whatever is needed.
2. Be pleasant—Smile when you are speaking on the phone and this smile will come through in your voice.
3. Be natural—Speak in a natural way. Don't try to use technical terminology, for it will only confuse the caller and certainly won't impress anyone. Be careful, however, not to use slang.
4. Speak distinctly—Talk into the telephone mouthpiece and pronounce your words slowly and clearly.
5. Be expressive—Speak in varying tones. Speaking in a monotone will not excite the caller about the hotel and its services, but speaking with vitality and enthusiasm will.
6. Answer promptly—By answering the telephone promptly, you will build confidence in the hotel and demonstrate efficiency to the caller.
7. Introduce yourself—When answering the phone, you can get the conversation off to a good start by introducing yourself and offering to serve the caller. Calls should be answered with a greeting similar to the following: "Good morning, reservations, Pat speaking. How may I be of service to you?"
8. Be personable—As soon as you get the guest's name, use it throughout the conversation.
9. Listen—Listen to the caller carefully so he or she won't have to repeat words, and so that you get all of the information correctly.

Telephone sales of guest rooms are extremely difficult. When a guest is already at the hotel, it is difficult enough to sell the services of the hotel because of their intangible nature. Over the phone, this difficulty is multiplied. In order to sell rooms over the phone, the reservationist must verbally communicate ideas, impressions, and facts about the hotel. The best way to handle this task is to describe the room's size, location, special features, and any extras included.

Mail

Fewer reservations are made today by mail than were made in the past. This situation has come about because of the ease of making reservations using the other methods discussed here. Fortunately, this is the case, because with a reservation request made by mail, there is often a problem with rooms being available on the requested dates of stay. There may also be some confusion as to what the guest wants in terms of accommodations and, in this situation, there is an inability to upsell the guest to a higher-rate room.

Fax

With the proliferation of fax machines in businesses, there will be a growing trend to use this method of transmission to request room reservations. Some of the problems associated with mail reservation requests are still present. The fax method of communication opens up an excellent channel for reservations with international hotels. Now reservations can be made instantaneously and a reservation confirmation sent back to the caller all in a matter of a few minutes.

In Person

When a reservation is made in person, either by the future guest or his representative, a great many opportunities open up that did not previously exist. No longer is the reservationist faced with the dilemma of trying to explain only through verbal communication what the hotel has to offer. Now the person has an opportunity to actually see the hotel and experience its services. Whenever possible, the guest should be shown a room similar to the one he is making a reservation for. This is a perfect opportunity to make friends with the guest and to upsell him at the same time.

RESERVATION FORMS

Various forms are used throughout the reservation process to ensure that all accepted reservations will be accommodated. The two major forms we will discuss in this section are the reservation record and the confirmation form.

Reservation Record

The reservation record used in the reservation process is an extremely important document. Information contained on it is critical for satisfying the needs of the guest, for following up in the area of marketing, and for processing the charge on a guest that may become a no-show.

Exhibit 3-8 is an example of a reservation record. After the employee has confirmed the type of accommodations the guest desires, and the availability of the room on the dates requested, the next step is to complete the reservation record. The following information should be solicited from the prospective guest and recorded on the record:

ROOM RESERVATION

DATE _____

ROOM TYPE   S   D   P   VIP   RATE _____

NUMBER OF ROOMS _____

ARRIVAL DATE _____

DEPARTURE DATE _____

NUMBER OF PERSONS/ROOM _____

TRAVEL AGENT'S ID# _____

TRAVEL AGENCY NAME _____

ADDRESS _____

CITY _____ STATE _____ ZIP _____

PHONE _____

_____

GUEST NAME _____

_____

COMPANY NAME _____

ADDRESS _____

CITY _____ STATE _____ ZIP _____

PHONE _____

DEPOSIT REQUIRED _____

RESERVED BY _____

SPECIAL REQUESTS _____

CREDIT CARD NO. _____

Exhibit 3-8

- Date of Reservation—Record the date that the guest made the reservation on, using the format style of the hotel, such as either 9/8/90 or Sept. 8, 1990.
- Reservation Clerk—Write in the reservation clerk's name or initials, or the number of the clerk accepting the reservation. It is important to be able to go back and check with this person in the event that some of the information needs to be clarified.
- Arrival Date—Use the format set by the hotel. This information is critical and should be carefully entered. The time of arrival is important to know, especially if the hotel is overbooked on the date of arrival. A reservation with an A.M. arrival time that has not shown by late evening could indicate a no-show.
- Departure Date—In the event the guest is not sure, enter an approximate date with a question mark so it can be confirmed when the guest checks in.
- Number of Nights—Enter the number of nights the guest plans on occupying the room. This should correspond with the arrival and departure dates.
- Number of Persons—This number is broken down according to adults and children. Room rates will vary based on the number of guests. In many hotels there is no charge for children occupying a room with adults.
- Rate Confirmed—It is very important that the rate quoted to a guest be correctly recorded. The rate is usually made for the room without tax included. If this is the case, the guest should be made aware of the tax. In many areas of the country, the total tax on hotel rooms is higher than the state sales tax and can be 10 percent or more.
- Number of Rooms—The number of rooms requested and the type of room should be closely monitored when the rooms are removed from the available inventory in setting up the reservation for the guest's arrival. Various types of rooms should be explained to the guest with the possibility of upselling to a higher-priced room.
- Special Requests—These are only requests and should not be promised to the guest at this point. Such requests might include amenities, such as a room overlooking the pool, or rooms that are connecting or adjacent. The hotel should do everything possible to honor these requests.
- Telephone—A telephone number where the guest may be reached during the day should be recorded. Be sure to get the area code with the number.
- Name—Be certain to get the correct spelling of the guest's last and first name, and the middle initial. Any title used by the guest, such as "Dr." or a military rank, should be recorded. Be careful not to record the name of the caller if it is someone other than the guest.
- Address—Record the guest's home address. Be sure to get the street numbers, the post office box numbers, and the zip codes in their entirety.

- Representing—If the guest is on a trip other than vacation or personal business, record this information. Such information includes the name of the company or the name of the convention the guest is attending. When the guest is a business account, record the business address of the company.
- Reservation Guaranteed—If the reservation is guaranteed, calculate the cost for the guest room. For example, if the room rate is $110.00 and the tax rate is 7 percent and the guest intends to stay 5 nights, the guest would send $588.50, calculated as follows:

$110 × .07 tax rate = $7.70 tax per night
$110 + $7.70 = $117.70 room and tax per night
$117.70 × 5 nights = $588.50

If a travel agent is involved in a prepaid reservation, the commission may be deducted in advance. In this case, the five-night prepayment, less the commission, is remitted to the hotel. An example of this, based on a 10 percent commission to the travel agent, follows:

$110 × 5 nights = $550 × .10 commission = $55
$588.50 for 5 nights − $55 commission = $533.50

In this example, the travel agent would send the hotel a check for $533.50. However, when the hotel receives the check it must credit the guest's account for the full amount of $588.50. This saves the hotel the work of paying the commission. However, if the guest decides to check out before the five nights are up, the prepaid commission policy does complicate making a refund to the guest.

When the hotel accepts a reservation on a one-night deposit guarantee, the reservationist should request the guest to send the room rate and tax for the first night's stay. The reason for this is that if the guest is a no-show, the hotel will not lose anything by holding the room all night.

One very nice advantage to the deposit guarantee reservation is that the hotel can accumulate large sums of money in advance of the guest's arrival. This policy actually allows the hotel to use other people's money, interest free, until their arrival. With either type of deposit guarantee, there are certain procedures the hotel must follow to safeguard itself from loss. When accepting a deposit guarantee, the hotel must allow enough time for the check to reach the hotel and be deposited into its account. This ensures that the check will clear the bank. The hotel can accomplish this by setting a cut-off date by which time a deposit must be received, and by not accepting any reservations under the deposit guarantee that are made too close to the arrival date to allow for the clearing of the check before the guest's arrival. The hotel's local bank will be able to provide a listing that indicates the time needed for a check to clear, based on the location of the bank on which the check is written. With a credit card guarantee, the reservation is guaranteed once the phone call is over. The drawback with a deposit guarantee reservation is that once the reservation is taken, more steps must take place before the reservation is actually guaranteed. For instance, the guest must send the deposit, and the hotel has to process the check and record the information that the deposit has been received. When the hotel receives the deposit it sets up a credit on the guest's account for the amount of the deposit. This credit remains there until the guest checks in and uses the credit, or until the guest cancels the reservation and requests a refund.

Corporate

Hotels often set up agreements with different businesses to accept their reservations on a guaranteed basis. These agreements are usually in the form of a written contract between the hotel and the company. By entering into the contract, the company agrees to pay the hotel for all reservations booked, whether its representative shows or not. To effectively process this type of reservation, the reservation department and front desk should have a listing of all businesses that the hotel has set up accounts with, including the account number for each business. In addition to the name of the guest and the address, the account number of the business should be placed on the reservation. Corporate business is an extremely important part of many hotels' markets, thus extra care should be taken when processing these reservations to ensure complete guest satisfaction.

CANCELLATION POLICY AND PROCEDURES

For a variety of reasons, guests will sometimes find it necessary to cancel their reservations. Canceled business meetings, a change in vacation plans, and personal emergencies are just a few of the many situations requiring a cancellation. To best serve the guest and protect the hotel, it is necessary to have a cancellation policy in place. The policy should be made known to the guest when the reservation is made; in addition, the confirmation process should include a repetition of the policy. The individual needs of the hotel will depend both upon the history of how far in advance guests make reservations and the trend of the number of cancellations that the hotel receives. A sample cancellation policy is as follows:

> If you cannot stay with us, you can cancel any reservation by calling the hotel directly or by using the toll-free number (800) 555-0000. When you call, you will receive a cancellation number. All guaranteed reservations must be canceled 24 hours prior to your scheduled date of arrival in order for a refund to be issued.

Hotels may require more than the 24-hour cancellation notice. This is true where a special event is taking place in the area or during a holiday period. Resort area hotels are particularly concerned with advance notice of cancellations because of the destination vacation business that they rely upon.

The procedure to follow when a guest calls to cancel a reservation is as follows:

1. Obtain the guest's name and date of arrival.
2. Locate the reservation and mark on it "canceled," along with the date of the cancellation, the cancellation number, and the name of the person canceling the reservation.
3. Ask the guest if you can make another reservation for him or her at this time.
4. Refile the reservation and cancellation so there will be a record of it in the event a question arises later.

Remember, when a guest calls and cancels a reservation he or she is doing the hotel a favor by not being a no-show. Thus, the same level of courtesy should be given this customer as any other actual or potential guest. The reservationist's treatment of the cancellation may well come to bear upon the likelihood that the person canceling a reservation this time will consider the same hotel when planning his or her next vacation or meeting.

Cancellation Number

A cancellation number should be assigned for every reservation that is canceled, and it should be given to the guest for his or her records. One method of developing a cancellation number is to base it on the following information:

141—The hotel's property number of the chain.
030—The date of arrival based on the Julian calendar.
413—The number of total cancellations for the hotel for the year to date, including this one.
LD—The first and last initial of the clerk accepting the cancellation.

Cancellations should then be recorded on a cancellation record form that contains the cancellation number, name of the person that canceled the reservation, the name in which the reservation was recorded, the date on which the reservation was made, and the date the cancellation was made.

OVERBOOKING

Overbooking is a term that conjures up fear in the hearts of many involved in the hotel industry, as well as causing apprehension for potential hotel guests. By overbooking we refer to the act of accepting more reservations than a given hotel has rooms to accommodate. The main reason for overbooking is to ensure that the hotel will achieve 100 percent occupancy. Because of no-shows on nonguaranteed reservations, cancellations, and understays, many hotels find it necessary to involve themselves in overbooking. While no-shows are not as prevalent for hotels as for the airline industry (where as many as 30 percent of those persons holding reservations fail to show up for a flight), it is still a major problem. But before any hotel engages in overbooking, the hotel's attorney should be consulted, due to potential legal complications.

When a hotel overbooks, it is gambling that its overbooking percentage will be accurate enough so as not to have to "walk" any guests. The overbooking percentage rate, commonly referred to as OPR, is developed for each hotel based on its knowledge of current reservations, the business that is currently booked, its history, last year's trends, local events, area hotels' occupancy levels, the number of walk-ins, and the no-show rate. With this information in hand, hotels that wish to overbook are able to compute an OPR that will allow the hotel to maximize occupancy without displacing any guests. While it is possible to calculate the OPR for any hotel, this percentage is not fixed. The previously mentioned factors are constantly changing, making it necessary to recalculate the OPR almost daily.

When overbooking, a hotel must accept the fact that this procedure will not always work in its favor and some guests with confirmed reservations must be walked. When this occurs, the hotel has an obligation to the guest. The American Hotel & Motel Association has written a "Guest Reservation Pledge" that can be adopted by hotels. It reads as follows:

OUR PLEDGE

We will hold confirmed reservations until the specified arrival time in the reservation unless a later time of arrival is requested.

Prior to the time so specified, it is not our policy knowingly to offer for rent guest rooms for which we already have valid confirmed reservations.

If, for any reason beyond our control, a room should not be available for a customer who has a valid reservation, we shall assist in securing comparable accommodations at another property as nearby as possible.

THE MANAGEMENT

An approach taken by some hotels is to pay for the guest's room at the hotel to which the guest has been walked. This policy adds a cost consideration to the overbooking decision the hotel has to make. Holiday Inn, for example, adopted "The Holiday Inn Reservation Promise," which reads as follows:

> If your reserved room is not vacated by a previous guest, the host hotel will provide a room at, and transportation to, another hotel, and pay for a telephone call to notify your home or office of the lodging change. The host hotel also will pay any increase in room rate if you had a regular reservation (6:00 P.M. arrival), or the full cost of the first night's lodging if you had a Guaranteed All Night reservation or had made an advanced deposit.

Naturally, a policy such as the one above makes it more costly for the hotel to walk a guest than it would be to underbook by one room. But, more important, if the guest does have to be walked, there is less likelihood that relations will be destroyed. Yet, the danger of this is still there, even with the free room policy. The hotel might lose the guest as a repeat customer, but if the hotel is a member of a chain, the entire chain may suffer. The advantage of slight underbooking is clear when one considers the short- and long-term costs of walking a guest.

The Reservation as a Contract

The reservation has been viewed as a contract. The contracting parties are the hotel and the guest. The guest contracts to arrive as planned or to cancel the reservation by notifying the hotel prior to the planned arrival. The guest secures the contract by placing a deposit with the hotel. The hotel has its obligations as well. They agree to reserve a room, and to keep the room available until the guest either cancels, or arrives, or until some time or date when the guest is considered as a no-show. This is not a law book, but in general, the hotel is obliged to reserve a room for the guest. If the hotel overbooks and a guest arrives with no rooms available, the hotel is obliged to make alternative arrangements for the guest. Usually the hotel will forego the first night's room rent in light of the inconvenience to the guest for moving them. The hotel is under no obligation to do this (in most states), but this is one example (of many) where the law and the marketing reality differ.

If the guest fails to show and the hotel would have been fully booked (such as during a special event like the Kentucky Derby), then the hotel may charge the guest for the entire stay (that is, if the guest reserved a room for five nights the hotel can charge the no-show for the five-night stay). Case law places restrictions on this, and the likelihood of collecting is very small, but the hotel does have this right. In general, though, the hotel can remove itself from legal problems by supplying a guest who must be bumped with a room in another hotel of equal quality, and the hotel can then collect from the guest the normal room rate. In general, the hotel can charge the no-show for the one night's revenue, but collection problems and legal requirements make it very difficult to collect more than that.

DISCUSSION QUESTIONS

1. What are the differences between central reservations and property-level reservations in terms of making a reservation?
2. How do we determine room availability?
3. Describe one of the three most common methods of room inventory control.
4. Why do you think a computer system would be so useful in maintaining a density control system?
5. How might the cancellation policy of a hotel affect the hotel's revenue?
6. Who may initiate a reservation?
7. What kind of obligation do hotels have to guests holding confirmed reservations when the hotels overbook?

STUDY QUESTIONS

1. What are the components of the reservation system?
2. What information is the first thing needed by the reservations clerk from the caller to a central reservations office?
3. What do we mean by "selling up"?
4. What are the types of inventory control systems used by reservations?
5. Which two forecasts are specifically stated in the text as being prepared by the front office manager?
6. What might happen if the daily availability forecast were not performed early in the morning?
7. What is an "understay"?
8. What is a no-show?
9. Someone who reserves a room for a person who works for him or her as an employee is initiating a reservation under what category?
10. What are the four methods of contact used by potential guests or their agents while making a reservation?

PROBLEMS

1. If you had a 100-room hotel and you expected the following operational statistics for next Monday, how many reservations would you allow the reservations department to accept for that night? (Assume no overbooking is allowed.) Stayovers: 50 rooms; current reservations booked: 30.

2. Construct a density control sheet for a 100-room hotel (The Empty Arms Hotel) with the following room categories: Ocean front (35 rooms), ocean view (20 rooms), street view (35 rooms), tower suites (10 rooms).

3. If I pay a 10 percent commission to travel agents, how much commission would I owe the Fly-by-Night Travel Agency for a guest occupying two rooms for 14 nights at $100 per room?

CHAPTER 4

Room Rates

CHAPTER OBJECTIVES

After reading this chapter you will understand:

- Why the establishment of the proper room rate structure is so important to a hotel.
- What categories of room rates are usually seen in a hotel.
- How room rates are determined in a hotel.

IMPORTANCE

When one considers room revenue, there are two major factors taken into consideration. They are the percentage of occupancy and the average room rate. While there are many areas of the country where occupancy has been on the decline, the percentage of occupancy has been relatively stable nationwide over the past decade. On the other hand, the average room rate has increased considerably.

In many cases in the past, too much emphasis had been placed on the percentage of occupancy and not enough on the area of room rate maximization. This chapter will focus its attention on the factors involved in maximizing the average room rate. The room revenue of a hotel is by far the most significant in achieving financial success. We can easily see this by showing the amount of revenue brought into a hotel through the rooms division as a percentage of a hotel's gross profit. The following example compares the gross revenue and the contribution from the rooms division and the food and beverage division.

In a 400-room hotel that has a total annual revenue of $10 million, the breakdown of the revenue would appear as follows:

Total Revenue	$10,000,000	Total Revenue	$10,000,000
Rms Revenue %	× 60%	Food & Bev. Rev. %	× 33%
Rms Revenue	$6,000,000	Food & Bev. Rev.	$3,300,000
Rms Expenses %	× 25%	F & B Expenses %	× 80%
Rms Expenses	$1,500,000	Food & Bev. Expenses	$2,640,000
Rms Income	$4,500,000	Food & Bev. Income	$660,000

The rooms division represents 60 percent or more of the hotel's total revenue, whereas the food and beverage area makes up around 33 percent. The remaining 7 percent comes from the other revenue-producing areas of the hotel. Even more dramatic is the fact that of the 60 percent brought in, 75 percent of this is rooms division income. In the previous example, this would be $4.5 million, compared with only $660,000 from the food and beverage area. Thus, it is not difficult to see the importance of the rooms division. There are several reasons for this. One important reason is that the labor cost in the food and beverage area is higher than in other areas. Also, product costs in the food and beverage area are a direct cost of that division, whereas the cost of the rooms, for instance, is not a direct departmental cost.

ROOM RATES

The average room rate in a hotel is achieved by charging a variety of different types of rates. These rates are set up for many different reasons, which will be discussed as part of the following exploration and analysis of each type.

Rack Rate

The rack rate is the standard rate of the rooms in the hotel. These rates vary, usually based on the type of room or location of the room within the hotel. This rate type represents the highest rates that are quoted to walk-in or advance reservation guests who are not part of a guest classification that receives special rate considerations.

Corporate Rate

Corporate rates are less than the standard rack rates of the hotel. These reduced rates are given to develop repeat business from the corporate market segment. In any hotel, there are various corporate rates, depending on the amount of business with which the particular company provides the hotel. The more business that is provided, the greater the discount offered to the company. A hotel's attempt to attract business to itself over other hotels in the same locale results in a high level of competition among hotels in corporate rates. In many cases, the difference of a few dollars can be the deciding factor in obtaining a company's business. For this reason, corporate rate schedules are kept as confidential as possible. Sometimes hotels will have available one corporate rate for all business people that inquire. Additionally, these hotels will have even lower rates that are referred to as *preferred rates*. A preferred rate will bear the name of the company it is attached to, such as the "IBM rate."

Off-Season Rate

Off-season rates are most often found in hotels that are located in tourist destination areas. These rates are lower than rates quoted during the rest of the year because of the lack of business during the off-season. For example, in many parts of southern Florida, the summer time is a very slow period. Rooms can then be found for half the normal rate charged in the winter time when business is booming.

In-Season Rates

These rates are the opposite of the off-season rates mentioned above. Depending on the hotel's location, the rates will bear the name of the peak season. For example, on Cape Cod, the highest rates paid are in the summer time when tourism is at its peak. Consequently, these peak season or in-season rates are called *summer rates*.

Weekend Rates

Weekend rates are those rates quoted for Friday and Saturday nights. In many city hotels, these weekend rates are quite a bit lower than the weekday rates that are charged when occupancy is at its highest due to the work week business. This, however, is not always the case. Many times if there are special events, such as football games, room rates will actually be higher than weekday rates. In many locations, such as Las Vegas, the weekends are extremely busy and rooms are at a premium. Thus, hotels in such areas can have weekend rates as high or higher than their weekday rates.

Premium Rates

These rates are higher than the standard rates quoted because of the type of accommodations and services provided. In this category, one finds rooms located in what is called the *tower's level* or *concierge floors*. Here guests receive more services and personal attention. A lounge area and a separate check-in area are examples of the extra services that may be provided.

Group Rates

Group rates are lower than the standard rates quoted because this type of business results in a large number of rooms being taken by the same organization. Examples of organizations receiving group rates are group tours run by tour operators who buy up blocks of rooms during different periods of the year, and social groups that are having a special function that requires many rooms.

Other Rates

Other rates that fall into the lower rate level because of the high volume of business are government rates, airline employee rates, and military rates.

Reduced Rate Formula

When management makes the decision to offer a reduced rate to a special category or group of guests, it must do so with a plan of action. This plan will quantify the decision and provide a rate that is going to benefit the hotel as well as satisfy the guest. The two main factors that must be taken into consideration are volume and demand. Using these two determinants, the hotel can utilize a predetermined formula to help establish the rates:

1. *Volume:* When evaluating the volume portion of the formula, the hotel must consider the following:
- Existing large accounts.
- The number of room-nights to be taken by each account.
- The competition and their expectations for the business.
- Any past experience with these accounts.
- The desires of the accounts.
2. *Demand:* When evaluating the demand portion of the formula, the hotel must consider the following:
- Past occupancy trends.
- Competitors' occupancy trends.
- Number of room-nights available in the area.
- Any changes expected in the area or business overall.
- Any changes in special events.
- Any changes that would affect the economy in general.

The formula would appear as follows:

$$S = R - [(V \times D) + (R \times DF)]$$

where S is the special rate, R is the rack rate, V is the volume from the account, D is the discount, and DF is the demand factor. To utilize this formula, the hotel would have to assign values to the volume and demand components.

The following is an example of this formula in use for a hotel that is in a strong season for business. The rack rate is $100, the volume of business coming from the account is 100 rooms, the discount is 10 percent of the volume, and the demand factor would be 5 percent off the rack rate when the demand is high. The application formula would occur as follows:

$$X = \$100 - [(\$100 \times .10) + (\$100 \times .05)]$$
$$X = \$100 - [\$10 + \$5]$$
$$S = \$85$$

Using the above mentioned volume and demand factors, the reduced rate would be $85 for this business.

RATE DISCOUNTING

All of the rates explained above are given for a special reason. They must be differentiated from what is called *rate discounting*, which is done in hopes of stimulating room business from the masses of people that would normally be quoted the rack rates. Naturally, one hopes that discounting rates will motivate people to choose the hotel with the discount over other hotels. However, it is the opinion of many in the business that rate discounting does nothing more than provide a lower rate to guests who would otherwise pay the standard rate. Critics of rate discounting also argue that it does nothing to stimulate growth in the industry overall. Such growth, they say, can only be accomplished by adding more guests to the marketplace. Many see rate discounting as analogous to the "gas wars" engaged in by the gasoline station industry in the early 1980s. Such price wars were created when one gasoline station lowered its prices to increase business and another then followed suit, until the prices were so low that no one was making any money.

In the hotel industry, more emphasis needs to be placed on the idea of a price value relationship. When guests are given excellent personal service and many extras, they will be willing to pay the price and will probably return to pay it again. A problem arises when the guest does not feel that what he or she is receiving is worth the price. Amenities such as turndown service, express check-out, baggage handling, and complimentary coffee and newspapers are extras that connote value.

The basic argument against rate discounting is based on the belief that the demand for hotel rooms is *inelastic* as opposed to elastic. *Elastic demand* refers to the percentage change in the price of an item that results when a larger or smaller percentage of the items are sold. Lowering prices by 10 percent, for example, could result in a sales increase of 50 percent. *Inelastic demand*, on the other hand, occurs when the percentage change in the price of an item is greater than the percentage change in the number of items sold. For instance, lowering prices by 10 percent might, if demand is not elastic, result in a sales increase of only 10 percent or less. The equation that represents this principle for rooms sold would be:

$$\text{Demand elasticity of rooms} = \% \text{ change in number of rooms sold} \div \% \text{ change in price}$$

Most hospitality experts are of the opinion that the demand for hotel rooms is, over the long run, inelastic. The basic argument is that hotel rooms are a perishable quantity and cannot be bought tonight and saved up for later usage, as are commodities that can be saved in some other types of businesses that have elastic demand for their products. For an example of elastic demand, we can look at the grocery store industry. In this business, a store can lower the price of a product like canned peas and experience a substantial increase in sales. Why? Unlike hotel rooms, the canned peas can be purchased today and stored for consumption later. On the other hand, while hotel rooms may be reserved for the future, they must be occupied (consumed) on a specific date.

Thus, when management decides to discount room rates, it must do so with an understanding of the relationship between rate reduction and the accompanying increase in occupancy that will be needed to offset the reduction in total room revenue. The factors involved here are the percentage that the room rate will be reduced, the additional cost associated with renting each additional room sold, and the new occupancy that must be achieved to bring the revenue up to the current level of profitability. A formula to calculate the needed new level of occupancy is as follows:

$$NO\% = PO\% \times (RR - AC) \div [RR \times (1 - R\%)] - AC$$

where $NO\%$ is the new occupancy percentage, $PO\%$ is the present occupancy percentage, RR is the rack rate, AC is the additional cost of renting each room, and $R\%$ is the percentage the room rate will be reduced. For a hotel that is currently operating at a 70 percent occupancy level with an average rack rate of $100 and a cost of $15 for each additional room sold, they would have to achieve an occupancy of 92 percent to reduce their rates by 20 percent.

$$NO\% = 70\% \times (\$100 - \$15) \div [\$100 \times (1 - 20\%)] - \$15$$
$$NO\% = 92\%$$

A 400-room hotel that is averaging 70 percent occupancy per night is generating sales of 280 rooms per night, or 400 rooms $\times$ 70 percent = 280 rooms. Now if the plan above is implemented and rates are reduced by 20 percent, an average of 368 rooms per night must then be sold (400 rooms $\times$ 92 percent = 368). This additional 88 rooms per night will be extremely difficult to fill with only a 20 percent rate reduction.

Exhibit 4-1 is a rate-cutting chart designed to be used when the additional cost of renting rooms is equal to 25 percent of the current room rate. To use this chart, one must locate the hotel's present occupancy percentage, by which rates will be reduced. The occupancy is the new level that will have to be attained in order to make up for the reduction.

SETTING ROOM RATES

The setting of room rates for a hotel is a task upon which all good hotel managers place a great deal of attention. When room rates are being set, there are

EXHIBIT 4-1   THE CONSEQUENCES OF RATE CUTTING

Current Occupancy Percent	Occ % Required if Rate Reduced 5%	Occ % Required if Rate Reduced 10%	Occ % Required if Rate Reduced 15%	Occ % Required if Rate Reduced 20%	Occ % Required if Rate Reduced 25%
76%	81.4	87.7	95.0	103.6	114.0
74%	79.3	85.4	92.5	100.0	111.0
72%	77.1	83.1	90.0	93.2	108.0
70%	75.0	80.8	87.5	95.5	105.0
68%	72.9	78.5	85.0	92.7	102.0
66%	70.7	76.2	82.5	90.0	99.0
64%	68.6	73.8	80.0	87.3	96.0
62%	66.4	71.5	77.5	84.5	93.0
60%	64.3	59.2	75.0	81.8	90.0
58%	62.1	66.9	72.5	79.1	87.0
56%	60.0	64.6	70.0	76.4	84.0
54%	57.9	62.3	67.5	73.6	81.0
52%	55.7	60.0	65.0	70.9	78.0
50%	53.6	57.7	62.5	68.2	75.0

Example: If current rate is 70%, you would need a 75% occupancy rate to produce the same net income if you reduce the room rates by only 5%. Note how quickly a rate reduction can drive required occupancy levels to impossible levels (i.e., how can you have more than 100% occupancy?)

some basic considerations that must be made. The rates charged have to be high enough to cover the expenses of operating the hotel and return a large enough profit to satisfy the ownership of the hotel. Also, the rates must be attractive enough to motivate the guest to choose the hotel.

There are various methods used in setting room rates in hotels. Some of these are quite simple and could be considered guessing; others are very complex, employing sophisticated mathematical computations. The first group of methods explored here are those known as *qualitative*, in that they do not rely on the use of any quantitative tools. The second group of methods discussed rely quite heavily on mathematical support and are classified as *quantitative* methods of room rate analysis. No single method should be or is intended to be used alone. It is only through a mixture of the different methods at different times that one is able to establish rates that will be effective.

Qualitative Methods

Pied Piper

This approach uses the competition as the basis for rate setting. Rates are set according to what other hotels in the area are asking for similar accommodations. It is important to remember that, while attention must be paid to the competition, placing too much emphasis on the competition may prove to be a serious error. Although the rates for the competition are readily attainable, the corresponding expenses are not. So while two hotels may have similar rates, if one has a higher level of expenses, the bottom line of that property will be negatively impacted. Additionally, while two hotels may seem to be similar in accommodations, it is ultimately the consumer who will decide if the value received is comparable.

Hit or Miss

When using the hit or miss approach to pricing, the hotel's rates will be allowed to fluctuate up and down. At each different pricing level, the occupancy will be recorded. Then after a period of time, an analysis will be carried out to determine which rate range produced the most profitable level of occupancy. The problem here is that levels of occupancy fluctuate for more reasons than the changing of rates. Things such as weather and seasonality of business produce fluctuations as well. A derivation of this method is the process used when the rates are lowered until the occupancy moves up to an acceptable level, after which the rates are raised until occupancy drops too low. At this point, the rate-reduction technique is repeated.

Gouge 'Em

This approach to rate setting relies on a rate schedule that is below the market level most of the time. This is done in an attempt to lure business away from the competition. Then, when rooms are at a premium during special times of the year, the rates are inflated to an abnormally high level. The problem with this approach is twofold. First, the hotel is selling below the rate that it could receive most of the time, and second, when the rates are overinflated, almost any guest forced to accept these rates will not return to the property in the future because of the high price.

Percentage Increase

When a hotel uses the percentage increase method, the first step is to list the rates that were charged in the previous year. Next, management will consider factors such as the rate of inflation, payroll increases to be given, and the new cost of supplies to be purchased during the year. From this information, a percentage increase will be calculated. This increase will be applied to each rate category from the previous year. For example, if last year, the rate for a king-size room during the summer season was $70 per night, and the percentage increase calculated above was 9 percent, the new rate for the king-size room during the summer season would be $76.30 or 9 percent more than last year.

Quantitative Methods

Quantitative methods used in room rate determination go from very simple calculations that require little information and time to compute, to quite complex formulas requiring a tremendous amount of information. These complex room rates determination methods yield a variety of information that can be used on both a short-term and long-term planning basis. With the continued utilization of computers in the hotel industry, many new methods have been developed and some old ones simplified. The more commonly used methods of room rate determination will be discussed in this section. While a hotel may not rely on all of these in determining its room rates, the calculation of rates based on these will provide a basis of comparison with which to work.

$1 Per $1,000

The $1 per $1,000 method of room rate determination was developed by Horwath and Toth. This formula is often referred to as the *building cost rate formula*. It relies on cost information of the hotel to establish the ideal average room rate.

The starting point in this formula is the cost of the hotel, which includes costs for building, land, land development, furnishings, and equipment. After these costs have been determined, the total is divided by the number of rooms in the hotel. This yields a cost per room for the hotel. Next, this cost per room is divided by $1,000. The product of this is the average rate that needs to be attained in order to meet all costs and provide a fair return. For a 400-room hotel project that costs $28 million, the average room rate would be calculated as follows: $28 million ÷ 400 rooms = $70,000 cost per room. In this case, using the $1.00 per $1,000 formula, the $70,000 cost per room is then divided by $1,000 to determine the average room rate at approximately $70.

Several factors must be taken into consideration when this formula is used. First of all, it is only a "rule of thumb" and does not provide a definite answer. The formula is based on the hotel averaging a 70 percent occupancy rate so that if the occupancy drops below this level, the rates would have to be raised. Also, there has been some discussion lately as to validity of the rule because of rising interest rates. This formula may be made more precise for an individual hotel if it is calculated from the beginning. That is, the cost per room would be calculated by considering the cost per room for the building, land, furniture, and equipment. Then the carrying costs would be calculated: the property taxes and insurance, the depreciation on the building, furniture, and equipment, and the return on investment. The total carrying costs per room would then be divided by the percentage of income available to cover the carrying costs. This yields the amount of revenue generated by each room over a one-year period. If this amount is divided by the average number of days per year that each room will be occupied, the result is the average room rate for the year.

Hubbart Formula

The Hubbart formula was developed by Roy Hubbart in the late 1940s in response to a need established by the American Hotel Association to develop a formula that could be used to compute hotel room rates. It was published in 1952 by the American Hotel Association, which is today the American Hotel & Motel Association. In the design and use of the formula, the focus was on determining an average room rate that, if met, would cover costs of operation and yield a fair return to the ownership of a hotel. The association stressed that although room rates are set by hotels based upon competition and economic conditions in a given area, it was still necessary to determine room rates based upon some quantitative method.

Schedule I of the formula appears in Exhibit 4-2. In this schedule, the total amount of revenue derived from room sales is calculated. This total revenue will cover costs and provide a fair return to the owners of the hotel based on the present fair market value of the hotel. The various aspects of the schedule include the following:

> Operating expenses—These expenses are for the various operating areas of the hotel, excluding the costs of operation for other revenue producing departments that are dealt with later in the formula.
>
> Taxes, insurance, and other similar costs—Expenses in this area of the formula are for the taxes and insurance costs as indicated.
>
> Depreciation—In the formula in Exhibit 4-4, the depreciation expense is computed based upon the present fair value of the hotel. This is what it is

EXHIBIT 4-2   THE HUBBART FORMULA FOR DETERMINING ROOM RATES
SCHEDULE I: FINANCIAL CALCULATIONS

	Example	Property
OPERATING EXPENSES:		
Rooms Department	$442,730	
Telephone Department	14,990	
Administration and General	271,620	
Payroll Taxes & Employee Benefits	36,850	
Advertising & Promotion	46,250	
Heat, Light, and Power	167,570	
Repairs & Maintenance	158,030	
Total Operating Expenses:		$1,138,040
TAXES, INSURANCE, ETC.		
Real Estate and Personal Property Taxes	$96,240	
Franchise Taxes	3,000	
Insurance on Building and Contents	9,220	
Total Taxes, Insurance, Etc.:		$108,460
DEPRECIABLE ASSSETS AT BOOK VALUE:		
Building	$92,400	
Furniture, Fixtures, and Equipment	61,600	
Total Net Book Value of Depreciable Assets:		$154,000
FIXED & DEPRECIABLE ASSETS AT FAIR MARKET VALUE: (over book value above)		
Land		
Building		
Furniture, Fixtures, and Equipment		
Total Fair Market Value:		$450,000
TOTAL:		$1,474,030
DEDUCT: (Income obtainable from sources other than rooms revenue.)		
Income from Store Rentals	$52,590	
Profit [Loss] from Food & Beverage	248,640	
Miscellaneous Income	75,240	
Total Credits from Other Sources:		$376,470
AMOUNT REQUIRED FROM GUEST ROOM SALES TO COVER COSTS AND PROVIDE A REASONABLE RETURN TO FAIR MARKET VALUE:		$1,474,030

worth in today's market as opposed to the book value. These costs for depreciation may be calculated using the amounts that are reported by the hotel for tax purposes in place of the fair market value.

Return on present fair value of the property—A rate of return will be calculated for each individual hotel operation. This rate of return not only covers a rate of return on the owners' equity, but also includes consideration of return on the portion of the hotel's value that is outstanding under debt.

Credits from sources other than rooms—These credits are from the other areas of the hotel that produce revenue. If these revenue producing costs are less than the direct operating expenses, there will be an income derived from this area that should be deducted from the amount of revenue needed to be received from the sale of rooms. On the other hand, the amount of any loss shown by these departments should be deducted from the other credits. In a case where all of the other revenue-producing areas show a loss, this figure would be added to the amount of revenue needed to be produced by rooms sales. When these credit amounts are calculated, care must be taken to include only income that will continue. Any income that represents a one-time occurrence should be dealt with separately.

The figure that is obtained by adding the four areas of the schedule and then deducting the credits represents the amount of income that will have to be obtained from rooms revenue. In recent years, this approach has been modified to appear as an "upside-down" income statement, which is to determine the level of rooms revenue that is needed in order to obtain a required net income after taxes. Although the formula is three decades old, its basic assumptions still hold true. It can be, and still is, used today at many properties, though altered to suit the particular needs of the hotel.

Schedule II of the Hubbart formula appears in Exhibit 4-3. This calculation is designed to determine the average rate that will have to be obtained in order to achieve the needed rooms revenue so that all costs are covered and a fair return given to the owners of the hotel. The amount of rooms revenue needed is already known from the calculations made in Schedule I. The next step is to determine the number of room nights the hotel has available to sell in the year. This is calculated by multiplying the number of rooms in the hotel by the number of days the hotel will be open for business. Next, the hotel must project the percentage of occupancy that it expects to achieve for the year and multiply this percentage by the number of room nights available for sale in the year. The product of this calculation is the number of room nights that the hotel projects selling in the year. The number of room nights thus projected is then divided into the total room revenue needed, resulting in the average room rate that must be achieved in order to obtain the targeted revenue figure. Yet the average room rate figure is only that—an average. Other factors that go into achieving the rooms revenue figure are the percentage of double occupancy, the mix of the rates charged, the frequency of selling the most expensive rooms first, and the discounting policies of the hotel. Thus, while the average room rate derived is a starting point, it does not indicate what the hotel should charge for its various different types of rooms. Nor does it indicate the rates involved when rooms are discounted.

EXHIBIT 4-3   THE HUBBART FORMULA FOR DETERMINING ROOM RATES

Schedule II: Computation to Determine Average Daily Rate per Occupied Room Calculation	Example	Property
(1) Amount Required from Guest Room Sales per Schedule I:	$ 1,474,030	
(2) Number of Guest Rooms Available	100	
(3) Number of Available Rooms on an Annual Basis (Item 2 multiplied times 365)	36,500	100%
(4) Less: Allowance for Average Vacancies	9,125	25%
(5) Number of Occupied Rooms Based on Estimated Occupancy Percentage	25,375	75%
(6) Average Daily Rate Required to Generate Desired Income: (Item 1 divided by Item 5)	$ 53.80	
(7) Actual Average Rate in Market	$ 49.50	
Required Occupancy Percent Based on Market Rate:		79%

Schedule III included in the formula, Exhibit 4-4, allows for an alternate method of pricing rooms to achieve the desired room revenue. In this schedule, the total square footage of the hotel that is allocated to guest rooms is calculated. The total square foot area for rooms is then multiplied by the percentage of vacancy during the year. This figure is then deducted from the total square footage, yielding the square footage that will account for the room revenue produced. Then, by dividing the total rooms revenue needed by the square footage to be rented, one may arrive at an average rooms revenue amount per square foot per year. When this yearly amount is divided by 365 days in the year, an average rooms revenue amount per square foot per day is determined. This method of calculation is more appropriate for a residential hotel than a transient one. In a transient hotel, the rates charged, in most cases, vary more according to location and furnishings than according to size.

EXHIBIT 4-4   THE HUBBART FORMULA FOR DETERMINING ROOM RATES

Schedule III: Rental Required on a Square Foot Basis Item	Example	Property
(1) Amount Required from Guest Room Sales per Schedule I:	$1,474,030	
(2) Square Foot Area of Guest Rooms	206,000	100%
(3) Less: Allowance for Average Vacancies	51,500	25%
(4) Net Square Foot of Occupied Guest Rooms	154,500	75%
(5) Average Annual Rental per Square Foot	$ 9.54	
(6) Average Daily Rental per Square Foot	$ .026	

Minimum Acceptable Average Room Rate

The minimum acceptable average room rate formula (MAARR) in Exhibit 4-5 is used to determine what the lowest average room rate attained should be. The first step in setting up the formula is to determine the different rate categories and the number of rooms to be allocated to each category. Next, a double occupancy percentage must be forecasted for each category. The double differential in the formula represents the difference between the single and double rate. The revenue is then calculated at 100 percent occupancy for the hotel. This assumes that an equal percentage of rooms will be sold from each category. This will be the case if the proper number of rooms is allocated to each category and the rates are set at the appropriate level.

In our example, the percentage of double occupancy is set at 20 percent for all rates. In an actual model, the percentage would vary and more rate categories would exist. After calculating the total revenue of $49,200 for a day when 100 percent occupancy is achieved, the total revenue is divided by the number of rooms in the hotel. Here we see that the MAARR would be $82.

The basic assumption behind the formula is that if the rates have been set at the correct level and the correct number of rooms is assigned to each level, an equal percentage of rooms will be sold from each level. If the average room rate achieved is lower than the MAARR, the reservations department may not be selling across the rate categories, but instead, selling from the bottom up. The front desk staff may also be following this approach to achieve guest acceptance with the least amount of work involved. Sale of the least expensive rooms first

EXHIBIT 4-5   MINIMUM ACCEPTABLE AVERAGE ROOM RATE

	Number of Rooms	Single Rate	Double Rate	Double Differential
	100	$60	$ 75	$ 15
	300	$75	$ 95	$ 20
	200	$90	$120	$ 30
Total:	600			

Given 100% Occupancy with 20% Double Occupancy

(100 rooms × $60) + (20 rooms × $15) = $ 6,300

(300 rooms × $75) + (60 rooms × $20) = $23,700

(200 rooms × $90) + (40 rooms × $30) = $19,200

Total Rooms Revenue = $49,200

$$\frac{Total\ Rooms\ Revenue}{Rooms\ Sold} = Minimum\ Acceptable\ Average\ Rate$$

$$\frac{\$49,200}{600} = \$82.00$$

could also be a sign that the rates are too high if, in fact, reservations and the front desk are doing their jobs.

When selling takes place from the top down, the attempt is to sell the most expensive rooms first. Although many hotel managers believe this is the way to sell, there may be problems created by using this method. For example, if a guest calls and is quoted the highest rate, he may be scared off and not stay on the phone long enough to be quoted a lower rate. Such a situation means, of course, that the sale is lost altogether. Yet a high level of success in selling from the top down can mean that the hotel's highest rate is too low for the guest making a reservation during that period of time. The trick here is to balance the rates and the number of rooms in each rate category to maximize revenue. A MAARR is only a control point that when triggered should be cause for investigation.

Room Rate Structure Formula

The methods discussed so far in the determination of room rates have yielded an average room rate that must be achieved for the hotel to be profitable. In reality, a great many rates will be charged in order to attain this average. This is the purpose behind the room rate structure formula—to determine what the rate structure of the hotel needs to be in order to achieve a given level of income at predetermined levels of occupancy and double occupancy. The factors that must be taken into consideration in this formula are the percentage of occupancy, the percentage of double occupancy, the rate spread, the double differential, and the different rate categories.

Percentage of double occupancy is the percentage obtained when the number of guests in the hotel is divided by the number of rooms sold. Room rates must be structured with this variable in mind. The greater the percentage of double occupancy a hotel experiences, the more revenue it may be able to attract in the other areas of the hotel, such as in food and beverage area. Every hotel will experience this percentage to a different degree. In addition, each will have its own percentage of double occupancy, which will vary by rate category and by day of the week and time of year.

Rate spread refers to the difference between single-rate categories in the hotel. If the single-rate for a room with one queen bed is $60 and a room containing one king bed is $77, the rate spread is the $17 difference between the two rooms.

Double differential is the difference between the single rate and the double rate for each category. Each rate category will have its own double differential. For example, if the queen-bed room's single rate is $60 and the double-bed rate is $72, the double differential for this rate category would be $12—the difference between the two rates.

Rate categories are all of the different rates charged for the rooms in the hotel. Every hotel has a number of different rates that are charged for its guests rooms. These different rates are based on factors such as the type of room, the location of the room in the hotel, the number of guests occupying the room, the type of guest, and many other variables, some of which may be specific to an individual hotel. For example, the rate will normally be higher for a room with two double beds than it would be for one with a queen-size bed. Similarly, an ocean-front room will cost more than one with an inland view, and a corporate rate guest will be charged less than a noncorporate rate guest.

Thus far, room revenue has been discussed in relationship with achieving a predetermined average room rate. The question that remains to be answered is the following: How much will have to be charged in the various rate categories of the hotel in order to achieve this average room rate, which will, at a given occupancy level, enable the hotel to attain the required room revenue figure? A related question also presents itself at this point: How much should be charged for each of these different types of rooms and guests to enable the hotel to achieve its budgeted average room rate? The room rate structure formula in Exhibit 4-6 can be used to determine the answers to these questions. The formula has been designed with consideration of the following factors:

1. Different room rate categories.
2. Sales mix for each room rate category.
3. Single-rate spread between categories.
4. Percentage of double occupancy.
5. Rate double differential.

In this example, the different room rate categories are identified in Exhibit 4-7. Four categories have been set up, three of which are rack rates set by the type of beds in the rooms. The fourth category is for a corporate rate guest. This represents an oversimplification of the formula in that as many categories

EXHIBIT 4-6 ROOM RATE STRUCTURE FORMULA

(1) Room Rate Categories (See Ex. 4-9)	(2) Projected # of Room Nights (See Ex. 4-9)	(3) Single Rate by Room Category (See Ex. 4-9)	(4) Double Rate by Room Category (See Ex. 4-9)	(5) Projected Room Revenue (Cols. 3 plus 4)
Q	1,260	S +	$[(.30 \times 1,260) \times (.20 \times S)]$	?
K	1,260	$(S + \$20)$ +	$[(.30 \times 1,260) \times .20(S + \$20)]$	?
D/D	1,890	$(S + \$30)$ +	$[(.30 \times 1,890) \times .20(S + \$30)]$	?
Corp.	1,890	$(.80 \times S)$ +	$[(.30 \times 1,890) \times .20(.80 \times S)]$	?
			Total Projected Room Revenue:	$409,500.00?

By solving the four equations for S we know that $S = \$51.40$.

EXHIBIT 4-7   ROOM RATE CATEGORIES

Room Code	Description
Q	Room with a queen-size bed
K	Room with a king-size bed
D/D	Room with two double beds
Corp.	Corporate rate

as needed can be entered; most hotels will have a need for many more than four.

The projected sales mix for these different rate categories is based on the history of the hotel and future trends. For example, if last September there were 1,260 room nights for the Q rate category out of 6,300 total room nights sold, this would represent a 20 percent sales mix based on the following formula:

Number of room nights sold in category ÷ total room nights
sold × 100% = Percent sales mix of category
(1,260 ÷ 6,300) × 100% = 20%

In Exhibit 4-8, we are projecting 6,300 room nights being sold. This projection is derived by using the following formula:

Number of rooms in the hotel × number of days in the month × projected percentage of occupancy = room nights sold
300 rooms × 30 days × 70% = 6,300 room nights sold

In Exhibit 4-9, the data section is set up for this illustration. Within this data section is the single-rate spread. The single-rate spread is the difference between a base room rate (in this case the queen room) and the other room rate categories at single occupancy. The single rate for the king room is $20 more than the queen, and the single corporate rate is 20 percent less than the

EXHIBIT 4-8   PROJECTIONS FOR THE MONTH OF SEPTEMBER, 199_

Room Rate Categories	Monthly Room Nights @ 70% Occupancy		Projected Sales Mix		Projected # of Rooms Occupied
Q	6,300	×	20%	=	1,260
K	6,300	×	20%	=	1,260
D/D	6,300	×	30%	=	1,890
Corp.	6,300	×	30%	=	1,890
	Total:		100%	=	6,300

EXHIBIT 4-9 DATA SECTIONS FOR ILLUSTRATION

Number of Rooms in the Hotel	300
Overall Occupancy Percentage	70%
Rooms with Double Occupancy	30%

Single Rate Spread	Room Rate Categories	Single Rate
Single Rate	Q	S
plus $20	K	$S + \$20$
plus $30	D/D	$S + \$30$
20% Discount	Corp.	$.80 \times S$

Double differential is 20% of the single
rate for each room type.

single queen rate. These differences are based on the competition, room amenities, and other factors as determined by past experiences. The double differential is the difference between the single rate and the double rate for each category. In this example, a double differential of 20 percent will be applied to all rate categories. This differential percentage is determined by using the same criteria that was applied to the single-rate spread. A double differential is computed for each category by multiplying the single rate by the established percentage. Optionally, a fixed dollar amount may be established instead.

In Exhibit 4-10, the room rate structure formula is illustrated using the information from Exhibits 4-8 and 4-9. The formula can be established with as many different room rate categories as the hotel has. For each rate, a line is set up in the formula. The sum of the room rate category lines is equal to the budgeted room revenue. When the formula is worked through, S—the single rate for the queen room—is solved. In this example, S is $51.40.

EXHIBIT 4-10 ROOM RATE STRUCTURE FORMULA AFTER SOLVING FOR S

(1) Room Rate Categories (See Ex. 4-9)	(2) Projected # of Room Nights (See Ex. 4-9)	(3) Single Rate by Room Category (See Ex. 4-9)		(4) Double Rate by Room Category (See Ex. 4-9)	(5) Projected Room Revenue (Cols. 3 plus 4)
Q	1,260	S	+	$[(.30 \times 1,260) \times (.20 \times S)]$	$ 68,650.00
K	1,260	(S + $20)	+	$[(.30 \times 1,260) \times .20(S + \$20)]$	$ 95,350.00
D/D	1,890	(S + $30)	+	$[(.30 \times 1,890) \times .20(S + \$30)]$	$163,100.00
Corp.	1,890	(.80 × S)	+	$[(.30 \times 1,890) \times .20(.80 \times S)]$	$ 82,400.00
				Total Projected Room Revenue:	$409,500.00

EXHIBIT 4-11 ROOM RATE STRUCTURE

Room Rate Categories	Single Rate Calculation	Double Rate Calculation (Double rate differential times single rate)
Q	$S = \$50.40$	$(1.20 \times S) = \$60.50$
K	$(S + \$20) = \$70.40$	$(1.20 \times (S + \$20)) = \$84.50$
D/D	$(S + \$30) = \$80.40$	$(1.20 \times (S + \$30)) = \$96.50$
Corp.	$(.80 \times S) = \$40.30$	$(1.20 \times (.80 \times S)) = \$48.40$

The room rate structure is computed in Exhibit 4-11. By adding the single-rate spread for the other rooms to the single rate of the queen room, all of the remaining single rates can be calculated. To arrive at the double rate for each category, the single rate is increased by 20 percent. This increased price may be calculated by multiplying the single rates by 1.2. After these calculations are performed, the hotel has the rate structure needed to reach its desired average room rate and, more important, achieve its budgeted room revenue. During the course of the month for which these calculations have been worked out, this formula can be reworked for the remaining days of the month whenever the occupancy level is not being met. The intention here is to adjust the rate structure so that the desired room revenue is achieved.

Evaluating Room Rates

The word "minimum" in the minimum acceptable average room rate formula explained previously does not describe the situation achieved as often as management would like to be the case. The reasons for this were mentioned previously, as well as the discounting that was discussed earlier. To evaluate the average room rate that is achieved, some formulas have been developed along with the reports. These are used by management to help in the future planning of room rate maximization. One formula that may be used is calculated by dividing the average room rate achieved by the minimum acceptable average room rate. For example, by using the MAARR from above and taking an ADR (average daily rate) of $70, we can see the result:

$$(\$70 \div \$82) \times 100\% = 85\%.$$

The ADR was only 85 percent of what it should have been according to the MAARR. Each hotel should set up percentage ranges to work with in evaluating the rates achieved. In a given property, a 100 percent to 94 percent range may be acceptable. If this range moves to the 93 percent to 87 percent range, however, further investigation of the variance may be needed. If the percentage achieved equals 88 percent and there has not been a great deal of discounting of rates for that day, then a need to retrain the reserva-

ROOM REVENUE HISTORY
Day of the Week History

Date	Premium Transient	Discount Transient	Package	Contract	Non-Revenue	Group	Total Occupied	Turnaways	% of Occupancy	Indiv. Avg. Rate	Package Avg. Rate	Contract Avg. Rate	Group Avg. Rate	Total Hotel Avg. Rate	Total Hotel Revenue

Exhibit 4-12

tions staff and the front desk staff on proper selling techniques may be indicated.

Exhibit 4-12 is an example of a form that can be used to track the rooms sold and the average rates charged for each of the different types of rooms. From this information, management is able to see the effect that each of the different rate categories has had on the average rate of the hotel. This information may be used in planning rates and room allocation to these rate categories in the future.

Room Rate Discrepancy Report

Date of Report: _____ , 19_____ .

Room Number	Rack Rate	Rate Charged	Variance (Col 2 – Col 3)	Reason for Variance
TOTAL:				

Exhibit 4-13

Room Rate Discrepancy Report

An example of a room rate discrepancy report is seen in Exhibit 4-13. This report lists all of the rooms in the hotel, along with, in the next column, the current rack rate for each room. Following this is the rate that was charged for the room on the night in question. If there is a discrepancy between the two rates, the fifth column is used to give the reason for this discrepancy. Some of the more common of the various reasons for a discrepancy include a lower rate due to a discount or a room having been booked under a reservation prior to a rate increase. Management will review this report daily and follow up on any discrepancies that seem to be inappropriate. By totaling up this report, management is better able to see the potential revenue that was sacrificed due to these discrepancies. Management's judgment about whether or not all of the reduced rates were necessary will help in determining whether such reductions will continue to be offered in the future.

Additional Exercises

Calculating room rates is not so easy that you can do it correctly without a little practice. Let's try a few sample room rate calculation problems and see if you can come up with the same answers that we do.

Problem 1: A Roadside Inn

Let's assume there is a roadside inn with two types of rooms. Let's assume that this is a 100-room property and that the usual mix of sales is 40 percent type A and 60 percent type B. We anticipate a 75 percent occupancy for the month of December. We charge $20 more for a B single than for an A single. What room rate structure should we have for the hotel in order to achieve a room revenue of $169,750 for the month? Double occupancy is 30%. The double differential is 20% of the single rates.

Answer:

Step One   Calculate room occupancy forecast:

$$(31 \text{ days in December}) \times (100 \text{ rooms}) \times (75\% \text{ occupancy}) = 2,325 \text{ rooms occupied}$$

Step Two   Calculate number of singles versus number of doubles:

ROOM RATE STRUCTURE FORMULA
(A) ROOM RATE CATEGORIES

Room Code	Description
A	Single occupancy
B	Double occupancy

(B) PROJECTIONS FOR THE MONTH OF SEPTEMBER, 199_

Room Rate Categories	Monthly Room Nights @75% Occupancy		Projected Sales Mix		Projected Number of Rooms Occupied
A	2,325	×	40%	=	930
B	2,325	×	60%	=	1,395
	Total:		100%		2,325

Step Three   Set up formula in Exhibit 4-9:

ROOM RATE STRUCTURE FORMULA
(C) DATA SECTIONS FOR ILLUSTRATION

(1) Room Rate Categories	(2) Projected Number of Room Nights	(3) Single Rate by Room Category		(4) Double Rate by Room Category	(5) Projected Room Revenue (Columns 3 plus 4)
A	930	S	+	$[(.30 \times 930) \times (.20 \times S)]$	?
B	1,395	$(S + \$20)$	+	$[(.30 \times 1,395) \times .20(S + \$20)]$	?
				Total Projected Room Revenue:	$169,750

By solving the two equations for S we know that $S = \$56.86$

DISCUSSION QUESTIONS

1. Room rates and occupancy percentages are the two main factors in determining hotel profitability. Which does the text consider to be most important? Do you agree?
2. Why do we offer so many kinds of reduced rates? Do you think that offering reduced rates is a good idea?
3. Discuss the weakness inherent in rate discounting.
4. You are the general manager of the newest hotel in Orlando, Florida, home of Disney World and other attractions. What would you consider the strengths and weaknesses of establishing your rates via the Pied Piper method of rate setting?
5. Discuss what factors might prevent you from obtaining a room rate that would cover costs and provide a fair return on the owner's investment?

STUDY QUESTIONS

1. Why is rooms revenue better than revenue from food and beverage departments?
2. What do we call a rate used in localities where business is very good at one time of year and very bad during another time of the year?
3. Why do we offer corporate rates?
4. What would be the consequence to a hotel with a current occupancy rate of 66 percent if it reduced its rates by 15 percent overall?
5. What is the difference between qualitative and quantitative methods of rate setting?
6. If my hotel cost $16 million to build, and I have 128 rooms and have determined that my average room rate should be $125 per night, what room rate formula did I use in making this determination?
7. Which quantitative method focuses on determining an average room rate that, if met, would cover costs of operation and yield a fair return to the ownership of a hotel?
8. Why is the average room rate determined by the Hubbart formula just a starting point in rate determination?

9. Which rate method determines the lowest acceptable rate that must be obtained?

10. What is the only rate determination formula that can tell you the complete rate structure for a hotel?

PROBLEMS

1. If you owned a hotel with $20 million in annual revenue, of which 75 percent was derived from rooms revenue and 25 percent came from food and beverage, what would be your operating revenue assuming costs of 25 percent for the rooms department and 75 percent for the food and beverage department?

2. Use the reduced rate formula in order to find out what rate you should charge given the following conditions: The rack rate is $150, the volume of business coming from the accounts is 100 rooms, the discount is 15 percent of the volume, and the demand factor is 10 percent off the rack rate when the demand is high.

3. Using the "rule of thumb" method for room rate calculation, suppose you had a hotel worth $25 million with 250 rooms. What would be the average rate you must charge assuming 70 percent occupancy?

4. Assume you have determined that you need $5 million in guest sale revenues in order to meet the requirements of the Hubbart formula. Compute the average daily rate per occupied room using the second part of the formula and the following facts: rooms available 250, occupancy rate 70 percent, market rate $65.

5. Using the same information from Problem 4, what annual square foot rent is required if the total square foot of all guest rooms is 500,000 square feet?

6. Using the following information, determine the minimum acceptable room rate given a double occupancy of 30 percent.

MINIMUM ACCEPTABLE AVERAGE ROOM RATE

Number of Rooms	Single Rate	Double Rate	Double Differential
50	$60	$70	$15
150	$65	$85	$20
100	$70	$95	$25
Total: 300			

CHAPTER 5

Registering the Guest

CHAPTER OBJECTIVES

After reading this chapter you will understand:

- Why the check-in of a guest is so important to a hotel.
- How a guest checks into a hotel.
- What procedures are followed at check-in and why.
- Who within the hotel must be made aware of the check-in and why.

INTRODUCTION

Among the most important parts of the rooming process in any size hotel are the registration and room assignment procedures. Both the short-term and, ultimately, the long-term success of the hotel depends on the grace and ease with which guests are guided through the rooming process and the degree to which this important initial contact with the hotel fulfills their expectations. Whether these expectations are based upon a previous visit, a travel agent's information, or a hotel brochure, the guest arriving at the hotel has a preconceived notion of what his or her stay is going to be like. If this notion has come from the experiences he or she had last time at the hotel (which were obviously pleasant enough to cause the guest to return), the hotel must make sure the subsequent visit—from beginning to end—equals or exceeds the quality of the last stay. When the guest is coming to the hotel for the first time, he or she also has an image of the type of service that he or she will be receiving and it is, again, the responsibility of the employees involved in the rooming process to ensure that the guest's expectations are met. In this chapter, we will focus on the employees, procedures, and equipment involved in the rooming process. Although these procedures will vary among hotels, the basic flow of events is the same. In addition, employee behavior and equipment are somewhat standard among hotels.

GUEST ARRIVAL—UNIFORMED SERVICES

When the guest arrives by his own automobile at a full-service hotel, a member of the uniformed services staff will greet her or him. Usually this person will be one of the valet parking attendants. At this point, the attendant will welcome the guest to the hotel and ask if the guest wants his or her car to be parked in the hotel's parking garage. In cases where there is no parking garage, there is usually a valet attended parking lot that serves the same purpose. Then the attendant will fill out a parking ticket and give the guest his or her part of the ticket. There are several parts to this ticket. Another part of this ticket is kept with the guest's keys so that when he or she returns to claim the car, the keys and car are easily located. The front desk cashier will receive notification from the garage that the guest has his car parked there. This needs to be communicated to the front desk so that the guest will be charged the parking fee. Before moving the car to the garage, the valet parking attendant along with the doorperson, will remove the guest's luggage from the car and place it on a luggage cart. The doorperson will ask the guest his or her last name and send the guest to the front desk, and the doorperson will then turn the luggage over to a bellperson. If a bellperson is available, the guest should be escorted to the front desk. When a bellperson is not available, the doorperson should write the guest's name down and keep it with the luggage until a bellperson comes to claim it. In some large hotels, the guest will be given half of a luggage claim check with a number on it. Then when the guest is in his or her room, the guest simply calls down to the bell stand and gives his claim number and room number. A bellperson will then be assigned to deliver the luggage to the room.

Another scenario is that the guest first registers for the room. When the registration process is completed, a bellperson is called to the desk and given the guest's name and room key and told to escort the guest to the room. While there are variations to the above mentioned steps, the basic idea remains the same. Whatever set of procedures provides the best level of service to the guest is the one that should be used.

GROUP ARRIVALS

When a group arrives at a hotel, the bell staff will assemble all of the luggage in one area. Then, by using the rooming list, which shows the guest's name and room number, the bell staff will set up the luggage for delivery to the guests' rooms. Groups must be informed ahead of time by the hotel sales area that all luggage must have the guest's name on it. If it does not, then each guest must identify his luggage as it is unloaded. With a group arrival, the hotel may want to set up a special room where the guests can go for refreshments and receive their room keys. This gives the bell staff time to place the guests' luggage in their rooms.

REGISTRATION PREPARATION

There are certain events that must take place prior to the guest's arrival to ensure that the rooming process will go smoothly. During the night audit shift or first thing in the morning, information from the reservations department must be transferred to the front desk area. A list of arrivals for the day, along with the reservations, will be sent to the front desk in a noncomputerized system. These reservations are arranged in alphabetical order to speed up the process of locating the reservation when the guest arrives. Some hotels keep a rack of reservations arriving for the day. Then in the morning the entire rack is sent to the front desk. The front desk must allocate rooms for the arriving guests, but additionally, there must be an allocation for walk-ins—people arriving without a reservation. These walk-ins will be discussed in more depth later in the chapter.

Preregistration is the process whereby guests that have reservations will already have a registration card filled out prior to their arrival at the hotel. These cards are kept at the front desk in alphabetical order. Some hotels use a packet that combines the reservation, registration card, folio, information slip, and room rack slip. This system cuts down on the steps involved in the registration process. All of these different forms will be covered in detail later in this chapter.

Prior to the start of the first shift (which usually runs from 7:00 A.M. to 3:00 P.M.), a list will be made up of all guests who have indicated this day as being their check-out date. This list will be useful in tracking the check-outs. When check-out time gets close, the front desk staff must look more closely at this list. As we discussed in Chapter 3, if the hotel is planning on achieving 100 percent occupancy, these guests must check-out to make way for the guests coming in with reservations.

Throughout the day, the front desk will constantly be tracking how many rooms are left to be sold for that day. Close monitoring of this will allow the hotel to sell rooms throughout the day, even though they may not be able to be occupied until later. Guests that become understays cause an excess of available rooms and may, if not closely watched, cause the hotel to do less than 100 percent occupancy.

FRONT OFFICE RACKS

There are various racks used in a noncomputerized front office system. Some of these racks are still used when a computer system is first installed, then later removed when the computer system is being fully utilized. Others will be kept, either because of their usefulness or for the sense of security that they provide. Some of the racks that we will discuss in this section are the room rack, information rack, key rack, mail rack, and voucher rack.

Room Rack

Prior to the introduction of the computer into the front office area, the room rack was the most important piece of equipment at the front desk. In the many hotels without computers, the room rack remains the single most important item on the equipment list. The room rack is the inventory of all the rooms in the hotel. In addition, it also indicates the condition and status of each room.

Exhibit 5-1 Room Rack   *Source:* Courtesy of the Concord Resort Hotel.

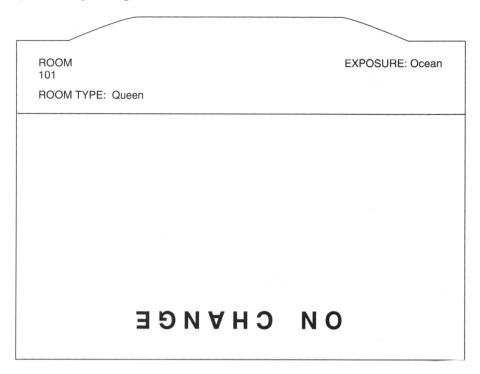

ROOM
101

EXPOSURE: Ocean

ROOM TYPE: Queen

ON CHANGE

Exhibit 5-2   Room Rack Card

Exhibit 5-1 is a photograph of a room rack. The typical room rack is a metal tray made up of many small slots or smaller metal trays. Each slot or small tray is used to represent a room in the hotel and is designated by a room number at the side. A room rack card is in each slot or tray. This card contains the room number in the upper left-hand corner and may contain various information regarding the contents of the room. A room rack card is featured in Exhibit 5-2. These cards come in different colors and most hotels establish their own color-coding system to differentiate room type. The following listing gives the color of the room rack card, the type of room represented by the color, and the abbreviation used to represent that type of room:

Color	Type of Room	Abbreviation
Yellow	One Queen Bed	Q
Orange	One King Bed	K
Green	Two Double Beds	D/D
Red	Parlor	P

The following list represents a continuation of types of rooms and a possible abbreviation for them:

Type of Room	Abbreviation
One Double Bed	D
Two Queen Beds	Q/Q
Murphy Bed	M
Studio	ST
Water Bed	W

Room Condition or Status

On the bottom portion of the room rack card are the words "On Change." These words are used to indicate the condition of the room. The process by which the room rack is used to communicate the condition of the rooms is explained below. First, however, it is important to understand what is meant by condition of the room. Condition or status of a room refers to the room's availability for occupancy at any given time. There are five main conditions that a room rack will indicate a room to be in at any given time. These include the following:

1. clean, unoccupied, and ready to be rented
2. clean and under reservation
3. currently occupied
4. unoccupied and unclean—not ready for occupancy
5. out-of-order

The room rack card will communicate this information regarding the room's condition or status to the front desk staff, provided the staff has properly updated the status of the rooms as they have changed them.

When a room is clean, unoccupied, and ready to be rented, the room rack card for the room will be the only thing in the slot and it will be rightside up, displaying the room number. Thus, when a desk clerk is checking to locate a room for a guest who is checking in, all the clerk must do is locate a room rack card as just described. He or she will locate the cards indicating which rooms are "clean and under reservation." This status is indicated by a room rack card being in the room rack along with a reservation block in front of it. The reservation block will have the date of arrival written across the top, with the guest's name below that. The word "hold" in the upper right hand corner will indicate that the reservation is a guaranteed one, whereas the signal "6:00 P.M." will indicate that the reservation is only to be held until 6:00 P.M. This will help to ensure that all 6:00 P.M. reservations will be released for sale by 6:00 P.M. Exhibit 5-3 is an example of a room rack reservation block.

When a room is occupied by a guest, the room rack card will be turned upside down so that the words "On Change" are on top. In front of the room rack card will be the guest's registration card, or if the tray type of rack is used, the

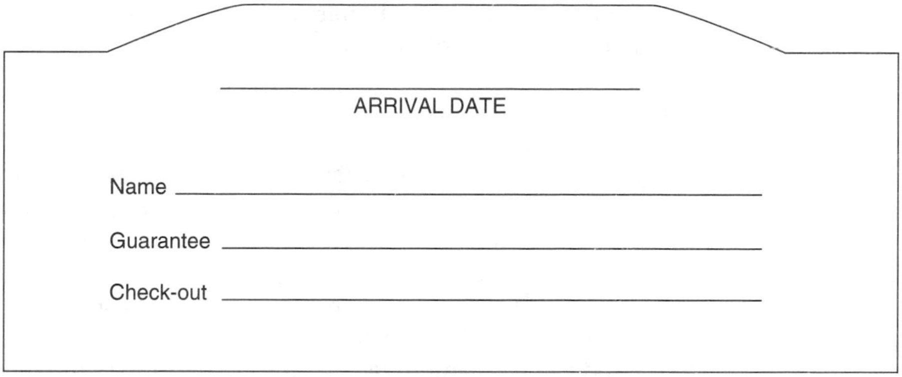

ARRIVAL DATE

Name _____

Guarantee _____

Check-out _____

Exhibit 5-3   Room Rack Reservation Block

rack slip from the folio packet will be placed in front of it. Either way, the room rack card must be turned over so that "On Change" is showing. This is done so that when the guest checks out, the registration card or slip is removed, leaving the room rack card showing "On Change." When a clerk sees the "On Change," he or she knows not to allow a guest into the room until housekeeping lets the front desk know the room is made up. This is the "unoccupied and unclean—not ready for occupancy" condition discussed earlier. A room in this condition can be rented when no others are ready, but the guest must be told of the condition and forewarned that they will have to wait until it is ready before they can enter it. A flag must be put in front of the registration card in the room rack indicating that the room was not ready when the guest checked in, and that a key should not be issued until the room is made up.

In the situation where the guest checks out and another guest is not checked into the room, the front desk will wait for housekeeping to indicate that the room is made up. We refer to this as a "ready room." At this point, the front desk clerk will turn the room rack card around so that the room number is displayed and "On Change" is on the bottom and not visible.

The "out-of-order" condition prohibits the renting of a room or rooms for a variety of reasons. When a room is out-of-order, it is flagged as such on the room rack as well as indicated by the turning of the room rack card to the "On Change" position. In the next section, the flagging of rooms will be discussed in more detail. Rooms are put in the "out-of-order" condition when something in the room is malfunctioning, such as the plumbing or electrical systems, or if a guest who previously occupied the room had caused some damage that requires repair work prior to renting it again. When the hotel is running close to 100 percent occupancy, an "out-of-order" room must be gotten ready quickly to prevent the loss of revenue. During the off-season, hotels will put several rooms out of order: often entire floors will be closed off for deep-cleaning, painting, recarpeting, and other work that needs to be completed to bring the rooms up to standard. The important point to be made here is that out-of-order rooms must be clearly indicated on the room rack and never rented.

Flagging Rooms

Rooms are flagged for a variety of reasons. Flagging a room means placing something in the room rack in front of the room rack card to draw attention to a room's special condition. Many hotels will use a triangular shaped piece of plastic in different colors to represent varying situations. For instance, flags are put in when a rollaway or crib is placed in a room. This way, when the guest checks out, the staff will be notified that the crib or cot must be removed. The flag ensures that the front desk will remind housekeeping of the crib or cot in the event that housekeeping does not notify the desk of their removal. For example, if a green flag is used to represent a crib, the clerk checking in a guest who requests a crib would place a green flag in the slot for this room. Then, all during the guest's stay, the whereabouts of this crib will be known. At check-out, the crib is still accounted for in that room, until housekeeping removes it and notifies the desk. Without this procedure, a 300-room hotel staff may find itself doing some searching for a missing crib that has been previously left in a guest room.

Flags are also used at check-in to temporarily block a room so that two front desk clerks will not sell the same room at the same time. In addition, rooms are flagged when they are out-of-order. Flagging may also be done on a room where the occupants have been causing problems or where the number of guests requires housekeeping to keep an eye on the room.

Other Room Rack Signals

Rooms that are connecting (that is, a room which has an inside door that connects one guest room with another) are indicated on the room rack. A common way of showing this is with arrows on both room cards pointing from one room to the other.

Another situation in which a room rack signal is helpful occurs when a guest checks in and registers for another room (or rooms) on one account. In this case, a registration card or rack slip will be placed in the slot for the lowest number room. In the other room's slot (or slots) a cross-referencing slip will be placed to indicate that the clerk should refer to the other room's card. For example, if a guest has rented rooms 220, 224, and 226, a rack slip or registration card would be placed in room 220's slot. In the two other rooms' slots, a flag would be placed. The indication "C-220" would be written on the flags, meaning that one must "see" room 220 for all of the guest information and charges that would be on the guest's registration card and folio.

Some room racks will have information about each guest room on the rack itself. Different codes or abbreviations will be used to represent the type of beds in the room. Abbreviations will be used to indicate where the room is located or the view from the room. For example, the letters "OV" would stand for "ocean view" and indicate that the room looks out on the ocean.

Most codes and abbreviations used in the lodging industry differ from property to property. There is no standardization of this information that would allow an employee working at one hotel to go to another one in a different company and see the same codes used. However, the systems do, in most cases, have a great deal of similarity, and it is quite easy for an employee to move from one front desk to another, and to pick up the differences very quickly.

Room Numbering

The system by which room numbers are given to the rooms and the way that they appear on the room rack do follow a logical sequence. The room rack is laid out according to the actual physical arrangement of the rooms on each floor of the hotel. This makes it easier for the clerk to determine the location of a room he or she is selling to a guest. Clerks should have a layout of the different floor plans available at the front desk so they can check for room location if needed. This is especially needed now that computers are doing away with the room rack. In many hotels, rooms closest to the elevators will have the lowest numbers, and the room numbers get larger as one moves away from the elevators. Even numbers may be on one side of the hallway, with odd numbers on the opposite side. There should always be signs on the walls to assist the guests, once they are on the floor, in finding their rooms.

In the United States, the lobby is almost always on the first floor or ground level. Recently, there are more exceptions to this, especially in the new hotels being built in some urban areas. For example, the lobby area of the Marriott Marquis in New York City is located on the eighth floor. This means that room numbers may start much higher than the tradition room number 2. In addition, guest arrival, luggage handling, and check-in may deviate from the traditional methods employed at most hotels. In many other parts of the world, hotels start the first floor of guest rooms with the Number 1 and consider the floor below to be the lobby. Under this system, room number 120 would not be on the first floor (ground level) of the hotel, but would be the first floor containing guest rooms. Most U.S. hotels number from the ground floor up. So, even though the lobby is located on the ground floor and is called the lobby level, it is counted as the first floor when the remaining floors are numbered. Thus, a room with the number 202 would be on the first floor of guest rooms but on the second floor of the hotel. Following the logic stated earlier, room number 202 would be close to the elevator and across the hall, or opposite, from room 203.

Many hotels have left out the number 13 when numbering the floors. This is done out of tradition more than anything else. But the number 13 as part of the number of the room is far more common. With the lodging industry expanding into other parts of the world more rapidly than ever before, and with more international visitors coming to this country, it is important that we continue to be aware of other people's attitudes with regard to room numbering.

Information Rack

The information rack is another one of the racks that has in many cases been replaced by a computerized property-management system. An information rack is pictured in Exhibit 5-4. This rack is created for use by the people who are operating the switchboard, as well as by any front desk employee that needs to locate a guest's room number. As explained in the previous section, if information is needed about who is in a particular room, the room rack will supply this information. This room rack runs in numerical order by room number.

An information rack keeps track of information in alphabetical order. The information stored here is the guest's name, kept alphabetically by last name, and the room number that the guest is occupying. When a guest checks in, the information is placed in the rack. Then when someone calls for a guest, the call can be transferred through to him or her. With the use of computer systems, an information rack is not needed. The computer can search and display the guest's name and room number. Either way, front office employees must always remem-

Exhibit 5-4   Information Rack   *Source:* Courtesy of the Concord Resort Hotel.

ber that a guest's room number is *never* to be given out. When someone asks for it at the front desk, he or she should be referred to the house phone and then connected to the room, but he or she should *never* be given the guest's room number.

Key and Mail Rack

The traditional key rack is displayed in Exhibit 5-5. This rack is used to hold guest room keys and mail (except during the check-in and check-out periods). The key rack in most hotels does not receive much use. Most people living in the United States hold on to their key until check-out. On the other hand, travelers from Europe and Asia are in the habit of leaving their room key at the front desk when they go out, and stopping by to pick it up when they return.

The traditional key rack has been replaced in recent years by the key drawer. This is a lockable drawer at the front desk where guest room keys are kept. The hotel of the future will not have a need for a key rack, key drawer, or any storage place at all, as guests will be able to use their credit cards to gain access to their rooms. This system will be covered in Chapter 8.

The traditional key rack also served as a mail rack. When a letter was received for a guest, the information rack was utilized to find the guest's room number. Then the letter was put in the cubbyhole used for the key for that room. With the advent of the key drawer, the mail cubbyhole was replaced by a group of alphabetically arranged cubbyholes. When mail is received, it should be

Exhibit 5-5   Key Rack   *Source:* Courtesy of the Concord Resort Hotel.

stamped with the date and time. (As we will see, much of the paperwork completed in the front desk area is stamped with the date and time.) Mail is stamped so that guests will be able to see when the mail arrived for them. The guest's mail is then filed alphabetically by last name. A notice is then placed in the guest's room, informing the guest that there is mail at the front desk. The guest may call the front desk to arrange for picking it up, and then it is retrieved from the cubbyhole. Over the years, fewer guests have been receiving mail at hotels, so this smaller system has been able to fill the void quite well. With the proliferation of fax machines, less and less mail will be received for guests.

Voucher Rack

The voucher rack is kept in the front desk area. When vouchers are received at the front desk from other areas, they are posted by cashiers to the appropriated guest account. These vouchers are then filed in the voucher rack according to the type of voucher. For example, all paid out vouchers are kept in the same cubbyhole. The night auditor will then go through these when completing the night audit.

THE HOTEL DAY

Many new employees, as well as some hotel guests, have a difficult time understanding exactly what period of time constitutes a hotel day. In many hotels there is a fixed check-in and check-out time. Other hotels will only focus on the check-out time as being the important one. Most city hotels and resort hotels will state both of these times. For example, check-out time may be set at 11:30 A.M. and check-in will be at 2:00 P.M. This gap of two and one-half hours is set up to allow housekeeping enough time to make up the rooms, and to prevent a large check-out from colliding with a large check-in.

With a situation such as the one described here, the hotel day that the guest is paying for is shorter than a 24-hour period. In most cases the day is considerably less than a 24-hour day, since many guests arrive later than the check-in time. Upon request, most hotels will allow a departing guest an extension of time over the scheduled check-out time. The standard extension is about one hour. Guests can be accommodated in this way since the maids will not finish making up all of the check-out rooms by the scheduled check-out time. Even when an extension cannot be given for an entire amount of time a guest requests, the hotel can usually provide for the guest's needs. For example, when a guest does not have a flight out until the evening, he or she may store luggage at the hotel with the bell staff until ready to leave for the airport. When a group has to check-out and depart later, they will be given a hospitality room. In this case, the hospitality room is provided for the guests' relaxation, if needed, before their flight leaves. This is done as a courtesy in appreciation for the group's business.

Hotels that find they are having many individual guests with similar needs may open a hospitality lounge for these people. This would be a plus in the area of customer service.

When a hotel has a fixed check-in time, it must also be flexible to prevent the loss of business. If, for example, a person walks into the hotel at 9:00 A.M. requesting a room and the hotel has vacancies, the person should be checked in. In some hotels located by the highway, guests may want to be checking in even earlier than this time. Each hotel needs to assess its situation and provide the best possible service to its guests.

REGISTRATION PROCESS

The flow of a guest through the hotel's cycle begins as soon as he or she makes a reservation for a room. Following that, the next stage in the cycle is the arrival. In the beginning of this chapter, we discussed the procedures followed once the guest arrives at the entrance to the hotel. In this next section, we will go through an in-depth analysis of the registration process. We will discuss the manual and semiautomated approaches to the registration process. Chapter 8 goes into detail on the computerized process so it will only be briefly mentioned here.

Legal Aspects

The registration process in many states is required by law. Hotels located in such states are required to keep written proof of a guest's registration for a specified period of time. The guest must give the hotel his or her name and address, and the hotel must record the data and time of arrival and departure. These hotels are also responsible for keeping the guest's registration information confidential both during and after the guest's stay. If anyone requests the information, the hotel should contact legal counsel to determine what course of action to take. This is particularly important because of the variance in legal requirements among different areas of the country. Although a state may not require a hotel to have guests register and keep these registrations, it is extremely rare to find a hotel that does not require its guests to register when checking in.

Another legal issue that arises regarding the registration process is that of the right of the hotel to refuse accommodations to a guest. Common law states that due to the nature of the hotel business, innkeepers are required to accept into the hotel those people wishing to be received as guests, assuming that those people wishing to become guests are well comported. Guests who are not well comported can be refused accommodation at the hotel. In addition to the common law requirements, the civil rights laws of the different states and the Civil Rights Act of 1964 prohibit discrimination based upon race, color, religion, national origin, and gender. In the past, many hotels had on the registration card a statement similar to the following: "This hotel is privately owned and operated and the owner reserves the right to refuse service to anyone." This statement clearly goes against the nondiscriminatory policies described above, and such statements should not be used in any hotel.

However, there will be times when a hotel will want to refuse accommodations to guests for a variety of reasons. Laws in many areas have provided for this by indicating certain conditions or situations that may constitute a reason to deny accommodation or service. Guests may be refused accommodations in the following situations:

If an individual who is requesting a room is drunk or behaving in a way that is disorderly, to the point of causing a public nuisance, the hotel does not have to rent this person a room. The hotel has to be concerned about the safety of its guests, employees, and property. So when an individual such as this arrives at the hotel, care must be taken in dealing with him or her. A person that has a contagious disease can also be refused a room for the same reasons.

When a person wants to bring something into the hotel that is not usually allowed, he may be refused a room. For example, if pets are not allowed at the hotel, a guest with a pet may be refused. Firearms and explosive materials are examples of items that are dangerous to the hotel and its guests. Therefore, a person possessing such materials may be and should be refused a room.

Hotels may also refuse accommodations to guests who are unable or unwilling to pay for the room. Thus, if a person attempts to check-in without the means to pay for the room, the hotel may refuse him a room. This situation may present itself when a person has no money and requests that the hotel extend him credit and, after his stay, send him a bill for all services rendered. Most hotels today require a guest at check-in to either pay for the room in cash or allow the front desk to imprint their credit card. If a person refuses to accept these conditions, he may be refused accommodations. This is done to protect the hotel from skippers. A *skipper* is a guest who departs the hotel without going through the formal check-out procedure and paying for all of the charges he has accumulated. With the requirement of paying in advance and the heavy use of credit cards, the number of skippers are much lower today than in the past.

In cases where the hotel is full, that is, when all the rooms are sold or under reservation, the hotel is not obligated to provide rooms to people who walk in. Otherwise, the hotel could be held liable for breach of contract to those who have reservations. A situation in which a hotel may not refuse to rent a person a room is at a late hour. Hotels are, by the nature of their business, presumed to be open at all hours to receive people. In situations such as described above, where a hotel's right to refuse service is concerned (as well as in all matters that involve legal issues), a hotel should seek legal counsel to ensure that the requirements of the law are being met.

Welcoming the Guest

The front desk clerk will be the next employee of the hotel to greet a guest after the parking valet, the doorperson, and a bellperson. It has been said that close to

99 percent of what a guest thinks about a hotel is influenced by the employees that the guest comes in contact with. With this in mind, one can easily see why so much emphasis should be placed on training the front desk staff in proper guest relations. Front desk employees must understand that the guests arriving at the hotel may be upset from their long trip getting there. In cases where a guest arrives at the hotel upset, the employees of the hotel will have an even more difficult time pleasing this person. If the clerks can achieve success in calming and cheering distressed in-comers, however, the hotel will have gained a satisfied customer.

Guest should be greeted by the front desk staff as soon as they approach the desk. Clerks should be taught to smile and say "good morning," "good afternoon," or "good evening," and "welcome to the DeVeau Hotel." If the clerk is unable to serve the guest at once, he should tell the guest he will be right with him or her. This way the guest at least knows his or her presence is recognized. Many hotels set up rope lines for the guests to wait in until an available clerk can service them. This practice allows hotels to eliminate a situation where all arriving guests are huddled around the desk and experiencing nothing but confusion. Hotels can make this waiting a more pleasant experience by serving coffee, tea, and (during the late afternoon and early evening hours) champagne. The Stouffers Hotel in Orlando, Florida, is one example of a hotel that has adopted this practice to encourage relaxed and happy customers.

After greeting the guest, the clerk needs to determine whether the guest has a reservation or is a walk-in. When the guest does have a reservation, the clerk will ask the guest for his or her last name. Once the last name is known, the clerk should use it throughout the check-in process. By repeating the guest's name, the clerk will put the guest at ease and make him feel welcome. This will also help the employee to remember the guest's name for future encounters. A person's name is a very important part of one's identity and most people love to hear it repeated.

Reservation Check-in

When a guest has made a reservation, the next step in the check-in process is to locate the reservation or the registration card. Hotels that preregister their guests will have the registration card filled out and filed in alphabetical order at the desk along with the reservations. Those that don't preregister will have their reservations filed in alphabetical order.

A preregistration packet in a noncomputerized system will contain a registration card and folio, with the slips for the room rack and information rack. The clerk will present the registration card to the guest and ask him to check all of the information for correctness. Also at this time, the clerk should confirm with the guest the type of room or rooms reserved, the length of stay, and the rates quoted: "Mr. DeVeau, we have reserved for you a room with a queen-size bed for three nights at a rate of $85 per night plus tax. Is that correct, sir?" Various other revenue producing techniques may also be applied at this point in the process.

Selling Up

Selling up, or convincing the guest to accept a more expensive room, may be attempted here. This can be done by offering a larger room or one with a better view for only the additional amount: "Mr. DeVeau, if you would like, we have a very nice king room available at this time that will provide you with more space for only $95 per night." The idea is to push the rooms with the higher rates, while making the guest feel that he is getting something extra special for just a small additional amount of money.

Internal Selling

Internal selling involves selling the services and products of the hotel to the guest after arrival. All guest-contact employees are involved in this type of promotional selling, but the desk clerk and bellperson are two of the most important. During the check-in process, internal selling can be done very casually. For example, the clerk might suggest to a hotel's new guests that they try, for instance, the Rib Room if they would enjoy a nice steak dinner. In the case of a repeat guest, a new special on the menu at the Rib Room might be mentioned. When internal selling is utilized by employees, they must be taught to be natural and to not sound as if they are reading a prepared speech. Also, guests should not feel that they are being pressured. This can be accomplished if a remark is made by the service employee about the restaurant or other service, for example, and then advertising is placed inside the elevator or guest room that will help to reinforce the product or service in the guest's mind.

Registration Card

The second step when dealing with a preregistered in-comer is to present the registration card to the guest and ask the guest to verify the information on it for correctness. Is the name correct and spelled correctly? Is the address correct? Is the company name correct? If there is no company name listed, is there one to fill in now? Does the guest have a car? If so, the registration information for the car should be filled in at this time. The guest should then sign the card at the bottom where the signature is required. The clerk will then take the card back from the guest, thanking him or her for checking it. Next, the clerk will ask the guest how he or she will be paying for the room, and the method of payment should be indicated on the registration card. The clerk will fill out the additional information, such as room number, room rate, number of guests, date of arrival, date of departure, and other information as needed. All of the paperwork used during the registration process should be time and date stamped, using the machine at the front desk.

If the hotel does not preregister guests, the clerk will present the guest with a blank registration card to be completed. Some registration cards are separate from the guest's folio. However, in a semiautomated system, the folios and registration cards come together in a packet. There is a perforation where the registration card meets the folio and the clerk separates them when the guest arrives. A folio is the guest's bill, where all of the guest's charges and payments will be recorded during his or her stay. The folio will be covered in greater detail in a later chapter.

The registration card and folio have the same number printed on them. When the guest checks out, the registration cards are filed in alphabetical order by month of arrival and the folios are filed in numerical order. This way, there is a numerical and alphabetical cross-reference of these forms.

The contents of a folio packet vary by hotel. However, it is quite common to see it includes a registration card and a folio made up of a hard copy kept by the hotel and two soft copies to be given as guest receipts or to be used for billing the account. Also in the folio packet are two smaller slips to be used as information rack slips and room rack clips. These appear at the top of the registration card.

Walk-ins

A walk-in guest is one that arrives at the hotel without a reservation. With this type of guest, it is often possible to charge a much higher rate than may have been quoted to a person that has made a reservation far in advance. Here is where "selling from the top down" really pays off in improving the hotel's revenue. Walk-ins are registered in much the same way that guests are in a hotel that does not preregister its guests who are arriving with a reservation. The difference is that instead of clarifying information, this process involves obtaining all information about the guest as new information. Naturally, there are some differences. Most especially, walk-ins post the problem of perhaps complicating room assignments for guests arriving later in the walk-in's stay. That is, a walk-in may be welcome today, but what happens if there is a large group arriving tomorrow and the hotel will be full? The problem of what to do with the walk-ins (which can be a substantial part of the business of some hotels) and how to accommodate them, while still being sure that there are enough rooms available for reservations that will be arriving during the walk-in's stay, was, prior to the computer, a very important part of the front desk's planning and a rooms division manager's headache. Computers allow the front desk to access the room utilization forecasts for the length of stay of the proposed walk-in and to quickly ascertain if the walk-in's entire stay can be accommodated.

One mitigating factor concerning walk-ins is that they often are very transient, sometimes staying for only one night. Of course, there is a downside to this as well. Often scam artists and other criminals arrive via walk-in, so the hotel must be even more alert to credit fraud and other types of fraudulent behavior. Registration procedures and especially the establishment of credit must be closely adhered to with regard to walk-ins. While the vast majority of walk-in guests probably pose no additional security risks than the average guest, it should be noted that hotel rip-offs often can be traced to walk-ins. With a fully functioning PMS (property management system), the potential for rip-offs is greatly reduced.

Room Selection

While the guest is completing the registration card, the front desk clerk should be locating a room for the guest and retrieving the room keys. Many hotels will block off the rooms in the hotel for specific guests prior to their arrival. Thus, when a guest checks in, a room has been preselected for him or her. However, guests should always be told what type of room they are getting and its location, and then asked if it will satisfy their needs. If a guest then requests a different situation, it is the job of the front desk staff to accommodate the guest. For example, a guest may ask for a room with an ocean view, or a room on a higher or lower floor than the one selected. The room clerk should also use his judgment when selecting a room for a guest. For example, an elderly guest should not be put in a room that is farthest away from the elevator.

Rooming Slips

A room slip may be given to the guest after the registration process, or it may be given to the bellperson to leave with the guest upon arrival at the room. Information about the guest and his stay with the hotel is on the rooming slip. It is put there so that the guest can confirm the spelling of his name. In addition, this allows the guest to make sure the clerk agrees with his plans. The room rate is also on the slip, as well as the room number and number of guests in the room.

Many hotels have expanded the rooming slip of old into a small booklet the size of a passport. In fact, many hotels refer to it as the hotel passport. Included in it is the information found on the rooming slip plus the following: a layout of the hotel, the location of various guest attractions (such as the swimming pool) along with their hours of operation, the food and beverage outlets in the hotel and their hours of operation, and any of the additional information a guest may want to know about the hotel and the area around it.

Methods of Payment

As discussed earlier, most hotels today want some sort of payment at check-in. If a guest is paying cash, the clerk will encourage the guest to pay for his entire stay at check-in. The first night's payment will be required at check-in, with the other nights being paid for prior to check-out time the next day. When a guest is paying with a credit card, the card will be imprinted at check-in and authorization will be obtained for the projected charges. A guest who is paying by credit card may charge purchases made throughout the hotel to his or her room. In some cases, the guest is given a hotel credit card that has his or her name, signature, and room number on it. When the guest uses a hotel service such as dining in the hotel restaurant, he or she may charge the meal to his or her account simply by showing the hotel credit card and signing for the charge. This charge is then transferred to the front desk for payment at check-out along with the rest of the charges.

Innovations in Registration

There have been a great many improvements in the registration process since the days of the manual system and guest register book. In this section, a few of the latest innovations will be mentioned.

One way the registration process has been speeded up is through automatic credit card readers that interface with a hotel's property management system. With this piece of equipment, the clerk need only run the guest's credit card through the card reader. This automatically accesses the guest's reservation information, thus eliminating the need to enter in the initial information through the keyboard.

Another means by which registration may be facilitated is through radio communication during the guest's ride from the airport to the hotel. Many hotels provide complimentary van or limousine service to the hotel from the airport. Recently, hotels have started to have their drivers radio guest information to the front desk so that the guest is preregistered by the time he or she reaches the hotel. Then, when the guest reaches the front desk, he or she is greeted by name and very quickly roomed.

Guest self–check-in/check-out systems are used in an attempt to cut down on the amount of time a guest must spend waiting in line at the front desk. The repeat business traveler to a hotel, for example, can benefit greatly from this system. Since this guest already knows his or her way around the hotel and usually has a limited amount of luggage, he or she probably does not need the assistance of a bellperson. A self check-in/check-out terminal is about the size of a typewriter and can be placed easily throughout the lobby area.

Terminals are accessed easily by the guest who simply walks up to the terminal and reads the instructions. The only requirements are that the guest has a reservation at the hotel and uses a credit card that is accepted by the hotel. The instructions on the terminal instruct the guest to slide his or her credit card through the card reader on the terminal. The property management system selects a room according to the information obtained, and then the reservation that was made is confirmed by the guest at that time. This is much like an automated teller machine at a bank that allows its user to confirm and update information. As long as the guest confirms the reservation information on file with the automated computer system, the guest's information from the reservation is transferred at this time to the registration file. Then a registration slip is printed out of the terminal for the guest to take to the desk in order to pick up the room key. If there is any problem or question, the guest may receive assistance from the front desk staff at any time during the process.

As more hotels adopt room locking systems activated by the guest's personal credit card, the self–check-in/check-out process becomes even more convenient. The new credit card–access guest room locking system uses the guest's credit card to open the guest room door. This system will be discussed in Chapter 10. The importance of this type of locking system is that a hotel can eliminate the need for a guest to go to the front desk to get a room key. As soon as the guest has run his credit card through the automated registration terminal, he or she has made the credit card into a room key at the same time. Through the interface with the property management system, the terminal also permits the credit authorization of the guest's credit card. It is anticipated that in the near future, these terminals will be placed in hotel vans and airport luggage areas. Check-out, of course, can be accomplished in the same way. Then, when the guest runs his or her credit card through the terminal at the time of departure from the hotel, the terminal prints out the guest's folio.

Group Registration Procedures

The registration of a large group can be a relatively simple process if some basic steps are followed. If these steps are ignored, however, it can also be a front office manager's greatest nightmare. Planning for a group's registration takes place long before the date of arrival and requires the cooperation of the sales department. If the group itself or group leader will accept responsibility for all charges made by group members, this will eliminate the need for imprinting each group member's credit card at check-in. Imagine the difference a simple arrangement such as this can make when one is checking in a group of 100 guests into 60 rooms.

DISCUSSION QUESTIONS

1. "Quality" has often been associated only with "luxury," yet Japanese cars come in all price ranges. How might hotels interpret "quality" as it relates to registering a guest, even if the hotel is an economy property?
2. Can you describe or draw a flowchart of the usual sequence of events in the registration process?
3. In what ways does a group arrival differ from individual guest arrivals?
4. Room racks are a holdover from precomputer days. Yet many hotels still maintain them. Can you come up with a reason for this? Does it make sense?
5. Can you name a few disadvantages of having the lobby on a floor other than the first floor? Can you name at least one advantage?
6. How might we accommodate a guest who has a 6:00 P.M. flight home?

STUDY QUESTIONS

1. Who is the first person to greet a guest arriving by automobile?
2. What should the doorperson do if a bellperson is not available right away in order to take the arriving guest's luggage?

3. What is meant by the term *preregistration*?
4. Of the five possible room conditions, which three mean that the room is unavailable to an arriving guest?
5. If your room is located on the third floor, what number would your room begin with?
6. Should the check-in time be flexible?
7. Can a guest who is obviously loud, abusive, even drunk be denied a room?
8. How important is it to greet a guest in a nice way upon that guest's arrival at the hotel?
9. Can you describe "selling up"?
10. What method of payment usually requires the hotel to charge for all rooms up front? (That is, the guest must pay for his or her entire stay upon registration.)

CHAPTER 6

Accounting
for
the Guest's Stay

CHAPTER OBJECTIVES

After reading this chapter you will understand:

- What accounting functions take place at the front desk.
- Why these accounting activities take place at the front desk.
- How the front desk performs these accounting functions.
- What the accounting functions mean.

INTRODUCTION

The front office is the focal point for the accounting activities of the entire hotel. It is often divided into two subdepartments—the front desk and the reservations department. As we have seen in previous chapters, in the front office guest reservations are handled, rate quotes and room assignments are made, and guests are registered. When there is no concierge or guest services subdepartment, the front office often provides guests with information regarding local events and addresses. Because of its central position in the hotel's organizational structure, it is the source of most of the information concerning what is occurring within the hotel as well. Therefore, it is only logical that instructions to the rooms department should emanate from the front office, and that the front office should be the central repository for all information concerning a guest's stay at the hotel.

The front office is the natural source for most of a hotel's accounting information and operating statistics regarding sales. This information is used to make current decisions, such as room assignments and rate quotes, and it is accumulated for inclusion in various reports about the history of the hotel's business that serve as guides to management when preparing long-term plans and making long-term policy decisions.

In this chapter we will look at the process of accounting for a guest's stay in a hotel. We will do this from the point of view of a manually operated accounting system, even though this type of system is outdated, because it enables us to explain on a step-by-step basis the processes involved. Mechanical and computer systems go through the same steps, but they compress these steps so that it is difficult for the student to understand what is occurring. Students should understand the underlying basic processes involved in a manual accounting system. Also, computer systems tend to be designed specifically for each hotel, which makes it difficult to teach about them in any but the most general terms. However, those who understand a manual accounting system will find it easier to understand mechanical and computer systems when they encounter them. Many hotels today start up with manual accounting systems, and then, once the personnel is trained in the manual system, they switch to a computerized system. Furthermore, it is important for front office personnel to understand the flow of information in a manual accounting system because computers often break down, sometimes for many days. If front office personnel are not familiar with the flow of information, they will be at a loss during the breakdown period. In each chapter, where it applies, and in Chapter 8, there will be discussions of mechanical and computer systems in as much detail as is logically feasible.

This chapter will begin with a brief discussion of the objectives of an accounting system and a brief review of the basic accounting process involved in recording sales and collections. We will then look at the different types of charges and credits that can be made to a guest's account and discuss the documents used to record these charges and credits. This will include a detailed analysis of the flow of accounting information through a hotel's manual accounting system. The differences in information flow through a mechanical system and a computerized system will be reviewed briefly toward the end of the chapter.

OBJECTIVES OF FRONT OFFICE ACCOUNTING

Generally the objectives of a hotel's accounting department are to do the following:

1. Record accounting information.
2. Process this accounting information.

3. Verify that accounting information is being properly recorded and processed.

4. Assist management in evaluating the hotel's performance.

Although the accounting department is responsible for providing these support services to all hotel departments, in this text we are concerned with how these objectives are applied in the rooms division, of which the front office is a subdepartment. Furthermore, in so far as the rooms division is concerned, the verification function of the accounting department is fully explained in Chapter 7, "The Night Audit," and the evaluative function of the accounting department is explained in Chapter 12, "Budgeting in the Rooms Department." This chapter and Chapter 9, "Check-Out and Collections," will deal only with the recording and processing of accounting information. The accounting procedures required to record sales activities in the rooms department during a guest's stay are explained here. Chapter 9 will explain the check-out and post–check-out phase of a guest's stay.

REVIEW OF BASIC ACCOUNTING PROCEDURES
FOR RECORDING SALES

The term *accounting procedures* can be used to refer to the recording and processing of both expenses and revenues. However, this text deals with front office procedures, and in the front office, with the exception of certain minor expenses (paid as petty cash expenditures by cashiers), only sales and collections information is generated. Therefore, our basic accounting review will concentrate on recording and processing sales and collections. Accounting information is taken from various source documents and initially recorded in a journal. The journal is summarized and is subsequently transferred to a ledger account in the General Ledger. The General Ledger may sometimes have subsidiary ledgers associated with it to provide a detailed breakdown of the information stored in any given account. These components of an accounting system are described below and in Exhibit 6-1.

Source documents are the various receipts, tickets, charge slips, and so forth, generated through guest transactions. The guest may eat a meal in the coffee shop, thus generating a source document (the restaurant voucher). Or the guest may have checked in and a rack slip was created showing that guest's room rate. (In this case, the guest never actually sees the source document, but he or she has acknowledged the legitimacy of the charge through accepting the reservation confirmation, checking in, and signing a registration card.) There are numerous documents generated, all of which must eventually find their way to the front desk, where clerks post the charges to the appropriate journal.

Journals, used as initial records of similar accounting transactions, can be of many different formats and sizes, but they all have three things in common.

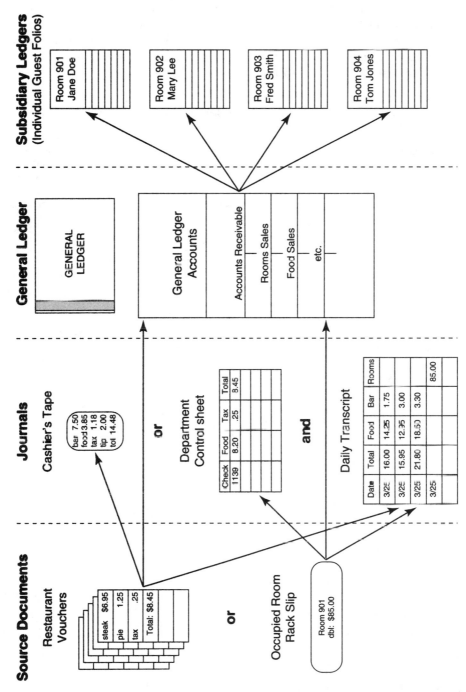

Exhibit 6-1 Components of Nonroom Accounting System — Room Sales and Restaurant Credit Slips

Journals are designed to record similar types of transactions easily and repetitively; they are the first place where accounting information is systematically recorded; and they are designed so that the information is always recorded in chronological order, that is, in the order in which transactions occur. A traditional manual sales journal format is shown in Exhibit 6-2.

EXHIBIT 6-2
A TRADITIONAL MANUAL SALES JOURNAL (ILLUSTRATION SHOWS A FOOD AND BEVERAGE JOURNAL)

Ticket Number	Sale Date	Total Amount	Food Sales	Beverage Sales
34	11/05/98	$15.67	$11.02	$4.65
35	11/05/98	$13.22	$8.57	$4.65
36	11/06/98	$4.65		$4.65
37	11/07/98	$12.48	$9.48	$3.00

With the advent of the electronic cash register, this journal was replaced by a cash register tape that looks as shown in Exhibit 6-3.

Receipt tape from
dining room register

Tapes printed on
kitchen workstation

```
        RECEIPT
SERV #              2
TBL #              34
GUESTS             2
TRANS          19396
DATE        10/01/98
T/C # 10019900121
ESCARGOT         7.25
CAESAR/2         8.95
P RIB RARE      12.95
SALMON          10.50
CHEESECAKE       2.50
CREPE FORST      4.75
COFFEE           1.50
COFFEE           1.50
FOOD TOTAL      49.90
CHRG TIP        10.00
TOTAL           59.90
VISA/M.C.       59.90

4751129657460719
EXPIRE: 02/99
```

```
----KITCHEN----
ESCARGOT
CAESAR/2

D1 02 19396 T34
10/01 18:55 01
```

```
----KITCHEN----
P RIB *RARE*
BAKED *NO VEG*
SALMON
*SAUCE ON SIDE*
RICE

D1 02 19396 T34
10/01 19:08 17
```

```
----KITCHEN----
CREPE FORST

D1 02 19396 T34
10/01 19:44 52
```

Exhibit 6-3   A Sample Electronic Cash Register Tape and Remote Kitchen Station Tape

Electronic cash registers have a receipt tape printer in them; often they have two. When there are two tapes, one receipt tape is kept inside the machine and removed at the end of each shift (or at the end of the day). The other receipt tape is given to the customer. Other cash registers use a two-part receipt tape, one part of which is given to the customer. Regardless of the procedures used, the main receipt tapes contain the same information on them; a receipt number, the date, the shift or time of day, the server/cashier number, and the amount of food, bar, tax, tip, and total charges incurred. Some machines print out other additional information, such as the items ordered and their price, thank you messages, and a host of other information. Also, tapes come out of the remote work stations. These remote stations may be terminals located in other parts of the establishment. Exhibit 6-3 shows both a cash register tape indicating the dollar value of sales and a remote kitchen terminal tape used to transmit guest orders to kitchen personnel when the server enters an order in the dining room electronic cash register (ECR).

Although the cash register tape replaces the manual sales journal, as all journals should, it provides a means of recording the initial entry of transactions, on a repetitive basis with a minimum effort, and chronologically. Journals of original entry also allow accountants, or computer accounting systems, to easily determine the total entry to a general ledger account by simply totaling the various columns of the sales journal in a manual system, or, when an ECR is used, by printing out the totals stored in each of the ECR's separate memory registers, one for each type of sale, taxes, etc. Information is directed to the individual memory registers when it is keyed into the ECR by depressing the food key, beverage key, etc. By providing a totaled record against which to compare individual vouchers, sales journals also serve to verify that all credit sales vouchers have been included with the shift business sent to the front office for posting to the individual guest folios, as described later.

Once a transaction has been entered initially in a sales journal, it must be transferred to its proper General Ledger account. Accounts are used to gather, in summary form, all transactions of a similar nature and to maintain these summaries for inclusion in various financial reports. Transferring data from a journal to an account in the General Ledger is called "posting." An account can be presented in what is known as a "T-Account" format (rarely used in business but a good way to illustrate what is happening to those unfamiliar with accounting), or it can be in General Ledger format. In the T-Account format, debits are posted to the left of the vertical line and credits to the right. The balance is calculated by subtracting the smaller of the debit or credit total from the larger total and writing the difference, or balance, in the account below a single line on the side with the larger total. When using the General Ledger format, debits are posted in the debit column and credits are posted in the credit column and the balance is posted in the balance column. Both of these formats are shown in Exhibit 6-4, along with a commonly used computer-generated account format.

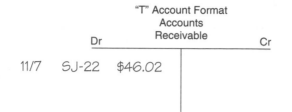

"T" Account Format
Accounts
Receivable

Dr   Cr

11/7   SJ-22 $46.02

General Ledger Format

Account Name: Accounts Receivable

Date	Description/Source	Debit		Credit		Balance	
11/9	SJ-22	46	02			931	03
11/9	SJ-22	16	32			947	35

Computer Format

```
Transaction report

Date      Ref.     Source        Amount        Account
- - - - - - - - - - - - - - - - - - - - - - - - - - - -

11/07     0193     SJ-22          46.02         1-1010-3
11/07     0194     SJ-22          16.32         1-1010-3
11/07     0195     SJ-22           2.85         1-1010-4


General Ledger Listing

Account   Trans.   Debits      Credits       Balance
- - - - - - - - - - - - - - - - - - - - - - - - - -

1-1010-3  0193     46.02                       931.03
1-1010-3  0194     16.32                       947.35
```

Exhibit 6-4   Various Account Formats

In Exhibit 6-1 we saw how accounting information originates with source documents and is gathered in journals (such as a cashier's tape and the daily transcript). From there, totals are transferred to the appropriate General Ledger accounts. It is important to note that at the same time information is being transferred to the General Ledger control accounts, it is also being entered in the individual guest subsidiary ledger folios. This provides management with a detailed breakdown, by guest, of the total in the accounts receivable control account. This breakdown is useful to management in a variety of ways, which we will indicate in this chapter and in the next. It is also of obvious use to the guest, as it represents the total amount that the guest owes at any point in time.

As you may remember from your basic accounting classes, the T-Account is mainly used as a learning tool, whereas the General Ledger format is the account format formally used in all practical accounting systems. You may also recall from your accounting courses that the General Ledger is the book of final entry, as opposed to the journals, which are records of initial entry. It contains all the accounts of the hotel grouped together either as a continuous list (computer-generated) or in a loose-leaf book (a manual system). In either case, there is usually a debit column and a credit column, plus a balance column, which indicates to a manager the balance in the account. In some computer-generated General Ledgers, the debits and credits are posted in a single column with credits preceded by a minus sign.

As you may already know, the hotel industry has developed a Uniform System of Accounts for Hotels, which lists all the accounts a hotel is likely to need, and specifies what charges are to be posted to each account and how these accounts are to be presented in financial statements. Some accounts used to record hotel revenues in the rooms division are listed in Exhibit 6-5.

EXHIBIT 6-5   REVENUE ACCOUNTS USED IN THE ROOMS DIVISION

Revenue Accounts Rooms Division Sales	*Balance Sheet Accounts* Accounts Receivable
Transient Regular	Guest Ledger
Transient Group	City Ledger
Permanent	
Other Rooms Revenue—	
Other Departments	
Telephone Charges	
Laundry Charges	
Valet Charges	
Garage Charges	

The rooms revenue accounts accumulate sales information by guest type. A more detailed subdivision of revenue accounts can also be made. For instance, transient-group sales may be subdivided into convention, corporate meetings, or tour groups. Transient regular sales may be subdivided into regular tourist, corporate (guaranteed rate), or military (guaranteed rate). Permanent sales can be made for specific rooms, or, if they are for a specific category of room, they may be called *contract transient revenue.* You may ask why nonrooms revenue accounts are listed in Exhibit 6-5, if we are only going to discuss rooms division front office activity. The reason is that when credit sales are made in these other departments, they are posted to a guest's account through the front office, as we shall see later when we discuss the flow of accounting information in the rooms department.

The accounts receivable category also needs to be subdivided. The accounts receivable category in a hotel's General Ledger only tells a manager the total amount owed to the hotel. It doesn't tell the manager who the debtors are and how much each one owes. Therefore, most hotels have two or more additional sets of ledgers, called *subsidiary ledgers.* These contain ledger pages or cards called *folios,* which show a detailed listing of all credit purchases and payments made by anyone at the hotel, as well as the balance in each guest's account. A sample folio is shown in Exhibit 6-6. Folios enable a manager to know how much each guest owes. The two most frequently used ledgers, called the *guest ledger* and the *city ledger,* serve to record transactions of guests staying at the hotel and the transactions or amounts owed by patrons not currently staying at the hotel. These and other subsidiary ledgers will be discussed later in the chapter.

The individual balances in each of these subsidiary ledgers, or folios, must total to the balance in the corresponding accounts receivable General Ledger account, sometimes also called the *accounts receivable control account.* It is so called because it serves to verify that none of the ledger folios are missing and that the balances in all the subsidiary ledger accounts are correct. Thus the total of the balances of all the subsidiary guest ledger folios must equal the balance in the General Ledger guest accounts receivable account, and the total of the balances of all the city ledger folios must equal the balance in the General Ledger city accounts receivable account. Before concluding our review of basic accounting, we will refresh the reader's memory concerning the journal entries required to record sales in the rooms division. These journal entries are quite simple; however, there is one peculiarity inherent in hotel accounting that needs to be pointed out: both cash and credit sales generated in the hotel are posted to the accounts receivable General Ledger control account and the subsidiary ledger folios. This differs from the normal procedure for posting cash sales, which involves a debit to cash and a credit to sales. For cash sales generated in the rooms division, such as the prepayment of a room, the accounts receivable control account and the guest's subsidiary ledger folio are still debited just as if the sale were a credit sale. To offset this entry in the case of cash sales, a second entry is made crediting accounts receivable and debiting cash. This transfer from accounts receivable to the cash ac-

ROOM 321	NAME KURY, CLAUD				100	**41782**	
NO. PARTY 2	STREET ADDRESS 178 PINE ST.				RATE	FOLIO NO.	
DEPART 01/14	CITY, STATE, ZIP WESTFIELD, NJ 07090				01/12/98 13:54:06		
ARRIVE 01/12	PAY TYPE VISA	SAFE BOX 32	LICENSE PLATE JMH 321 (NJ)		DATE STAMP		

BALANCE FORWARD - FOLIO NO.		AMOUNT		-0-
DATE	DESCRIPTION	DEBIT	CREDIT	BALANCE
01/12	Room	100.00		-0-
01/12	Tax	6.00		100.00
01/13	Room	100.00		106.00
01/13	Tax	6.00		206.00
01/13	Restaurant	30.00		212.00
				242.00
01/14	VISA		242.00	-0-

Thank you

The STAGGAR INN

17875 Beach Blvd.
Miami, FL 33133
Tele. (305) 495-0505

Where Our
Guests
Get Dry

Exhibit 6-6   A Sample Folio

count takes place when the deposit is made in the bank. Thus, the balance in the accounts receivable control account and the guest's subsidiary ledger folio is not affected. The same procedure is used for posting cash sales when a sale is generated in a department other than the rooms division. The front office is advised of the cash sales through the shift reports sent to the front office along with the charge slips. Cash sales in the restaurant, for instance, are sent to the front office to be posted to accounts receivable and a ledger folio is made out to "daily cash." This "daily cash" folio, in the city ledger, records a temporary debit for cash sales made to nonguests of the hotel because they have no individual accounts receivable ledger folio. This procedure allows the night auditor to audit all sales as well as all receivables postings, so that the accounting department has a daily sales journal posting to the General Ledger, which has been prepared by the night auditor (a level of internal control not available to most businesses).

Thus, $50 in restaurant sales, $5 in valet charges, and $15 of telephone charges, all credit sales, would affect the hotel's accounts as follows, assuming a 6 percent sales tax (see Exh. 6-7). The sales tax payable account is a credit account because it represents funds that are collected on behalf of the state or local government and must eventually be remitted to that government.

EXHIBIT 6-7   POSTINGS TO THE GENERAL LEDGER

	DR	CR
Accounts receivable		
{Control Account}	$74.20	
Restaurant Sales		$50.00
Valet Charges		5.00
Telephone Charges		15.00
Sales Tax Payable		4.20
Totals	$74.20	$74.20

If these amounts were charged by two guests, say a Mr. John Doe and a Ms. Mary Jane Roe, then their subsidiary ledger accounts (their folios) would be affected as shown in Exhibit 6-8.

EXHIBIT 6-8   POSTINGS TO SUBSIDIARY LEDGERS (THE FOLIOS)

	DR	CR
John Doe Ledger Folio		
Restaurant Sales	$30.00	
Valet Charges	5.00	
Sales Tax	2.10	
Mary Jane Roe Folio		
Restaurant Sales	$20.00	
Telephone Charges	15.00	
Sales Tax	2.10	

If one night's stay were paid for in advance, this would constitute a cash sale and would be recorded as shown in Exhibit 6-9, along with the credit to the appropriate sales tax payable account.

EXHIBIT 6-9   POSTINGS TO THE GENERAL LEDGER

	DR	CR
Accounts Receivable	$106.00	
Room Sales		$100.00
Sales Tax Payable		6.00

ENTRY TO SUBSIDIARY LEDGER

	DR	CR
John Doe Ledger Folio		
Room Sales	$100.00	
Sales Tax	6.00	

Notice that the debit to the accounts receivable control account is equal to the total debits to the subsidiary ledger account. Since this is a cash sale, a second entry, representing the collection of payment on the cash sale, would be made to debit the cash account and credit the accounts receivable account as shown in Exhibit 6-10.

EXHIBIT 6-10   POSTINGS TO THE GENERAL LEDGER

	DR	CR
Cash	$106.00	
Accounts Receivable		$106.00

ENTRY TO SUBSIDIARY LEDGER

	DR	CR
John Doe Ledger Folio		
Payment		$106.00

If accounts receivable are collected at a date later than the date the sale is made, the accounts receivable control account is credited and the cash account is debited in exactly the same manner as above, except that the collection entry is made at a later date. Thus, the collection entry for both a cash sale and a credit sale is the same.

Another type of transaction that can generate charges to accounts receivable and a guest's ledger folio involves a cash advance to a guest, or the payment on behalf of a guest for packages delivered to the hotel. If the hotel paid $40 for a package delivered to a guest, the accounts receivable control account and the guest's ledger folio would be charged for this as if it were a cash advance, as shown in Exhibit 6-11.

EXHIBIT 6-11   POSTINGS TO THE GENERAL LEDGER

	DR	CR
Accounts Receivable	$40.00	
Cash		$40.00

ENTRY TO SUBSIDIARY LEDGER

	DR	CR
John Doe Ledger Folio		
Cash Advance	$40.00	

VARIOUS TYPES OF CHARGES AND CREDITS AND THE FRONT OFFICE ACCOUNTING FORMULA

In this section of the chapter we will provide a more complete discussion of the various events that can generate charges and credits on a guest's folio, along with an explanation of these different charges and credits. Before continuing, it is recommended that the reader study Exhibit 6-12.

Room Sales

Of course the most common source of debits to a guest ledger is room sales. Every night that a guest stays at a hotel, the guest's ledger folio is debited for the room rate of his or her room. As discussed previously, many rates can be charged for the same room depending on the following:

- double or single occupancy
- the rate plan
- the season of the year
- the type of guest
- package plans

Most hotels have a slightly higher rate if there is more than one occupant per room. Because this rate is only slightly higher than the single rate, it usually is a bargain for two people to share a room. The difference between the single rate and the double occupancy rate is known as the *rate spread*. There are three basic rate plans:

- the European Plan (EP)
- the Modified American Plan (MAP)
- the American Plan (AP)

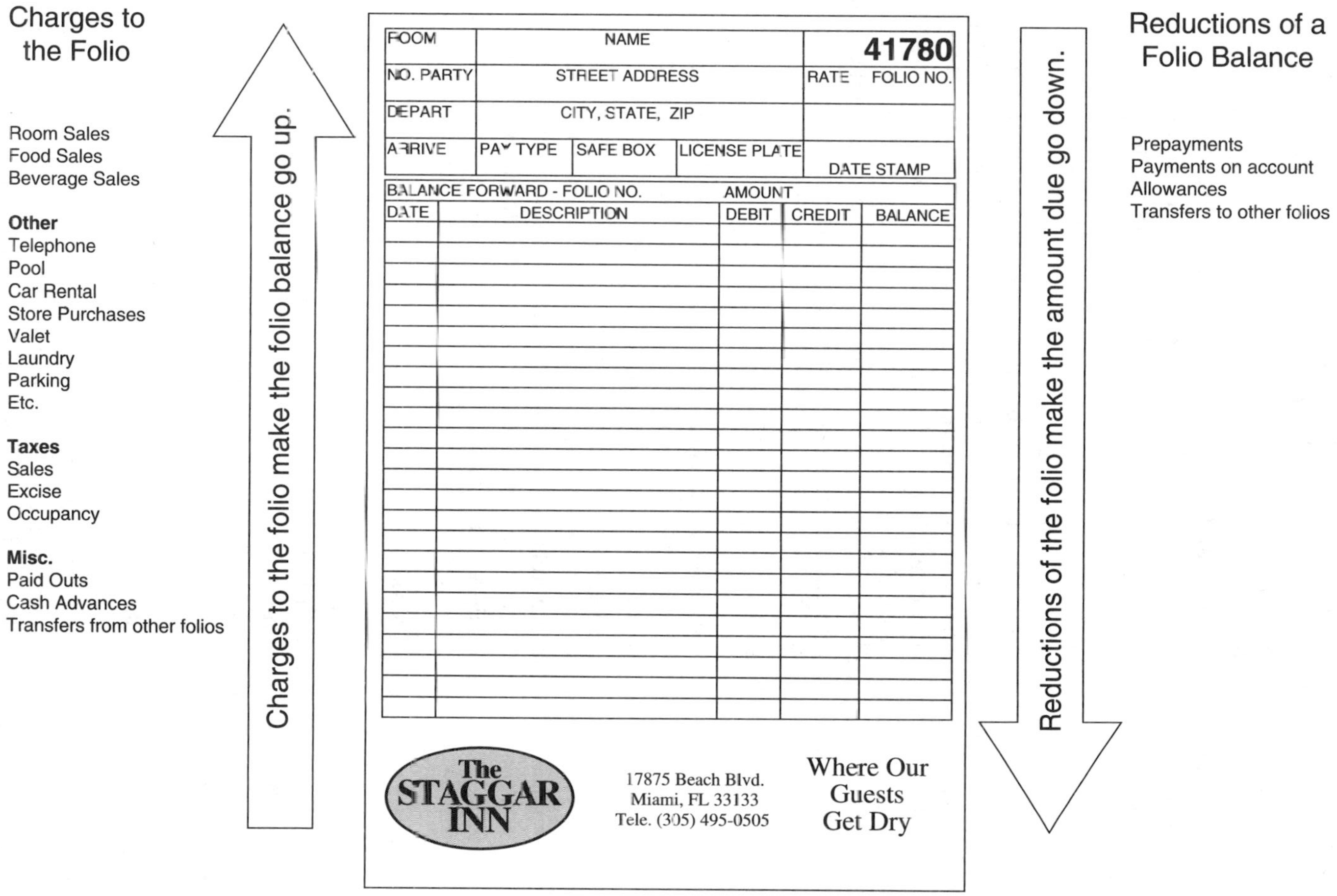

Reductions of a Folio Balance

Prepayments
Payments on account
Allowances
Transfers to other folios

Reductions of the folio make the amount due go down.

ROOM	NAME		41780
NO. PARTY	STREET ADDRESS	RATE	FOLIO NO.
DEPART	CITY, STATE, ZIP		
ARRIVE	PAY TYPE	SAFE BOX	LICENSE PLATE

DATE STAMP

BALANCE FORWARD - FOLIO NO.

		AMOUNT	
DATE	DESCRIPTION	DEBIT	CREDIT	BALANCE

The STAGGAR INN

17875 Beach Blvd.
Miami, FL 33133
Tele. (305) 495-0505

Where Our
Guests
Get Dry

Exhibit 6-12 Activities That Affect a Room Folio

Charges to the folio make the folio balance go up.

Charges to the Folio

Room Sales
Food Sales
Beverage Sales

Other
Telephone
Pool
Car Rental
Store Purchases
Valet
Laundry
Parking
Etc.

Taxes
Sales
Excise
Occupancy

Misc.
Paid Outs
Cash Advances
Transfers from other folios

Rates quoted under the European Plan include room only, no meals. In Europe, there is an ever-less-popular modification of the European Plan called the Continental Plan, which typically includes a light breakfast of pastry and coffee. Rates quoted under the Modified American Plan include breakfast and dinner. The American Plan rates include all three meals in the price of the room.

The season of the year sometimes affects the rate charged for a room. This is usually true of resort hotels. In peak season the same room may be sold for as high as a 50 percent premium over the minimum rate charged in the slack season. The type of guest is also an important factor in determining the room rate. Although usually less than 10 percent of guests fall into this category, the walk-in guest with no group connections is usually quoted the highest rate deemed appropriate for the hotel's current demand situation. Groups are often quoted lower rates or given some other consideration, such as free meals or drinks, because of the volume of rooms being sold to the group. Also, corporations or government agencies may receive guaranteed rates for their employees, which may be lower than the individual rate for that day, because of their frequent use of the hotel. Rooms that are permanently occupied and are used as apartments, almost nonexistent in large hotels, receive special low rates. It is interesting to note that the Waldorf Astoria in New York is one of the few large hotels with rooms in this category.

Finally, rates may also vary according to special amenities requested by a guest, such as an extra portable bed, color TV, special cable TV stations, or any other special treatment or service the hotel may offer for an additional fee.

As explained in Chapter 4, "Room Rates," in view of the current emphasis on yield management, which attempts to realize the maximum dollar sales potential of each room, large hotels today may have hundreds of room rates to cover not only the variety of rooms but also a variety of client categories and service requests, as well as the different demand conditions they may be experiencing.

Food and Beverage Sales

Sales of food and beverage that are signed for by a guest are charged to the guest's subsidiary ledger folio. When food and beverage purchases are paid for on a cash basis, the same procedure is followed except for the subsequent offsetting entry (see pages 130–131) to transfer the balance from accounts receivable to the cash account.

Other Department Sales

Sales may be generated in other departments of a hotel, such as the valet department, telephone department, laundry department, garage, swimming pool, or tennis club. These sales are also charged to the corresponding accounts receivable subsidiary ledger folio.

Sales Tax

In those states where there is a sales tax, the hotel acts as collection agent for the government. A charge is made on the corresponding guest or city subsidiary ledger folio for the amount of the sales tax on all sales subject to the tax. This amount is shown separately on the subsidiary ledger folio. The collected amount is then paid to the government periodically by the hotel.

Occupancy Tax

More and more states and cities are also levying an occupancy tax (sometimes referred to as a "tourist tax"). This tax varies and may be levied as a flat dollar amount per room-night, or as a percentage of sales. Occupancy taxes are handled in exactly the same way as sales taxes.

Cash Advances and Paid-Outs

If a hotel gives a guest a cash advance or pays for merchandise delivered to the guest on a C.O.D. basis, the amount paid out is charged to the guest's subsidiary ledger folio. Guests may also tip personnel using the paid-out method (that is, by charging the tip to their folio). Similarly, a guest may purchase the services of an outside vendor. For example, the hotel may not have a golf course but may have made arrangements so that the guests may use a nearby course. In these cases the hotel wishes to make it appear to the guest that this is a hotel service, so the hotel does not require the guest to pay the vendor directly. The vendor is paid by the hotel and the charge is applied to the guest's folio. Another source of cash advances occurs when the guest cashes a check at the front desk. The check is usually posted as a payment on the folio, and the cash is posted as an advance. This posting allows the hotel to maintain a record of checks processed by the front desk and assures the hotel that the cashiers are only cashing checks for registered guests of the hotel.

Allowances

Sometimes a guest will receive a reduction in rate after the room rate has been posted, or after other purchases have been recorded on his or her ledger folio. This is called an *allowance*, and a separate credit entry is made in the credit column of the ledger folio for the amount of the reduction. Coupons, two-for-one specials, and all manner of sales promotions are handled this way. Also, many hotels offer rates that are reduced for longer stays; hence, the rate may be $100 per night but $600 per week. An allowance slip must be posted to the folio to reduce the rate accordingly. Since this represents money that is "given back" to the guest (that is, sales for which the hotel is not receiving payment), the usual hotel policy is to require the authorization of a manager on the slip. Usually front desk clerks are not allowed to post allowances on the folio balances without such signed authorization.

Transfers

If a guest pays with a credit card, the balance in his or her guest ledger folio is transferred to the credit card company's folio on the city ledger. This is done by crediting the guest's folio and debiting the credit card company's folio. Or, if one guest pays another guest's bill, the balance in the folio of the guest whose bill is being paid is removed with a credit, and it is charged (debited) to the paying guest's folio. Transfers must be verified by the night auditor for their appropriateness. Clerks may be tempted to transfer off a balance from a folio for which the guest has paid cash and to put the balance onto another folio, in the hopes that the other guest will not notice the charge (thus enabling the clerk to pocket the cash payment). Such tricks, while not common, are inhibited when the clerk knows that all transfers are verified during the night audit.

Also, for those rare cases when the front desk fails to establish the means of payment at check-in and a guest leaves the hotel without paying his or her bill, the amount owed is credited to the guest ledger folio and is charged to another folio in the delinquent ledger under that guest's name. This is the transfer of a bad debt whose collection is doubtful, another reason for a complete audit of all transfers.

Payments

When a guest makes a payment on his or her account, the amount paid is credited to that guest's subsidiary ledger folio by entering it in the credit column of the folio.

THE FRONT OFFICE ACCOUNTING FORMULA

All of the above types of debits and credits are related to each other on the folio page by what is known as the *front office accounting formula*. This formula states that folio charges and credits are related as follows:

Beginning Balance + Charges − Credits = Ending Balance

Thus the folio in Exhibit 6-6 indicates the guest had a beginning balance of zero, and that on January 12th, $100 was charged to the folio (for a room) and $6 was charged (for sales tax on the room). On January 13th, another $100 (room) charge was made, plus the $6 (sales tax), and $30 was charged (for food in the restaurant). Finally, on January 14th, the guest checked out and paid the bill, a total amount of $242. Items in parentheses indicate possible sources for charges and credits. These transactions would appear as shown in Exhibit 6-13 when expressed in the front office accounting formula.

EXHIBIT 6-13   THE FRONT OFFICE
ACCOUNTING FORMULA

Beginning Balance	+	Charges	–	Credits	=	Ending Balance
-0-		$100.00		-0-		
		6.00				$106.00
$106.00		$100.00		-0-		
		6.00				
		30.00				$242.00
$242.00		-0-		$242.00		-0-

FRONT OFFICE ACCOUNT FORMS

Before continuing on to describe the flow of accounting information in the rooms division, let us review the forms most commonly used in the front office, which we have previously mentioned, plus some new forms such as the *cash sheet*, the *transfer journal*, and the *error sheet* or *correction sheet*.

General Ledger

The General Ledger is the book of final entry. It is composed of all the individual accounts in a hotel's accounting system. Information is transferred to the General Ledger from journals, books of original entry where the information is accumulated in chronological order. A sample General Ledger page format was shown in Exhibit 6-4. This format is basically the same for both manual accounting systems and computerized accounting systems. In both cases, there is a date column, description column, debit column, credit column, and balance column. Sometimes, in a computerized system the General Ledger may compress the debit and credit columns into one column, showing credits with a minus sign. The balance will be shown either in a separate column to the right of the combined debit/credit column, or it may appear as a total beneath this column.

The Subsidiary Ledger Folio

We have learned that some accounts need to have their contents broken down into subgroups for management purposes. One of these accounts is the Accounts Receivable General Ledger account. Management not only needs to know the balance in the Accounts Receivable General Ledger account, but must also know how many individuals owe the hotel and how much each one owes. The Accounts Receivable General Ledger account, therefore, is broken down into subaccounts—one for each guest or patron of the hotel with an unpaid balance. These subaccounts are called the subsidiary ledger. The subsidiary ledger is usually made up of individual folio pages, such as the one shown in Exhibit 6-6. Each page contains charges, credits, and the balance in the account—related to each other by the front office accounting formula.

The individual folios are kept in a container called a *bucket* or *pit* in order to minimize the chances of their being lost. Hotels keep folio pages grouped in three categories: (1) the guest ledger, (2) the city ledger, and (3) the delinquent ledger. The guest ledger is kept at the front office. Guest ledger folio cards are organized in the bucket by room number or by account number. The city ledger and delinquent ledger are kept in the accounting office and are organized in alphabetical order or by account number.

There are different types of folios as well. The *guest ledger* consists of guest folios. The *city ledger* is made up of nonguest folios to record credit purchases made by patrons of the hotel who are not staying at the hotel, and to record payments with credit cards. For example, credit card companies have individual accounts in the city ledger, to which balances from the guest ledger are transferred when a guest checks out and pays with a credit card. Also, if the hotel grants direct credit to a guest, the guest's individual account will be transferred to the city ledger if the account is not paid at check-out time. The city ledger may be subdivided into the city ledger proper and the *delinquent ledger*, containing the folios of guests who dispute their bills. The accounts of guests who, because of an oversight or due to a hotel's lax policies, were allowed to check in without establishing a method of payment and did in fact leave the hotel without paying are also kept here. Finally, there are also *master folios*, which are used to record charges for groups, and A and B folios for split billings. These will be explained later in the section on sales to groups and conventions.

Vouchers

Information is transferred to the ledger folios from vouchers sent by each of the other departments of the hotel. Two typical vouchers are shown in Exhibit 6-14. Vouchers show the date, type, and amount of a transaction plus the signature of the guest, or nonstaying patron, making the purchase.

Cash Sheet

Cash sheets are maintained by each front office cashier to keep track of all money received and paid out during a shift. A sample cash sheet is shown in Exhibit 6-15. Basically, the cash sheet is divided into the left and right halves, with the left-half used for recording cash receipts (debits to the cash account) and the right-half for recording payments (credits to the cash account) made by the cashier. In addition to the cash receipts and cash disbursements columns, there are columns to record explanations of receipts and payments.

Transfer Journal

Sometimes, where there are many transactions of this nature, hotels keep track of transfers from one folio to another by maintaining a *transfer journal*. A transfer journal is shown in Exhibit 6-16 and is used to keep track of all transfers and to

Miscellaneous Sales

Date: _09/23/98_   Room: _516_

Charge: _Purchase in gift shop_   Amount: _$0.25_

Initial: _NP_   Guest's Signature: _Jane Doe_

This slip is white.

Valet

Date: _09/24/98_   Room: _401_

Charge: _2 suits, 1 pants_   Amount: _$14.50_

Initial: _PD_   Guest's Signature: _Alfred Smith_

This slip is yellow.

Exhibit 6-14   Two Typical Vouchers

Front Office Cash Sheet

Cashier _Charles Riley_   From _3_ AM / **PM**   To _11_ AM / **PM**   Date: _January 11_   19 _98_   Rev 12/93

| MISCELLANEOUS | | CASH RECEIPTS | | ACCT. NO. | ROOM NUMBER | | | Name | Room No. | Cash Disbursements ☑ | EXPLANATION |
EXPLANATION	Amount ☑	Guest Ledger ☑	Sundry Acct's Rec ☑		On Acct.	Paid in Adv.	On Depart. ☑				

Exhibit 6-15   Front Office Cash Sheet

A Sample Hotel

Transfer Journal

Posting Date	FROM				TO				Reason
	Folio #	Room #	Voucher #	Amount #	Folio #	Room #	Voucher #	Amount #	
01/24/93	45170	131	1983	65.18	44301	Sales	1983	65.18	Lunch with client
01/24/93	45291	219	1984	129.58	45313	306	1984	129.58	Moved room
01/24/93	45305	208	1985	301.20	45590	CL #12	1985	301.20	City ledger
01/25/93	45461	212	1986	8.16	44302	Errors	1986	8.16	Didn't use phone
01/25/93	45498	321	1987	21.03	44301	Sales	1987	21.03	Drinks
01/25/93	45552	Deposits	1988	1,000.00	45601	CL #92	1988	1,000.00	Wedding reception
01/25/93	45606	335	1989	21.12	44301	Sales	1989	21.12	Drinks
01/26/93	45508	212	1990	8.16	44302	Errors	1990	8.16	Didn't use phone
01/27/93	45591	108	1991	16.30	45592	217	1991	16.30	Wrong room
01/27/93	45592	217	1992	45.00	44301	Sales	1992	45.00	Room discount
01/27/93	45663	219	1993	21.12	44301	Sales	1993	21.12	Drinks
01/27/93	45648	150	1994	9.60	44302	Errors	1994	9.60	Didn't use minibar

Exhibit 6-16

ERROR CORRECTION SHEET

MACHINE NO. _____

ROOM NO.	VOUCHER NO.	NAME	AMOUNT POSTED	CORRECT AMOUNT	AMOUNT OF ERROR	DEPT. KEY DEDUCTION	EXPLANATION OF ERROR	OPER-ATOR

Exhibit 6-17

ensure that all amounts credited to one folio have in fact been charged to another folio. By writing them down in the transfer journal there is a trail, known as an *audit trail*, that can be traced in case any question should arise concerning where an offsetting charge or credit was made.

Error Sheet

Another form that is used to maintain an audit trail is the *error sheet*. Whenever an error is made in posting to a folio, the person who discovers the error (it is hoped that it is the person who made the error) enters it on the error sheet. This enables the night auditor to verify that errors are properly corrected. A sample error sheet is shown in Exhibit 6-17.

THE ACCOUNTING FLOW FOR BILLINGS

As stated earlier, there are three different types of accounting systems currently in use by hotels—manual, mechanical, or computerized accounting. The manual system is now only used in the smallest hotels. Because the steps involved in the manual system are more visible and explicit, however, we will use it to explain the forms and flow of data involved in accounting for the guest's stay. Once the manual system is understood, any variations in procedure and forms due to the use of mechanical or computerized systems are more easily assimilated. Our description of the accounting flow for billings will be divided into (1) room sales, (2) nonrooms department sales, (3) posting sales to the General Ledger, and (4) processing nonsales charges.

Room Sales

Because of the greater complexity of group and convention sales they will be dealt with separately from sales to individuals.

Sales to Individuals

Room rates and taxes are posted to folios either during the day by the billing clerk, or during the night shift by the night auditor. If a guest pays in advance, or if the guest checks out after the designated check-out time, then the room rate is posted by the billing clerk at the front office to record payment and update the guest folio. Designated check-out times vary from 11:00 A.M. to 3:00 P.M. Some hotels will charge a half-day rate when the guest checks out between the designated check-out time and 6:00 P.M., and a full day's rate thereafter.

The billing clerk on the evening shift reconciles the housekeeper's afternoon report with the room rack to detect and correct any occupancy errors. The night auditor then posts room rates to folios and balances the total with the total obtained by adding all the *rack slips*. Since the rate marked on the *rack card* may not be the rate that is charged, the actual room rate charged is obtained from an additional slip of paper, called the *rack slip*, which is attached to the rack card. The night auditor is informed of any rate changes by a new rack slip, which is attached to the rack card on top of the old rack slip. The old rack slip is preserved in order to maintain an audit trail. Rack slips are also used to enter codes that identify the guest category and rate basis. These codes are later used to generate guest statistics.

During the night shift, the night auditor totals the column corresponding to that day on each folio and calculates the cumulative balance as of that day. At the bottom of the folio, debit and credit columns total charges, and total payments and other credits pertaining to the guest are also shown. When payments and credits exceed the charges on any particular day, the balance is a credit balance and is shown in parentheses or in a circle. This means the hotel owes the guest the amount of the credit balance. Otherwise, the balance represents an amount receivable by, and owed to, the hotel. As stated above, and as will be more fully explained in Chapter 7, "The Night Audit," the night auditor uses the copy of the departmental sales record, whether it is a tape or control sheet, to verify that all vouchers have been received and posted.

The folios are placed in the bucket or pit according to room number order. Several copies are prepared. In extreme situations as many as seven copies are prepared. One is the guest's bill that he or she receives. The other copies are kept for future billing or as a permanent record by the hotel and may be filed by guest name and/or room number and/or credit card company. When a guest pays with certain credit cards, or when the guest enjoys extended credit privileges directly from the hotel, one copy of the folio may be given the guest at check-out, one transferred to the city ledger, and the third mailed out with the bill at the end of the month. Credit cards have their own receipt form that is mailed to the credit card company during the billing cycle, making it unnecessary to send a separate folio copy. Sometimes the guest registration card is attached to the folio. When this is done, it is removed at check-out time and sent to the room clerk as notification that the room is on *on-change* status. On-change status means the room is not ready to be sold because it is being cleaned.

Since the folio is the only record the hotel has of the charges made by a guest at the hotel, it is extremely important that a folio not be lost or misfiled. Also, because they are given to guests as receipts of payment, it is important for accounting internal control purposes that all folios be accounted for in order to verify that the correct payment was actually received by the hotel. A folio numbering system helps to achieve this control since it is easier to detect missing numbers. In those cases where a guest stays longer than one week, special folios called *transfer folios* or *supplemental folios* may be used. These do not have a number and are attached to the original numbered folio.

Rates may change during a guest's stay due to the arrival of other guests, the sharing of a room, the use of a portable bed or a color TV, or for other reasons. In these cases, a rate change card or slip should be attached to the folio, indicating the effective date and amount of the new rate. If an additional guest, who will be billed separately, stays in a room, a new folio card should be prepared for the new guest. If this produces a rate increase, then the new rate may be split evenly on the two folios, or only the double-rate differential may be posted on the second guest's folio, or the entire room rate may be posted to one account, according to instructions from the guests. Even if all charges are to be made to one folio, usually hotels require preparation of a separate rack slip for statistical information purposes when nonfamily members occupy the same room.

After verifying that individual folios have had all charges posted to them, the night auditor prepares a recap of all the guest folios on a spreadsheet called the *daily transcript* (see Exhibit 7-8). This daily transcript is then used by the accounting department to post charges and credits to the accounts receivable account, the various sales accounts, and the cash General Ledger account. The daily transcript will be discussed at length in Chapter 7.

Sales to Groups and Conventions

Sometimes groups will require *split billing,* that is some charges will be included in the group rate and other charges will be charged to the individual members of the group. In these cases, there is a folio for group charges and separate folios for individual charges. For example, the group *master folio,* called the *A folio,* might be used to charge common activities, such as banquets, speakers' rooms, food, and meeting rooms. The individual members of the group have separate folios, called *B folios,* for their room and personal charges. In other cases the rooms and basic food charges may be covered by the group and entered on the master A folio, and personal incidental expenses are charged to the individual B folios. This occurs, for instance, when tourists have booked as a tour group. The travel company selling the tour has already collected the room and tax amounts from the travelers, so the hotel bills the tour company for those charges. But the travelers may incur charges on their own, for example, when they call home. These charges are the responsibility of the individual tourist, so the charges are put on a B folio. It can get even more complicated. For example, tourists sometimes travel two to a room, but are not otherwise sharing expenses. In this case, each guest in the room has a separate folio (a B and C folio). Front office posting machines often allow for up to nine subsidiary folios per room.

Sometimes, when large corporations form a group or are part of a convention, they may each give their own functions and offer their own amenities. This requires that several master folios be maintained, in addition to the individual folios. It is important that proper signature authorization cards be maintained in these cases, and that hotel personnel be made aware of their existence in order to avoid rendering services that may later prove controversial or unchargeable.

Special entries in the General Ledger may be required for groups and conventions when the overall group fee includes certain meals or other amenities. In these cases, the hotel gives members of the group coupons or vouchers to claim these meals or amenities. Subject to the agreement between the group and the hotel, unused vouchers, called *breakage,* either reduce the group charge or accrue to the benefit of the hotel. When they reduce the group charge, the master folio is charged for the overall group room charge plus any individual vouchers as they are used.

However, if unused vouchers or coupons do not reduce the overall **group** charge, then the hotel needs to set up a special *voucher income account* with a credit balance on the General Ledger when the group charge is recorded. This account is credited with the total value of all the vouchers distributed to group members. As members use these vouchers, they are debited to the voucher income account and are credited to the various department sales accounts on the General Ledger. Most such vouchers are usually issued to enable guests to buy food and beverages at the hotel, and are credited to the food and beverage departments as they are used. The value of unused vouchers is left in the voucher income account, since no services were provided and the hotel is entitled to keep the money received for the vouchers. Used vouchers are not posted to any folio. They are sent to the accounting department to be debited to the voucher income account and credited to the appropriate departmental sales account.

Nonrooms Department Sales

In this section of the chapter, the accounting flow for nonrooms department sales to guests will be differentiated from the accounting flow for nonguest patrons of the hotel who enjoy credit privileges at the hotel, either through direct credit from the hotel or through the use of credit cards.

Nonrooms Department Sales to Guests of the Hotel

The billing procedure for other department sales is diagrammed in Exhibit 6-18, which uses a restaurant as an example. The first step in a sale is the origination of the voucher. When a guest or patron tells the restaurant cashier he or she wants to charge the purchase to his or her account, the cashier requests that a voucher be signed (often the sales check itself serves as a voucher). The guest is then requested to write his or her room number on the voucher (check). Guests who have paid for their room cash-in-advance do not enjoy credit privileges at a hotel. If there is any doubt concerning the legitimacy of the guest's right to charge a purchase, the cashier should call the front office information clerk to verify the guest's name, room number, and possibly even the signature. The sale is then recorded on the cash register using the credit or charge key. This will enable the cash register to total credit sales separately at the end of the day. The cashier will then make a record of the charge on a control sheet. A copy of this sheet is forwarded to the front office at the end of the day along with the signed vouchers. Vouchers are prepared in duplicate. One copy is sent immediately to the front office for posting to the guest's account. The other copy is kept by the originating department and sent to the front office at the end of the day with the control sheet. This procedure is followed by all the nonrooms departments of the hotel.

It is essential that the sales charges from different departments be communicated to the front office as soon as possible after the sale is made. This minimizes the possibility of a guest checking out before a nonrooms department charge has been posted to the guest's folio. A constant stream of sales information also enables the billing clerk to maintain a constant work pace, which would not be the case if sales information arrived in batches. Pneumatic tubes (a hollow capsule sent through a tube by air pressure) or runners (messengers) were two ways used to send sales vouchers to the front office. These, however, have mostly been replaced by computer systems, which communicate charges instantaneously.

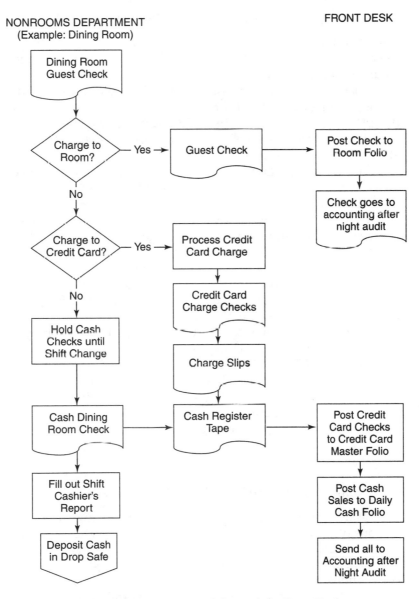

Exhibit 6-18   Nonroom Sales and the Front Desk

Some record of the sale is kept by the originating department and the sales vouchers are forwarded to the front office. At the end of the shift an adding machine tape or copy of the department sales control sheet is forwarded to the front office. This latter enables the night auditor to verify that all vouchers have been received and posted by the front office.

Posting Nonrooms Department Sales to Guest Folios

Upon receipt of the vouchers at the front office, a billing clerk then posts them to the appropriate ledger folio. For sales made to nonguests who enjoy credit privileges at the hotel, their vouchers are entered on the daily transcript (see Chapter 7 for a description of the night audit) in total, and are then sent to the accounting department for posting to the individual city ledger folios next day. At the end of the day, the night auditor posts any vouchers that have not been posted during the day and, by preparing the daily transcript, verifies that all vouchers have been posted to folios. As explained previously, credit sales, from whatever department, are posted as charges (debits) to the accounts receivable account and to the appropriate subsidiary ledger folio.

A manual folio is shown in Exhibit 6-6. As charges originate in the different departments the date of the transaction is entered in the date column, the type of charge or the department where the charge is made is entered in the description column, and the amount of the charge is entered in the debit column. Credits, returns, allowances, payments, or other reductions of the guest's account are entered on the folio in the credit column. The balance due the hotel should be recalculated every time a new charge or credit is entered on a guest's folio. After posting them to the proper folio, the billing clerk then *validates* them. In a manual system this is done by stamping them or by writing in the initials of the billing clerk who posted them. This eliminates the possibility of posting a voucher twice.

In Chapter 7 there is a description and illustration of a folio page used in a mechanical posting system. If you compare it to the manual folio page illustrated in this chapter, you will notice that the mechanical posting folio shows individual charges, whereas the manual folio only shows the daily total of all charges from each department. Under a manual system, therefore, the original vouchers must be kept at the front office in case guests wish to verify the individual amounts being charged to their account.

Nonrooms Department Sales to Nonguest Patrons

Many hotels make credit sales to patrons not registered at the hotel. These patrons of the hotel may pay with credit cards, or they may enjoy direct credit from the hotel itself. The latter privilege is usually granted to large corporate clients, whose employees frequent the hotel for business lunches, meetings, and conventions. Since these are not guest accounts, transactions from such clients are recorded on a folio in the city ledger instead of the guest ledger. If patrons pay with credit cards, then their sales are charged to the city ledger folio for the credit card company whose card is being used. If direct credit from the hotel is involved, then each patron will have his or her own folio in the city ledger.

Nonguest patron credit transactions are reported to the front office in exactly the same way as guest charges. The signed charge vouchers or credit card slips are sent to the front office, where they are separated from the guest vouchers. If there are not many charges, they are entered individually on separate lines of the daily transcript by the night auditor. Alternatively, these vouchers may be entered on summary sheets that serve as intermediate records so that the night auditor only needs to enter totals on the daily transcript. These summary sheets must show separate totals for credit card slips, hotel credit vouchers, and advance guest deposits, when these are deposited through the front office cashier instead of with the hotel's general deposit in the accounting department. Summary sheets should also show other miscellaneous city ledger entries.

Another solution similar to the above is to prepare a *city journal*. This journal is used to record debits and credits to the city ledger accounts receivable control account. The city ledger often takes the form of a separate "bucket" in the "pit" at the front desk, where folios are maintained for the various in-town people with house charges. One hotel on Miami Beach has considerably more local business than guests in house; the ratio is about 2:1! This can present quite a billing problem, when the front office transfers up the city ledger folios at the end of the month and the accounting department mails them out to the city ledger customers. The payments must then be run through the front office system as payments on the folios at the front office. The procedure for posting nonrooms department cash sales to nonguest patrons is explained on pages 130–131. It consists of debit columns and credit columns with headings for the various types of sales generated by the hotel. The debit columns indicate debits to the account receivable control account. The heading of the debit column indicates what sales account is to receive the offsetting credit. For example, a $200 entry made in the debit column marked "restaurant" would indicate that a $200 debit needs to be made to the city ledger accounts receivable control account, as well as to the customer's subsidiary city ledger folio. It also indicates that a $200 offsetting credit must be made to the restaurant sales account. Conversely, if an entry is made in a credit column, it means that the accounts receivable control account must be credited and the offsetting debit must be made to the sales account corresponding to the column heading where the credit was made. The headings and first line of a city journal for a hotel with rooms and food departments would look like this:

City Journal

Debits		Credits	
Rooms	Food	Rooms	Food

POSTING SALES TO THE GENERAL LEDGER

We have seen how charge and cash sales in both the rooms division and the non-rooms departments are initially recorded. Before going on to discuss how these charges and credits are recorded in the book of final entry, the General Ledger, let us summarize what has been said so far.

We have been dealing with six types of transactions, each of which had its own flow of transaction information:

1. Credit sales in the rooms division
2. Cash sales in the rooms division
3. Credit sales in nonrooms departments
4. Cash sales in nonrooms departments
5. Credit sales to nonguest patrons of the hotel
6. Cash sales to nonguest patrons of the hotel

Credit sales in the rooms division (room rates and taxes) are posted directly to the subsidiary guest ledger by the billing clerk and/or the night auditor. Cash sales in the rooms division (rooms paid in advance) are first recorded on the front office cash sheet and then posted to the guest ledger in the same way as payments on credit sales. Credit sales in nonrooms departments are sent to the front office in voucher format and are posted to the guest ledger by the billing clerk and/or the night auditor. Finally, nonrooms department cash sales are sent directly to the accounting department for direct debit to the General Ledger cash account and credit to the various sales accounts.

Of the above, we have traced only nonrooms department sales to the General Ledger. We have traced the other three types of sales only as far as the subsidiary guest ledger. These three types of sales are entered on the General Ledger from the guest ledger via the daily transcript. As previously stated, the daily transcript and its preparation process will be described more extensively in Chapter 7. However, a brief description of its content and preparation, however, will be given here. In Exhibit 7-8 it is evident that the daily transcript is divided into a left-hand and right-hand portion. The left-hand portion contains columns for all possible charges on each individual guest ledger folio and the right-hand portion contains columns for all possible credits on each guest ledger folio. Tedious as it may seem, under a manual accounting system (not so under a mechanical or computerized system), the night auditor must copy all the charges and credits from each folio card onto a separate line of the daily transcript. Then the night auditor must use the front office accounting formula (beginning balance + charges − credits = ending balance) line by line, page by page, and for the entire transcript, to verify that all charges and credits have been included on the transcript. This transcript then becomes the sales journal for cash and credit room sales and advances, plus credit sales in the nonrooms departments.

The daily transcript is also used as the accounting record of initial entry for nonguest charges. As explained previously, this type of charge is posted individually on separate lines at the bottom, in the city ledger section, of the daily transcript when they are few. When they are many, then only totals are entered in the city ledger section of the daily transcript (see Exhibit 7-8).

The daily transcript is sent to the accounting department where, on the following day, the totals of each of the columns in the daily transcript are posted to the proper General Ledger accounts to complete the posting cycle. The guest ledger accounts receivable control account is debited for all charges made by guests staying at the hotel, and the city ledger accounts receivable control account is debited for amounts included in the city ledger section of the daily transcript that contain the nonguest charges. In those hotels where the city ledger is kept in the accounting office, individual charges must also be entered on their corresponding city ledger folios. After posting these amounts to the General Ledger, the hotel will know how much it is owed in total (according to the accounts receivable General Ledger control account), as well as how much it is owed on an individual-by-individual basis (according to the individual subsidiary guest ledger folios).

PROCESSING NONSALES CHARGES

So far we have been discussing charges to folios as the result of room sales or other department credit sales. There are three other sources of charges or debits to folios: (1) paid-outs and advances, (2) charges transferred in from another folio, and (3) error corrections.

Advances and Paid-outs

Advances are loans given by the hotel to a guest to be repaid when the guest settles the bill. The guest signs a voucher for the amount of money received. *Paid-outs* are cash amounts that are paid-out for various reasons on behalf of a guest. Paid-outs and advances are disbursed by the front office cashier and are recorded by the cashier on the *cash sheet*, which was explained earlier. Guest paid-outs may result from any one of the following types of transactions:

- A C.O.D. delivery is received for a guest (for purchases, luggage delivery, and so forth). (Usually these are accepted only when the guest has prearranged for it with the hotel.)
- A collect telegram is received (also subject to being prearranged for by the guest).
- Tips for bellpersons or tips for other hotel employees are paid on behalf of a guest (usually done for tour groups or when prearranged for by a guest).

- When guest purchases from hotel concessionaires are paid for by the hotel.
- A cash-paying guest leaves earlier than expected, resulting in an overpayment of his or her bill, which requires a refund to the guest.

Some of the above transactions, such as purchases from concessionaires or overpayment refunds, are often automatically preauthorized. However, most hotels do not authorize paid-outs, and those that do have stringent authorization policies. Care should be exercised in observing them. In all of these cases the cashier pays funds to a third party (bellperson, store, concessionaire, or delivery service) who signs for the money received. These paid-outs are listed on the cashier's cash sheet, where the guest's name and room number, the amount, and an explanation are entered on a line on the right side of the cash sheet. The cash sheets are totaled and audited during the night audit. At that time, the night auditor picks up any advances or paid-outs that were not posted to the folios at the time of the advance or pay-out, and he or she then charges them to the appropriate guest folio. Advances or paid-outs that have not been posted could only be the result of an oversight by the billing clerk, since all charges to guest folios should be posted immediately after being made.

Advances on Behalf of Parties Not Registered at the Hotel

In addition to making cash advances on behalf of guests, cash advances can also be made in the name of some third party, such as Western Union's Flash-Cash service. This service enables a guest to send a money order to him- or herself. If the hotel is enrolled in this service network, Western Union will call the hotel to authorize a cash advance to the guest, thus eliminating a trip to the nearest Western Union office for the guest. Since Western Union is the debtor of the hotel under this arrangement, instead of the guest, this type of advance is charged to Western Union's city ledger accounts receivable control account and also to Western Union's city ledger folio. Advances of this kind are entered on the cash sheet by the cashier as an advance to Western Union. They are then picked up by the night auditor and forwarded to the accounting department on the daily transcript for posting to the city ledger.

Transfers In

Charges can also be made to a folio as the result of transfers into a folio. If one guest wishes to pay for another guest's account, then the paying guest's account is charged with the other guest's account balance, resulting in a charge. Such transfers should be cross-referenced on both the folio from which the transfer is made and the folio to which the transfer is posted. For obvious reasons, it is essential to have the authorization of the guest whose folio is being charged. If such transfers occur frequently, a transfer journal may be used to provide a history, or audit trail, to facilitate verification that amounts transferred out of one folio were transferred into another folio, and that the correct folios were involved. Exhibit 6-16 presents a sample transfer journal.

Error Corrections

Another source of charges may be error corrections. If a room rate below the actual rate were charged to a folio (a single rate for a double occupied room for instance), an additional charge can be made to correct the situation. Or a mathematical error may have been made in calculating a previous balance, which now needs to be increased. Again, in order to keep a history of errors and/or corrections made during the day, most hotels keep an error sheet. Both the transfer journal and the error sheet enable the night auditor to post and/or verify that these types of transactions are properly recorded in the correct guest folios. Exhibit 6-17 presents a sample error correction sheet.

COLLECTIONS AND CREDITS

In addition to the sales charges and other billing debits to guest folios, which we have discussed thus far, there are various types of credits that may need to be posted to the guest folios. Credits to folios have four sources: (1) payments on an account, (2) allowances, (3) transfers out of a folio, and (4) error corrections. These will be discussed here. Additionally, payments on account and transfers out will be dealt with in greater depth in Chapter 9, "Check-Out and Post-Check Out Procedures."

Cash Payments on Account

The most common source of credits to a folio is the receipt of payments on the account. When a guest checks out of the hotel, or makes a periodic partial payment on his or her account, the debit balance on the folio card is reduced by the amount of the payment credited to the folio. As you will recall, credits can be indicated by a minus sign or by posting in a credit column of the folio, if such a column exists.

When payment is made in cash, the payment is received by the cashier and recorded on the cash sheet. In those cases where the payment is an advance payment for a room or a late check-out, the cashier also posts the room rate and any other unposted vouchers to the folio. When guests pay in advance, the cashier usually gives them a copy of their folio at the time of payment and the room is automatically placed on on-change status the day they are scheduled to leave. Such guests are not allowed to make charge purchases at the hotel without a corresponding deposit. If the payment being received is a partial payment on account, then the cashier gives the guest a standard receipt form instead of the receipted folio sheet. Most hotels have a policy of collecting payment from their guests when credit limits are exceeded, or whenever an inordinately large amount is charged to the folio. A message is placed in the guest's mailbox or in their room. In these cases also, a receipt is given to the guest, instead of the folio page itself, when an additional payment is made.

The special treatment required by more complex forms of payment, such as with personal and traveler's checks, credit cards, foreign currency, and travel vouchers will be dealt with in Chapter 9.

Collections from Parties Not Registered at the Hotel

Payments received from nonguest patrons or third parties, such as Western Union, are credited to the city ledger accounts receivable control account and to the corresponding city ledger folio. If it is hotel policy for the front office cashier to receive these payments, they are entered on the front office cash sheet during the day. The night auditor then posts them to the city ledger folios, if these are kept in the front office, or he or she reconciles the totals and sends them with the cash sheet for posting to the city ledger folios in the accounting department.

Reservation Deposits

Reservation deposits present their own problem. If the check is filed until the guest arrives, instead of being deposited, there is risk of losing the check. Also there may be no record that the money was received, and the hotel loses the use of the money until the guest arrives. If the check is deposited and a folio is opened in the guest's name with a credit balance in it, then the numerical sequence of prenumbered folios is difficult to verify on a weekly basis (as explained earlier), because a long time may transpire until the guest arrives and the folio number sequence will have advanced in the meantime. If this method is chosen, however, not only is the money deposited, but also there is a record of having received the check since it appears on the cash sheet when received. Under this method, the folios are kept in the back of the pit as a separate group until the guest arrives, at which time they are filed with the other folios in room number order.

A better variation of this method is to enter all reservation deposits on a single folio card. When the guest arrives his or her deposit amount is transferred to a new folio and filed in room number order. This method has the advantage that it does not tie up folio numbers over long periods of time, thereby placing them out of sequence and making numerical sequence verification more difficult. This folio is usually maintained in the accounting office. Reservation slips for reservations that have been paid for in advance are coded in some way, usually by color, and the deposit amount is written on them so that when the guest arrives, the front office knows the amount of the deposit. Also, since checks are received by the reservations office, this office informs the front office cashier and the accounting department of the expected date of arrival. If the guest is a no-show, the cashier informs the accounting department. If the guest does arrive, the front office cashier includes the amount of the deposit on that day's cash sheet as a transfer deposit, in order to inform the accounting office that the guest arrived and to inform the night auditor that the payment must be credited to the new folio card. When the cash sheet arrives at the accounting office, a debit is made to the General Ledger cash account to offset the credit being made on the new folio.

Allowances

Another source of credits to guest folios are allowances. These may be for unsatisfactory services or for other reasons, such as authorized rate reductions if a guest stays at the hotel for specified periods of time. Allowances may also be given in connection with different meal plans, such as the American Plan or Modified American Plan. Discounts for unsatisfactory services require filling out a credit voucher that must be signed by a manager. These vouchers are prepared at the front office and are posted to the folios there. The proper use of every allowance voucher should be verified by a manager.

Often a hotel grants certain individuals or organizations the use of a room free of charge. A list of these *complimentary rooms* should be maintained. Other than this, no accounting records are kept of complimentary rooms. A daily report listing complimentary rooms is prepared by the night auditor for management information purposes.

Allowances are posted to folios either during the day or by the night auditor. They represent credits to the accounts receivable General Ledger account, and debits (charges) to the various sales accounts.

Transfers Out

When one guest pays another's bill, the folio of the guest whose bill is being paid receives a transfer credit that is equal to the transfer debit given to the folio of the guest who will pay. As stated earlier, in many cases a transfer journal is used to provide an audit trail of these transfers for the night auditor to verify. Transfer out credits are also made when a guest pays with a credit card. The guest folio in the guest ledger is credited for the balance in the folio and the city ledger folio of the credit card company is debited for the same amount. Also, if a guest leaves without paying the bill, his folio balance is transferred to a folio in the delinquent ledger if the guest does not enjoy extended credit privileges at the hotel, or to the *hold ledger* if the guest's departure was authorized and the guest intends to return to the hotel. There is hardly any difference between the hold ledger and the city ledger, so most hotels just use a city ledger to record hold-type charges. When a guest is granted credit directly by the hotel, instead of through a credit card company, the guest folio balance is transferred to the city ledger by making a credit on the guest ledger card and a charge (debit) on a folio card in the city ledger.

OTHER FUNCTIONS OF THE CASH SHEET

The front office cash sheet has been discussed so far as a means of recording advance payments, partial payments on account, full payment at check-out, payment of room sales, or paid-outs to or on behalf of guests or third parties, such as Western Union. In this function, it serves as an initial record for cash charges and credits before they are subsequently posted by the night auditor to the guest ledger if the guest has arrived, or to the city ledger if the guest has not arrived or has already left, or if a third party is involved. However, the front office cash sheet can be used to record petty cash expenditures and cash received by the cashier on behalf of the hotel itself. This is the case when the general cashier uses the front office cashier to make miscellaneous cash disbursements because the general cashier does not have a cash fund.

Petty Cash Expenditures

Certain minor hotel expenses are paid in cash rather than by check. When this occurs the front office cashier prepares a petty cash voucher similar to the one in Exhibit 6-19, which is signed by the person being paid by the cashier.

Daily the cashier "sells" these petty cash vouchers to the general cashier in exchange for an equivalent amount of cash to replenish the cash fund. The general cashier obtains this cash by writing a check for the total amount of the vouchers and cashing it at the bank. No entry is made on the cash sheet for these petty cash vouchers. They are posted to the proper General Ledger account by the accounting department the following day. A debit is made to the appropriate expense or asset account, and a credit is made to the bank account.

In some hotels the petty cash vouchers are recorded on the cash sheet. In this case, no separate petty cash reimbursement is required since these payments

---

PETTY CASH VOUCHER

Date: _____   No. 19791

Paid to: _____   Amount: $_____

Reason for pay out: _____

Approved by: _____   Cashier: _____

Exhibit 6-19

become part of the daily cash count and reconciliation. The proper account is charged in the accounting department based on information contained in the cash sheet.

Miscellaneous Receipts

Miscellaneous receipts can be from over-the-counter sales of items such as cigarettes and newspapers, or coin deposits from vending machines. In these cases the cashier simply records cash receipts in the appropriate columns on the left half of the cash sheet and disbursements in the appropriate columns on the right half of the cash sheet, with a brief explanation for each receipt or expenditure.

RECONCILING THE CASHIER'S REPORT

At the end of the day all cashiers prepare a cash report to send to the accounting department. These reports summarize all the day's transactions and reconcile them with the cash on hand. The cashiers' reports from all departments are then summarized into one report in the accounting department. This summary cash receipts report is used for making the debit entry to the cash General Ledger account and to make the daily deposit. The cashiers' reports are audited by the night auditor that night, before sending them to the accounting department, and they are again audited by the income auditor in the accounting department the following day to enable them to verify that all money received was accounted for and deposited. After preparing their daily reports, cashiers should be left with a predetermined amount of money called the *bank*, although sometimes they turn in more money than they received during the day when they want the general cashier to break down large bills into smaller denominations. When this occurs it is known as a *due back*. The due back amount is returned to the cashier in small denominations as requested. Each cashier's permanent bank balance is different depending on that particular cashier's needs. Bank amounts usually vary from $500 to $5,000, although lower and higher amounts are also possible.

Nonrooms Department Cashiers

Nonrooms department cashier's reports are simpler to prepare because they usually only contain cash sales, since credit sales vouchers are forwarded to the front office for eventual reporting to the accounting department. Exhibit 6-20 shows a combined nonrooms department cashier's report/envelope. It has a space for listing the different denominations of currency enclosed, plus a section for listing checks and miscellaneous expense vouchers representing small hotel expenses paid out by the cashier. The money and vouchers enclosed with the report is called the *turn-in*. The turn-in usually equals the amount of receipts unless a cashier wants big bills broken down into smaller currency, as explained

CASHIER'S REPORT

Date . . . . Watch . . . . A.M.
                                                                                                              P.M.
Cashier . . . .

RECEIPTS		
LESS-DISBURSEMENTS		
NET RECEIPTS		

CONTENTS OF ENVELOPE

CHECKS AND LIST ENCLOSED		
CURRENCY		
COIN		
HOUSE VOUCHERS (List Separately)		
TOTAL AMOUNT ENCLOSED		
LESS-NET RECEIPTS		
EXCHANGE DUE CASHIER		

EXCHANGE WANTED

CURRENCY–		
$20–and over		
10–		
5–		
1–		
COIN–		
.50		
.25		
.10		
.05		
.01		
TOTAL		

Exhibit 6-20

above, in which case there is a due back amount. The report is accompanied by the cashier's tape readings at the beginning and end of the shift, which, when subtracted from each other, indicate the amount of cash sales (receipts) during the cashier's shift. Any *overage* or *shortage* should be reported on a separate line of the envelope. An overage occurs when the original bank amount has increased by more than the cash sales amount, and a shortage occurs when the opposite happens.

Rooms Division Cashiers

Rooms division cashiers' reports are more complex than nonrooms department cashiers' reports because several types of transactions are handled at the front office. Basically there are four calculations that need to be made when preparing a cashier's report. These are the following:

- Net receipts (total receipts − total disbursements, excluding house vouchers)
- Overage or shortage (correct amount of cash on hand − actual amount of cash on hand)
- Turn-in (may be more than, but not less than, the total of cash in excess of the bank amount, checks, and vouchers)
- Due bank (amount needed to restore original bank balance).

Let's look at an example to better understand how these calculations work. For the following front office bank situation, the previously listed four calculations are shown subsequently in example situations:

Permanent bank amount = $1,000
From front office cash sheet it is evident that:
RECEIPTS

Advance room payments	=	$100
Guest account payments	−	$550
City ledger payments	=	$2,300
Coin machine collections	=	$400
Total Receipts	=	$3,350

PAID OUT

Advances to guests	=	$200
Paid for office supplies	=	$50
Total Disbursements	=	$250

A cash drawer count reveals it contains:

Cash	=	$849
Checks	=	$3,250
Guest voucher	−	$200
Petty cash voucher	=	$50
Total in drawer	=	$4,349

The four calculations would give the results below:

(1) Net Receipts	=	$3,350 − $200	=	$3,150
(2) Shortage	=	$1,000 + $3,150 − 4,149	=	$ 1
(3) Turn-In	=	$3,250 + $200 + $50	=	$3,500
(4) Due Bank	=	$1,000 − $849	=	$ 151

MECHANICAL POSTING

Throughout this chapter we have been discussing the flow of accounting information required for a guest's stay under a manual accounting system. In this section of the chapter we will consider the impact on accounting forms and information flow resulting from the use of a mechanical, or machine, posting system. Basically, four forms change under a mechanical system: (1) the folio, (2) the voucher, (3) the cashier's report, and (4) the daily transcript. Examples of these forms are shown in Exhibit 6-21 through Exhibit 6-24.

Charge and credit information is posted chronologically from the top to the bottom of the folio, instead of from left to right, as occurs in the manual folio. Also, instead of having specific lines for the different departments (rooms, food and beverage, and so forth), the description of the charge or credit is printed next to it. Finally, there are separate columns to enter debits, credits, and the balance in each folio, instead of entering this information at the bottom of the folio, as is the case with the manual folio. The mechanical voucher (see Exh. 6-22), although different from the manual voucher in design, contains the same information. The different layout is necessary because it is inserted into the posting machine for mechanical validation when it is posted to the folio, instead of having a clerk initial or stamp the voucher. The cashier's report (see Exh. 6-23) is designed to record total receipts and paid-outs at the beginning and end of a cashier's shift, thereby permitting a manual calculation of the net cash received. Finally, the daily transcript (see Exh. 6-24), called the *D card* in mechanical posting terminology, is also oriented vertically, as opposed to the horizontal orientation of the manual daily transcript. Instead of having the departments listed across the top of the transcript, they are listed from top to bottom. Chapter 7, "The Night Audit," explains more fully the preparation of a mechanical daily transcript as well as the process for correcting errors on folios and the D card. Aside from these differences in format on some of the accounting forms, there is no difference in the flow of accounting information between a manual and mechanical accounting system. In fact, mechanical accounting systems are called posting systems because essentially that is all they do—they post and accumulate totals in different registers corresponding to the various hotel departments and different types of sales (guest ledger credit sales, city ledger credit sales or cash sales.)

PRESS HARD - YOU ARE MAKING MULTIPLE COPIES

(LAST) NAME	(FIRST)	(INITIAL)		

ROOM			RATE	OUT	FOLIO NUMBER	
ADDRESS	STATE	ZIP	GUESTS A ¦ C	FROM FOLIO	
CLERK	FIRM		IN	TO FOLIO	
	ADDRESS			ADVANCE PAYMENT	

DATE	REFERENCE	CHARGES	CREDITS	BALANCE	PREVIOUS BALANCE PICK-UP

ROOM _____

RATE _____

LAST
BALANCE IS
AMOUNT DUE

SPECIAL BILLING:

SIGNATURE _____

CHARGE TO _____

ADDRESS _____

CITY _____ STATE _____ ZIP_____

SAFETY DEPOSIT BOX NO. _____

Exhibit 6-21   163

CITY LEDGER VOUCHER

GUEST NAME: _____   C/L ACCT: _____   DATE: _____

DEPARTMENT	VOUCHER NO.	AMOUNT

CLERK _____   GUEST SIGNATURE _____

Exhibit 6-22   Mechanical Posting Machine Voucher

COMPUTERIZED ACCOUNTING

There are several types of computerized accounting systems. The most basic has individual microcomputers at the front office and possibly at the various department cashiers' stations. They are not connected and so the information must be transported from the departments to the front office on diskettes, if the departments have their own computers, or in the same way as in manual systems, in voucher format, if they do not. This is known as a *batch processing* system. The next step up from this type of system is a network of microcomputers and/or dumb terminals all communicating with each other. Here again we may have two levels of sophistication. In the more basic system, the nonrooms department computers (or terminals) must be told to update their information to the front office computer (host computer). The more sophisticated system, called an *on-line* system, enables the terminals to constantly and automatically update the main data memory of the host computer in the front office. These terminals can retrieve information as well. They are called point-of-sale (POS) terminals because they introduce data into the accounting system directly and continuously at the point of sale.

Interconnected computer systems obviously eliminate the need to physically transfer sales vouchers from the nonrooms departments to the front office. They also greatly simplify the work of the night auditor because the hand or machine prepared folios are replaced by a similar folio in the computer's memory. Therefore, the night auditor does not have to post room rates and taxes. The

CASH REPORT

CLASSIFICATION	DATE	TRANS. SYMBOLS	NET TOTALS	CORRECTIONS	MACH. TOTALS	
PAID						
CLOSING						
OPENING						
CASH RECEIVED						
PAID OUT						
CLOSING						
OPENING						
CASH PAID OUT						
NET CASH						

ON DUTY _____

OFF DUTY _____

CASHIER _____

Exhibit 6-23

165

D NIGHT AUDITOR'S MACHINE BALANCE NO. _____

DEPARTMENT	DATE	DESCRIPTION	NET TOTALS	CORRECTIONS	MACHINE TOTALS	
ROOM						
TAX						
TELEPHONE						
LONG DISTANCE						
LAUNDRY						
VALET						
GARAGE						
TELEGRAM						
BEVERAGE						
MISCELLANEOUS						
RESTAURANT						
TRANSFER CHARGE						
PAID OUT						
TOTAL DEBITS						
TRANSFER CREDIT						
ADJUSTMENT						
PAID						
TOTAL CREDITS						
NET DIFFERENCE						
OPENING DR BALANCE						
NET OUTSTANDING						
TOTAL MCH. DR. BALANCE						
TOTAL MCH. CR. BALANCE						
NET OUTSTANDING						
CORRECTIONS						

DETECTOR COUNTER READINGS   ☐ DATE CHANGED

AUDITOR'S CONTROL: _____   ☐ CONTROL TOTALS AT ZERO

MACHINE NUMBER: _____   ☐ MASTER TAPE LOCKED

    ☐ AUDIT CONTROL LOCKED

AUDITOR

_____

Exhibit 6-24

computer knows which rooms are occupied, their rate and tax, and automatically posts this data to the folios, either guest ledger or city ledger, which it keeps in its memory. As stated earlier, the night audit process will be explained more fully in the following chapter.

In an interconnected system, sales data from the nonrooms departments is also posted by computer to these folios. Payments and paid-outs are posted to the folios through the cashier's computer. The front office and other department computers can also be connected with the accounting department's computer. When this is the case, the computer system automatically posts to the General Ledger. Finally, the computer updates the status of each room as guests check in and check out. Exhibit 6-25 is a computer-generated guest folio. It contains the same information as the manual or machine-generated folio. Since there are printers at the various stations of the hotel, computer generated folios may be printed out at any time. In addition to requiring less personnel in the front office, a computer system produces more complex reports, and on a more frequent basis, than was previously justifiable, due to the large amount of work the manual and machine-posted reports entailed.

One Really Big Hotel Company
Anywhere, USA

NAME: Mr. Robby T. Robot

ADDRESS: 11731 Kendal Drive
Oswago, PA 21281

	IN	OUT	FOLIO
	07/13/99	07/22/99	130359
	RATE	ROOM	
	$165.00	0706	

DATE	DESCRIPTION	ID	REF. NO	CHARGES	CREDITS	BALANCE
07/13/99	ROOM RATE 706	XAP		165.00		165.00
07/13/99	ROOM TAX 706	XAP		16.50		181.50
07/13/99	700-379-1314	XA2	18:42	5.43		186.93
07/14/99	ROOM RATE 706	XAP		165.00		351.93
07/14/99	ROOM TAX 706	XAP		16.50		368.43
07/14/99	RESTAURANT	XRZ	4575	21.50		389.93

Exhibit 6-25

QUESTIONS AND PROBLEMS

Discussion Questions

1. To what subsidiary ledger would the following transactions be posted?

   (a) A businessperson who is not a guest of the hotel, but whose company (ABC, Inc.) has an account with the hotel, invites a potential customer to eat lunch at the hotel. The bill is $50.

   (b) A guest is disputing certain charges made by the hotel after checking out of the hotel. The guest's account is seriously past due.

   (c) A guest of the hotel charges the $5 purchase of suntan lotion at the hotel pool shop to his room number.

   (d) A guest of the hotel charges a $20 dinner eaten at the hotel's restaurant to her American Express charge card.

2. Describe in a step-by-step process how the charges described in Question 1 (above) move in a manual system from the point of sale to their appropriate subsidiary ledger and General Ledger accounts. Are these procedures different for a mechanical posting system? In general terms, how do they differ in a POS computerized system?

3. Who usually reconciles the housekeeper's afternoon report with the room rack? Why is this done?

4. What is the function of the rack card and rack slip?

5. Define the following terms

   (a) bucket

   (b) validate

   (c) split billing

   (d) breakage

6. What are the five types of charges and four types of credits that can be made to a guest folio?

7. Aside from recording cash receipts, what other function may the front office cash sheet serve?

8. What four basic forms are different in a manual system and a mechanical system? How do they differ?

9. How does a POS computer system differ from a batch-processing computer system?

10. Describe in general terms how the flow of accounting information in an on-line computer system differs from the flow in a manual or mechanical system?

11. Who verifies that all vouchers have been received and posted to guest folios in manual and mechanical systems?

12. What is the daily transcript?

13. In what order are folios usually filed?

14. "The cashiering function at the front desk is very similar to the duties performed by a bank teller." Do you agree or disagree with this statement? Why?

15. Do you think that a front office manager should have some accounting background? In what ways are the front desk employees working with the same tools as bookkeepers? Could they be called "Bookkeepers with personalities"?

Problems

1. Prepare the journal entries to indicate what accounts should be debited and credited as a result of the following transactions. Be sure to prepare entries for subsidiary ledger accounts as well as for General Ledger accounts.

   (a) A businessperson who is not a guest of the hotel, but whose company has an account with the hotel, invites a customer to eat lunch at the hotel. The bill is $50.

   (b) A guest of the hotel makes a $150 payment on her account at the hotel.

   (c) A guest of the hotel charges a dinner eaten at the hotel's restaurant to her American Express charge card. The cost is $20.

   (d) The American Express company sends a $25,000 payment to the hotel on its account.

2. Show how the following transactions would appear in the front office accounting formula format. Assume the beginning balance on June 15 is zero.

   (a) June 15—A guest of the hotel has a $120 room charge recorded on his folio.

   (b) June 16—A guest of the hotel charges the $5 purchase of suntan lotion at the hotel pool shop to his room number.

   (c) June 16— A guest of the hotel has a $120 room charge recorded on her folio.

   (d) June 17—A guest of the hotel charges a $20 dinner eaten at the hotel's restaurant to her room.

   (e) June 17—A guest makes a $100 payment on his account.

3. Assume the charges and payments in Exercise 2 were all made by the same guest. Draw a manual guest folio (or use the blank guest folio at the end of these exercises), post the charges and payments listed in Exercise 2 to the folio and calculate the daily balances of the folio. Then do the same thing using a mechanical folio.

4. Draw a front office cashier's cash sheet for July 25, 1999, and make the following entries in it:

   (a) John Doe in room 345 paid $548 on his account without checking out.

   (b) Mary Jane in room 212 asked the cashier of the hotel's beauty parlor for $45 in cash and to charge it to her bill. The front office manager agreed.

   (c) Bill Westmon in room 109 obtained authorization from the front office manager to have the cashier pay for a purchase of $149 that was to be delivered to him C.O.D.

   (d) The cashier paid $29 cash for some office supplies ordered for the front office.

   (e) The cashier cashed a $500 check for William Hemptun, a guest in room 187.

   (f) The vending machines in the hotel were emptied of their cash which amounted to $936. The cash was given to the front office cashier.

   (g) Wilma Kord checked out of room 396, and paid the balance of $441 due on her account.

   (h) Dora Sowder had no credit cards or traveler's checks. Since the hotel does not accept personal checks, she had to pay $150 in advance for her room (number 605).

   (i) Ron Norman, a guest in room 157, checked out of the hotel. Yesterday he had paid $240 in advance for a two-night stay at the hotel. He decided to stay only one night, however, so the cashier refunded $120 to him.

5. From the following summary of the cash sheet on August 6, 1999, and the cash drawer count below, prepare the four equations that perform the following reconciliations:

   (a) Net receipts

   (b) Over or short

(c) Turn in

(d) Due bank

Assume the permanent bank amount is $2,500.

Also, assume the general cashier in the accounting department "buys" hotel petty cash vouchers at the end of each shift and posts them to their proper account directly in the accounting department.

August 6, 1999

RECEIPTS	
Guest payments on account	$3,422
Advance room payments	465
Vending machine collection	1,112
City ledger payments	4,677

PAID-OUTS	
Advances to guests	$505
Paid for minor repairs	246
Paid for office supplies	178
Paid for packages delivered to guests	731

CASH DRAWER COUNT	
Cash	$10,560
Traveler's checks	1,000
Personal checks	610
Guest vouchers	1,236
Hotel petty cash vouchers	424
Total in drawer	$13,830

Use the following form in solving problem 6.3

ROOM	NAME			41782		
NO. PARTY	STREET ADDRESS			RATE	FOLIO NO.	
DEPART	CITY, STATE, ZIP					
ARRIVE	PAY TYPE	SAFE BOX	LICENSE PLATE		DATE STAMP	

BALANCE FORWARD - FOLIO NO.			AMOUNT			
DATE	DESCRIPTION			DEBIT	CREDIT	BALANCE

The
STAGGAR
INN

17875 Beach Blvd.
Miami, FL 33133
Tele. (305) 495-0505

Where Our
Guests
Get Dry

CHAPTER 7

The Night Audit

CHAPTER OBJECTIVES

After reading this chapter you will understand:

- The importance of the night audit.
- Who performs the night audit.
- The procedures for performing a night audit.
- How the night audit can detect fraud.

INTRODUCTION

As explained in Chapter 6, the front desk is the information center for account transactions made by guests in the hotel. Not only are room charges posted to a guest's ledger at the front desk, but also all other credit charges are posted, as are reductions to outstanding balances, through such things as payments made for guest accounts. Naturally, with so much financial information being transmitted through the front desk, it is a focal point for errors. If for no other reason than to detect and correct any mistakes that may have been made in posting charges or credits to a guest's account, an audit of transactions posted at or through the front desk would seem to be called for. Good accounting control also argues in favor of a nightly audit of all transactions. Because they deal with the verification of accounting transactions, night auditors are usually members of the accounting department rather than the rooms department.

Traditionally, this audit has been performed during the night shift because that is the time of least activity, and doing it at this time causes the least amount of disruption at the front desk. Also, the night audit nicely closes out the day's business—the fundamental time period for all accounting activity. This fact gave rise to the name "night audit." The night audit takes four to eight hours to complete. It begins between 11:00 P.M. and 1:00 A.M. and ends sometime before the morning front desk shift begins (about 7:00 A.M.). The length of the audit is a factor of the size of the hotel, the amount of charge business, and the accuracy of postings by the day clerks. Naturally, on nights where the front desk clerks have made a particularly large number of mistakes (or ones that are particularly hard to find and correct), the night audit may last longer, occasionally well into the next day. Normally, one auditor is needed for every 200 occupied rooms. In a large hotel, the night audit team may consist of a head auditor, two or three assistants and one or two food auditors. A whole audit team is sometimes needed because the night auditor, or night audit team, not only performs the night audit functions, but also actually takes over the operation of the front desk, replacing the desk clerk, cashier, and even the telephone operators. As we shall learn later, with today's fully automated accounting systems, at least some of the objectives of the night audit can be accomplished at any time during the day without noticeably disrupting front desk operations. This considerably reduces the number of personnel required for the night audit. A discussion of the typical hotel day is found in Chapter 5, and the reader may wish to refer to that chapter throughout the following discussion.

OBJECTIVES OF THE NIGHT AUDIT

The objectives of the night audit are broader than the verification function mentioned above. When a manual accounting system exists, the night audit function may encompass as many as five general objectives:

1. Verifying room status and no-show reservations for all rooms.
2. Posting or verifying the posting of daily transactions to guest ledgers.
3. Balancing or verifying account balances (the detection and correction of accounting errors).

4. Performing various activities, such as verifying that credit limits are observed, taking department cash register readings, preparing guest invoices, and performing the duties of the night manager.

5. Generating summary and statistical activity reports for management use.

Which objectives, of those listed above, apply to the night audit function in a particular hotel depends on the type of accounting system in use at the hotel. Hotel accounting systems can be divided into three types: (1) manual, (2) mechanical, and (3) computerized. Even among the computerized systems there is a broad range of variation. In the most primitive systems, the computers throughout a hotel are not connected to each other, in which case information from each computer must be transferred manually. In the most sophisticated systems, all computers are interconnected in a network. Sales information is entered in the network at the point-of-sale (POS) and information is transferred instantly. Computer programs based on artificial intelligence have been developed to perform some of the analytical functions previously reserved to management. Computerized accounting systems are rapidly becoming the norm in large hotel corporations. Furthermore, with the price of microcomputers dropping dramatically in recent years, soon few manual or mechanical systems will be in use even in smaller properties.

Nevertheless, we will review night audit procedures from the point of view of a manual system initially, since a manual system enables us to observe in detail the accounting transactions that need to take place at or through the front desk, be they performed manually, mechanically, or electronically with a computer. Once the reader understands what takes place in a manual night audit, we will discuss the impact of mechanical and computerized accounting systems on these functions.

VERIFYING ROOM STATUS

Since one of the objectives of the night audit is to post, or verify the posting of, room rates and taxes to individual guest accounts, the auditor must first ascertain the status of each room in the hotel. This is done by looking at the room rack. The room rack has itself been previously verified by a night clerk who has compared the room rack to the *housekeeper's evening report*. After completing this verification process the night clerk prepares the *evening rooms report*. See Exhibit 7-1 for a diagram of the reports used in this process. The night auditor then updates the rooms report for late arrivals, if necessary, and checks it before sending it to the accounting department.

This seems complicated, and it is. Remember, room sales constitute the primary revenue for the hotel. It is important that the amounts charged to guests be correct and that no rooms be given away. ("Given away" means the guest stayed in the room without the knowledge of management.) The reports included in

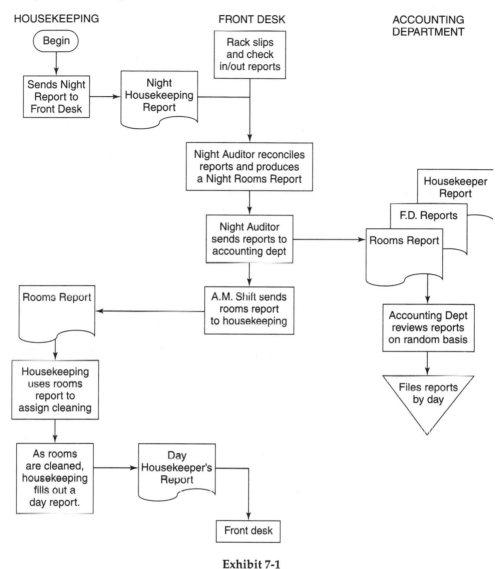

HOUSEKEEPING   FRONT DESK   ACCOUNTING
                                                                    DEPARTMENT

Begin

Sends Night
Report to
Front Desk

Night
Housekeeping
Report

Rack slips
and check
in/out reports

Night Auditor reconciles
reports and produces
a Night Rooms Report

Housekeeper
Report

F.D. Reports

Night Auditor
sends reports to
accounting dept

Rooms Report

Rooms Report

A.M. Shift sends
rooms report
to housekeeping

Accounting Dept
reviews reports
on random basis

Housekeeping
uses rooms
report to
assign cleaning

Files reports
by day

As rooms
are cleaned,
housekeeping
fills out a
day report.

Day
Housekeeper's
Report

Front desk

Exhibit 7-1

the information flow diagram presented in Exhibit 7-1, as well as some additional reports, will be discussed in this section.

The Arrivals and Departures Report

The Arrivals and Departures Report is really a journal maintained at the front desk that records every arrival and departure. It is used to verify the dates of occupancy of specific guests (guests sometimes call back months later wanting to

EXHIBIT 7-2 THE BASIC OCCUPANCY FORMULA FROM AN ARRIVALS AND DEPARTURES JOURNAL

Last Night's Occupancy	+	Today's Arrivals	−	Today's Departures	=	Tonight's Occupancy

know the exact dates they stayed at the hotel). More importantly, it is used to determine the occupancy of the hotel. Hotel occupancy is calculated using this journal as shown in Exhibit 7-2.

Naturally, it's not quite this simple. There can also be rate changes that take effect during the guests' stays. These changes do not change the total number of rooms occupied, but these changes do affect the total room sales for the day. These rate changes are shown in the Arrivals and Departures Jour-

---

The Really Nice Resort Hote
Arrivals & Departures Report

TODAY'S DATE: _____ 19 _____

Departures			Arrivals			
Room Number	Folio Number	Room Rate	Room Number	Folio Number	Room Rate	Balance Forward
					YESTERDAY:	$13,000.00
310	21020	315.00	450	24015	145.00	
315	23961	182.00	310	24016	315.00	
209	20318	88.00	117	24017	90.00	
151	21888	90.00	408	24018	130.00	
212	22050	85.00				
450	20989	130.00				
		890.00	SUBTRACT FROM		680.00	−210.00
Auditor _M R E_					Today:	$12,790.00

RECAP OF ROOM REVENUE

ROOM REVENUE CARRYFORWARD FROM PRIOR DAY:	$13,000.00
PLUS ARRIVAL ROOM RATES:	$680.00
MINUS DEPARTURE ROOM RATES:	$890.00
ROOM REVENUE FOR TODAY:	$12,790.00

Exhibit 7-3

nal on the bottom of the day's form (see Exhibit 7-3). The form has a section called "recapitulation," and we usually abbreviate the word as "recap." Here is where the basic formula shown in Exhibit 7-2 is used to calculate tonight's occupancy.

Housekeeper's Reports

The housekeeper prepares two reports—the evening or afternoon report and the morning or daytime report. The daytime report is sometimes called the *discrepancies report*. It consists of a report given to management of any rooms that the front desk reported as vacant but which the maid found to have been used. Naturally, this could be a sign of guests being housed at the hotel without payment being received by the company. Discrepancies are treated very seriously, and should be reported to the front office manager. Usually a discrepancy represents a clerical error and the matter is settled quickly. Occasionally a discrepancy was really a guest who checked out but returned later and used the room prior to actually leaving the hotel (perhaps checking out at breakfast, attending meetings during the morning, and actually vacating the room around noon). The vast majority of discrepancies are similar, nonthreatening instances. But the renting of rooms without the company collecting its proper rate is threatening to the health and well-being of the hotel, so every attempt is made to make the employees aware that management is checking, and that such activities as the illegal selling of rooms and the pocketing of the sale are cause for termination.

The *housekeeper's morning report,* or *discrepancies report,* is prepared in response to a *morning rooms report* prepared by the front office and sent to housekeeping early in the morning. This report indicates the number of rooms that should be unoccupied. When preparing the morning report, the housekeeper does not check every room, only those that are supposed to be unoccupied, in order to avoid disturbing sleeping guests. The housekeeper's morning report is also sent to the front office, where any discrepancies are reconciled.

To prepare the evening report, the housekeeper checks *all* rooms to determine their status. This also fulfills a legal requirement in many states that stipulates that all hotel rooms must be checked at least daily. The status of each room is marked on a sheet, and the housekeeper then sends the *housekeeper's evening report* to the front office as early in the evening as possible, in order to give the night clerks time to finish their work before the night audit begins. See Exhibit 7-5 for a sample housekeeper's report. The codes used are not standard throughout the industry, but this sheet uses room status codes that are self-evident as to their meaning. Since tour group members tend to leave on the same day, tour-group dominated properties do not always clean all rooms immediately upon departure. Some rooms are cleaned the next day to enable the hotel to maintain staffing levels (in other words, so the maids can work a 40-hour week).

The Dreamland Hotel
Night Auditor's Rooms Report

DATE _____   AUDITOR _____

Room Number	Condition	Number Guests	Room Number	Condition	Number Guests
101			301		
102			302		
103			303		
104			304		
105			305		
106			306		
107			307		
108			308		
109			309		
110			310		
111			311		
112			312		
113			313		
114			314		
115			315		
201			401		
202			402		
203			403		
204			404		
205			405		
206			406		
207			407		
208			408		
209			409		
210			410		
211			411		
212			412		
213			413		
214			414		
215			415		

Condition:	OOO	Out of order	RES	Reserved
	O/C	Occupied	VAC	Vacant
	CHG	On change	MIS	Miscellaneous

DISTRIBUTION:	Housekeeping	Rooms Control
	Accounting	Maintenance
	Telephone	Bell Department
	Food & Bev. Auditor	Maitre d' Hotel

Exhibit 7-4   Rooms Report

Room Codes
VC - Vacant & Clean
V - Vacant
ONC - On Change
OCC - Occupied
OOO - Out of Order

The Ocean World Hotel
Housekeepers Report

Date: _____ 19 _____

Report submitted by: _____

Room	Persons	Status		Room	Persons	Status
101				101		
102				102		
103				103		
104				104		
105				105		
106				106		
107				107		
108				108		
109				109		
111				111		
112				112		
113				113		
114				114		
115				115		
116				116		
117				117		
118				118		
119				119		
121				121		
122				122		
123				123		
124				124		
125				125		
126				126		
127				127		
128				128		
129				129		
131				131		

Exhibit 7-5   Housekeeper's Evening Report

The night clerk uses this report to verify the status of each room on the room rack, from which he or she prepares the rooms report. (See the previous discussion of this activity.) The housekeeper's report typically contains several columns: one for the room number, one or more for entering codes to indicate the status of the room, and a column to indicate the number of guests in the room. Two or more codes may be used in relation to one room. Some codes used by other hotels are listed in Exhibit 7-6.

EXHIBIT 7-6   HOUSEKEEPING ROOM STATUS CODES

OOO	=	out-of-order room
O	=	occupied room
V	=	vacant room
D	=	dirty room
B	=	sleep-outs (baggage in room but bed unused)
X	=	occupied room with little or no baggage
CO	=	check-out
P	=	permanent guest

Rooms Reports

As we have seen, two rooms reports are prepared by the front office—a *morning rooms report* and an *evening rooms report*. The evening rooms report is usually prepared by the night clerk, or by a clerk on the last shift of the day, the swing shift. It is prepared from the previously verified room rack and lists all the occupied rooms, as well as the number of guests in each room. The night auditor may have to add any late arrivals to the rooms report.

Then the night auditor must compare the rooms report with the housekeeper's report and the room rack on a test basis to verify that the night clerk's verification was performed correctly. If there are any discrepancies, the night auditor must reconcile them. After this, the auditor uses the reconciled rooms report to either post or verify the posting of room rates and taxes to each guest's ledger folio for that night.

The *morning rooms report* is sent to housekeeping to inform the housekeeper of any new arrivals and to prevent these arrivals being disturbed when the housekeeper checks the empty rooms. The report is also used to verify that the morning front office shift will have accurate rooms status information.

Discrepancies between the rooms reports and their respective housekeeping reports may arise due to one of several factors. When housekeeping reports an unused room that appears occupied, either

1. there is an error in the rooms report or the housekeeping report,
2. the guest checked out but the front desk clerk failed to record the check-out on the guest's ledger folio, or
3. the guest left without checking out, intentionally or unintentionally.

Open Balance

To determine the source of the error, the night auditor should look for the guest's ledger folio. If the guest's ledger folio has an open balance, then the auditor must check the rooms cashier's report to determine whether or not the guest paid. If the guest paid, then probably the front desk clerk failed to record the guest's check-out on the guest ledger folio. If no guest payment exists, then either there is a mistake in the housekeeping report, or the guest left without checking out.

No Open Balance

If the guest ledger folio indicates payment has been made and no open balance exists, then the room should appear as paid for in the rooms cashier's tape. Payment or nonpayment of an account can be verified later through the daily transcript reconciliation process. If an open balance exists and no payment appears for the room when the daily transcript reconciliation is made, then there is a strong presumption of theft on the part of the cashier.

The case may also arise where the housekeeping report indicates that a room is being used, but the room does not appear occupied in the rooms report. This situation is often called a "who," as in, "Who is in the room?" In this case either

1. there is an error in the rooms report or the housekeeping report,
2. the guest checked in but the front desk clerk failed to open a ledger folio for the guest, or
3. the guest's ledger folio has been misplaced.

If there is a guest ledger folio with an open balance for that room, then most likely the desk clerk made a mistake when preparing the rooms report. If there is no guest ledger folio, but there is a guest registration folio as of the date of the night audit, then most likely the front desk clerk failed to open a ledger folio for the guest at the time of check in. If there is no guest ledger folio, but the guest registration card bears a date prior to the night audit date, then most likely the guest ledger folio has been misplaced and should be located. If there is no guest ledger folio nor a guest registration card, then most likely the housekeeping report is in error. In this instance, the discrepancy should be noted for further verification the next day. If all else fails, the only remaining solution, albeit an embarrassing one, may be for the front desk to call the room at a reasonable hour during the day and ask who is staying there. It is not surprising that errors appear frequently in the housekeeper's report since, in many instances, the housekeeper's report may be based on maids' reports, thus rendering it a second-hand report with the additional error potential this implies.

Sometimes situations seem to indicate an error, when in fact there is none. If a guest slept out (for example, he or she went on an overnight trip to another nearby attraction and plans on returning and continuing his stay) and took his or her baggage along, then the room will appear to be empty when in fact it is not. Or if there is a guaranteed reservation on a room and the guest is a no-show, a room will give exactly the same impression as the above (except in this case no one showed up to take the room). The nonshowing guest usually loses his or her deposit in this case. The room rack may show it to be occupied, but there will be no check-in or baggage for the room.

Another way of verifying room occupancy is through use of the *rooms computation formula* (similar to Exhibit 7-2) presented below:

occupancy brought forward
from previous day   + arrivals − departures = tonight's occupancy

This formula can be expressed in (1) number of rooms, (2) number of guests, or (3) dollar amounts (room rates × occupied rooms). In making this calculation to determine how many rooms are available, as opposed to how many rooms are occupied, one must take into account that rooms from which a guest has recently departed are unavailable until cleaned, and others that were previously considered unavailable due to cleaning may again be used. These "changes," as they are called, must either be added along with arrivals or subtracted along with departures, depending on whether they represent rooms being taken out of service or being put back into service. When calculating this formula on a rooms and dollar amounts basis, two types of changes must be watched out for: (1) partial departures, where the departure of one among several guests causes the room rate to change, and (2) changes in Plan, for example, from European Plan to American Plan. Both of these changes cause rates to change and may appear as departures, but do not leave a vacant room.

Once all discrepancies have been resolved or identified, the night auditor is ready to proceed with the next objective of the night audit—posting or verifying the posting of the day's guest transactions in the hotel.

POSTING OR VERIFYING THE POSTING OF DAILY TRANSACTIONS

As we have seen, the front desk is the hub for a hotel's transaction activities. Although the volume of this activity depends on the number of departments, or profit centers, and on the number of guests, all transactions affecting a guest's account are summarized by the equation shown in Exhibit 7-7, often called the audit equation, or posting formula.

EXHIBIT 7-7   THE BASIC POSTING FORMULA

Previous Balance	+	Charges or Debits	−	Payments or Credits	=	Net Outstanding Balance
PB	+	DR	−	CR	=	NOB

Thus the transactions of a guest who has a previous balance of $1,000 in his or her account and is staying in an $80 room, has charged a $15 lunch at the hotel's restaurant, has bought a bottle of suntan lotion at the hotel pool for $5, and has paid $500 on the account would be recorded as follows:

Previous Balance	+	Charges or Debits	−	Payments or Credits	=	Net Outstanding Balance
PB	+	DR	−	CR	=	NOB
$1,000	+	80	−	500	=	$600
	+	15				
	+	5				

In a manual system, the first function of the night auditor is to verify that debits and credits from all hotel departments have been posted to the appropriate guest's account according to the above formula. This means that the night auditor must post amounts to a guest's account if they were not posted by front office personnel. The night auditor must be particularly attentive of unposted telephone charges and front desk cash transactions. Sometimes, there is a bill clerk in the front office responsible for these postings, or the cashier might have done the posting. But even when there is a bill clerk, in high volume hotels it is not unusual for the night auditor to be responsible for posting room rates to each guest's ledger folio.

Posting or Verifying Room Rates

Room rates are posted by referring to the previously verified rooms report. In those cases where the auditor does not post room rates, it is his or her responsibility to verify that the correct room rate and tax amount have been posted. This is often done with the aid of a room revenue report, which lists all rooms along with their rack rate, charged rate, and the number of persons in each room. Thus the night auditor can verify that occupants of rooms not being charged the rack rate, or maximum published rate, fall into one of the discount categories of the hotel, for instance, the group or government rates. The sales tax amount is verified by multiplying total room sales by the applicable tax rate. This should agree with the total in the tax column of the daily transcript.

No-show Reservations

In addition to posting or verifying room rate charges, the night auditor may also be responsible for posting charges to the appropriate ledger folio for no-show reservations when a room was guaranteed by the hotel and the guest did not arrive. Of course, this is a very sensitive area because if a guest cancels his or her reservation and the hotel does not record this fact, but posts no-show charges anyway, one or both of the following may occur:

1. the credit card company through which the charge was made may have second thoughts concerning doing business with the hotel, and/or
2. the person being erroneously charged may not want to do business with the hotel in the future.

Extreme care must therefore be used in posting no-show charges to client accounts.

Vouchers for Posting or Verifying Charges from Other Departments

For charges other than room rates, sales information is sent to the front desk by the various hotel departments in the form of sales vouchers, which are accompanied by an adding machine tape, cashier's tape, or sales journal. These show the calculation of the totals of all the sales vouchers. Before the night auditor posts and verifies that all activity has been posted to the corresponding ledger folios, he or she must first compare the vouchers sent by each department with the accompanying cashier's tape or journal for that department, to verify that all vouchers have been properly included in the tape total or sales journal. This is important because in a later step of the night audit, when account balances are verified, the night auditor must determine that all charges have been posted to client accounts by comparing column totals of the daily transcript with the totals from these cashiers' tapes or sales journals. If a voucher is missing, the night auditor will prepare a substitute or dummy voucher and post it, mentioning this in a handwritten report to the accounting department. If a voucher is not listed on the tape or accompanying sales journal, then it must be added to the journal. The auditor must also verify that all cash sales have been posted to the appropriate ledger folio.

Errors

In verifying voucher totals, as in all subsequent verification objectives of the night audit, mistakes are very likely to be due to errors in performing mathematical calculations. The two most common mistakes are misplaced decimal points and transposed numbers (for example, writing down a 43 instead of a 34). The best way to detect either of these two errors is to subtract one total from the other and then divide by 9. If the number is perfectly divisible by 9, then you are most likely dealing with one of the above two types of errors. Another helpful error-detecting technique is to divide the difference between the two totals by two.

You should then look for this amount on the voucher tape or whatever column it is that you are totalling. This amount may have been entered as a negative amount when it should have been a positive amount, or vice versa.

Cash Sheet

The front desk maintains a daily cash sheet or cash journal to record all payments of guests' accounts and all amounts paid out. This latter type of transaction may occur when a hotel is willing to pay for merchandise delivered to the guest at the hotel, or is willing to act as a bank for the guest by giving cash advances. They may also represent petty cash payments for small hotel expenses. In some hotels, however, petty cash pay outs are not shown on the cash sheets. Instead, the receipts for amounts paid out are considered to be part of cash. This cash sheet is divided into a cash receipts and cash paid out section. The night auditor must verify that paid-outs made on behalf of guests were posted to the appropriate guest folios and are properly supported by a voucher signed by a person receiving the pay out. Later, when preparing the daily transcript the auditor must also verify that the total of the cash receipts column in the transcript equals the total of the receipts columns of all the cashiers' sheets, and that the total of the cash paid out column of the daily transcript equals the total of the cash disbursement columns of all the cashiers' sheets.

Other Sources of Debits and Credits

Departmental sales vouchers and cash sheets are not the only sources of debits to a guest's account. Charges may be entered from a corrections journal used to make corrections for prior erroneous entries, or to transfer amounts into a guest's account from another guest's account. Similarly, in addition to credits that record cash or credit card payments made by a guest, credits to a guest's account may be made to correct errors or transfer amounts out of the guest's account to that of another guest, or out of the guest ledger to the city ledger or delinquent ledger.

Guest Ledger Folio

As explained in Chapter 6, "Accounting for the Guest's Stay," in order to keep track of all the debits and credits in guests' accounts, each guest is assigned a ledger folio. Remember, charges to the guest are posted in the debit column, credits in the credit column, and the new balance is calculated and entered in the balance column. By looking at a guest's ledger folio it is possible to know how much the guest owes the hotel. Other columns on the ledger folio indicate the date of each transaction and the department where the transaction originated. These folios are kept in a tray or trays. The guest ledger is used to maintain a record of balances owed by guests who are currently staying at the hotel and do not enjoy extended credit privileges at the hotel (that is, they must pay their account when they leave).

City and Delinquent Ledgers

A hotel may have some guests, however, to whom the hotel grants direct credit (not through a credit card company) and who are allowed to leave without paying their bills. The ledger folios for these guests are kept in what is known as the *city ledger*. They are handled exactly the same way as guest ledger folios but are kept in a separate location, either in a seperate ledger bucket or in the accounting office instead of at the front desk. Also, when a guest pays with a bank or travel credit card, the balance due on that account is transferred to that credit card company's city ledger folio. Finally, the city ledger is used to record charges to accounts of customers who use the hotel's services, such as the restaurant and pool, on a credit basis without being staying guests at the hotel. As we learned in Chapter 6, the "daily cash" folio in the city ledger is used to record temporary debits for cash sales to nonguest patrons (see pp.130–131).

As part of the city ledger, there is usually a *delinquent ledger*, which may have its own tray, or may share a tray if it doesn't contain many accounts. As explained in Chapter 6, the delinquent ledger contains the ledger folios of guests who are disputing their bills and who have not paid the hotel for an extended period of time, say 90 days or more.

Transfer Journal

As was also explained in Chapter 6, "Accounting for the Guest's Stay," sometimes it is necessary to make transfers from one guest account to another or from the guest ledger to the city ledger, then to the delinquent ledger, when a guest who does not enjoy extended credit privileges checks out of the hotel and disputes his or her bill. These transfers should always be cross-referenced in both folios or ledgers, indicating where the offsetting debit or credit entry was made. The auditor should verify that every transfer out of one folio or ledger has an offsetting transfer into another folio or ledger.

When there is a large number of such transfers, however, it is advisable to use a *transfer journal* to keep track of them. This journal can have four columns, one for the guest account number, one for transfers into or out of the guest ledger, one for transfers into or out of the city ledger, and one for delinquent ledger amounts. A new transfer journal can be prepared daily or weekly, depending on the volume of business. By referring to this journal the night auditor can verify that account balances have been transferred to the appropriate guest ledger or city ledger folios and that, in the case of transfers to the city ledger, the ledger folios have been removed from the guest ledger trays and sent to the accounting department for collection follow-up. It is the responsibility of the night auditor to verify that all of the above transfers are made and correctly recorded. See Exhibit 6-16 for a sample transfer journal.

DAILY TRANSCRIPT FOR BALANCING OR VERIFYING ACCOUNT BALANCES

Description

In order to understand the daily transcript, we need to refresh our knowledge of the basic accounting journal entry for recording credit sales. Basically, credit or noncash sales are always recorded as credits to the sales accounts and as debits to the accounts receivable account. If this were all there were to recording sales, it would be a simple matter to take all the totals from department sales tapes or sales journals and post them as one lump sum to the accounts receivable account in the General Ledger. However, it is essential not only to know the total amount owed the hotel by all guests, but also to know how much each individual guest owes. The main objective of the night audit is to verify that the sales (as represented by debits to guest folios) generated by the rooms department and the other hotel departments are all posted to the correct guest accounts, thereby generating separate balances in all the individual guest accounts. It confirms to management that the noncash sales revenue generated by the various hotel departments, and all room sales, have been charged to guests.

This process of balancing or verifying individual account balances is done in a manual system through the preparation of the daily transcript. The daily transcript is a spreadsheet-type schedule, based on the posting equation, that permits verification of charges and credits made to each guest's account. A sample manual daily transcript is shown in Exhibit 7-8.

The transcript is divided into a left and a right side, divided by a totals column (column O). The side to the left of the totals column is for entering charges or debits to guest accounts, and the columns to the right of this total column are for entering payments or other credits to a guest's account. There is another total column (column U) containing a total of all credits to guest accounts.

Let us take a close look at this transcript. The first column (column A) lists guest accounts vertically by account number (room number) and may be followed by a column (column B) for the number of guests in each room and a column for the folio number (not shown in this example) for guests who have used more than one ledger folio. The balance brought forward from the previous day is copied into the next column (column C), followed by columns for charges from the rooms department (columns D and E), for the food and beverage department (columns F and G), for the telephone department (columns H and I), for miscellaneous charges (column J for the amount of the charge, and column K for a description of the charge), for parking and valet charges (columns L and M), for transfer debits (column N), and for the total of all daily charges (column O). The columns to the right of the totals column are used to record credits to a guest's account. These credits may be of three

Report Date: December 12 ____ 19 97

The Sample Inn
Daily Transcript of Guest Ledger

Report by: MRE

Room No.	No. of Guests	Opening Balance DR (CR)	Room	Room Tax	Food	Bar	Telephone Local	Telephone Long Dist.	Misc. Charges Amount	Misc. Charges Department	Parking	Valet	Transfer Debits	Total Daily Charges	Cash Receipts	Credit Card Transfers	Allowances	Trans. to City Ledger	Transfer Credit	Total Credits	Closing Balance
A	B	C	D	E	F	G	H	I	J	K	L	M	N	O	P	Q	R	S	T	U	V
101	2		45.00	2.25		7.50					3.00			57.75					45.00	45.00	12.75
102	3	102.50	45.00	2.25	13.50	2.75		3.95	6.00	Cot				73.20						0.00	175.70
103														0.00						0.00	0.00
104	1	753.21	50.00	2.50	9.98		.50	6.92			3.00			72.90						0.00	826.11
105	2	112.80	45.00	2.25	2.75						3.00			53.00						0.00	165.80
106	1	47.25	comp			21.50	2.50	13.75	44.00	gift			850.50	866.75						0.00	914.00
107	1	0.00	45.00	2.25										117.75						0.00	117.75
108												5.00									
109																					
110																					
Sub-total:		1,015.76	230.00	11.50	26.23	31.50	3.00	24.62	50.00		9.00		850.00	1,251.35		500.00				500.00	1,757.11
Departures																					
Rm 107		212.90	2.25	2.25	7.50		0.50				3.00			58.25	270.65		0.50			271.15	0.00
Sub-total:		212.90	2.25	2.25	7.50	0.00	0.50	0.00	0.00		3.00	0.00	0.00	58.25	270.65	0.00	0.50	0.00	0.00	271.15	0.00
City Ledger:		1,706.58			395.90	218.75			25.00	candy			500.00	1,139.65	218.21					218.21	2,628.02
Total All Posting		2,935.24	13.75	15.75	429.63	250.25	3.50	24.62	75.00	0.00	12.00	5.00	1350.50	1,139.65	288.86	500.00	0.50	0.00	0.00	989.36	4,385.13

Exhibit 7-8 Daily Transcript

types, each having its own column on the transcript. Those reflecting a payment on the account are entered in "cash receipts" (column P), while credit card payments are shown in column Q. Allowances or discounts granted are entered in column R, and when prior charges are transferred out of the account to another guest's account or to another ledger, they are entered in "transfers" (column S for a transfer to the city ledger in this example, and column T for other transfers out). Notice that there are two types of transfer columns—one type on the debit side of the transcript for entering transfers in, and one type on the credit side of the transcript for entering transfers out. The form concludes with a column for the total of all credits (column U) and a column for the closing folio balance for the day (column V).

The bulk of the night audit will consist of copying data from each individual guest account onto the transcript, verifying that all transcript column totals are correct, and correcting all discrepancies found. It is important to keep in mind that corrections must not only be made in the daily transcript, but also in every incorrect supporting record on which transcript data is based, be it a guest ledger folio, department sales voucher, department sales tape, cashier's report, rooms report, or housekeeper's report. Therefore, unless the mistake was made directly in posting to the transcript, it is never enough to merely correct the transcript. The process of preparing this transcript and verifying column totals and making corrections will be explained here.

Preparing the Daily Transcript

The night auditor takes each ledger folio out of its tray and proves today's ending balance by beginning with the previous day's balance, adding new charges or debits and subtracting new credits. If the ending balance on the folio is correct, the auditor transfers all the information from the folio to the appropriate columns of the transcript, recalculates the ending balance using data entered on the transcript, and repeats the process with the next ledger folio. When he or she has transcribed all the data from all the ledger folios to the transcript, the night auditor must total each column of the daily transcript.

Next, the night auditor must enter the information from the departure folios. This information usually consists of a few charges (most often breakfast charges) and the settlement of the folio prior to departure. The total of all departures is entered on a single line.

When data from all ledger folios has been entered in the transcript, the night auditor must enter data from the city ledger folios. Since they are usually few in number and have little activity, city ledger amounts are entered as a total on a single line at the bottom of the daily transcript recapitulation, or "recap," sheet. Delinquent ledger folios are entered on another line, again as a single total. Then the auditor can proceed to verify column totals.

The total of the rooms-occupied column (if there is one) and the guests-in-house column must agree with the previously verified and reconciled rooms report. The total of each column dedicated to a hotel department must agree with the cashiers' sales tape totals from that department. Recall that the auditor previously verified and reconciled these tapes with vouchers from each department. If the auditor finds that the column totals in the transcript for any department are lower than those on that department's sales tape, it's probable that a folio was omitted or a voucher was not posted to a guest folio. Another source of error that is difficult to detect is a voucher that is posted to a guest ledger in a prior day's column. Since the auditor does not normally verify transactions prior to the current day, it is easy to overlook this kind of mistake, and very time-consuming to find.

Totals in the cash receipts and cash paid out columns must agree with totals of all previously verified cashiers' reports, and the totals in the transfer columns must agree with transfer journal totals. Also, the closing balances of the individual ledger folios should be totaled and compared with the total in the closing balances column of the daily transcript. When the ending balance in the daily transcript agrees with the balance on each guest's ledger folio and when the column totals of the daily transcript agree with the cashiers' tape or report totals from the various departments, it indicates that all charges sent in by the various hotel departments have been posted to some guest ledger folio. But this does not prove that they were posted to the correct ledger folio. Other than exercising care, there is no way to systematically detect errors in posting to wrong ledger folios except through guest complaints. Finally, the total of the ending balance column in the daily transcript must agree with ending balance totals of the guest ledger and city ledger folios, indicating that all individual ledger folios have been included in the transcript.

As stated earlier, the city ledger is made up of guests who are not staying at the hotel but who enjoy house credit privileges and by guests who have left the hotel without paying their account because they enjoy extended credit privileges. The activity for these accounts is not copied to the daily transcript account by account. Usually transaction amounts for these accounts are totaled and posted to a single line of the daily transcript, or, if there is one, to the daily transcript recapitulation sheet, the purpose for which is explained below. The reason for this is that city ledger folios are often kept in the accounting department. The restaurant and other purchase vouchers are sent to accounting with the daily transcript for posting to the individual folios there. Departures are shown in the daily transcript on separate lines. In Exhibit 7-8 Room 107 was vacated and reoccupied the same day.

Also, the accounts of guests who leave the hotel without paying, and do not enjoy extended credit privileges, are transferred to the delinquent ledger. The total of these accounts is entered on the daily transcript recapitulation sheet on a single row at the bottom, next to the city ledger row.

Daily Transcript Recapitulation Sheet

Typically 30 to 40 guest accounts can be entered in each daily transcript page. Therefore, when several daily transcripts are required (seven daily transcript pages are not uncommon) because of the large number of guests, a daily transcript recapitulation, or "recap," sheet is prepared, which summarizes the data included on all the individual transcripts. This sheet can also include a summary of all the cashiers' reports, the transfer journal previously discussed, and a section for making journal entries to record charges in the city ledger by nonguests, although these latter three items are sometimes included in the daily report, to be discussed subsequently. With the preparation of this sheet the night auditor concludes his or her second audit function, that of balancing and verifying account balances.

OTHER NIGHT AUDITOR RESPONSIBILITIES

Among the various miscellaneous objectives of the night audit is that of monitoring guest credit limits to determine that they have not been exceeded. These limits may be those of the credit card a guest is using or they may be in-house credit limits set by the hotel itself. In any case, it is the responsibility of the night auditor to monitor these limits, either when room rates are being posted or as a separate step in the audit, and to report to management (1) any accounts that have exceeded their limit and (2) any bills that have remained unpaid for more than a predetermined number of days. This can be done on a form sometimes called the *high balance credit report.* In some hotels the night auditor prepares bills for accounts in the guest ledger that have reached a predetermined credit balance, for express check-out guests, or for (automatically) all accounts on a weekly basis. An express check-out guest is one who advises the hotel in advance that he or she is leaving the next day. This enables the hotel to prepare their bill in advance and eliminates the wait at the front desk during the check-out.

The night auditor is also usually responsible for taking cash register readings in the various hotel departments. The auditor clears the registers, checks the date, and sends the old register tapes to the accounting department after using them in the night audit. He or she performs these same functions for mechanical posting machines when they are in use.

Generating Summary and Statistical Activity Reports

The final objective of the night audit is to prepare reports that inform management concerning the hotel's daily activities and assist management in making decisions. Reports prepared by the night auditor for management may be divided into two categories, although some reports may fall partially into both of these categories:

- Those reports that provide statistical information that is useful to management in making long-term decisions, but do not require immediate action, such as the daily report.
- Those reports that require some sort of immediate action on the part of management. A typical report requiring management action is the high balance credit report, indicating that some guests have exceeded either the hotel's or their credit card's credit limits.

Three of the reports prepared by the night auditor, the daily transcript, the daily transcript recapitulation sheet, and the high balance credit report have already been discussed. Other reports often prepared by the night auditor are described next.

The Daily Operations Report

The daily operations report, also called the *daily report*, is the front office statistical report. It contains a summary of the dollar sales of all hotel departments, as well as statistical information concerning each department, such as the average cover, average room rate, year-to-date totals, last year's amounts for today's date, or last year's year-to-date totals. A sample daily report is shown in Exhibit 7-9. It is prepared by the night auditor on a carry-forward basis, adding each day's data to the previous day's cumulative totals, where applicable. These operating statistics enable middle management to evaluate lower management performance by comparing the current season with other periods of this year and with the same period last year. They also serve as a basis for the preparation of subsequent years' sales projections and for planning expansions of the hotel.

Transaction Corrections Report

The transaction corrections report, also often called the *errors report*, should ideally be prepared by the clerks as they make and correct errors. The night auditor needs to verify that these errors were properly corrected, and, if they were not, that the corrected transactions be added to this report. The night auditor must also add any new errors discovered during the night audit, along with the appropriated corrections, to this report. (See Exhibit 6-17 for a sample errors report).

Comp Room Report

This report informs the front office manager of any rooms that are being used free of charge on a complimentary basis. The manager must be aware of these to prevent unauthorized use of rooms free of charge.

The Stagecoach Inn
DAILY REPORT

Feb. 9, 1999
TODAY'S DATE

Fred
REPORTED BY

Sales Summary

Department	Today	Month To Date	Year To Date	This Day Last Year	This Month Last Year	Last Year To Date
Rooms	$13,100	124,450	551.510	$11,528	109,516	485,329
Food	3,218	30,571	135,478	2,832	32,438	133,952
Bar	1,986	18,867	83,611	1,748	16,603	73,577
Telephone	182	1,729	7,662	160	1,522	6,743
Pool	104	988	4,378	92	869	3,853
Gift Shop	310	2,945	13,051	273	2,592	11,485
Other	50	475	2,105	44	418	1,852
Total	$18,950	180,025	797,795	$16,677	158,422	702,059

Statistical Summary

Department	Today	Month To Date	Year To Date	This Day Last Year	This Month Last Year	Last Year To Date
Rooms						
Available	198	1,778	7,903	198	1,760	7,899
Occupied	154	1,464	6,197	170	1,422	6,471
Occ. %	78.0%	82.3%	78.4%	85.9%	80.8%	81.9%
ADR	$85.00	$85.00	$89.00	$68.00	$77.00	$75.00
Food						
All						
Covers	495	4,549	20,627	424	4,960	19,555
Avg. Cov.	$8.50	$8.72	$8.57	$6.68	$6.54	$6.85
Cafe						
Covers	366	3,361	15,336	303	3,489	13,355
Avg Cov	$2.66	$2.76	$2.48	$3.70	$2.50	$2.50
Dining Rm						
Covers	89	822	3,631	121	1,121	4,525
Avg. Cov.	$12.47	$12.50	$12.66	$13.95	$12.37	$12.00
Banquet						
Covers	40	366	1,660	0	350	1,675
Avg. Cov.	$28.45	$30.11	$31.01	$0.00	$27.31	$26.98

Accounts Summary

Cash

Openings	$33,519.51
Deposits	$6,590.00
Checks	$7,383.23
Ending	$32,666.28

Receivables

Ledger	Today	Last Year
Guest	$16,591	$15,898
City	3,109	3,236
Direct Bill	6,585	7,589
Total:	$26,285	$26,723

Exhibit 7-9

Rate Discrepancies Report

The rate discrepancies report includes a listing of all rooms that do not follow a particular rate plan of the hotel. The purpose of this report is similar to the comp room report; namely, to keep rooms from being sold by front desk clerks at rates lower than those authorized by management.

Rooms Repairs Report

The rooms repairs report informs management of any rooms that are being repaired and therefore cannot be sold. This makes management aware of the percentage of total rooms available for sale. It also enables management to determine whether or not repairs are being performed on a timely basis.

Occupancy Forecast Report

This report gives the front office manager a rough and approximate estimate of how many rooms are expected to be sold in the near future, for example in the next three days. It is based on guests already staying at the hotel who are likely to extend their stay, as well as on confirmed reservations.

SUMMARY OF STEPS IN A TYPICAL MANUAL NIGHT AUDIT

Before proceeding to explain how machine accounting systems and computerized accounting systems affect the night audit, we will here summarize the various steps involved in a manual night audit. It must be kept in mind that because of the variety of hotel organizations, night auditors for different hotels are likely to adjust the content or the order of the steps listed below to suit their own organization. Generally, however, the steps shown below are performed in the manner and order in which they are presented.

1. Verify that the room rack has been properly reconciled with the housekeeper's report and rooms report, and reconcile all differences.
2. Post any unposted room rates, telephone calls, and taxes to the guest ledger folios based on the reconciled rooms report.
3. Verify that all vouchers have been sent by each department. This is done by totaling the sales vouchers sent by each department and comparing the total with the cashier's tape or accompanying department sales report. Make corrections to reconcile vouchers with departmental tapes or sales journals.
4. Check for vouchers that do not have a posting mark and post them to the appropriate guest or city ledger folio.

5. Verify totals of all cash sheets and determine that all cash entries have been posted to the appropriate guest ledger folio for hotel guests or to the city ledger for nonguests. Make corrections where necessary.

6. Verify that all discounts and allowances are supported by properly authorized vouchers and have been posted to the correct guest folios.

7. Total the charges and credits made that day on each ledger folio to verify that the current balance shown is correct. Then bring this balance forward to a new folio if necessary.

8. Copy the current data from each account folio onto the daily transcript, account by account. Begin with today's opening balance, post new charges and new payments or credits, and then copy today's ending balance.

9. Total all the columns of the daily transcript, including the beginning and ending balance columns.

10. Verify that all balances are correct by doing the following:

   • Total the balances on all the individual ledger cards and compare this total to the total in the closing balances column of the daily transcript.

   • Compare the column total for the opening balances column with the column total for the previous day's closing balances column.

   • Compare the totals of the departmental charges columns with the total of the adding machine tapes, cashiers' tapes, or sales journals sent by each department with the sales vouchers.

   • Compare the total of the cash advances, or paid-out, column with the front desk cash sheet totals.

   • Compare the cash receipt columns with the corresponding column totals on the cash sheet.

   • Verify that the allowances column and discount column totals agree with the totals of the allowance and discount vouchers.

   • Verify that the total of all the charge columns agrees with the total of the total charges column.

   • Prove the posting formula on the transcript by subtracting the totals of all the credit columns from the total of the total charges column to obtain the total of the ending balances column.

If the night audit has been performed correctly, the last two totals mentioned above will equal each other. Matching totals indicate that all vouchers have been charged and that all credits have been credited to someone's ledger folio. But remember that matching totals do not prove charges and credits were posted to the correct account. If the night auditor was careful in performing Steps 2, 4, 5, and 6, of the audit, however, there should also be assurance that charges and credits were posted to the correct guest folios.

HOW POSTING MACHINES AFFECT THE NIGHT AUDIT PROCESS

Basically, mechanical posting machines, such as the NCR 250 or 4200, have an effect on Steps 2, 4, 7, 8, 9, and 10 of the night audit procedure described earlier. Steps 2 and 4 are posting steps that involve posting to the individual ledger folios. Step 7 involves updating the balance on ledger folios after posting to them, and Steps 8 and 9 involve copying to the daily transcript and totaling it. All of these steps are performed simultaneously by the posting machine when charges and credits are posted to each folio card. The only function left for the night auditor is to perform some of the verification processes included in Step 10 of the manual audit.

Posting to Folios with a Mechanical System

Posting to folios with a mechanical system involves inserting the folio card in the NCR machine and properly aligning it so that the data will be printed by the machine in its proper place, although recent posting machines, such as the NCR 250, align the folio card for you. Charges are distributed to the different departments when the appropriate department key is pressed and the corresponding dollar amount is entered. The machine then prints the amount on the ledger folio card (coded by department), prints a new balance on the card, and maintains a running total for each department. If an error is made, the erroneous entry must be subtracted on the folio card and the correct amount reentered.

Although the cashier will post check-outs when they pay, and the clerk may have had time to post room rates, the night auditor must still post all unposted room charges and charge vouchers from other hotel departments, just as would be the case in a manual audit. The considerable amount of time saved when using posting machines can be appreciated when it is realized that this one mechanical posting step has eliminated five steps of the manual audit.

Machine Posting and the Daily Transcript

But the greatest saving in labor and time when using posting machines for the night audit comes from the fact that the daily transcript no longer needs to be prepared by hand. The posting machine produces a daily transcript in the form of the D card (see Exhibit 7-10). As can be seen from the illustration, this D card contains the totals row of the daily transcript, but oriented vertically in column format rather than as a row. The total sales for each department is listed along with transfers in and paid-outs, and there is a total debits line that reflects the total of all the previous lines. Then there are three credit lines: a transfers out line, an allowances line, and a paid line to record guest payments, followed by a total credits line. Finally, the difference between total debits and total credits is added (if debits are greater) or subtracted (if credits are greater) from the previous outstanding balance total to arrive at the current outstanding balance for all folios.

D   NIGHT AUDITOR'S MACHINE BALANCE NO. _____

DEPARTMENT	DATE	DESCRIPTION	NET TOTALS	CORRECTIONS		MACHINE TOTALS	R/R	30
ROOM			01	ROOM		10,731.00	Z	156
TAX			02	RMEX		207.00	Z	4
TELEPHONE			03	TAX		1,312.20	Z	159
LONG DISTANCE			04	PHON		32.12	Z	41
LAUNDRY			05	LOST		530.95	Z	120
VALET			06			.00	Z	0
GARAGE			07	DAYR		204.00	Z	3
TELEGRAM			08			.00	Z	0
BEVERAGE			09	COFF		386.44	Z	27
MISCELLANEOUS			10	MISC		734.20	Z	28
RESTAURANT			11	REST		211.11	Z	24
TRANSFER CHARGE			12	TRDR		196,977.98	Z	108
PAID OUT			13	POUT		368.53	Z	16
TOTAL DEBITS	15,217.55 ✓		14	DRS		582,774.23	Z	683
TRANSFER CREDIT			15	TRCR		196,977.98	Z	108
ADJUSTMENT			16	ADJ		56.39	Z	3
PAID			17	PAID		2,024.64	Z	39
TOTAL CREDITS	2,081.03		18	CRW		199,328.63	Z	154
NET DIFFERENCE	13,136.52 ✓		19			.00	Z	0
OPENING DR BALANCE	325,206.72		20			.00	Z	0
NET OUTSTANDING	338,343.24 ✓		21	DBCO		.00	Z	0
			22	CRCO		.00	Z	0
TOTAL MCH. DR. BALANCE	340,076.67		23			.00	Z	0
TOTAL MCH. CR. BALANCE	1,788.16		24			.00	Z	0
NET OUTSTANDING	338,291.51		25	INDR		320,578.70	Z	6

CORRECTIONS

51.73 SHORT

DETECTOR COUNTER READINGS

☐ DATE CHANGED

AUDITOR'S CONTROL: _____   ☐ CONTROL TOTALS AT ZERO

MACHINE NUMBER: _____   ☐ MASTER TAPE LOCKED

☐ AUDIT CONTROL LOCKED

AUDITOR

[signature]

Exhibit 7-10   Night Auditor's Daily Report

Since a cash register is maintaining the balances for the various columns that one would find in the handwritten daily transcript, there is no need to produce a daily transcript except for the lines marked "subtotal" (see Exhibit 7-8 for the location of those lines). In fact, some hotels where management hasn't fully given up on the manual system require the night auditor to enter the totals off the D card onto the subtotal lines of an otherwise blank daily transcript ledger page. The D card grand totals (otherwise known as a Z reading because this printing of a D card also results in the clearing of the machine totals to zero in order to begin a new day) match what in a manual system daily transcript would be the bottom line (the total receipts line). The reader can clearly see that the mechanized front desk register has simply automated the totaling up of the daily transcript ledger and does nothing more than produce a mechanized version of that form.

The auditor and/or audit team must still perform the other audit steps, which involve verifying that all rooms charges, allowances, cash sheet entries, and departmental vouchers have been posted to the individual ledger folios. Errors can be caused by failing to post any of the above, by posting wrong amounts, or by posting to the wrong folio. Some errors will have been caught by the clerk or cashier doing the posting during the day. These errors are not only corrected in the posting machine, but are also entered on a correction sheet (see Exhibit 7-11). Any additional errors discovered by the auditor are also entered on the error correction sheet and are corrected through the posting machine until all departmental totals equal the adding machine, sales journal, or cash sheet totals sent by each department. Also, the posting of all room charges must have been verified as described earlier.

Just as the night auditor in a manual system turns in the backup to the accounting office, the night auditor in a mechanized system turns in A, B, and C cards as well. These cards look like a D card but are the subtotals of all work done by each shift at the front desk during the day. They are the same as a shift report under the handwritten system.

COMPUTERIZED ACCOUNTING SYSTEMS

As explained in the beginning of this chapter, there are many degrees of computerization in computer systems. Some systems have small microcomputers located in the various departments of the hotel that do not communicate with each other directly. They may have a computer at the front desk, the restaurant, the sandwich shop, the banquet department, and the pool. But since they do not communicate directly with each other, the sales information they have stored must be physically transported, using so-called floppy computer disks, to the principal computer, usually located either at the front desk or in the accounting department. There the information is consolidated and merged into the necessary audit and management reports.

In other systems the computers are all interconnected into what is called a *network.* This is the most advanced type of computerized accounting system, often called an *on-line* system. In this type of system the various departments do not have microcomputers, but instead they have *terminals* connected to a minicomputer or a late-model microcomputer. Originally computer terminals had no data processing power themselves; they only served as messengers to transmit information to the main computer and therefore were called "dumb terminals." Lately, however, "intelligent terminals" have become more popular. These are microcomputers connected to the main computer. They can both process data themselves and/or send it to the main computer. In such a system, whenever

The Prince William Hotel

Night Auditor's Report
ERROR CORRECTION SHEET

Today's Date _____

Auditor on Duty _____

Revenue Clerk's Initials _____

Machine No.: _____

Room No.	Voucher No.	Name	Amount Posted	Corrected Amount	Amount of Error	Dept. Key Deduction	Explanation of Error	Error by Operator

NOTE: ATTACH CASHIER'S CORRECTION SHEET TO THIS AND TURN IN WITH NIGHT AUDIT

Exhibit 7-11

any information is entered into a terminal ("dumb" or "intelligent"), it can be immediately transmitted to the minicomputer, which processes the information and merges it with all other information contained in its memory. Thus all the accounting information generated in the various hotel departments under an on-line system is always instantly available to management for the preparation of reports and audits. In on-line systems, information can also flow from the main computer to the terminals. This enables hotel sales personnel to verify a guest's room number, for instance, or to verify whether or not reservations exist for that guest, or to obtain any other necessary information required prior to processing a particular transaction. Systems that generate computerized accounting data at the point of sale are called *point-of-sale* systems (POS systems).

Recently, computer hardware and software programs have advanced to the point where they are no longer limited to performing mathematical calculations on data. Because of increased processing speed, larger memory capacity, and more sophisticated programming techniques, computers are now beginning to perform some of the more complex logical functions formerly limited to humans. They can analyze ratios, predict room demand and availability, arrive at conclusions, and recommend action. This type of deductive logic programming is called *artificial intelligence.*

THE NIGHT AUDIT IN COMPUTERIZED ACCOUNTING SYSTEMS

As we saw earlier, mechanical posting machines eliminate the five night audit steps related to posting charges and credits, and they automate the preparation of the daily transcript. They do not, however, reduce any of the posting verification steps required to determine that all charges and credits have been entered on folio cards, nor do they eliminate the posting process itself. A computerized accounting system that is on-line does away with this step of the night audit.

This is so because in a computerized accounting system it is usually unnecessary to post sales vouchers and other charges and credits to the individual guest folios one by one, either manually or through a posting machine. The host computer receives the sales data generated at the points of sale throughout the hotel without human intervention. In an on-line system, the main computer is constantly receiving this information throughout the day and is posting it to the various guest ledger folios. Also, room charges and taxes are automatically posted daily by the computer when instructed to do so by the night auditor.

In such a system there is not only less labor involved, but also less chance for error. This is true, not only because transcription errors are eliminated, but also because the system itself will block certain types of errors. For example, computers will not allow cashiers to charge purchases to room numbers that do not exist or are not occupied.

Some verification is still required in an on-line system, however. For example, cashiers can still post to another occupied room by mistake. And so, in a computerized system, the night auditor's work is mostly limited to verification.

Because computerized systems can be so individually tailored to particular hotels, there is no one general routine followed by the night auditor on a computerized system. A sample of one of the many routines that can be followed is listed here:

1. Print a *D sheet* from the computer. This is the equivalent of the D card in a mechanical system.
2. Verify cashiers' work.
3. Instruct the computer to post room rates and taxes to each guest folio.
4. Perform one or more of the following verification steps:
   (a) Verify that the housekeeper's reports and rooms reports were properly reconciled to each other and to the room rack.
   (b) Verify that purchases and advances have been posted to the correct room number.
   (c) Verify transfers from one folio to another. It is easy for charges to "disappear" on a computer system as a result of such transfers.
   (d) Verify that all credit card vouchers are on hand and reconciled to the day's credit card sales.
5. The night auditor might then instruct the computer to perform all the chores involved with closing out the current day, and to begin a new day with the next day's date.

A computerized system has its disadvantages as well. The complexity of the system is its major disadvantage. It not only requires better-trained personnel to input the data correctly, but it also requires highly capable and trained individuals to interpret the vast amount of data in the many, and often complex, reports that computers print out. A computerized room rack printout, for instance, requires some experience to read and understand. Variations in room rates that do not fit any of the hotel's plans can, therefore, be hidden more easily. On the other hand, if the unauthorized rate is clearly visible to all desk clerks, as it is in a manual room rack, such "hidden" room rates do not occur. Transfers among accounts and ledger folios can also be more easily hidden and be made to "disappear" on a computer system. The following chapter, "Technology in the Rooms Division," contains a more extensive discussion of hotel computer systems.

QUESTIONS AND PROBLEMS

Discussion Questions

1. What are the five objectives of the night audit?
2. How many different categories, or types, of accounting systems are there?
3. Why is it important that the room rack be accurate? How can its accuracy be verified?

4. Name three reasons why the housekeeping report may indicate an unused room that appears to be occupied in the rooms report.

5. What is a "who"? Name three possible causes of a "who."

6. What is the rooms computation formula and what is it used for?

7. Write down the posting formula and explain what it describes.

8. Who are primarily responsible for posting room rates to guest folios?

9. How does the night auditor verify that all purchase vouchers have been posted?

10. What is the purpose of the front office cash sheet?

11. Besides the cash sheet and nonrooms department vouchers, what other sources of debits to guest folios are there? What other sources of credits may there be, besides guest payments on their accounts?

12. What is the purpose of the transfer journal?

13. What is the purpose of the daily transcript?

Problems

1. Use the rooms computation formula and the statistics below to determine how many occupied rooms there should be:

    (a) Occupancy brought forward from previous day = 240

    (b) Arrivals = 132

    (c) Departures = 122 (included in these departures is a guest who occupied a room with a relative)

2. List the ten steps of the night audit; describe them and explain why they are necessary.

3. Based on the following data, prepare a daily transcript for August 4, 1999.

    (a) The following opening balances existed:

Room No.	Opening Bal.	Room No.	Opening Bal.
251	$876	377	$1120
293	732	462	135
348	341		

    (b) The following charges were made to guests at the hotel.

Room No.	Room Charge	Tax	Restaurant	Beverage
348	$45	$5	$68	$12
462	85	9		39
293	75	8	93	

		Telephone		
	Local	Long Distance	Laundry	Valet
377	$6	$25	$10	
420			8	$5
299	3	15	7	4

(c) Room No.	Payment Amount	Allowances
348	$100	$35
293	150	
420	?	

(d) Below are given the room rates and taxes for the occupied hotel rooms as indicated by the room rack:

Room No.	Room Rate	Tax
251	$75	$8
293	75	8
348	45	5
377	55	6
420	85	9
462	85	9

(e) The following additional information concerning certain rooms was obtained from the front office cash sheet and transfer journal:

Room No.	Information
462	Transferred $19 of restaurant check and related tax to Room 293.
293	Received a $50 cash advance from the hotel.

CHAPTER **8**

Technology in the Rooms Division

CHAPTER OBJECTIVES

After reading this chapter you will understand:

- What a Property Management System (PMS) is.
- What hardware and software are used by a PMS.
- Some functions of a PMS.
- Sample output from a PMS.

PROPERTY MANAGEMENT SYSTEMS

Computer systems in the lodging industry are developed to perform two basic functions. First, they are designed to store data in a convenient and easily retrievable way. Second, they then process this data in such a way that management will receive information conducive to effective decision making. Over the years, the computer systems found in hotels have taken on the generic name "Property Management System." The term means many things to many people but, for the sake of clarity, we will take it to mean an integrated computer system, which, at least, includes the computerization of the front desk processes, and, at most, the control of virtually all operations in the hotel, including the telephone, in-room movies, the use of electricity, and the monitoring of motors and other mechanical devices. Such a system would also control food and beverage operations and information, remote (that is, away from the front desk) point-of-sale equipment, management information systems, back-of-the-house accounting and decision-support systems, and systems that link the hotel into worldwide information networks, such as a 1-800 reservation system, an on-line computer system, and the general international communication system known as the Internet. While implementation of PMSs in hotels can be as small as one personal computer at the front desk or as big as networks within the hotel numbering 30 or more machines, they all have certain common characteristics, and they can benefit a property in four major ways:

1. The operation of the hotel can be improved by the reduction of repetitive tasks.
2. The information needed by management to make decisions is current and easily accessible.
3. The service provided to guests can be improved with regard to the timing and accuracy of pertinent information. Another benefit to customers is the added personalization of the service, due to the specific information on individual guests that can be kept in a guest history file.
4. The internal operations of the hotel can be kept in a standardized way that is easy to control and would be almost impossible to duplicate in a manual system.

Property Management Systems are not a cure for a poorly designed manual system. In order to implement a computerized system, a well-conceived manual system run with skilled employees must be present for a smooth transition. The germ *GIGO*, "garbage in–garbage out" applies to hotels as well as other businesses; if the hotel systems are a mess before computerization they will become an even bigger mess after computerization. This being said, thousands of successful computer installations have shown us exactly what the benefits of computerization are to a hotel.

PMS Components

A PMS is made up of software that instructs the second part of the system—the hardware. Software "tells" the hardware how to process the data that is input into the system by the users. There are many Property Management Systems available to hotels today. Some of the basic requirements of the software are outlined below:

- Growth and Flexibility. When purchasing a PMS, one should buy one that will handle one's present needs as well as grow with the hotel as needed. A good way to allow for this growth is to purchase a system that functions as needed at the time of purchase and also offers the capacity to add on other options at a later date.

- User Friendliness. In the front office area, there tends to be a high turnover of employees due to promotions and terminations. The ease of training new employees on the system is an essential feature if a PMS is to be effective. Some of the features that will increase the ease of operation are well-designed menu prompts, self-explanatory input screens, help functions, and simple error correction.

- Operating System. Since operating systems differ, not all software will run on the same hardware. Thus it is important to select the software before selecting the hardware system.

- Multiuser. In a multiuser environment, several people can have access to and enter data into the system at the same time. A hotel system is almost always multiuser except in the tiniest of establishments.

- Report Generator. The report generator provides access to the information stored in the PMS, either through predesigned reports of the system or through reports that are developed to meet a hotel's own special needs. The software should provide reports that are meaningful to management as well as provide the capabilities to produce special reports as the need arises.

- Stability. The software should be stable (that is, free from bugs). The hotel should be assured that the software will operate without "crashing" or without unexpected stoppages. Data can be lost during crashes, and customers can become frustrated waiting for the system to be reinitialized (restarted) so they can pay their bill. Stability often can be measured by the number of other hotels which have installed the same software. A large user base indicates that the software has probably been debugged to the point where it is stable.

Hardware

Once you have selected the software part of the PMS, the next step is to select a compatible hardware system. The choice of a software package has already started to narrow the choice of hardware, but in no way makes it a simple decision.

The size of a hardware system needed is dependent upon the PMS functions that will be used, the number of people that will be working on the system, the number of terminals the hotel will have on-line, the amount of data to be stored on the system, and the speed needed in processing the data.

There are two broad categories of computers most commonly utilized by hotel Property Management Systems. They are microcomputers and minicomputers. Each of these types has its own set of advantages and disadvantages.

A microcomputer (or more commonly referred to as a PC) is a desktop computer. While these systems are small in size, technological advances have provided them with a great deal of power. In fact, many smaller hotels can be run quite effectively in the PC environment. The advantages of the microcomputer are its low unit cost, small size (so it fits easily on a desktop), ease of installation and movement, and ease of operation. Two disadvantages are that *networking* (the connection of many PCs together in order to share information) tends to be difficult and that it must be done so one PC can communicate with another (which requires special hardware and wiring). Power is reduced further when PCs are networked, since some of the PCs' computational ability must be dedicated to running network software. Additionally, the software written for the PC systems often has fewer features than does software written for minicomputers. This last disadvantage is becoming less noticeable with the advent of even more powerful PCs.

Minicomputers are based on the same setup as mainframe computers. There is a central processing unit (CPU) that is shared by all of the users through their terminals. This allows the users to function at the same time on similar and on different tasks. Some of the major advantages of the minicomputer environment are the amount of data that can be stored on it, the increased computational power as compared with the PC, and the growth that is allowed by the addition of more terminals. (Some PC networks are limited in the number of PCs that can be hooked up to them.) Major disadvantages include the increased cost of the system, and the larger size of the equipment as compared with the PC. Some very large hotels experience problems with computer capacity limits, and neither computer system is useful. These very large hotels use a mainframe computer. As far as the user is concerned, there is little difference between the minicomputer and a mainframe. There is a noticeable difference between the minicomputer and the microcomputer and the user will notice these differences immediately.

PROPERTY MANAGEMENT SYSTEM MODULES

The software in a Property Management System is made up of several modules. Each of these modules of the software is designed to be used in a particular area of the hotel or to serve a general purpose for all or most of the areas. In Exhibit 8-1 we see the main menu for the Computerized Lodging Systems (CLS), a type of Property Management System, as it appears on the computer screen. This system is made up of eleven different modules. The first module, for example, is for the reservation area, which is accessed when module number 1 is selected. One advantage of this modular approach to software design is that various properties may decide to initially use only a few of the modules. This creates a far less daunting task than computerizing the whole hotel at once. One can keep reservations on a manual system while one computerizes the front desk, for example, thus allowing management to concentrate its efforts in one area of the hotel.

In this section, we will go through the various modules. Our intention is to explain the different functions available in each module as well as analyze some

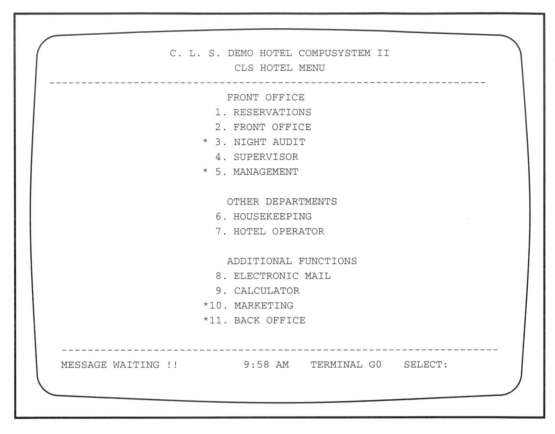

```
                C. L. S. DEMO HOTEL COMPUSYSTEM II
                        CLS HOTEL MENU
--------------------------------------------------------------------

                        FRONT OFFICE
                   1. RESERVATIONS
                   2. FRONT OFFICE
                 * 3. NIGHT AUDIT
                   4. SUPERVISOR
                 * 5. MANAGEMENT


                        OTHER DEPARTMENTS
                   6. HOUSEKEEPING
                   7. HOTEL OPERATOR


                        ADDITIONAL FUNCTIONS
                   8. ELECTRONIC MAIL
                   9. CALCULATOR
                 *10. MARKETING
                 *11. BACK OFFICE


--------------------------------------------------------------------

MESSAGE WAITING !!            9:58 AM    TERMINAL G0    SELECT:
```

Exhibit 8-1 Main Menu for CLS *Source:* Courtesy of CLS (Computerized Lodging Systems)

of the reports that are produced in each module. We are not trying to "sell" the CLS system, but it is a very good tool for showing the reader what is available. All hotel software is very similar when operated because, as mentioned previously, all hotel software has a common origin in the manual systems in use by hotels at the time of conversion. "Then why should a hotel computerize?" one might ask. Because a computerized hotel system provides managers with reports on a more timely basis. It is through the reading and analysis of these reports that management really experience the benefits of a computerized Property Management System.

Reservations

In Exhibit 8-2, the menu is displayed for the reservation module. There are a total of sixteen functions that can be accessed from this main reservation menu. This portion of the PMS has eliminated many of the manual processes mentioned in Chapter 3.

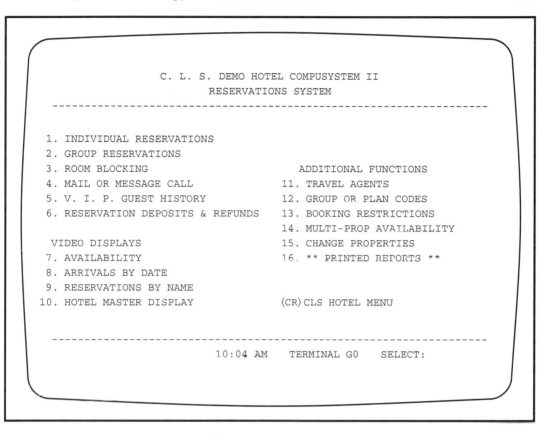

```
              C. L. S. DEMO HOTEL COMPUSYSTEM II
                    RESERVATIONS SYSTEM
----------------------------------------------------------------

 1. INDIVIDUAL RESERVATIONS
 2. GROUP RESERVATIONS
 3. ROOM BLOCKING                    ADDITIONAL FUNCTIONS
 4. MAIL OR MESSAGE CALL         11. TRAVEL AGENTS
 5. V. I. P. GUEST HISTORY       12. GROUP OR PLAN CODES
 6. RESERVATION DEPOSITS & REFUNDS   13. BOOKING RESTRICTIONS
                                 14. MULTI-PROP AVAILABILITY
  VIDEO DISPLAYS                 15. CHANGE PROPERTIES
 7. AVAILABILITY                 16. ** PRINTED REPORTS **
 8. ARRIVALS BY DATE
 9. RESERVATIONS BY NAME
10. HOTEL MASTER DISPLAY         (CR) CLS HOTEL MENU


----------------------------------------------------------------
                10:04 AM    TERMINAL G0    SELECT:
```

Exhibit 8-2   Menu for Reservations

Individual Reservations

When a prospective guest calls to make a reservation, this is the portion of the system that is accessed. The program for individual reservations allows the clerk to enter, change, or cancel a guest's reservation. Exhibit 8-3 is the screen that appears when the clerk is ready to enter a reservation for a guest. The first thing that a clerk does is to check availability, that is, to see if the type of room wanted is available on the dates that the guest wishes to stay. To perform this function, the clerk enters the number of rooms, the type of rooms, the date of arrival, and the number of nights the guest wishes to stay. After this information is entered, the system will indicate on the screen whether the accommodations are available to match this request. If they are, the system will inquire of the clerk whether space is to be booked. At this point, the clerk may check the rates on the room by invoking the "rates" section of the program.

Once the guest decides to reserve a room, the clerk is now ready to enter the information needed to complete the screen in Exhibit 8-3. When the group code is entered on the reservation, the rate that has been set for that group will

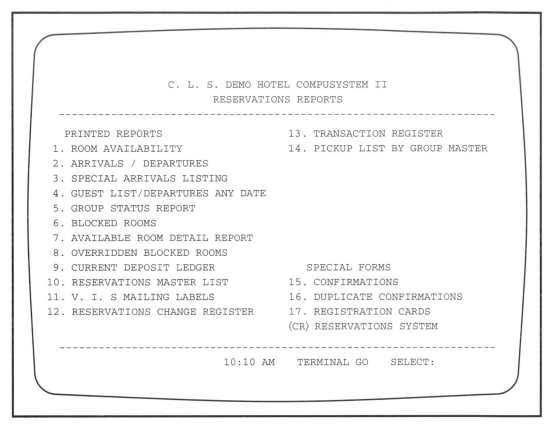

```
            C. L. S. DEMO HOTEL COMPUSYSTEM II
                     RESERVATIONS REPORTS
---------------------------------------------------------------
    PRINTED REPORTS                13. TRANSACTION REGISTER
 1. ROOM AVAILABILITY              14. PICKUP LIST BY GROUP MASTER
 2. ARRIVALS / DEPARTURES
 3. SPECIAL ARRIVALS LISTING
 4. GUEST LIST/DEPARTURES ANY DATE
 5. GROUP STATUS REPORT
 6. BLOCKED ROOMS
 7. AVAILABLE ROOM DETAIL REPORT
 8. OVERRIDDEN BLOCKED ROOMS
 9. CURRENT DEPOSIT LEDGER              SPECIAL FORMS
10. RESERVATIONS MASTER LIST       15. CONFIRMATIONS
11. V. I. S MAILING LABELS         16. DUPLICATE CONFIRMATIONS
12. RESERVATIONS CHANGE REGISTER   17. REGISTRATION CARDS
                                   (CR) RESERVATIONS SYSTEM
---------------------------------------------------------------
                  10:10 AM   TERMINAL GO    SELECT:
```

Exhibit 8-3   Menu for Individual Reservations

be displayed. For example, if a guest is coming as part of an association's conference for which a special rate has been set up, this special rate would already be
entered into the system. It will immediately appear when accessed by the association name (or other reference phrase) entered as part of the reservation. This
also applies to special packages the hotel has available. In addition to the rates,
other features will be displayed, such as a free breakfast, inclusion of tips, a
sightseeing tour, or other amenities that are being offered as part of the package.

   If the reservation is being made by a travel agent, this information must
also be included by the clerk at this time. Simply entering the travel agency's
code or phone number will bring up the name and address if the agency is on file
with the hotel.

   The "commission deducted" section will record the amount of commission
that the travel agency has deducted prior to sending a deposit. This will prevent
the hotel from paying more than the amount agreed upon as commission.

   If the type of room requested by a potential guest is not available at the
time of reservation inquiry, the guest's name may be put on a waiting list. A re-

port of the names on this waiting list may be printed out later to use in attempting to accommodate the guests. Another feature is used during the many times that hotels require a two- or three-day minimum stay during a holiday or special event period. If, when the dates of stay are entered, this period of time has a minimum stay attached to it, the system will indicate this on the screen. In the "deposit required" section, the clerk will enter the amount of deposit requested. This will then appear on the guest's confirmation. Even more important, a report can be printed that will indicate the reservations for which a deposit has not yet been received. The "paid-to-date" section will be filled in when a deposit has been received. This occurs automatically when the deposit is posted.

A reservation system also has the ability, when the reservation is taken, to indicate if a confirmation is to be printed. These confirmations will be printed at the end of the day and prepared for mailing. A space is provided at the bottom of the screen for the "guest history" and comment line. Information placed here can be saved in the "guest's history." If a guest has a special request with regard to the type of room he or she wants, the system will allow for blocking a room at this point or at any other time.

A "share-with" reservation is used when two or more people will be occupying the same room under separate folios. With the "share-with" reservation, separate reservations, confirmations, folios, and registration cards will be printed. Also, there is a feature that allows the clerk to copy the same reservation information from one reservation to another. This is useful when several people from the same company are making separate reservations. By simply typing in the information the reservation screen requests, a clerk has booked the room, deleted it from inventory, blocked a specific room, and set up a confirmation to be sent. If using a manual system, several forms would have to be completed, books checked and rechecked, and more than one employee would be involved. The advantages of a computerized reservation system are readily apparent.

When a reservation must be canceled, the procedure is quite simple with the computerized system. Everything is completed through the keyboard with the "cancellation" function of the program. The system will retain the cancellation on file until the arrival date, just in case the guest should show up. If this were to happen, the clerk could access the canceled reservation and give the details of its cancellation to the guest.

Multiples, as they are called, give the hotel the capability to make as many one-day reservations in a row as needed. This feature was designed for companies and airlines that have different people coming in each day for one-day reservations. A "Transfer" refers to the ability to transfer a reservation and deposit to another hotel in the same company when using a multiproperty system.

Group Reservations

There are several different ways in which a group reservation is booked and handled. First, the total group of rooms is booked by one person who is, in most cases, a travel agent, an association representative, or a company representative. In the case of a tour group, the tour operator will send a rooming list that indicates what type of room each guest requires. For an association, individual guests will phone in to reserve one of the rooms that has been put aside in the block. Both of these situations are easily handled in a computerized reservation system. In addition, a running total is kept that shows how many rooms have not been "picked up" from the block of reserved rooms. Expedition of billing may be accomplished through the transfer of charges from individual guest folios to a group master folio at check-out. A cut-off date will be established, by which rooms will be released from the block if they are not picked up. It is possible also to get a printout that will assist in this process for the various groups. The hotel can decide for each group if room availability is to be affected either when rooms are committed to the group or when the rooms are actually picked up. When the reservation is booked, it is possible to specify the different types and numbers of rooms reserved and rates quoted, or to use the "run of the house" method and charge one set price for any one of several different types of rooms. Whenever a group reservation is canceled, it is possible to reinstate the reservation and any individual pick-ups off the group at any time prior to the original reservation date. If a reservation is deleted, however, it may not ever be retrieved. To book a pick-up of a group reservation, the clerk goes into the pick-up section and simply adds the correct information for the guest. Everything in the group reservation will be updated.

A subprogram of the group reservation—called *Billing*—controls charges that go from the individual folios to the group master folio. For this to work, all charges to be transferred must be stipulated ahead of time. Then these charges will go from the individual to the master folio and all other charges will remain on the individual folios. These instructions may be changed anytime up until check-out.

Room Blocking

Once a reservation has been entered into the system, it is possible to go back and assign a room to this reservation through the "room blocking" area. If the clerk does not know what room to block, the system will lead the clerk through several steps to find the type of room the guest is requesting. It is even possible to list the rooms least used in any given year so they can start to be rented, thereby making it possible to even out the wear on the guest rooms.

Mail or Message

Before computers, when a guest with a reservation had a message, it was paper clipped to the reservation until the guest arrived. Now, when a guest due to arrive receives a message or mail, a notice can be placed on the reservation by simply accessing the reservation and typing it in. When the guest arrives, the messages may be printed off and given to the guest at check-in.

VIP Guests

When a guest is indicated to be a VIP, the information from his reservation card and charge totals will be transferred into a guest history. This serves as a database of information to be used by the hotel when dealing with this guest in the future. In a multiproperty system, all hotels may share this information. Also, mailing labels can be printed from this database to be used in direct mailings to these guests.

Deposits and Refunds

When a deposit is received at a hotel that processes deposits manually, a series of many steps must take place. In a computerized environment, the same task is completed very quickly with a much higher degree of organization. The reservation deposit screen is brought up on the system. At this point, the reservation clerk enters the reservation number that the guest was given when the reservation was made. If the number is not known, the reservation may be located by using the guest's last name. The system will search for this last name, after which the clerk can access the reservation by selecting the guest's name from the list of guests generated. When the reservation is selected, the information from the reservation will fill up the screen that is used to post the deposit.

When a guest with a reservation deposit cancels his or her reservation, the deposit can be refunded through the system. Refunds can only be made on reservations that have a deposit applied to them. This is an internal control measure to prevent checks being issued incorrectly. The guest's reservation is accessed the same way as when a reservation is posted. When the deposit is refunded through a computer system, the deposit is taken off the reservation, a message goes into the VIP section of the reservation to indicate the deposit refund, and the deposit is deducted from the advanced reservation deposit ledger. Then, when the night audit takes place, the city ledger will be updated, and a check for the refund will be issued by the accounts receivable refund function. Sometimes, a guest will cancel a reservation but will not want a refund, requesting instead that the hotel credit his deposit to another reservation held by a friend or associate. A computerized system has the capability to complete this transaction electronically.

Availability

In a computerized Property Management System, there are several screens that show availability in a variety of different ways. One such screen displays the availability for one day only. This provides a detailed picture of that day's availability and occupancy situation. On this screen the following information can be seen: number of rooms sold, percentage of occupancy, out-of-order rooms, rooms due to check out, and number of rooms left to sell. In addition, the system supplies a breakdown of the types of rooms under reservation, the type of reservation guarantee, the number of each type that is a stayover rather than a new arrival, and the forecast rather than the actual occupancy. This screen may be seen in Exhibit 8-4. A screen similar to this one, with the exception of the house-count information, is available for planning reservations into the future. Information such as this is extremely useful in planning one's strategy to achieve a full house. A manually prepared form containing the same information takes a great deal of time to prepare and update.

   A 15-day availability graph provides information for 15 days into the future. It contains the occupancy percentage for these days, the number of rooms available, the rooms that are part of a group block that have not been released, and the number of rooms that are under a 6 P.M. guarantee.

   The screen that can be used to check availability in detail when answering a reservation request is the 18-day spread. Included in this screen is the type of rooms in the hotel, their availability, and the rates for an 18-day period beginning with the date of arrival. A screen such as this contains a great deal of useful information in an easy-to-read format.

```
-------- ROOMS AVAILABLE FOR  12-05-86  ----FRIDAY    -- 1:16 PM-----
        TIER PRICING IN EFFECT:  TIER 3  RATE RANGE:  100-130
-------------------------------------------------------------------

        TOTAL ROOMS:        86      ---TYPE-----000-AVAIL-RS-G RSNG SOLD
        SOLD/RESERVED       85      KING  ( 22)      8-  20    2    8
        AVAILABLE:           1      QUEEN ( 17)      9    1    0    7
        % OCCUPANCY:        99 %    DBDB  ( 22)     13-   1   30    4
                                    PRLR  ( 12)      3    5    2    2
        OUT OF ORDER:        1      EXEC  ( 13)     10    1    0    2
        DUE TO DEPART       12      BLK   (  )       0    0    0    0
        ROOMS TO SELL       12- *   WAIT  (  )       0    0    0    0
                                                    ---  ---  ---  ---
                                    SUMMARY          1   28   34   23
-----------------------------------------------
-* HOUSE COUNT *         (PLANNED) (ACTUAL)-
- ARRIVALS TODAY             7          0 -
- WALK-INS                   —          1 -
- DEPARTURES                12          0 -
- DEPARTURES-UNEXPECTED     00          0 -
- STAYOVERS                 24         36 -
- OUT OF ORDER               —          1 -
- VACANT ROOMS              55         48 -
    <CR>=CONTINUE  <P>=PRINT  SCREEN:
```

Exhibit 8-4 Rooms Availability Screen *Source:* Courtesy of CLS

Another type of screen is used in assigning rooms to guests and setting up reservations. This particular screen displays the room numbers, types of rooms, and the status of each room on a specific date. So, for example, if a guest requests a specific room, such as room number 325, the clerk can check this screen to see the status of the room on the dates in question. A screen is also available that gives the status of a particular room for up to a year ahead. Many computer systems have the ability to display information on other properties in a hotel situation.

Travel Agents

Several functions are available to deal with the business generated from travel agents. Some of the options in this area are the entry of travel-agent data, such as name, address, and phone number; listings of travel agents that do business with the hotel and the amount of the business they generate for the hotel; and commission statements. One advantage of this feature is that after the commission statements are produced, the commission checks can automatically be generated.

Groups and Plans

Groups that are coming in will have a code associated with them. This allows the individual reservations to be given this code number so it is recognized as part of the group. A "plan" code or number is for a "plan" package that the hotel has put together. With the use of this number, the revenue will be split out from the plan package price into the different revenue areas of the hotel that should receive the credit. For example, if a charge on a weekend plan package is $200, the revenue would be split out as room charge, $110; tax, $11; beverages, $30; breakfast, $15; and dinner, $34.

Reservations Module Reports

Various reports are available through the reservation module in a computerized Property Management System. Exhibit 8-5 is the menu from a system by CLS that indicates the reports possible.

Under "availability" different reports can be produced. The first one gives a breakdown of rooms sold and reservations guaranteed and not guaranteed, all by the type of room. Another report is produced for an entire month, which shows the occupancy and number of rooms available by the type of room. This information can also be displayed in graphical form.

Arrivals and Departures

These two reports will list the guests that are due to depart and arrive on a date specified. Other information about the length of stay and type of guarantee is also indicated. Also, it is possible to print a list of arrivals for 6 P.M. guaranteed

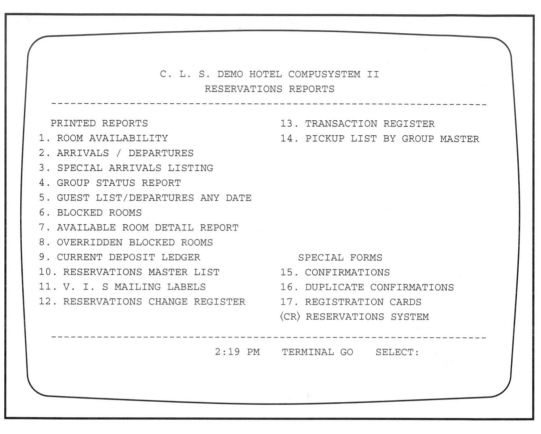

```
              C. L. S. DEMO HOTEL COMPUSYSTEM II
                     RESERVATIONS REPORTS
    -----------------------------------------------------------------

    PRINTED REPORTS                   13. TRANSACTION REGISTER
    1. ROOM AVAILABILITY              14. PICKUP LIST BY GROUP MASTER
    2. ARRIVALS / DEPARTURES
    3. SPECIAL ARRIVALS LISTING
    4. GROUP STATUS REPORT
    5. GUEST LIST/DEPARTURES ANY DATE
    6. BLOCKED ROOMS
    7. AVAILABLE ROOM DETAIL REPORT
    8. OVERRIDDEN BLOCKED ROOMS
    9. CURRENT DEPOSIT LEDGER              SPECIAL FORMS
    10. RESERVATIONS MASTER LIST      15. CONFIRMATIONS
    11. V. I. S MAILING LABELS        16. DUPLICATE CONFIRMATIONS
    12. RESERVATIONS CHANGE REGISTER  17. REGISTRATION CARDS
                                      (CR) RESERVATIONS SYSTEM

    -----------------------------------------------------------------
                      2:19 PM    TERMINAL GO    SELECT:
```

Exhibit 8-5 Reservations Reports Menu *Source:* Courtesy of CLS.

reservations only, or a list of all reservations that are to be billed directly. These reports can be very helpful in preparing for these or other guests' arrivals.

Group Report

The group report can be printed for all group reservations or just the one indicated by the reservations clerk. These reports are run according to arrival and or departure dates. The advantage is that information that normally would take hours to gather manually, can be prepared in a matter of seconds in report format. Information such as the number and types of rooms committed to the group, and the number and types of rooms picked up to date, may be included in the report.

Departure List

This is a list of guests due out on a specific day. A blocked rooms report is a printout for each room in the hotel indicating whether the room is blocked or open for an 11-day period starting with the date entered. The report will indicate if there is a conflict between a guest currently in a room and a guest assigned to check-in to the same room.

Master List

A master list of all reservations coming into the hotel can be printed out by date of arrival. Also, it is possible to print out reservations based on date of arrival if information on only one day's reservations are needed.

Front Desk and Cashier Systems

The front desk and cashier functions will be discussed here as being part of the same menu. With this setup, the cashier locations can serve as check-in terminals during busy periods and cashier functions can be conducted from any terminal. The assigning of rooms in a computerized front desk system is, in most systems, automatic. Rooms are selected based on least amount of use, any special locations or features of the room, and guest room floors in the hotel.

When a guest who has made a reservation arrives at the hotel, check-in can be completed on the computer with as few as 10 key strokes on the computer keyboard. This is quite a change from the manual process used in a noncomputerized environment. After the guest is checked into the hotel, his or her information may be accessed through any of the programs in the front office program. When the housekeeping department needs to communicate with the front desk regarding the status of a guest room, this may also be done through the computer system. This eliminates the need for the front desk to contact someone in housekeeping to find out the status of rooms, or the need for housekeeping to have to phone or go to the front desk with these updates. The status of a guest room can be updated by using the telephone in the guest room. To do this, the maid simply enters in his or her code, the status change code, and the room code. This new information will now be in the system when the status of a room is checked. Information needed by housekeeping, such as which rooms have checked out, can also be obtained through the computer system.

The process of checking out a guest can also require as little as 10 strokes on the keyboard. This includes settling the account as well as updating the status of the room and all other areas of the system that contain information about the guest. These systems also have the ability to give the guest a printout of his folio showing room and tax, even before the night audit is completed. The system may be set up to obtain a final copy containing all of the guest's charges on one folio or on separate folios for charges such as food and beverage.

Exhibit 8-6 is a sample menu of the functions, displays, and reports available to the front desk and the cashiering areas.

Registration or Change

The registration program is utilized by the front desk to check in guests with a reservation or without one. Guest room assignments may be made auto-

```
                  C. L. S. DEMO HOTEL COMPUSYSTEM II
                           NIGHT AUDIT
   -----------------------------------------------------------------

   AUDIT PREPARATION                 THE ONE-BUTTON SEQUENCE
1. NIGHT AUDIT CHECKLIST          *13. ONE-BUTTON NIGHT AUDIT
2. DOWNTIME REPORT SEQUENCE
                                      MASTER FILE MAINTENANCE
   ADDITIONAL FUNCTIONS            14. CONDENSE FOLIO TO BALANCE FWD
3. NIGHT AUDIT REPORT MENU         15. REBUILD AVAILABILITY
4. CREDIT CARD TRANSFERS           16. REBUILD GUEST BALANCES
5. POSTINGS TO CITY LEDGER         17. REBUILD GUEST CROSS-REF FILES
6. VERIFY GUEST FOLIO BALANCES     18. MAINTAIN BUDGET FOR 'D' CARD
7. GUEST VOUCHER TRIAL BALANCE     19. INTERFACE / GHOST TASKING
8. AUDITOR'S JOURNAL ENTRIES
9. SHIFT AUDIT DISPLAY / UPDATE       FOR EMERGENCY USE ONLY
10. REVIEW UNEXPECTED STAYOVERS   *20. ONE-BUTTON AUDIT BACK-UP MENU
11. REVIEW FOLIO FROM HISTORY FILE *21. CHANGE SYSTEM DATE OR TIME
12. PURGE FOLIO HISTORY FILE      (CR) CLS HOTEL MENU


   -----------------------------------------------------------------
                  8:27 AM   TERMINAL GO   SELECT:
```

Exhibit 8-6 Night Audit Screen   *Source:* Courtesy of CLS.

matically by the system or manually by the front desk clerk. When a guest has a reservation and is using a credit card at check-in, the process can be handled in just a few seconds. Many times there are charges for which a guest will have to be assessed each day, such as for parking or a roll-a-way bed. In these cases, the system can be set at check-in so that the charges will be automatically posted every day. One reason for the speed of the computerized system is that all the information on the reservation screen is transmitted and utilized in the registration area as well.

When a guest notifies the hotel at check-in that he or she will be paying for another guest's room at check-out, this information can be input into the system so that the cashier will be notified by the system at check-out. The system may also be set at check-in time to notify the night auditor to print out the folio as an express check-out. An express check-out is a situation where the guest will receive his or her copy of the folio before the expected check-out time. This enables the guest to depart the hotel without going to the front desk.

At registration, if the guest requests a specific type of room or location, the system has the ability to search for one that is available during the guest's stay.

For example, if the guest requests a king room on the tenth floor with an ocean view, the system can be prompted to search for a room meeting these requirements.

Selecting a Room

In a noncomputerized system, the room rack is used by the front desk staff to determine which rooms are available to be rented at any given moment. The use of a computerized system does away with the need for this room rack. An inventory of rooms in the hotel is housed in the program designed to accommodate this information. This room-selection program enables the clerks to select rooms based upon such criteria as type of room, status (whether the room is made up or not), location, and other special factors as needed. Some systems have a feature that enables the system to sort through those rooms listed as sold the night before to determine which rooms will be available for rental the next day. These rooms will be prioritized for renting by factors such as rate, type of room, and number of times rented so far in the year. Special codes are used to indicate the type of room that is being sought. The code OV could be entered to indicate that a room with an ocean view has been requested.

Transferring a Guest

There are times when a guest checks in and is not satisfied with the room assigned, or the guest may have to be moved to another room because of a problem with the room. When this change is recorded on a manual system, the clerk is required to change the room number on the folio, change and move the rack slip in the room rack, and change the information rack. With the computerized system, the clerk enters the information in the "transfer" function to update all of these areas of information in the computer, now that the guest is occupying the new room. The status of the room that the guest has been moved from is then updated to its new condition.

Message and Mail

The message and mail function allows the front desk staff and PBX operators to record messages on the guest's folio and later to retrieve these when the guest requests them. There is also a printer setup available that allows the guest's messages to be printed when requested.

Six PM Hold Reservations

Six PM Hold reservations are those held only until 6:00 P.M. and then released. In a manual system, the clerk is required to go through the records to cancel these reservations. With the computerized system, all Six PM Hold reservations may be canceled at once. There is also the option that allows the clerks to review them individually and cancel only those chosen. Another advantage is that even after the reservation is canceled, the information for the reservation is not deleted when canceled, but the room is put back in the available inventory of rooms to be sold. Thus, the late-arrival guest can still be checked in provided a room is still available.

Billing of Groups

In the billing of group members, all the charges can be posted to individual folios, or some or all can be posted to the master folio kept for the group leader. This is an option available for each individual group. At check-out, folios can be checked out by individual group member, or all folios can be checked out at once using these options.

Locating a Guest

In a computerized system, there are various functions that take the place of the room rack and information rack in a manual system. One such function allows the staff to locate a guest's room number by entering the guest's last name. This will produce a list of guests with this last name. Another such function displays the names of the guests occupying a room, the status of the room, and the rate, simply by the entering of the room number into the system. Additionally, there are functions that allow for the listing of all guests in a group, that show the status of guest rooms in the hotel, and that display the room rates for the different types of rooms.

Posting Charges

There is usually a separate program for posting the following: guest charges, long distance charges, guest account settlement, correction, allowance, and balances to the city ledger.

Printing in the Cashier Area

During the check-out process, the cashier will have to perform different functions at various times. Sometimes it will be necessary to display the guest's folio to check for certain charges before printing a copy. Many times a guest will want to review a copy before agreeing to the balance indicated by the cashier. Finally, the guest will be checked out and the final copy of the folio issued. When checking a guest out, the cashier should always ask the guest if he or she has made any charges recently and whether he or she would like to review a copy of the bill. If a guest should happen to return to the hotel during the same day as he or she checked out, it is possible to cancel the check-out and to reinstate him or her as a continuous registration. This may happen if a guest misses a flight, or has a sudden change in plans.

Night Audit

The advantages of a computerized Property Management System as discussed thus far are slight in comparison to the advantages seen when the system is used to perform the night audit. In a noncomputerized system, room and tax must be posted for each room in the hotel one by one. Readings must be taken and numerous reports completed by hand. If there are errors, this process can take more than the eight-hour shift allocated to it. With the computerized night audit, all of these tasks can be completed by the simple pressing of a few keys on the keyboard. This action will post room and tax to all rooms, and print all of the desired reports needed by management.

Exhibits 8-6, 8-7, and 8-8 indicate the various functions and reports available during the night audit process. Some of the more important features and reports will be covered in the following section.

During the night audit, confirmations for reservations will usually be run and set up for mailing. Registration cards for the guest arriving the next day will be printed in alphabetical order. Folios for guests scheduled for check-out can be printed and, where appropriate, be distributed in an express check-out system.

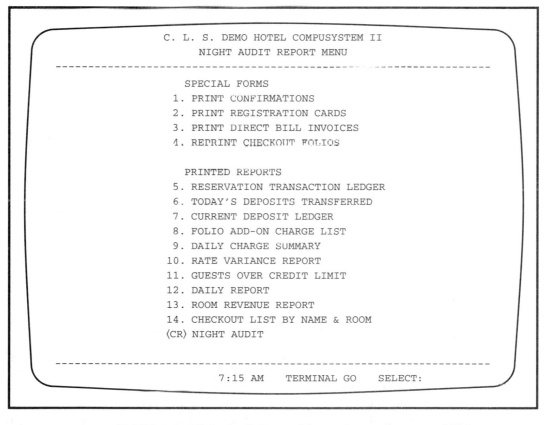

Exhibit 8-7   Night Audit Report Menu   *Source:* Courtesy of CLS.

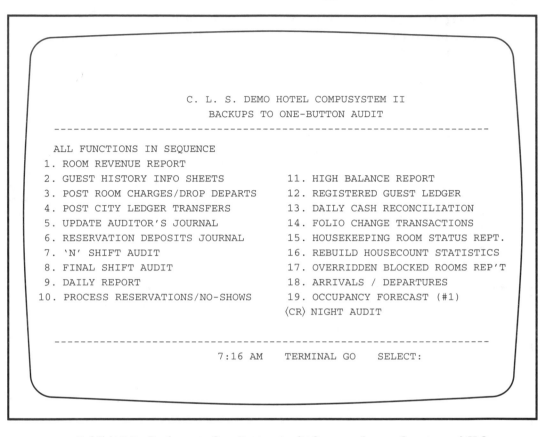

```
              C. L. S. DEMO HOTEL COMPUSYSTEM II
                    BACKUPS TO ONE-BUTTON AUDIT
    ---------------------------------------------------------------

    ALL FUNCTIONS IN SEQUENCE
 1. ROOM REVENUE REPORT
 2. GUEST HISTORY INFO SHEETS          11. HIGH BALANCE REPORT
 3. POST ROOM CHARGES/DROP DEPARTS     12. REGISTERED GUEST LEDGER
 4. POST CITY LEDGER TRANSFERS         13. DAILY CASH RECONCILIATION
 5. UPDATE AUDITOR'S JOURNAL           14. FOLIO CHANGE TRANSACTIONS
 6. RESERVATION DEPOSITS JOURNAL       15. HOUSEKEEPING ROOM STATUS REPT.
 7. 'N' SHIFT AUDIT                    16. REBUILD HOUSECOUNT STATISTICS
 8. FINAL SHIFT AUDIT                  17. OVERRIDDEN BLOCKED ROOMS REP'T
 9. DAILY REPORT                       18. ARRIVALS / DEPARTURES
10. PROCESS RESERVATIONS/NO-SHOWS      19. OCCUPANCY FORECAST (#1)
                                      (CR) NIGHT AUDIT


    ---------------------------------------------------------------
              7:16 AM    TERMINAL GO    SELECT:
```

Exhibit 8-8   Backups to One-Button Audit Screen   *Source:* Courtesy of CLS.

Room Rate Variance

This is an important report that should be reviewed by management every day. The report shows the guest's name, room number, rate charged, rack rate, and the difference between the two rates—the *variance*. All variances must be accounted for as part of the night audit process.

Credit Limit Report

It is important to keep track of all charges made by guests to ensure that they are not allowed to go over the credit limit set for them by the hotel or credit card company. This report will show guests who are over their credit limit. It is also possible to get a report listing all of the guests that are prepaid. Different outlets in the hotel should be provided with these lists so each knows which guests do not have charge privileges.

D Report

The D report is the daily report of operations for the hotel. It lists the different revenue areas in the hotel for the day and usually for year-to-date. Information regarding the day's deposit, guest ledger, and city ledger are also included.

Room Revenue Report

This report lists the rooms in numerical order indicating the room rates and other statistical information for the day's business.

City Ledger Activities

There are several different programs and reports used during the night audit that deal with the city ledger. One such program automatically transfers credit card check-outs to the city ledger. This removes these balances from the guest ledger and begins an accounts receivable for them in the city ledger. Another program allows screen viewing of all balances before they are posted to the city ledger and/or printing of all folios for the last time before they are transferred to the city ledger. There is also a report that is run to get a detailed listing of all vouchers posted to guests' folios during the day. This report is then compared with the guest ledger, with which it should agree.

Interfacing

Property Management Systems are quite often interfaced with point-of-sale systems throughout the hotel. During the night audit, these systems will be polled so that the information from that area can be included in the daily report. With the newer Property Management Systems, parts of this information can be input directly into the daily report. This interface capability also functions with an energy management system and a cost-call accounting system. The cost-call accounting system enables the hotel to mark-up guests' phone calls electronically.

Checklists

All Property Management Systems include a checklist for different operations. A checklist for the night audit is probably the most important one of all. Hotels will have to tailor the checklist for the night audit to fit their particular needs. These checklists are not only in a hardcopy form; many systems have a checklist built into the system to use as the procedures are being completed.

Housekeeping Functions

The housekeeping portion of a Property Management System has greatly reduced the amount of leg work that is required under a manual system. In the manual situation, housekeepers had to constantly be on the run to find out and communicate the status of the guest rooms to the front desk. With the computerized system, this communication is done by retrieving the information from the computer. The PMS will update the status of the guest room after a guest checks out. Thus, when housekeeping needs to find out which rooms have checked out at any given time, all they have to do is print the report from the computer system. When the front desk needs to know the status of any guest room, the desk clerk simply checks the computer to obtain this information. These room status reports that are computer-generated have greatly reduced the time that was lost in communications between the front desk and the housekeeping department. Housekeeping is now able to obtain from the system a report of rooms remaining to be cleaned. This information can be used to better schedule the number of maids that will be required later in the day. Much of the communication on the maid's part takes place using the phone in the guest room. The following information and reports are examples of what a Property Management System can do to improve the housekeeping area.

Room Status Changes

All changes to the status of guest rooms are made through the "room status" function. One room or a group of rooms can be changed. If a room is put into the out-of-order status, the system requests an explanation about what is wrong with the room. Another status function of these systems is one that enables the operator to view the status of any room in the hotel. If a guest is in the room or if a guest has checked out, the folio may also be viewed. Guests that were scheduled to check out will often decide to stay over instead. When this happens, this information is stored in a report that housekeeping can review during the day to determine if any guests have fallen into this category. Out-of-order rooms can be seen when the function that lists these rooms is displayed. This is an important display in that it enables maintenance to keep track of the rooms which need their attention. If 100 percent occupancy is going to be achieved, this type of communication is definitely needed. Using a room-status floor display, a hotel can have access to information about every room on a chosen floor, along with its status. This is helpful when a guest is checking in and requesting a particular floor.

Discrepancies

The use of a discrepancy report makes it possible to avoid losing revenue or checking a guest into an already occupied room. If housekeeping reports a room to be vacant when the front desk shows it as occupied, or if housekeeping reports a room to be occupied when the front desk shows it as vacant, there is a discrepancy in status. When this situation goes undiscovered, a potentially dangerous situation exists. The discrepancy report will indicate which rooms do not agree in status. It is then possible to back track and determine where the error is located. It is even possible, using the housekeeping portion of the system, to assign rooms to the individual maids for the day. If need be, these assignments can be changed manually by a supervisor.

Telephone Department

In the telephone department, the PBX operators must have access to various information and be able to record information for guests. Calls will come into the hotel to see if a guest is registered at the hotel or whether a guest has checked in yet. When a guest is not in his room, the PBX operator will very often be requested by the caller to take a message for the guest. Also, guests of the hotel will often request a wake-up call from the PBX operator. A request for a wake-up call is, of course, when the guest calls to the PBX switchboard operator and asks to be awakened at a specific time. Some automated systems allow the guest to use the room phone to place the call with the computerized wake-up system. In these cases, the guest uses the key pad on the room phone to record the time the wake-up call is needed. PBX operators will have a terminal for the PMS to achieve all of the items covered above. This terminal can be limited in that it will not be possible for operators to access other parts of the system. A decision such as this is to be made by management.

Some of the various displays and reports are discussed subsequently. The operator can search for a guest in the hotel by entering the guest's last name. All guests that have names spelled similarly to the name entered will be displayed on the screen. It is also possible to search for a guest by using the room number. When the room number is entered, the guest registered in that room will be indicated along with the room rate and room status information. Guests having a reservation for arrival may be accessed as well. Using this function, the clerk enters the guest's name into the system, after which the guest's reservation will be displayed. When wake-up calls are entered into the system, the guest's name will be displayed to ensure accuracy of entry. A list of all wake-up calls can be displayed on the screen or printed out at any time. When a guest receives a message, his folio will contain it. These messages may be viewed or printed at the PBX area or at the front desk area.

Front Office Management Access

In the hotel, the front office manager, or another member of management, will be assigned responsibility for the Property Management System. There is a function within the system that gives this person a quick update on the status of the system and the hotel at a particular point in time. This function summarizes the events of the previous day. Areas covered in this summary include availability, special requests, walk-ins, and statistics for the previous day. The availability information may include the current day's information, plus 15 or more days into the future.

A report of the rooms occupied by walk-ins should be checked against the reservations due in. This is to make sure a guest with a reservation is not treated as a walk-in. If this occurred, the guest could mistakenly be billed as a no-show.

It is also possible to get a printout of the arriving guests by last name, in alphabetical order. The manager can then check this list for guests desiring special attention. Throughout the check-out time, it is necessary for management to keep track of the guests who had previously indicated they would be checking out but have not as yet. As it gets close to the check-out deadline, these guests must be checked to see if they are overstays.

An out-of-order report can be accessed that shows the reasons for the rooms being out-of-order. This enables the manager to determine which rooms need maintenance first and to decide which rooms will not be available for sale on that day. A room rate variance report allows the manager to see what has happened in terms of discounting prior to a guest's arrival.

For hotel supervisors arriving after the check-out period, a report is available for them that allows this manager to investigate all late check-outs. It is important to monitor how late guests are allowed to stay and which clerk is allowing this to happen. A report can be run that recalculates availability based on new information such as overstays and understays. Walk-ins can be controlled by the manager when the hotel gets close to 100 percent occupancy. This system will alert the clerks to contact the supervisor before accepting any more walk-ins.

As you can see, the computer offers the advantages of time-lines, accuracy, and in-depth reporting (that is, highly more detailed reports).

Interface Concerns

One problem area with any PMS is in interfacing with the back-of-the-house (let's call it BOH). The system described so far in this chapter is a front-of-the-house system which handles the record-keeping and information processing from the point of initial guest contact (when the guest makes a reservation) through to guest check-out. All along this path there has to be a standard accounting system maintained in the BOH. If you think of two distinct systems running parallel to one another, you begin to see how the interface between the two systems is so important. (By *interface* we mean the cross-communication between the systems that allows both systems to be synchronized.) If the reservation system records that the guest sent in a check for $100 as a deposit, it is important that the BOH accounting system have a record in their advanced deposit account showing the $100. Should a guest cancel their reservation, the refund of the deposit must be reflected both at the front desk and in the BOH. This is but one transaction, the hundreds and thousands of transactions which take place every day in a hotel must all be similarly tracked by both systems. You may begin to see how easily the two systems can get out of "synch." The primary point of synchronization, both physically and from an organizational point of view, is the front desk. It is here that the "point man" for the accounting function should synchronize the two systems on a daily basis. This "point man" we are referring to is the night auditor. Too often we have seen accounting systems where some transactions take place on one system or the other and the two systems go out of synch. If all revenues are posted at the front desk, and all refunds or deposits or other charges to accounts receivable are posted there too, the two systems cannot go out of synch without the night auditor noticing it. We therefore *strongly recommend* that when the accounting office receives a check—say from a credit card company—that they write up a miscellaneous charge slip and take it down to the front desk along with the check and run it through the front desk cashier, just like *any* outside person's check would be run through if they were paying off their city ledger account or checking out of the hotel. By doing this, all revenues posted to the General Ledger are posted through the PMS, and an audit trail is complete. Outside auditors can follow the paper trail through both systems and easily verify that all moneys coming into the hotel were properly accounted for. The night auditor on a nightly basis produces a report that the bookkeepers in the BOH can use to directly post to the General Ledger all revenues and changes to accounts receivable on a daily basis. Having done this, the only other side of the cash equation, the cash disbursements side, can become the focus of outside auditing. We cannot emphasize enough that this simple procedure of having the accounting department run *all* incoming checks through the front desk will allow the night auditor to reconcile the two systems (the PMS and BOH system) nightly. If this is done they should never be out of synch for more than a few hours at most.

DISCUSSION QUESTIONS

1. What are the common characteristics of all Property Management Systems?
2. What are some of the basic requirements to look for when purchasing a Property Management System?
3. What are some of the advantages and disadvantages of microcomputers versus minicomputers?
4. Describe how one makes an individual reservation using the CLS reservation module.
5. According to the text, the activity which benefits the most from a computerized hotel system is the night audit. Why do you think this is true?

STUDY QUESTIONS

1. Define the term *Property Management System.*
2. What does the term GIGO mean?
3. What do we call software that is easy to learn and use?
4. What is a CPU?
5. If someone is making an individual reservation as part of a convention, how does one handle this in a computerized reservation system?
6. Who prints out express check-out folios?
7. When there is a difference between the rack rate and the rate actually charged, we have what is called a _____.
8. What does BOH stand for?

CHAPTER 9

Check-Out and Collections

CHAPTER OBJECTIVES

After reading this chapter you will understand:

- Why the check-out phase of the front desk cycle is so important.
- How various guests are checked out of the hotel.
- What kinds of records are maintained concerning guests.

INTRODUCTION

The first part of this chapter will deal with the objectives of the check-out and post–check-out process and the actual steps involved in these processes, as well as the responsibilities of the cashier and the forms involved. The process of updating room status, creating a guest history, and distributing check-out information to the appropriate hotel personnel or departments will also be discussed.

The second part of the chapter will discuss forms of payment and the credit and collection process in greater depth than was discussed in Chapter 6. The proper handling of payments by traveler's check, by credit card, in foreign currency, with travel vouchers, and by personal check will be addressed. The im-

portance of establishing proper credit-granting policies and collection procedures for city ledger and delinquent ledger accounts will also be discussed. Finally, the procedure for calculating bad debt expenses will be discussed.

OBJECTIVES OF THE CHECK-OUT PROCESS

The check-out process has three objectives:

1. To collect payment from the guest for all services rendered by the hotel.
2. To create a positive parting impression on the guest and to obtain information from the guest that might be useful to the hotel in improving its
   services and encouraging the guest to return.
3. To update room status, create a guest history, and distribute check-out
   information to the appropriate hotel departments.

The primary objective of the check-out process is to obtain payment from
the guest for all services rendered by the hotel. This may not be quite as simple
as it seems. For instance, if the hotel does not have an efficient communication
system, some last minute charge vouchers may not have been forwarded to the
front office by the various hotel departments. These are called *late charges* and
will be discussed later in the chapter.

Although creating a positive last impression with a guest is listed second
among the above objectives, it cannot be emphasized enough. Failure to bill a
guest for a particular service at check-out is an inconvenience and may imply
monetary loss for the hotel, but it is much less of a loss than the potential loss of
future business might be, due to the unpleasant impression created by an overly
aggressive or intrusive cashier. It must be remembered that one of the strongest
impressions a guest will take away with him or her is that created by the employees of the hotel, and, aside from the bellperson, the cashier is the last employee a guest is likely to encounter. In fact, because of the importance of the
position, the cashier's attitude is likely to create a stronger impression than that
of the bellperson. The owners of the hotel may be wonderful people, but guests
seldom meet them. It is the employees who must act as goodwill ambassadors,
and it is they who must create a pleasant and service-oriented atmosphere in the
hotel by being warm and efficient when dealing with hotel guests.

Reservations clerks are usually located in the back of the front office. It is
wise to either give them access to the front desk, or (in case they are not uniformed), give departing guests access to them through a house phone. Assisting
the departing guest in making continuing reservations, or even return reservations at the hotel, is another way to leave a favorable impression on a guest and
perhaps simultaneously create repeat business.

An integral part of inspiring goodwill in a guest is to ask for some feedback
from the guest concerning his or her impression of the hotel and the service re-

ceived. This is particularly important because it is the most inexpensive way to obtain an objective appraisal of the hotel. Guest comment cards should be made available at check-out time, and the guest should be gently requested to fill one out. Additionally, this gives hotel personnel the opportunity of apologizing and/or making restitution for any unsatisfactory service or unpleasant experience the guest may have had.

The third and final objective of the check-out process is to update the room's status and create a guest history. The housekeeper needs to know that the room will no longer be occupied so that the maid can clean it and prepare it for inspection before it is resold.

A guest history is useful in soliciting future business from prior guests of the hotel. Knowing the patterns of their stays at the hotel enables the hotel to plan promotions accordingly. It also enables the hotel to award free stays or discounts for frequent visits at the hotel. If the guest history file is efficiently updated, the front desk clerk or cashier can inform guests personally at check-out time of any bonus the hotel has awarded them. This is more effective than informing guests later by mail.

THE CASHIER'S CHECK-OUT FUNCTIONS

With the above in mind let us go through the actual check-out process. Checking out guests is one of the cashier's duties. There are six types of check-out that a cashier must deal with. Each involves a slightly different approach on the part of the cashier. The six check-out procedures are the following:

1. the regular in-person check-out
2. the express check-out
3. the in-room video check-out
4. the late check-out
5. the group check-out
6. the payment in advance check-out

Special procedures associated with the various methods of payment, such as payments by credit card, traveler's checks, foreign currency, and other payment methods will be discussed in the second part of the chapter in the section entitled "Forms of Payment."

Regular In-person Check-out

For an in-person check-out the cashier pulls the guest's folio from the pit, or, in computerized accounting systems, calls it up on the computer screen. The cashier will then ask the guest if he or she has recently purchased anything at the hotel. This enables the cashier to verify that the charge was made on the folio. If a purchase was made but not charged to the folio, the cashier should ask the room clerk if there are any unposted vouchers belonging to that room. If not, then the cashier must communicate with the department where the sale was made to obtain the sales amount. If this is impractical, then the cashier should take the guest's word for the amount. In either of the latter two cases, the cashier should prepare a *substitute voucher* for the amount posted to the folio. When the actual voucher is received the accounting department should be informed of any difference. A difference in favor of the guest is refunded, and a difference in favor of the hotel is either posted to miscellaneous expenses and absorbed by the hotel (up to $5), or it is billed as a late charge on the guest's credit card, or billed to the guest by mail. It should be kept in mind that usually guests are just as eager to have all charges posted as the cashier is. Guests have been known to mistakenly tell the front desk clerk at check-out that they have no additional charges when in fact they do. These additional charges, when they become known, are called *late billings*. Late billings are time consuming and can create additional problems for travelers on expense accounts, even though credit card vouchers provide a space for entering late charges. Most late billings are detected by the front desk prior to the end of the day of check-out. These late billings are posted to a folio and their amounts are added to the charge cards. If the guest checked out with cash, a city ledger account is established in the guest's name and the amount due is posted to the city ledger. If the late billing is discovered the next business day (this can happen with a charge to the in-room service bar for example), then the amount due is posted to a city ledger account. In the absence of a credit card voucher, it is not deemed worth the cost of writing a letter to collect amounts of $5 or less, and, in fact, most late billings not postable to a charge card are rarely collected.

After determining that all charges have been posted to the guest folio, the cashier will receive payment, either in cash or by check, credit card, or any of the other forms of payment (to be discussed later in this chapter). If payment is in cash or by check, it is entered on a cash sheet similar to the one shown in Chapter 6, either manually or by computer. The amount of the payment is entered in the column headed "Guest Ledger," the room number in the column headed "Room Number—Departure," and the name of the guest is written in the column headed "Name." The cashier's name has been entered previously at the top of the cash sheet, along with the date and the time of the shift. This makes that cashier responsible for all entries on that cash sheet. The night auditor, or a billing clerk, picks up the payments from the day's cash sheets and credits them to the appropriate guest folios before transferring folio activity to the daily transcript. The accounting department then debits the General Ledger cash account from the *summary cash receipts form* and credits the guest ledger accounts receivable control account from the night auditor's daily transcript. The summary cash receipts form is a summary of all the hotel's individual cashiers' reports.

If payment is by credit card, then instead of entering the payment on the cash sheet, the cashier enters the payment by debiting a transfer journal (see Chapter 6) used for summarizing debits and credits to city ledger accounts (in this case the credit card company's city ledger account) and crediting the guest's folio. This zeros out the guest folio just as it was done for a cash or check payment. Again, the night auditor picks up city ledger folio activity on the daily transcript. This in turn is used by the accounting department both to debit the city ledger accounts receivable control account and to credit the guest ledger accounts receivable control account. In a computerized system, of course, all of this occurs instantaneously since the computer does all the posting and prepares the night audit "D" sheet once the information is entered. The computer generated "D" sheet is the equivalent of the mechanical posting system's "D" card and the manual system's daily transcript.

After payment has been received, the cashier then posts the payment amount on the folios, either manually, through a posting machine, or by computer. Then the cashier enters the new zero balance, stamps all copies of the folios as paid, initials them, and gives one copy of this validated folio to the guest to serve as a receipt. The other copies are kept by the hotel as part of its guest history.

In some instances the guest may have a credit balance in his or her account. This may happen when a guest has a guaranteed reservation or has been asked to pay in advance and then decides to leave earlier than expected. When this is the case the cashier debits the guest folio for the amount of the credit balance and writes a check for the credit amount, or pays the credit amount in cash. This is recorded on the cash sheet as a cash disbursement, along with a brief explanation.

Express Check-out

Many hotels have what is called an *express check-out* procedure to avoid congestion at the front office during the peak morning check-out times (see Exhibit 9-1). In this case the guest calls the front desk the night before departure to request that the bill be prepared. The bill is then either slipped under the guest's door early on the date of departure, the guest picks it up quickly at the front desk, or it is mailed to the guest's home address. The room key is either left in the room, handed in at the front desk, or left in a special box. The guest then departs without waiting in line to pay his or her bill.

When the cashier is informed of an express departure, he or she pulls the guest's folio from the bucket in a manual or mechanical system, or calls it up on the computer screen in a computerized system. The cashier then verifies that all vouchers have been posted to the folio, checks for any late charges, and posts these to the folio. Then the cashier transfers the balance in the folio to the credit card slip, and enters a credit for an amount equal to the folio balance on the guest folio, thus zeroing out the account exactly as it was done for the in-person check-out. To assure that the credit card company is billed for this charge, the cashier also debits the city ledger folio of the credit card company or informs the accounting office to make such a debit through the use of a transfer journal.

Express Check-Out

To expedite your departure, we bring to your attention <u>The Concord Express Check-Out Service.</u>

Any guest who has left a signed imprint of their credit card on arrival and has informed us of their intention to use Express Check-Out may utilize this service providing <u>no changes</u> were made regarding the scheduled day of departure.

If you have not done so at check-in, you may notify the cashier by leaving an imprint of your credit card at your convenience during your stay. On your scheduled day of departure, simply drop your keys in any of the conveniently located key drops found throughout the hotel. An itemized copy of your bill and credit card voucher will be mailed to you. <u>All other guests not using Express Check-Out must settle their bill with the cashiers before departing.</u>

If you have any questions, please contact the Assistant Manager.

Thank you for choosing The Concord Resort Hotel. We hope you have a pleasant stay, and wish you a safe trip home.

Guests vacating their rooms after the 2:30 P.M. check-out time may be subject to additional charges.

Exhibit 9-1   *Source:* Courtesy of the Concord Resort Hotel.

In the case of an express check-out, it is often hotel policy to cancel all charge privileges in the dining rooms and other departments after the issuance of the express check-out bill. This can cause some guest complaints when they attempt to charge a breakfast, for instance, in the morning. One way to avoid these embarrassing situations is to post the policy and clearly state that the guest will no longer be able to charge to his folio after the express check-out bill has been issued. Guests may be encouraged to use the preordered breakfast slips found in many hotels today, where the guest indicates a breakfast choice the night before and places the slip on the door knob to the room.

In-room Video Check-out

This check-out procedure is similar to the express check-out but is available only when a computerized system is in use at the hotel. When checking out the guest uses a video terminal or TV screen located either in the lobby of the hotel or in the guest's room to review the bill and inform the hotel of his or her departure. This information may be transmitted to the computer via an in-room or lobby keyboard or via telephone using synthesized voice technology. Such terminals are similar to the self-registration, in-the-lobby terminals mentioned in Chapter 5. The in-room procedure is to use a spare channel on the TV set and have the guest enter items on the screen in an interactive mode. The terminals, regardless of their location, are connected to the hotel's computer, which then credits the payment to the proper guest ledger folio and debits the credit card company's city ledger folio. The computer distributes the check-out information to all appropriate hotel personnel and departments so that no further charges can be made to that room. In this case, a computerized property management system (PMS) can easily block further charges in all outlets in the hotel. Those properties where the food and beverage computers are not fully integrated into the front desk system may find the in-room check-out to be impossible to control. A canceled copy of the guest folio can be picked up by the guest at the front desk or it may be slipped under the guest room door early in the morning.

The Late Check-out

A special problem may be posed by guests who check out later than the posted check-out time on the day they are scheduled to leave. The check-out time is usually set to allow the departing guest the maximum amount of time in the room on the day of departure, while still allowing the hotel enough time to clean the room so that it can be sold again that evening. The housekeeping staff ends its afternoon shift at 4:00 to 6:00 P.M., so that there is little time between then and the usual check-out time of 12:00 to 2:00 P.M. to clean vacated rooms when there are many to be cleaned. If there is not enough time for housekeeping to clean and prepare the room for sale that evening and the hotel is full, it may mean a day's lost revenue on the room. This must be explained to guests who check out late and are required to pay for the additional day's use of the room. Also, hotels should post the designated check-out time prominently at the front desk and on the back of guest room doors. Many hotels only charge an additional half day if the guest leaves after the designated check-out time but before 6:00 P.M. In many cases a front office manager may ultimately have to negotiate such charges with the guest. Since the guest folio must be updated before the late-departing guest pays the bill, in manual and mechanical systems late charges are posted by the billing clerk or cashier instead of waiting for the night auditor.

Group Check-out

Another type of guest that presents special problems at check-out time is the group or convention guest. Special agreements between the hotel and the group govern the way charges will be billed in these cases. The cashier must be familiar with these agreements in order to be able to verify that charges were properly made to the master folio and individual folios, in addition to charging the voucher income account when required. Usually various copies of the agreement are provided for the various hotel cashiers. Also, the front desk must be sure to notify members of the group that they are responsible for paying their individual charges before they leave the hotel.

As explained in Chapter 6, groups or conventions require setting up two types of folios, the master folio, usually called the *"A" folio,* for recording all charges covered by the group or convention, and individual folios, usually called *"B" folios,* for incidental charges by individual group members. As was also explained in Chapter 6, sometimes the group charge covers both room and specific meals (or other hotel) amenities. In this case, the group members are given *meal vouchers.* Depending on the agreement between the group and the hotel, unused meal vouchers, called *breakage,* either accrue to the benefit of the hotel, or benefit the group by reducing the group charge. When the group receives the benefit of unused vouchers, then the group folio is only charged the agreed-upon fee as each voucher is used. If the hotel receives the benefit of unused vouchers, then a *voucher income account,* created when the group charge is recorded, is charged with the value of used vouchers. In any event, there is usually some degree of chaos associated with a group check-out as the front desk is briefly very busy (all members of the group seem to come down at the same time to check out), and some tour guests seem never to fully understand the rules and attempt to leave the hotel without paying their incidental charges. These stragglers must be rounded up and brought to the front desk and their accounts cleared. Many hotels devote a separate lobby area for group check-outs due to the confusion and activity which seems to surround a group departure (or a group arrival, for that matter).

In other cases, the agreement may include a fixed overall charge for rooms, but the hotel will bill the group folio for the going rate on specific meals taken at the hotel. In this case, group members sign their meal tickets and the regular value of the meal is charged to the group folio.

Sometimes a hotel will, by agreement with a group or as the result of creating its own package, act as intermediary between the group and other hotels or local restaurants, sightseeing tours, golf courses, tennis courts, and so forth. Honeymoon packages are good examples of this type of sale.

Payment in Advance Check-out

Walk-in transient guests who do not have a credit card or have not been granted extended credit directly by the hotel are required to pay for their room and any purchases at the hotel in advance. Such guests do not enjoy charge privileges in the hotel. In a computerized system the guest would be flagged so that when the various department cashiers query the computer, the no-charge status of the guest is reflected. In a manual or mechanical system each department cashier must call the front office to verify guest charge authorization. If the paid-in-advance guest wishes to make charge purchases in the hotel, an additional advance is usually requested to cover the value of the expected purchases. Of course, in a noncomputerized system it is clumsy, if not impossible, to keep track throughout the hotel of such a guest's remaining available charge balance. Some lower-class hotels and motels actually lock out their guests at check-out time to make sure they pay for the following day's stay.

When advance payment is received the cashier again cannot wait for the night auditor to post the debit to the guest's folio. Both the debit for the charge and the credit for payment are posted by the cashier when payment is received in advance so that a copy of the folio can be given to the guest at the time of payment. This makes it unnecessary for the guest to return to the front office to check out.

Late Charges

Late charges are charges made by a guest that were not included on his or her folio at check-out time. This may have occurred because the guest charged something after an express check-out and then forgot to go to the front desk to pay for it, or perhaps the hotel was slow in posting recent charges to the guest's folio and the guest overlooked the charges when checking out. It could also be due to an intentional effort on the part of the guest to defraud the hotel. If the hotel is constantly late in posting charges to guest folios, something should be done to change the system. This problem is not likely to arise in a computerized system because charges are automatically posted to the guest folios as soon as they are made. A computer system also helps eliminate post–check-out charges by guests, because the hotel department cashiers can use their computer terminals to verify the status of the guest.

At any rate, in a manual or mechanical system, the cashier should be careful to check for any unposted vouchers and should check room movie-use meters and telephone monitoring equipment to make sure all charges have been posted. If time permits, perhaps calls to the restaurant or bar can be made to ask for unforwarded charges. *Late charge vouchers* are often marked "LC" or "AD," for "after departure." As explained earlier, late charges are either added to the credit card voucher in the designated space for late charges, are billed by mail, or are charged to miscellaneous expenses and absorbed by the hotel (if $5 or less).

GUEST STATISTICS AND GUEST HISTORY

The next step in the check-out process is the preservation of the guest's registration card as part of that guest's history with the hotel. Most states require that the registration card be kept on file for one year. A copy of the guest's folio may also be kept on file for a prudent period, and many hotels file several copies, one by folio number, one by guest, and one by credit card company. Guest preferences and peculiarities used to be kept as part of the guest history, but today there is little time for this, and guest loyalty to a particular hotel has greatly diminished due to the amount of competition.

A basic guest history, however, is useful to the sales and marketing department for mailing out future promotional literature. If enough information is obtained from guests, it can also be used to create a profile of the typical hotel guest. At a minimum this file gives the hotel some idea of the geographic distribution of its guests by identifying guest zip codes. Statistics can also be kept by point of origin abroad. The guest history file is, of course, confidential and should not be released to third parties.

Some hotel chains have *frequent traveler discounts*. In these cases, the guest is assigned a number in the system so that his or her frequency of stays with the chain can be easily determined by querying a central computer databank. Usually points, such as 10 points per $1 spent, are assigned to each guest.

Guest Comment Cards and Reservations Assistance

A review of a guest's history may be due when hotels give bonuses to frequent visitors. This can be done by front office personnel as the guest is checking out, and it provides the front office with the opportunity to ask the guest for a comment card on the hotel and its services. A guest comment card is shown in Exhibit 9-2. This feedback enables a hotel to provide better service in the future and to apologize and make restitution for any inadequate service. Whenever appropriate, the guest should be informed what corrective action is being taken by the hotel to prevent a reoccurrence of the unpleasant incident.

The front office clerk should also ask if the guest needs assistance in making reservations at their destination or at the hotel for the return trip. The hotel should put the guest in contact with a hotel reservations clerk if necessary. As explained earlier, gestures such as these leave a positive parting impression with a guest, increasing the likelihood of repeat business.

YOUR COMMENTS ARE APPRECIATED

Dear Guest:

We are delighted to have you with us and hope that you are pleased with our facilities and services.

It is our desire to provide you with the latest hotel conveniences in a courteous and friendly atmosphere. To help us live up to these goals we ask for your kind assistance.

Would you take a few minutes to reply to our questionnaire. Thank you for your cooperation. Please leave this in the room, or at the Management Offices.

Room No. _____ Date _____

Have you stayed here before? _____

What encouraged you to stop here? _____

☐ Travel Agent   ☐ Newspaper Ad
☐ Another Traveler   ☐ Radio Ad
☐ Local Recommendation   ☐ Television Ad
☐ Travel Directory   ☐ Other_____

Did you receive friendly and courteous attention from:

Room Clerk _____   Telephone Operators _____
Cashier _____   Bellman _____
Maids _____   Doorman _____

Comments: _____

_____

Were your accommodations clean and comfortable? _____

If not, what was wrong? _____

_____

How was the food? _____

Was the Restaurant, Coffee Shop, Cocktail Lounge

Clean? _____

If not, what was wrong? _____

_____

Would you stay here again? _____

Remarks: _____

_____
_____

Thank you for this courtesy and please come back soon!

Exhibit 9-2   Guest Comment Card

DISTRIBUTION OF CHECK-OUT INFORMATION

The final step in the check-out process is to notify other hotel departments that a guest has checked out. Housekeeping receives a morning housekeeper's report from the front office manager indicating which rooms are *on-change*. This means the room is being cleaned and should not be resold until the housekeeping department advises that it is ready for resale. If a rapid turnaround is required, then the front office manager will inform the housekeeper by phone. Also, the room must be flagged at the front office room rack as being on-change.

When a manual or mechanical accounting system is in use, other hotel personnel or departments, such as the telephone department, also need to be informed of a guest's departure so that they will not accept any more charges to that room until a new guest arrives. The accounting and collection departments must, of course, be notified since they may need to bill for any unpaid balance. In the case of a computerized system, the computer terminals in each department inform their personnel that a guest is no longer at the hotel. In this case, no special effort need be made to inform these sales departments of a guest's departure.

FORMS OF PAYMENT

As we learned in Chapter 6, guests can settle their bills in various ways. The simplest, but ever-more-infrequent, method is to pay cash. The most common methods of payment are traveler's checks and credit cards. Personal checks are no longer accepted in the vast majority of hotels, but will be discussed here since some hotels do continue to accept them. The more complex and unusual methods of payment involve foreign currencies, travel vouchers, or direct credit from the hotel. Whenever a hotel accepts payment in any other form than cash in local currency, it is incurring an additional risk. For this reason it is imperative that cashiers be knowledgeable concerning the intricacies involved in these other forms of payment, and they should be made aware of how to reduce the hotel's exposure and how to minimize risk when accepting them. The first step in this process is for the registration clerk to request that each guest identify, when they register, the means of payment he or she will use. This gives hotel personnel time to evaluate the validity of the guest's payment medium.

Traveler's Checks

Although safer than personal checks, a cashier must take some minor precautions even with traveler's checks. When they are purchased the checks are signed in the presence of a person from the issuing organization. This signature must be the same as the second signature of the guest when the check is presented in payment or to be cashed. If possible, the cashier should subtly cover the first signature, perhaps offering assistance in holding the check, when the guest countersigns a traveler's check. As an additional precaution some form of identification may be requested from the guest. In the case of American Express Traveler's Checks, they have raised letters, red dots are visible when the check is held up to the light, and moisture applied to the denomination on the back left side will smear the check. Also, all traveler's checks have a dull black magnetic code and the first number on the check is always 8000. The next three numbers identify the specific issuer. For example, 005 indicates American Express and 001 indicates a Bank of America traveler's check. Remember, a traveler's check is not always honored by the issuing bank, and stolen checks will be returned to the hotel. The hotel should verify that the checks are not stolen by calling the issuing bank (just as they verify a credit card).

Credit Cards

There are three types of credit cards, although today the difference between two of them is rapidly disappearing. These three types are (1) bank cards, such as Visa and Mastercard; (2) travel and entertainment cards, such as American Express; and (3) other cards, such as hotel chain cards, gasoline cards, and others.

Most bank card credit slips are almost as good as money as far as the hotel is concerned. If the issuing bank is a local bank, then when credit slips are deposited, the bank transfers funds from its own account to the hotel's account immediately, just as if the hotel had deposited cash. If the issuing bank is not a local bank, it is part of a network of authorization centers set up throughout the country and abroad. Local banks wire these centers, or communicate with them by computer, requesting them to transfer funds immediately so that the hotel's account can be increased by an amount equal to the value of valid credit card slips deposited in the local banks. In both cases, the total credit card commission for all the credit slips deposited is periodically charged to the hotel's bank account and appears as a reduction of the hotel's balance on the bank statement. This commission can vary between 1 percent and 6 percent, depending on the volume of business and the importance of the hotel to its bank.

Travel and entertainment cards do not provide this "instant cash" privilege, although some of them are beginning to provide it for high-volume hotel chains. Also, the commissions charged the hotel by travel and entertainment card companies tend to be higher than those charged by banks on their credit cards. Traditionally, the charge card slip for travel and entertainment cards is mailed to the charge card company, and the company mails back a check for the value of the valid charge slips received minus the appropriate commission. Also, the third type of charge card always operates this way. Thus the hotel benefits more when a guest uses a bank card instead of a non–bank card. The travel and entertainment cards not only charge a higher commission, but also the hotel must wait up to 30 days for payment by the charge card company. Hotel personnel should bear this in mind and try to steer guests toward the use of bank cards. Even if fast payment is negotiated with the travel and entertainment cards, it costs an additional commission to do so.

Another difference between bank cards and travel and entertainment cards is that the former encourage the card holder to use the extended payment privileges offered by the cards. (On such balances, the banks charge higher interest than they would on normal loans.) The travel and entertainment cards require immediate payment of the total balance when it is due. Here, again, the difference is becoming blurred, as some non–bank cards are also offering extended payment options directly, or on a parallel card issued by a subsidiary.

Although credit cards tend to reduce nonpayment of accounts, they require their own precautionary steps. The first precautionary step is to obtain an impression of the guest's credit card at registration. This gives the front desk clerks the opportunity to review lists published weekly by credit card companies that show cards that are stolen and credit card owners who have exceeded their credit limit. If the card is acceptable, then the imprinted credit slip provides the hotel with a means of collecting payment. When a guest's charges are about to exceed the amount automatically accepted by a credit card company, or the hotel's internally set limit, the next step is to call the credit card company, on an 800 number it supplies, to clear additional charges. The company will give the cashier a clearance number that should be written in the designated box of the credit card slip. Theoretically, the signature on the back of a credit card should be com-

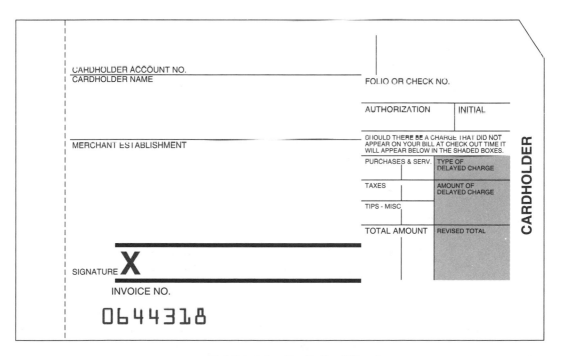

Exhibit 9-3   Credit Card Voucher

pared with the signature on some form of identification, although in practice this is seldom done. Exhibit 9-3 shows a typical credit card voucher slip.

Recently, the credit card terminal has begun to be widely disseminated. The credit card is slipped through a slot in the terminal and the amount of the transaction is key-punched in. The terminal then reads the magnetic strip along the back of the credit card and transmits that number along with the amount of the purchase to a central clearing station. If the charge is approved, a return message instructs the terminal to print the name of the guest and the amount of the charge on the credit card slip. Despite the convenience, not all establishments have such a terminal because of the installation cost.

Special Credit Card Problems

When payment is received via credit card, some additional problems need to be dealt with by the hotel. One problem is whether the hotel should pay the credit card company its commission on tips charged on the credit card, since it is the hotel that is advancing the money to its own employees. This situation is subject to negotiations between the hotel and credit card company. Another problem is whether to require employees to refund tips when there is a credit card *charge back,* that is, when the credit card company refuses to honor the credit slip. Although theoretically correct to do so, it is probably impossible to do so in practice without demoralizing the staff. An employee should not be made to bear the risks of the entrepreneur, unless some employee deficiency is responsible for the charge back. This may sound trivial, but large hotels (and especially hotels associated with casinos) may have hundreds of thousands of dollars in credit card–charged tips each year. Paying a 1 percent commission on $100,000 in tips is $1,000 in lost profits.

Credit Card Procedures

A checklist similar to the one in Exhibit 9-4 should be posted where it is visible to the cashier and other hotel personnel involved with credit card acceptance. The checklist approach is useful not only in catching bad or stolen cards, but also in avoiding charge backs, which are credit slips dishonored by the credit card company because they were improperly charged. These can prove costly to the hotel if it cannot eventually collect from the guest. In addition to displaying a checklist, the hotel should take measures to assure that credit card companies are billed promptly, thereby minimizing the amount of money that the hotel is, in effect, lending to the credit card company interest-free.

Foreign Funds

Although many hotels do not accept payment in foreign funds, the front office cashier should understand the implications of receiving such funds.

- Observe the card for signs of alteration or other indications that it is fake.
- Verify that the card is not on an invalid card list.
- Look at the expiration date embossed on the card to verify that the card has not expired.
- Verify that the amount of the charge does not exceed the maximum amount that the credit card company will automatically approve.
- Make sure the card machine has imprinted all information clearly and correctly on all copies.
- Use the credit card slip corresponding to the credit card being used.
- Compare the signature on the back of the credit card with the guest's signature, either on the registration form or on a sales ticket.
- Do not divide charges higher than the automatic approval limit into two or more charge slips in order to avoid the required verification procedure.
- If the original charge was made on a credit card, a credit slip should be issued to the credit card company instead of giving a cash refund to the guest.

Exhibit 9-4   Credit Card Acceptance Checklist

Foreign funds received by a hotel must eventually be converted into U.S. dollars. This is done by buying dollars from a bank or other foreign money broker. These brokers quote two different rates—the rate at which they will buy a foreign currency and the rate at which they will sell it. The difference between these two rates is their profit. A money broker or bank might offer to buy German marks (DM) at U.S. $0.50 per mark (2 marks per dollar) and might offer to sell them at U.S. $0.55 per mark, for instance. The five cents difference is the broker's, or bank's, profit. When hotels accept foreign currency, they usually accept it at an exchange rate that is somewhat lower than that of a money broker. Thus the hotel can itself make a profit in compensation for the additional trouble of having to convert the foreign currency into U.S. dollars. In the above circumstances, the hotel might accept German marks at U.S. $0.45 per mark. It will then sell them to the broker, or bank, for U.S. $0.50 per German mark and earn a five cent profit per mark on the transaction for its trouble.

Sometimes a hotel's discount will seem unreasonably large, but this may be necessary to cover an additional exchange fee charged by the bank or broker on top of the buying spread. Another eventuality the hotel needs to provide for is the possibility that the value of the foreign currency may fall between the time the hotel accepts it from a guest (buys it) and the time it sells it to the broker. For instance, in the above example, assume the hotel accepted 500 German marks (DM) at U.S. $0.45 per mark and their value dropped before the hotel sold them to the money broker, or bank. Suppose that as a result of the drop in value, the bank would only pay U.S. $0.40 per mark. Then the hotel would have a loss of U.S. $25.00 on the transaction. In order to spread out this loss over many foreign funds transactions, the hotel needs to factor in an additional discount every time it accepts (buys) foreign funds in payment. When it is hotel policy to accept payment in foreign funds, the cashier should be given proper exchange values on a daily basis for all foreign currency accepted by the hotel, since foreign currency values do fluctuate daily. Furthermore, it is extremely important, when foreign currency is accepted in payment, to resell the currency to a bank or money broker as soon as possible in order to avoid the risk of a drop in its value that might generate a currency exchange loss for the hotel.

Let us go through a sample foreign currency transaction. Suppose a guest pays the hotel's bill, amounting to $400, with $200 in U.S. currency and wants to know how many German marks he or she will have to pay to cancel the remaining $200 balance. Assume the hotel's exchange rate is $0.45 per mark. The amount of German marks needed to pay the balance of the bill is calculated by dividing the $200 balance by the exchange value of one mark, that is, U.S. $0.45, as follows:

$$\text{U.S. } \$200 \div 0.45 = \text{DM } 444.44$$

Thus the guest would have to pay an additional DM 444.44 (German marks) to cancel the $200 balance of the bill.

Travel Vouchers

In order to assure some return business from clients, advertising companies, airlines, and travel agencies, hotels and others sometimes pay their suppliers in vouchers that can only be used to pay for services performed by the issuing company. Thus a hotel may pay for $1,000 worth of advertising by issuing vouchers (*due bills*) to the advertising company for equal value. These vouchers entitle the advertising company's personnel to pay for $1,000 worth of services from the hotel by turning in these vouchers. The types of services payable with vouchers may be restricted, for instance, to room charges only and may exclude payment for food at the hotel. Also, the dates and times of services payable by vouchers may be limited to nonpeak dates and times. Finally, due bills may be traded to third parties, or sold to brokers who make a business of buying and selling due bills. This is done in much the same way that foreign currency is traded by banks or money brokers. The due bills can be sold to brokers at less than their face value and the broker can then resell them for more than their purchase price, but still less than their face value. The receipt of payment in the form of due bills has federal and state income tax implications, so a tax professional should be consulted when due bills are accepted in payment. Furthermore, most due bills have expiration dates. If they have not been presented as payment for services before that date, they become worthless. The fact that a guest will pay with a due bill should become evident at registration when the clerk asks the guest to identify his or her payment method.

When a due bill is received in payment, the cashier does not enter it on the cash sheet, but attaches it to the guest folio, after crediting the folio for the amount of the due bill. The night auditor then picks up the due bills on the daily transcript as a credit to the guest General Ledger control account and as a debit to a liability account that was established when the due bills were issued. For instance, if $5,000 worth of due bills were issued in exchange for advertising, then upon their issue, a $5,000 debit to advertising expense and a $5,000 credit to an account entitled "due bills outstanding" is made on the General Ledger. At the expiration date of the due bills, any amount that has still not been used to tender payment is debited to the due bills outstanding account and credited to an unused voucher income or miscellaneous income account.

Personal Checks

Most large hotels no longer accept personal checks because when doing so they incur the following risks:

- The bank on which the check is drawn does not exist.
- The bank exists but the account is no longer open, or never was open.
- The account does not have sufficient funds to cover the check amount.
- The guest is not the person authorized to sign on that account.

Hotels that decide to accept personal checks must, therefore, establish a thorough verification process such as the one listed in Exhibit 9-5. When a guest registers at the hotel and indicates that the method of payment will be cash, the guest should be asked more specifically whether payment will be in currency or by check. This gives the hotel time to verify the guest's home address, telephone number, and workplace in telephone directories or credit services, and to look up the guest's previous history at the hotel before the guest checks out. Such information should be used to reinforce the checklist mentioned above, not as a substitute for it. Hotel personnel should not allow themselves to be intimidated by a guest. An honest guest will have no qualms about subjecting his or her check to any scrutiny the hotel desires and will cooperate with the hotel to expedite the verification process. This verification process should be followed both when guests use a personal check to pay their bill and when they request that a personal check be cashed.

Protection Against Check Cashing Fraud

There are several ways that a hotel can try to protect itself against check cashing fraud. Closed circuit television or conventional photographic cameras can be used to simultaneously record the check casher and check. Signs should be posted indicating the check protection methods employed by the hotel. Or a

- Be especially careful on holidays. Most bad checks are passed then. Beware of guests in a hurry or who ask you to cash checks that can more reasonably be cashed elsewhere.
- Only accept checks for the amount of the bill.
- Don't accept checks that are illegible or appear to be altered.
- Compare the signature and address on the check with that on the registration card.
- If the guest does not sign the check in front of you, ask that the check be endorsed on the back.
- Use a check cashing stamp and fill in all the required information (two forms of identification should be required, one of which should be a driver's license).
- Review all the information on the guest's driver's license and verify that the guest meets the description and that the signature on the check is the same as that on the driver's license. Ask the guest questions concerning some of the information. This may make a bad-check passer nervous.
- Don't accept checks written by a third party with the guest as payee.
- Compare the city the guest registered as being from with the city where the bank is located.
- Notice the number on the check. Checks with low numbers indicate recently opened accounts, and possibly greater risk.
- Compare the numerical amount of the check with the written amount.

Exhibit 9-5   Check-Cashing Checklist

sign can be prominently displayed indicating that passing a bad check is illegal and specifying what the penalties are. Often these signs will deter a novice from passing a bad check. A check stamp detailing the information to be requested of check-paying guests should also be used. The driver's license number is extremely important because a name is insufficient to identify a person for purposes of an arrest.

Check Cashing Verification Services

There are also local and national check cashing services, which may or may not be associated with a bank, to which a hotel may subscribe, such as Telecheck or Telecredit. These services guarantee checks for a fee. The required check information is sent by telephone or by a check verification terminal. If the company agrees to guarantee the check, a guarantee number is transmitted to the hotel and should be written on the face of the check. The hotel is thereby protected in case the check is not honored by the bank. The fact that the hotel subscribes to such a service should be prominently displayed. The bad check writer may not want to be recognized as such on a nationwide, regional, or even local network.

Other Types of Check Losses

Losses due to the acceptance of checks may result for reasons other than that the check is uncollectable. A check that is being held may be misplaced. If the check is made out to cash or left blank, whoever finds the check can cash it. To avoid this eventuality the check stamp should indicate that they are for deposit only to the hotel's account, and the stamp should be applied immediately upon receiving the check, thereby rendering it nonnegotiable by anyone else.

THE ACCOUNTS RECEIVABLE COLLECTION PROCESS

Most businesses have two types of sales—cash and credit. The hotel industry actually has three types of sales—cash, guest credit (credit extended during a guest's stay), and city ledger credit (credit granted to guests after they check out, or to nonguest patrons of the hotel). The usual procedure is to grant credit to guests up to the hotel's credit limit, the credit card company's credit limit, or until unusually large charges appear on an account. Folios approaching these limits are detected by the front office manager upon reviewing the night auditor's credit limit or high balance report (see Chapter 7).

Guest Ledger Credit

The collection process on guest ledger credit sales actually begins when a guest either makes a reservation at the hotel or walks in to the hotel. When a guest makes a confirmed reservation, and it is accompanied by a personal check, the home, business address, and telephone numbers may be verified and the guest's history at the hotel may be reviewed. Also the hotel has the opportunity to verify the existence of the bank, to determine whether or not the check is good, or to deposit the check. If a credit card number is given, then that may be verified. Because of the extra time available to study them, guests who make advance reservations are less of a credit risk than walk-in guests or guests who make reservations with very short notice.

In the case of the walk-in guest, the hotel does not have the time to perform the type of review described above. The registration cards of walk-in guests should be reviewed by the hotel credit manager before being attached to the guest's folio. In the absence of more concrete information, the guest's appearance and the manner in which the guest behaves and responds to simple questions posed at registration may become important indicators of the guest's credit-worthiness. Nevertheless, these factors are not important if the hotel only accepts payment by credit card, traveler's check, or cash-in-advance, as almost all large hotels do today.

Guests should be informed clearly what the hotel's billing policy is. Billing, of course, is a delicate matter and personnel should be trained to do it tactfully, explaining the hotel's position and why it needs to be reimbursed for its services on a timely basis. Adequate personnel training is extremely important because uncollected bills increase a hotel's need for borrowed or invested capital and because costly legal complications may arise if the hotel behaves too aggressively when attempting to collect payment.

City Ledger Credit

As explained in Chapter 6, "Accounting for the Guest's Stay," the city ledger is used to maintain a detailed record of the hotel's accounts receivable for patrons of the hotel who are not currently guests at the hotel. It also includes folios for the various credit card companies and for entertainers who are staying at the hotel. A more complete list of city ledger categories is presented below, segregated into accounts that are current in their payments and those that are past-due. The past-due category of accounts constitutes the city ledger:

CURRENT ACCOUNTS

1. Patrons who enjoy extended credit granted directly by the hotel (house credit)
2. Credit card companies
3. Guaranteed reservations (when check is deposited)
4. House accounts (entertainment and promotional accounts)

PAST-DUE ACCOUNTS (DELINQUENT LEDGER SECTION)

1. Guests who left without paying late charges
2. Delinquent accounts (bad checks and excessively slow payers)

Not all of the above categories represent money owed the hotel. For example, guaranteed reservations folios have credit balances in them, representing the check amount mailed in to the hotel to reserve a room.

To keep past-due accounts to a minimum, the hotel should have established operating procedures that tend to assure that the hotel will receive timely payment for its services. For example, to minimize late charges, the hotel should have a good communications system between the various sales-generating departments and the front office, so that charges are transmitted to the front office as quickly as they are made. Of course an on-line, point-of-sale computerized accounting system is the ideal in this regard.

For those guests who enjoy house credit, proper credit-granting procedures should be established and then proper collection procedures should be employed to follow up on the account. This helps assure that the account will be paid, and on time. A checklist providing good procedures to incorporate into hotel policy in order to facilitate the collection of both guest ledger and city ledger accounts appears in Exhibit 9-6.

Credit-Granting Policies

The first step to be taken before credit sales are accepted is to establish a credit-granting policy. The hotel must be prepared to perform a thorough check of the patron's credit history and payment ability. The hotel should

- Properly identify the guest and learn the method of payment when a guest checks in to the hotel.
- Establish a rapid and efficient communication system to transmit sales voucher information as soon as possible after the sale is made to the front office in order to minimize late charges.
- Establish an efficient system for settling disputes quickly.
- Monitor the guest's folio balance continually.
- Establish credit-granting policies and monitor their adequacy.
- Establish collection policies for smaller accounts.
- Establish collection policies for larger accounts.
- Engage the services of a good collection service, collection agency, and lawyer.

Exhibit 9-6   Summary of Collection Process

have a list of the minimum financial characteristics that anyone who is going to receive house credit must have. These may include a minimum income level, previous credit history, amount of current credit outstanding, profitability of this particular type of account, and other factors. Much of this information is available from credit bureaus, such as TRW, for a fee. Alternatively, the information can be generated internally by reviewing a guest's history. When house credit is established, an upper credit limit should be specified so that the client will know beforehand how much credit he or she enjoys at the hotel, thus minimizing future friction and/or embarrassment. Having a credit-granting policy keeps the hotel's credit manager from spontaneously extending credit to potentially unreliable credit risks out of enthusiasm to increase sales. Also, with regard to credit card charges, the hotel should have a house maximum that it will accept prior to obtaining further telephone approval from the credit card company or a cash payment from the guest.

The credit department should review the hotel's selectivity in this regard to keep it from being either too strict or too lax. If it is too strict, then potentially collectible sales will not be made and credit business will go elsewhere, and if it is too lax too many uncollectible sales will be generated. To determine whether the hotel is too lax in granting credit, an *accounts receivable aging schedule* should be prepared. This is a listing of all outstanding invoices in different columns classified according to the number of days they have been outstanding. A typical sample accounts receivable aging schedule is presented in Exhibit 9-7. This aging schedule indicates that most accounts are paid on time. Few accounts reach 90 days. But too high a percentage may be reaching the "over 120 days past due" column, and thus potentially becoming uncollectible. Whether or not this uncollectible percentage is too high depends on the hotel's sales. An uncollectible percentage in excess of 1 percent of room sales is certainly too high, and indicates that perhaps credit-granting policies or collection policies, or both, are too lax. A periodic review, at least monthly, of the accounts receivable aging schedule should be carried out to keep tabs

EXHIBIT 9-7 ACCOUNTS RECEIVABLE AGING SCHEDULE AT 12/31/99

Guest	Invoice Date	Invoice Number	Total	Current	31–60 Days	61–90 Days	91–120 Days	Over 120 Days
Jon Arsone	8/3/99	103456	792					792
Cynthia Klok	8/9/99	103531	1237					1,237
William Shaker	8/18/99	104052	947					947
Karl Numm	10/20/99	105873	414				414	
Thomas Monn	10/30/99	106624	736				736	
Gerald Font	11/4/99	106839	823			823		
Mary Marlos	11/12/99	107723	904			904		
Philip McGlocken	11/25/99	107891	437			437		
Sylvia Worren	12/02/99	108345	1576	1,576				
Ronald Alter	12/13/99	108456	2567	2,567				
Marly Marlos	12/20/99	108775	832	832				
Totals			11,265	4,975	2,164	1,150	0	2,976

on both the strictness of the hotel's credit-granting policies and the effectiveness of its collection policies.

Collection Policies

Even good credit risks can become slow payers if proper follow-up collection procedures are not practiced. Once reliable credit recipients have been established and credit has been extended, the hotel must establish a consistently applied and firm collection policy. The two cornerstones of a good collection policy are (1) to establish a quick, efficient, and fair procedure for clearing up disputed items, preferably before the guest leaves the hotel; and (2) to establish a quick, repetitive, and gradually more insistent collection process.

Asking the guest for feedback before departure helps identify any potential contested items. These can be settled personally by the front office manager much more rapidly and with less friction than can be done later by mail. In general, it is better to give a guest the benefit of the doubt on a small item than to risk a delay in the payment of the total bill while discussions over this small item take place by mail. Front desk employees should be trained to identify such items and, rather than put off the guest, they should immediately call the front office manager or credit manager. The front office manager or credit manager should, in turn, be given the authority to settle such matters quickly and at their own discretion.

As far as the collection process is concerned, it should vary according to the size of the debt. Who executes this collection process and how it is done are the two factors in question here. It is expensive to dedicate hotel personnel to collect accounts, and it costs as much to put individual collection effort into smaller accounts as it does to collect accounts of hundreds of dollars. Some cut-off limit, perhaps near the $200 mark, should therefore be established to separate those accounts that will be given personal attention if they are still uncollected after a predetermined period of time from those accounts that will be collected via correspondence throughout the entire collection process.

For all accounts the first billing should go out immediately after a guest departs from the hotel. In the case of nonguest patrons, the first billing should take place no later than 30 days after the sale. This initial billing should be followed up by periodic billings at 30-day intervals, which may be shortened to 15-day intervals if collection is not effected by the second billing cycle. The collection notices should also become progressively more insistent. This may be done by simple statements indicating the account is overdue or that this is the second or third request; or it may include statements to the effect that the hotel is aware of the client's desire to pay and cannot understand why payment has not been received.

If these progressively insistent form letters don't produce results, then the smaller accounts should be passed to a third party collection service, whose collection process is still under the control of the hotel and is paid on a fee basis. Bringing a third party into action often shames a reluctant debtor into meeting his or her obligations. Finally, those accounts still pending after this effort should be handed over to a collection agency that is remunerated on a percentage-of-collections basis. This latter step, of course, should be used only as a last resort since collection agencies often take cases to court, which may foster a negative image of the hotel.

Larger accounts still uncollected after two or three months should be given the personal attention of hotel personnel. If a group or convention is involved, then perhaps the marketing department should be brought in for the initial collection effort. Care should be taken, however, to disengage the marketing department and to transfer the collection process to the credit department if friction begins to develop, since this may work to the detriment of the marketing department when bidding for future sales from that client. If the hotel's personnel is unsuccessful, then a third party collection service and/or a collection agency should be brought into play with these accounts also. Legal action should always be taken reluctantly and with great caution. Often the costs of the action and the potential recovery amount do not justify the negative image such action may generate.

Legal Implications of the Collection Process

The hotel must always take into account the impact of the various federal and state laws when designing its credit-granting and collection processes. The first law to be considered affects a hotel's credit-granting policies. The Equal Credit Opportunity Act requires that there be no discrimination in granting credit based on sex, race, color, national origin, religion, or age. The hotel's collection policies are affected by libel laws, which prohibit any kind of action on the part of the hotel that might intentionally or otherwise publicize a client's payment delinquency and thereby damage the client's reputation. Collection notices or messages written on the outside of the collection envelope are in violation of postal laws.

The second piece of legislation to be considered is the truth-in-lending act. This act requires that the hotel inform debtors of its established procedures for settling disputes. It also establishes the time frame for following these steps and what to do if no settlement is reached. Any state and local laws that may exist must be taken into account as well. From the above, it is evident that the services of an attorney are essential when designing credit-granting and collection policies.

Bad Debt Expense

Finally, when all else fails, a delinquent account must be written off. Since accounts rarely become uncollectible in the same period that the sale is made, the first step before writing off an account receivable is to create a *contra-asset account*, called the *allowance for uncollectible accounts*, in the same accounting period that the sale is made. A credit is made to this account on the balance sheet, offset by an equal debit to a *bad debt expense account* on the income statement based on estimates of future uncollectible amounts. Thus the expense of uncollectibility is recorded on the income statement during the same period that the sale is made, without having to identify the actual amount that will eventually become uncollectible.

The amount in the balance sheet contra-asset account (the allowance for uncollectible accounts) can be calculated in two ways: (1) the percentage-of-sales method and (2) the aging-schedule method. The percentage-of-sales method is the simpler of the two methods and should be used to calculate the amount of bad debt expense for less formal financial statements, such as interim financial statements. It is applied by multiplying the current period's sales by an uncollectibility percentage derived from previous experience. If three-quarters of 1 percent of accounts receivable have proven uncollectible on average over the previous three years, for instance, then the current period's sales are multiplied by three-quarters of 1 percent to arrive at the amount of bad debt expense to debit on the income statement. There is of course an equal offsetting credit to the contra-asset (allowance for uncollectible accounts) account on the balance sheet.

The aging-schedule method is more accurate and should be used for more formal and definitive financial statements, such as year-end statements. It differs from the percentage-of-sales method in its objective. Where the percentage-of-sales method determines the amount of bad debt expense to include on the income statement and enters the offsetting balance sheet entry by default, the aging-schedule method calculates the balance that should be in the contra-asset (allowance for uncollectible accounts) account and enters the offsetting income statement debit to the bad debt expense account by default. The aging-schedule method differs from the percentage-of-sales method in another respect. The percentage-of-sales method does not take into account the existing balance in the contra-asset (allowance for uncollectible accounts) account. The aging-schedule method does take this balance into consideration. Thus, if the aging-schedule indicates that the balance in the contra-asset account should be $500 and the existing balance in the account is $600, then instead of increasing this balance it must be reduced down to $500. This is done by debiting the account contra-asset account for $100 and crediting the bad debt expense account (instead of debiting it) on the income statement for an equal amount. In Exhibit 9-8, the reader can see an example of how this calculation is made, based on the aging-schedule presented in Exhibit 9-7.

EXHIBIT 9-8 CALCULATING THE CORRECT BALANCE IN THE CONTRA-ASSET
ACCOUNT "ALLOWANCE FOR UNCOLLECTIBLE ACCOUNTS"

		Assumptions			

A. Previous two years' collection experience (amounts represent percent of accounts that were uncollectible)

	Current	31–60 Days	61–90 Days	91—120 Days	Over 120 Days
1997	1%	3%	8%	16%	30%
1998	2%	4%	9%	17%	25%

B. Amounts outstanding at 12/31/99 per Exhibit 9-7 grouped by age

	Current	31–60 Days	61–90 Days	91–120 Days	Over 120 Days
Total	$4,975	$2,164	$1,150	-0-	$2,976

C. The current balance in the "allowance for uncollectible accounts" is = $900

		Calculations			

Step 1—Calculate average uncollectible percentage for previous two years

	Current	31—60 Days	61–90 Days	91–120 Days	Over 120 Days
1997	1%	3%	8%	16%	30%
1998	2%	4%	9%	17%	25%
Average	1.5%	3.5%	8.5%	16.5%	27.5%

Step 2—Apply average uncollectible percent to corresponding balances

$4,975	$2,164	$1,150	-0-	$2.976
× 1.5%	× 3.5%	× 8.5%	× 16.5%	× 27.5%

Amounts estimated to be uncollectible

$74.63	$75.74	$97.75	-0-	$818.40

Step 3—Total the amounts estimated to be uncollectible

$74.63 + $75.74 + $97.95 + $0 + $818.40 = $1,066.52

Step 4—Increase the balance of the "allowance for uncollectible accounts" from the current balance of $600 to the required balance of $1,066.52 by making the following journal entry:

	DR	CR
Bad Debt Expense	$466.52	
Allowance for uncollectible accounts		$466.52

Once the contra-asset account has been established, then the specific accounts that eventually prove to be uncollectible in subsequent accounting periods can be written off against this "estimated" contra-asset account. The entry is a debit to the contra-asset account and a credit to the appropriate accounts receivable General Ledger control account. The corresponding folio card is also marked as uncollectible and is stored as part of the guest's history at the hotel.

QUESTIONS AND PROBLEMS

Discussion Questions

1. What are the three objectives of the check-out process?
2. How can a hotel create a positive lasting impression on a departing guest?
3. Why is a guest history important?
4. Who is responsible for checking-out a guest?
5. What are the six types of check-out procedure?
6. How can late charges be avoided and how can they be collected?
7. What are the six forms of payment that guests can request to use when settling their account at a hotel?
8. What is a *due bill* or *travel voucher*?
9. In addition to cash sales, how many types of credit sales does a hotel make?
10. What are the two cornerstones of a good collection policy?
11. What are the two methods of determining the balance in the contra-asset account (allowance for uncollectible accounts)?

Problems

1. From the following data prepare an accounts receivable aging schedule as of December 31, 1999. Divide all accounts into five columns as follows: (1) current, (2) 31–60 days, (3) 61–90 days, (4) 91–120 days, and (5) over 120 days. Accounts are considered to be current until 30 days after the invoice date. Be sure to total all columns.

	Guest	Invoice No.	Invoice Date	Amount
(a)	John Traveler	13578	12/13/99	$567
(b)	Mary Star	13200	11/12/99	$1,231
(c)	Paul Plodder	12984	10/20/99	$678
(d)	John Traveler	13001	10/30/99	$542
(e)	Wally Wiley	12503	9/11/99	$666
(f)	Ziegmund Pell	12372	8/3/99	$999
(g)	Ronald Runn	12888	9/28/99	$715
(h)	Martha Madd	13339	11/25/99	$2,385
(i)	Bill Plunge	13489	12/02/99	$1,576
(j)	Simon Peters	13775	12/20/99	$832

2. From the following accounts receivable aging schedule and related information, calculate the entry to record a bad debt expense, using the following methods:
   (a) The percentage-of-sales method
   (b) The accounts receivable aging-schedule method

Sales for the previous three years were as follows:

    1997 $45,678
    1998 $51,026
    1999 $74,269

The balance in the contra-asset (allowance for uncollectible accounts) account is $200 on December 31, 1999, before adjustment.

ACCOUNTS RECEIVABLE AGING SCHEDULE AT 12/31/99

Guest	Invoice Date	Total	Current	31–60 Days	61–90 Days	91–120 Days	Over 120 Days
Paul Pell	8/13/99	421					421
Wyandote Stot	8/24/99	333					333
James Ronn	9/22/99	1032				1,032	
Willa Kathor	10/13/99	853			853		
Rilly Smart	10/26/99	681			681		
Mary Sharp	11/04/99	736		736			
Sam Sole	11/25/99	1482		1,482			
Karla Knot	12/12/99	1576	1,576				
Felicia Peters	12/19/99	567	567				
Willa Kathor	12/24/99	832	832				
Totals		8,513	2,975	2,218	1,534	1,032	754
Uncollectible %							
1999			0.80%	1.60%	3.00%	5.00%	12.00%
1998			1.00%	2.50%	3.70%	6.00%	10.00%
Two Year Average			0.90%	2.05%	3.35%	5.50%	11.00%

3. Marie Ledance is checking out of the Restwell Hotel and her bill amounts to $632. She is from France and wishes to pay her bill with French francs (FF). Foreign exchange brokers are offering to buy French francs at $1.50. The hotel charges guests a 5 percent discount for the extra work involved in converting foreign currency into U.S. dollars and an additional 5 percent discount to cover the risk of unfavorable exchange rate fluctuations that may occur before the hotel converts the foreign exchange into U.S. dollars. Based on the above data, how many French francs will Marie Ledance have to pay to settle her bill at the hotel?

CHAPTER 10

Safety and Security of Guests and Employees

CHAPTER OBJECTIVES

After reading this chapter you will understand:

- What special laws apply to the hotel industry.
- How to make guests secure from harm.
- Basic ways to protect the hotel property from loss or damage.

INTRODUCTION

The safety and security of guests and employees of hotels has never received more attention than in the past ten years. There are a variety of reasons for this. For one thing, today's guest is more conscious of the dangers around him or her. Through the media, crime, fires, and earthquakes are brought to the attention of people in this country on a daily basis. In fact, whenever a fire takes place in a hotel, it becomes worldwide news. The lodging industry has responded to the increased attention to hotel safety by placing a tremendous amount of energy into making hotels safe for their guests and employees and into making the public aware of the added security and safety measures that are being taken. New hotels, with their sophisticated fire and crime detection and prevention systems, may be among the safest places of all facilities to occupy. Of course, this safety level does not allow any reduction in the attention this area should receive. Our society seems to be becoming more violent, and this increased violence must be met aggressively. It is the responsibility of all employees to keep the security of the guest foremost in their minds at all times. The focus of this chapter is to cover all of the major areas of safety and security in a hotel. As always is the case when a legal issue is involved, the hotel should check with its attorney before proceeding with the implementation of its safety plan.

LEGAL ASPECTS

Every hotel has the moral obligation to provide a safe place for employees to work and guests to stay. Beyond this duty, hotels are obliged by law to provide reasonable care so that guests of the hotel will not become injured. The following section will deal with those areas of the hotel where injury can occur. More and more hotels are satisfying the health-oriented guest by offering recreational and exercise facilities. In these areas, it is up to the hotel to provide reasonable care for the guests' safety. Management must always keep in mind that hotels can be held responsible for actions taken by their employees. This fact places a strong demand for proper hiring, reference checking, and training of guest-contact employees. Such harmful actions by employees may range from acts of physical violence taken out on guests to something as simple as the giving out of the wrong room key. The entire range, of course, can result in a multitude of problems. Hotels may also be held liable for injuries to guests by another guest if reasonable care could have prevented the injury. Such incidents as guests being attacked in the hallway or lounge, or even the parking lot of the hotel, may involve third parties and may result in a hotel being sued for damages. Employees should be cautioned about lax security. Keeping that door propped open to the outside or not watching the arrival and departure of people through the lobby are just two breaches of security that can be averted if management emphasizes the role security plays in overall guest satisfaction. If a guest complains that he or she shouldn't be kept waiting at the front desk when they ask for a key to their room, the clerk should politely remind the guest that it is to the guest's benefit that the hotel assures itself that the person receiving the key is in fact authorized to have a key to the room. Little things like this add to the overall feeling on the guest's part that he or she is secure in the hotel.

Hotels also have a responsibility to guests for the security of their property, although many states have adopted statutes that limit the hotel's liabil-

ity. Each hotel must base its policies on the laws of the state, carefully re-
searched by the hotel, in which the hotel is located. Many states require that
the statutes be posted either in the lobby, in the guest room, or in both
places.

Some guests will leave their property behind when they check out. When
this occurs, the hotel should hold it for the time specified by state law. Then, it
may be disposed of in the established fashion by law. Exhibit 10-1 contains parts
of Chapter 509, Public Lodging and Public Food Service Establishments for the
State of Florida, that pertain specifically to the lodging area:

Exhibit 10-1   Florida Statutes Chapter 509 Public Lodging and Public Food
Service Establishments Contents

509.101 Establishment rules; maintenance of guest register.—

(1)   Any operator of a public lodging establishment or a public food service establishment may establish reasonable rules and regulations for the management of the establishment and its guests and employees; and each guest or employee staying,
sojourning, eating, or employed in the establishment shall conform to and abide by
such rules and regulations so long as he shall remain in or at the establishment. Such
rules and regulations shall be deemed to be a special contract between the operator
and each guest or employee using the facilities of or at any public lodging establishment or public food service establishment. Such rules and regulations shall control
the liabilities, responsibilities, and obligations of all parties. Any rules or regulations
established pursuant to this section shall be printed in the English language and
posted, together with a copy of ss. 509.111, 509.151, and 509.161, in the office, hall, or
lobby or another prominent place of such public lodging establishment or public food
service establishment.

(2)   It is the duty of each operator of a public lodging establishment to maintain at all times a
register, signed by or for guests who occupy rental units within the establishment,
showing the dates upon which the rental units were occupied by such guests and the
rates charged for their occupancy. This register shall be available for inspection by the
division at any time. Operators need not make available registers which are more than 2
years old.

509.111 Liability for property of guests.—

(1)   The operator of a public lodging establishment is under no obligation to accept for
safekeeping any moneys, securities, jewelry, or precious stones of any kind belonging to any guest, and, if such are accepted for safekeeping, he shall not be liable for
the loss thereof unless such loss was the proximate result of fault or negligence of the
operator. However, the liability of the operator shall be limited to $1,000 for such loss,
if the public lodging establishment gave a receipt for the property (stating the value)
on a form which stated, in type large enough to be clearly noticeable, that the public
lodging establishment was not liable for any loss exceeding $1,000 and was only
liable for that amount if the loss was the proximate result of fault or negligence of the
operator.

(2)   The operator of a public lodging establishment shall not be liable or responsible to
any guest for the loss of wearing apparel, goods, or other property, except as pro-

vided in subsection (1), unless such loss occurred as the proximate result of fault or negligence of such operator, and, in case of fault or negligence, he shall not be liable for a greater sum than $500, unless the guest, prior to the loss or damage, files with the operator an inventory of his effects and the value thereof and the operator is given the opportunity to inspect such effects and check them against such inventory. The operator of a public lodging establishment shall not be liable or responsible to any guest for the loss of effects listed in such inventory in a total amount exceeding $1,000.

509.141 Refusal of admission and ejection of undesirable guests; notice; procedure; penalties for refusal to leave.—

(1)   The operator of any public lodging establishment or public food service establishment may remove or cause to be removed from such establishment, in the manner hereinafter provided, any guest of the public food service establishment or any transient guest of the public lodging establishment who, while on the premises of the establishment, is intoxicated, immoral, profane, lewd, or brawling; who indulges in any language or conduct which disturbs the peace and comfort of other guests or which injures the reputation, dignity, or standing of the establishment; who, in the case of a public lodging establishment, fails to make payment of rent at the agreed-upon rental rate by the agreed upon check-out time or who, in the case of a public food service establishment, fails to make payment for food, beverages, or services; or who, in the opinion of the operator, is a person the continued entertainment of whom would be detrimental to such establishment. The admission to, or the removal from, such establishment shall not be based upon race, creed, color, sex, physical disability, or national origin.

(2)   The operator of any public lodging establishment or public food service establishment shall notify such guest that the establishment no longer desires to entertain him and shall request that such guest immediately depart from the establishment. Such notice may be given orally or in writing. If the notice is in writing, it shall be as follows:

   "You are hereby notified that this establishment no longer desires to entertain you as its guest, and you are requested to leave at once. To remain after receipt of this notice is a misdemeanor under the laws of this state."

   If such guest has paid in advance, the establishment shall, at the time such notice is given, tender to such guest the unused portion of the advance payment.

(3)   Any guest who remains or attempts to remain in any such establishment after being requested to leave is guilty of a misdemeanor of the second degree, punishable as provided in s. 775.082, s. 775.083, or s. 775.084.

(4)   If any person is illegally on the premises of any public lodging establishment or public food service establishment, the operator of such establishment may call upon any law enforcement officer of this state for assistance. It is the duty of such law enforcement officer, upon the request of such operator, to place under arrest and take into custody for violation of this section any guest who violates subsection (3) in the presence of the officer. If a warrant has been issued by the proper judicial officer for the arrest of any violator of subsection (3), the officer shall serve the warrant, arrest the person, and take him into custody. Upon arrest, with or without warrant, the guest will be deemed to have given up any right to occupancy or to have abandoned his right of occupancy of said premises, and the operator of the establishment may then make such premises available to other guests. However, the operator of the establishment shall employ all reasonable and proper means adequately to care for

any personal property which may be left on the premises by such guest and shall refund any unused portion of moneys paid by such guest for the occupancy of such premises.

EMERGENCY PROCEDURES

The focus of this section is some of the preventive measures that can be instituted in an attempt to alleviate dangerous occurrences, such as fire. More important, it focuses on what must be done when emergencies happen.

Fire Prevention

There are three types of fires that are common to the hotel industry. The Type A fire is one that involves wood, cloth, paper rubbish, and plastic. Type B fires start when paint, oil, gasoline, or other flammable liquids ignite. Type C is an electrical fire found with electrical equipment, motors, and control panels. Exhibit 10-2 lists the type of fire and which fire extinguisher should be used to put it out. Three things needed to start a fire are heat, fuel, and oxygen.

One of the surest ways of preventing fires is to be aware of any coexistence of these causes. Especially important are cigarettes and where they are placed by guests and employees. This applies to both public areas and guestrooms. Employees should know where the fire extinguishers are located for the area they are working in. Additionally, employees should know the closest exit to their stations and their particular responsibility in the event of a fire.

Fire Emergency Plan

Prior to the 1980s, there was not a real concern in the hotel business about fire safety. In the early 1980s there were several hotel fires that took many lives. After these fires, the industry focused its attention on making hotels as safe a place as any could be from the threat of fire. One of the major achievements is the adoption of a fire emergency plan that indicates exactly what should happen in the event of a fire.

The following information should be contained in almost any fire plan. When a fire is found, the person finding it should pull the fire alarm and call the hotel operator to report the location of the fire. The hotel operator will call the fire department, the employees in the hotel's fire brigade, the general manager, and any others as identified by the manager. A fire brigade made up of hotel employees should try to put out or contain the fire if possible. During this time, the switchboard operator will stay in touch with the manager and follow his or her orders. The hotel fire brigade will assist in evacuating guests if so instructed by the manager on duty or by the fire department.

EXHIBIT 10-2   FIRE EXTINGUISHER TYPES

Ingredient	Type - A	Type - B	Type - C
Soda Acid	X		
Foam	X	X	
Water (Pump tank, cartridge, pressurized)	X		
Loaded Stream	X	X	
Dry Chemical		X	X
Dry Chemical (Purple "K")		X	X
Dry Chemical (A,B,C-Triple)	X	X	X
Dry Chemical (Foam Compatible)		X	X
Vaporized Liquid		X	X
Carbon Dioxide		X	X
Halon	X	X	X

The master keys for the hotel should be obtained by the manager on duty and be available for use by the fire department. The manager on duty will station herself or himself at the command center, which is usually at the front desk close to the switchboard. In this location, the MOD will be able to communicate with both the fire department and hotel employees. Bell staff can be assigned to the task of bringing the elevators down to the lobby and shutting them down. These employees will be able to direct the fire department into the hotel and to the fire floor. The security department will coordinate with the police, keeping unauthorized people out of the fire area, and they will prepare for a follow-up investigation of the incident. Employees from the housekeeping department should remove all carts and material from the guest room hallways. If needed, housekeeping should remain on the floors to assist guests in evacuating the hotel. Food and beverage outlets will wait until the manager on duty informs them to close down. When possible, they will prepare to supply guests and employees with refreshments.

The evacuation of a hotel is cause for concern on the part of all involved. Although the main objective is to put out the fire, it is the smoke from the fire that claims many lives. Thus, when an evacuation is called for, the goal is to get all people out as quickly and safely as possible. Guest rooms should contain, on the back of the door inside the room, a card that shows a floor plan for the floor on which that room is located and all of the exits, with the exit closest to that room prominently indicated.

Instructions for the guest in case of a fire should also be included. The important points about which the guests must be informed are as follows: First, the guest should be told not to open the door until he or she has felt it to see if it is hot. If the door is hot, the fire may be very close by. In such an event, the door should not be opened or it should be opened very slowly, with the guest being prepared to close it quickly if need be. Second, when trapped in the room, the guest should call the front desk to notify the hotel personnel of the guest's location. Third, the bathtub should be filled with water and wet towels placed around the door to keep smoke out. The guest must be instructed, also, never to open the windows to the room unless necessary to get air to breathe. When it is possible to leave the room, the guest or employee should make his or her way to the closest stairway, making sure that the door is not going to lock behind him or her. If it appears that the latch will lock, it must be unlocked or the door must be left slightly ajar. This is to prevent the person from being trapped in a smoke-filled stairway. If smoke is encountered while the person is descending the stairway, he or she should turn around and go back up, never attempting to go through the smoke. These basic rules can be used by guests and employees to save lives during a fire. All hotels should develop their own fire emergency plan and have it approved by their local fire department before putting it into use.

Emergency Medical Procedures

Medical emergencies will occur in the hotel at one time or another. It is important that employees be prepared to act quickly and responsibly. Emergencies may consist of many problems, such as a cut, fall, or heart attack. The important consideration employees should remember is not to take any chances. When in doubt, they should consider all situations an emergency. It is always easier to live down the ridicule of others for jumping too fast than it is to live with a death that could have been prevented if fast action had been taken.

When a guest calls the operator with an emergency, the operator should dial the local emergency operator, which in many areas of the country is the number 9-1-1. The operator must remain calm and give full information about and the location of the emergency in the hotel. After this, the operator should send the hotel's first aid team to the location to supply whatever first aid is needed until the emergency medical personnel arrive. The operator should notify the bell staff of the location of the emergency. At that point, the bell staff will bring down an elevator and hold it in the lobby until the emergency medical personnel arrive. They will then escort the crew to the location of the emergency. Employees should be informed never to make any comments regarding the incident, but instead, refer them to management.

The person waiting with the victim should not attempt to move the person. Hotels should have employees on staff who are trained in general first aid. Some employee must have training in specific first aid in helping a choking victim, in artificial respiration, and in CPR. With an increased concern for guest service in the industry, it would be nice if hotels were to follow through on all levels of safety and security for guests, with first aid training being one of the first priorities.

If an employee comes upon a guest who appears to be expired, or another guest reports this situation, the employee should not assume this to be true. Since neither an employee nor a manager is a doctor, the only course of action to take is to call the operator to summon the emergency medical service.

Bomb Threat Procedure

Any time the hotel receives a call threatening that there is a bomb in the hotel, or if something is found that looks like a bomb, all involved must react as if this is true. When a call comes in with the threat, the following must be ascertained: Where is the bomb located? What time is the bomb set to go off? What does the bomb look like or what is it inside of? What is it made of? What is the caller's motive? The person receiving the call should immediately call the hotel operator, who will call the police and will act as the command center for this emergency. The police will advise what should be done next.

Armed Robbery

Employees confronted by an armed robber must try to remain calm. The most important thing to remember is that whatever the robber wants can be replaced by the hotel, and that human lives must be protected and must receive priority over material objects. Employees must be trained never to resist the robber, for this could result in injury or death for the employee and guests in the area. As soon as the robber has left, the switchboard should be called. The switchboard operator will then notify the police at once. When the police arrive, employees should try to give as much information about the incident and robber as possible.

Hotel Evacuation Plan

When the hotel needs to be evacuated, the manager on duty will order the fire alarm to be set off. Any communication system of a public address nature will be used to announce the procedure to the guests. Many newer hotels have an emergency communication system that acts like a public address system in each guest room. Any announcement of this kind should tell guests to remain calm and to leave the hotel at once using the stairs—not the elevators. They should then be instructed to assemble outside the hotel in a predetermined location. The location chosen should be out of the way of any emergency vehicles that will be arriving. Hotel personnel should be stationed along the way to route the guests through the hotel and out.

Front office employees should split up the hotel floor by floor and start calling each room that is occupied to confirm the evacuation. Rooms that have handicapped guests will be turned over to special emergency crews at the hotel for evacuation assistance. After all rooms are called, the ones that are not contacted will be given to the emergency crew to check and handle if necessary.

Power Failures

During a power failure, there are many issues to be dealt with. Some of these are loss of heat, loss of air conditioning, loss of telephone, loss of lighting, and safety and security. Hotels should have battery-powered emergency lighting in public areas and guest room hallways to enable movement within the hotel for guests and employees. The best situation is to have an emergency generator that will provide power to locations as needed. Care must be exercised in the distribution of candles for guest room lighting. If candles are given out, proper holders should be included so burning candles will not fall over, presenting a fire hazard. Management has to provide for increased security during these power failures. Personnel should patrol the hotel inside and out constantly. No area of the hotel should be left uncovered at these times.

Locking Systems

Another important consideration in hotel security is that of the systems and controls used to protect access to guest rooms and other areas of the hotel that need to be secured. The lodging industry has come a long way from the early inns that did not even have a locking system on the guest rooms. There has been an increased concern for better locking systems since the court case involving singer Connie Francis in the early 1970s. Ms. Francis was the guest at a hotel, and the room she was in did not have an adequate locking system. This situation allowed a rapist entry into her room to perpetrate his crime. The court awarded her 2.5 million dollars. Cases like this one can be prevented with the selection and maintenance of appropriate locking systems.

History of Guest Room Locks

The following list shows the development of locking systems and security systems in hotels:

1800s   Pin tumbler cylinder development.

1920s   Key in knob lock invented.

1950s   Removable core lock is the first significant advancement in hotel security because the cores could be rotated from room to room, thereby easily changing locks to provide increased security.

1980s   Recodeable locks were introduced that allowed the cylinder to be recoded to use a new key without being removed. This was the first real advance in hotel guest room security. It provided the first real accountability system for key control.

1981   Recordable locks were introduced that used plastic key cards, significantly reducing key cost.

1982   The first electronic lock system entered the market. Most were optical types that would read the holes in punched cards. The major advance this system afforded was in the automatic rekeying of the lockset by the guest upon insertion of a hole-punched key card into the lockset.

1984   Vast improvements and decreased costs in electronic locks, including "look ahead" technology to eliminate sequence problems, static charge elimination, and the capability of extracting data from the lockset. This was a significant help to hotel management in uncovering and reducing internal theft. It also provided a high level of litigation protection by furnishing a paper trail of access to the room and keys issued.

1985   Introduction of the first on-line hardwired guest room lock systems, which provided bidirectional instantaneous communication between the front desk and the guest room. Also, the beginnings of integration of locking systems with other systems, such as passive energy management systems and smoke detector monitoring. Additionally, a change from the key card back to a metal key, and, in another case, no metal key or key card, but a numeric touch pad on the door.

1989   First on-line, nonhardwired guestroom lock system, which has all the capabilities of the hardwired systems but without a wire running to each door. One unique feature is that the system can use a bank credit card to operate the lockset. Another new development is the introduction of remote check-in areas, where guests check themselves into the hotel and receive a key card from a vending machine.

We have truly come to the age of computerization in the lodging industry. Computerized locking systems offer many advantages over the previous mechanical systems. These electronic locks are the tool needed by hotels to reduce thefts and improper room entry.

Key Control

In most hotels, there are three different types of keys based on the access allowed by each. The guest room key allows entry only to the guest room for which it is issued. A master key will open all guest rooms. An emergency key will open all guest rooms just as the master key and will also allow entry into all guest rooms that are double locked. The emergency key is the most highly guarded key in the hotel. This key should be kept in a locked location that is only accessible to the highest level of management. Additionally, a log book should be kept, and the emergency key signed out anytime it is removed from this locked location.

The master key is used throughout the day by various employees of the hotel, such as maids in order to clean rooms and maintenance employees to perform work ordered. Some master keys for housekeeping purposes are categorized by floor. For example, one master key may only open the rooms on the fourth floor. This key could then be given to housekeeping personnel needing access to rooms on this floor. This system protects the hotel from having to change the locks on all floors in the case of a lost master key. If the floor-specific master key is lost, management only has to change the locks for the rooms on that floor.

From a security point of view, the keys for guest rooms are the ones that cause the most concern for hotels. The hotel's employees must always remember that the guest room keys are a major responsibility. If one of these keys gets into the wrong hands, the guests of the hotel are placed at risk—that of the loss of their property or possibly even their lives. Thus, a system must be set up to reduce the loss of keys to a minimum and also to allow for easy detection by the hotel when one is lost.

Key control at the front desk starts by the keeping of the room keys in a key drawer that can be locked when it is not being heavily used. When a guest checks in, he or she should be given the room key. After this, if the guest returns to the desk to get another, he or she must be asked to show proper identification before a key is given out. During the guest's stay, hotel employees should always be on the lookout for keys left in the doors of the rooms. It is not uncommon for guests to be negligent and leave room keys in the door.

Years ago, hotel keys had plastic tags attached to them with the name of the hotel and room number on it. This presented a problem in that if the key was lost, a thief now knew which hotel it was from and what guest room it was for. Today, most hotels don't use tags, but instead, use an oversized key with the room number or some other code that indicates the room number.

At check-out, front desk employees should ask the guest for the room key. However, many guests at check-out may not be finished in their room so they keep the key or keys. Often guests forget to leave the key at the desk or in the room when they finally depart. For this reason, many hotels have placed drop boxes in the hotel by the exit doors and, if they have them, in their courtesy vans. The case remains that some keys will end up going home with the guests. In these cases, the missing keys probably do not represent a direct security problem. The problem is that the hotel does not know for sure where the key is and must assume the worst—that it is in the wrong hands. Thus, anytime a key is found to be missing, the hotel must change the lock on that guest room. There are three ways to handle this situation. First, the lock can be rekeyed. This is expensive and usually requires the use of a locksmith. A second way of solving the problem is to install a spare lock on the room that is kept for this purpose. The replaced, previous lock can then be kept as the spare. The third way is to rotate the lock of the room whose key has been lost with the lock of another guest room. In reality, most hotels keep several locks as spares.

The question that presents itself is how the hotel knows that a key is missing. As mentioned earlier, the keys are usually kept at the front desk in a key drawer. The number of keys kept in the drawer for each room should be established, and there should not be any deviation from this number. For example, if the number kept in the drawer is two keys per room, there should be two keys in the drawer after a guest checks out. If there are not, the front desk should contact housekeeping to see if they have any keys not yet returned to the front desk. When it has been established that there are no longer two keys for a room, the lock to that room must be changed. This may seem complicated, but it is the only way to safeguard the hotel and its guests.

Computerized Lock Systems

The basic variations in computerized locking systems are as follows:

Some are on-line and hardwired.

Some are on-line and nonhardwired.

Some are off-line and retain information.

Some will work outdoors and some will not.

Some types do interface with other systems.

Some use batteries, whereas others run on 110 volt alternating current.

Costs range from $200 to $800 per room.

The latest innovation in locking systems is the Card Access Control (CAC) and Security Management System (SMS) designed especially for the lodging industry by Cellular Control Systems Corporation. (See Exhibit 10-3.) This system combines radio packet network communications technology with the power of the microcomputer. It uses wireless communications to connect its central computer to an intelligent network of reader control units. By eliminating wiring between cardreaders and the central computer, it avoids the single largest cost of installing an on-line, real-time access control system.

This is a true access control system, as opposed to the older hotel card systems, which are merely off-line card-activated locks working in conjunction with a front desk computer operating a key control program. The card access system, as it is called, is capable of assigning both guests and employees to specific rooms on specific days for predetermined time periods. Card access assignments reside in the system, not in the card. Card access can be programmed differently for various cardreaders, and it can be changed instantly from the central computer by authorized personnel. All card transactions are relayed back to the central computer, where hotel management can generate powerful reports detailing who went where and when. The innovative use of a guest's standard credit card, such as American Express, Diners Club, MasterCard, Visa, and others, with its unique magnetically encoded number, provides high security and unique elec-

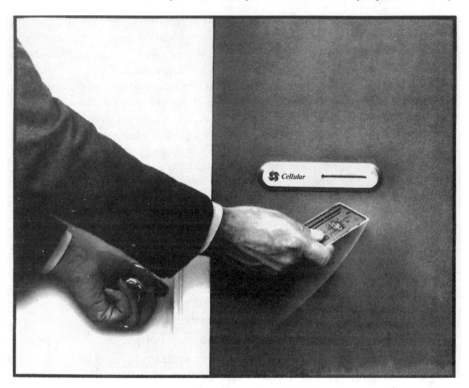

Exhibit 10-3   *Source:* Courtesy of Cellular Control Systems Corp. All rights reserved.

tronic rekeying of the room for each new guest. This eliminates the high cost of rekeying, key replacement, or replacing other types of access cards if they are lost or stolen. Once the guest checks out, his or her card is automatically or manually removed from the system. The lock code for a given room can be changed or removed without having to wait for a new guest to check in and carry the information up to the room via a coded card.

The use of the guest's own credit card is ideal because he or she is accustomed to carrying it and because the card number belongs uniquely to the guest. If a guest does not have his own credit card, or does not wish to use one for a room key, the hotel issues him a complimentary access card. These complimentary cards are very inexpensive; therefore, hotel management can either allow the guest to keep the card, or retain the card for repeat use by another guest. Each employee is likewise issued a magnetic strip employee badge that can also include a photo I.D. These cards are to be used in place of room keys or master keys, and can be traced back to the individual employee. The employee personnel information file can then be customized to meet a hotel's needs. Hotel management enters members of the hotel staff into the system by using a cardreader on the keyboard unit at the central computer. Information about the guest rooms and other system-controlled doors located in the employee's assigned work area are entered, together with the employee's work schedule. The system then is ready to relay employee-access information to the designated cardreader control units. Hotel management can use the system to print reports on the activity of an individual card user or the activity of an individual door, as well as reports on groups of cards and doors over any given period of time. This control of employee access assignments eliminates the need to issue master keys and master keys to specific floors to hotel staff. Also, there is no longer a need to create and keep track of employee access-level groups, which can become quite a cumbersome job.

Access to the system via the main video display terminal is restricted by requiring all desk clerks, security officers, and system operators to sign on to the system with a confidential password. Operators can be restricted to certain areas related only to their job functions. Each time a card is used, whether access is allowed or refused, the system records the card number, the room, the cardreader number, and the date and time. All of this information can easily be displayed or printed out at the central computer as transactions occur or later in report form.

To enter a room, the guest or employee inserts his card into a cardreader installed next to the door. If the card number is assigned to the room and is authorized for that time of day, the cardreader control unit opens the door. Each cardreader control unit makes its own access decisions instantly, independently of the central computer, and then reports all authorized entries, entry attempts, alarms, or intrusions to the central computer as they occur. The cardreader control unit also receives card access information updates from the central computer.

The cardreader control unit located at each door is a powerful microprocessor with sufficient memory to store 150 card numbers, together with unique time schedules, and authorized days to accommodate guests, hotel management, bell staff, security, maids, repairmen, outside contractors, and anyone else working in the hotel. The system is extremely flexible and easy to operate and provides custom individual access anywhere a cardreader is placed. It provides easy guest check-in, alarm, and card transaction reporting. It can provide property management reporting, long-term transaction history storage, and other capabilities far beyond those provided by typical hotel card lock systems. The central computer includes the main color video display terminal, a full function keyboard, a cardreader, a system unit featuring a hard disk for mass data storage, and a floppy disk drive for file backup and archiving.

When the system is interfaced with the Property Management System, all the work associated with card or key issuance at check-in will be eliminated. During the guest check-in process, the clerk enters the guest's card into the system by using the cardreader located at the compact terminal. The clerk types the registration information into a simple check-in form displayed on the terminal screen, which completes the guest's card assignment. This information can also be preprogrammed into the system at the time that an advance reservation is made. The central computer automatically transmits the access information and the time schedule across the network to the cardreader control unit at the assigned guest room.

The cardreader control unit uses these contacts not only to unlock the door for an authorized card, but also to act as a built-in alarm detector. When a guest or employee uses a card to open a door, the cardreader control unit automatically turns the door alarm detector off until the door is closed again. The cardreader control unit is designed so that when the guest or employee exits from the room, there is no alarm. This unit is programmed to send an alarm if someone enters without a card and not to send an alarm if someone is simply leaving the room from the inside.

Anytime an alarm condition occurs, such as when a door is forced open, the alarm is announced and displayed at the main video display terminal or at the alarm video display terminal. The display includes the location of the alarm and instructions to security personnel. When setting up the system, the security manager can program instruction messages to be displayed for each alarm, such as "Break-in at room 235. Send security team to investigate." A graphic map of the alarm area can also be displayed. Computer voice announcements of alarm messages are also available.

The system allows the use of a standard key to open a door in emergency situations only. This feature also allows the fire department to maintain their emergency fire lock box. When management, security, or fire personnel enter the room with a key, the system maintains security by announcing an alarm at the central computer. Maintaining the standard metal key function also allows for a backup system in the event of a cardreader failure. This ensures no loss of revenue due to the inability to access a guest room because of an inoperable cardreader.

The cardreader control unit is equipped with a backup battery that supports all functions for up to twelve hours in the event of a power failure. Power for the electric doorknob is supplied by concealed power transfer contacts located in the door jamb.

The cardreader control is also designed with an output control relay that allows the turning on and off of room power circuits (air conditioning, heating, and lighting). This can be accomplished through a keyboard command at the front desk or other location, or via special card command.

The system can provide numerous reports to maintain the integrity of the hotel. From providing information about a particular room's cleanliness and availability for occupancy to establishing important security facts, the CAC and SMS is extremely useful, to say the least. The following are some of the questions that can be answered using them:

To which areas is a guest allowed access, and when?

Which guests are from the XYZ Company?

Who owns the car with a particular license plate number?

When was a guest's card activated into the system?

Has a guest's lost card been used, and where?

Where has a certain employee been, and when?

Who is trying to access unauthorized areas, and when?

Which operator assigned a card to a given room?

Who has entered a room and when?

Is a room clean and ready for occupancy?

When did an alarm occur?

Who responded and what was the action taken?

Are any sensitive areas or exits unsecured?

Is there a power loss in the air conditioning unit?

With all of these features and security benefits it is not hard to see why this card access control and security management system will soon be the standard of the lodging industry.

Guest Room Sales

Naturally, hotel guests are concerned about the safety of their belongings in the guest room. Although virtually every hotel provides safety deposit boxes for guests, many guests do not use them. By providing guests an in-room safe, a hotel can increase the likelihood that guests will use the safes. It also reduces the traffic at the front desk area. In-room safes are attached from the inside of the safe, to the floor of the guest room. Most models work on a numerical key pad that accepts a six-digit security code the guest gives it.

Closed Circuit Television

The use of closed circuit television (CCTV) has increased tremendously over the past few years. CCTVs are video cameras placed to view locations that present a security risk, and they are connected to a TV monitor placed elsewhere in the hotel, where an employee can observe, from one position, all locations being monitored. A CCTV system can be hooked up to a video recorder as well, to record events for later playback if a security violation occurs. CCTV systems work out very well when used to monitor entrances, public spaces, and areas outside of the hotel. When the CCTV is used to monitor guest hallways, the results are not as good, nor do guests react well to their being observed. When the CCTV is used to monitor an outside parking lot, lighting must be appropriate and the monitors must be constantly observed if they are going to serve their purpose. However, it is important to remember that the CCTV is not an alarm system, and while it helps to add greater security to the hotel, it does not eliminate the need for an alarm system. Personnel costs will not be cut by adding a CCTV system because employees will have to be assigned to monitor the system. While these CCTV systems are helpful, hotels must be cautious not to place too much confidence in their ability to deter crime.

The Bell Staff's Role

There are several items the bell staff must be aware of with regard to safety and security. Members of the staff should always be careful, when lifting luggage, to use good body mechanics, bending their knees and using their leg muscles to lift rather than using their backs. When handling luggage, the bell staff must take care not to put the luggage down where guests may trip over it.

The bell staff and housekeeping staff get around the hotel's hallways more than any other employees. These employees should be the eyes and ears of the hotel in matters related to safety and security. For example, if a guest checks in with no luggage or luggage that is very light, the bell staff member should notify the bell captain, who will record this information and also report it to the front desk.

When a bellperson escorts the guest to the room, care must be taken if he or she is using the same elevator as the guest and utilizing a luggage cart, especially when getting on and off the elevator. Once at the guest room, the guest should receive an explanation on how to open the guest room door, particularly if the hotel has a newer computerized access system as discussed earlier. When inside the room, the bellperson should explain the locking system from the inside, indicate the location of the nearest exit to the room, and show the guest where the safety information is.

Guest Room Security

When the housekeeping department inspects a guest room after it has been made up, a check of the security equipment should be made as well. The door lock should be checked to make sure it is in good working order. The peep hole or door viewer must always be clear, allowing the guest an unobstructed view out into the hallway. A check should be made of the night chain to make sure it is secure and only removable when the door is closed. If the room has a connecting door to another room, the lock must be checked from both sides for security. Maids must be trained to leave the door to a guest room open when making up the room, and to leave the maid's cart in front of the room that is being cleaned. When a maid is cleaning a room, and must leave it to get something from the linen room, the room door must be closed and locked. When the room is a checkout, maids will have a metal locked box on their cart in which to drop any room keys that are left behind by the departed guest. If keys are simply left on the maid's cart, there is a chance that someone could walk by and steal them. While the maid is making up the room, a guest may return to the room. If this occurs, the maid must ask the guest to show her a room key for the room. If the guest does not have a key, the maid should refer the person to the front desk and then call security at once.

Garage and Parking Lot Safety and Security

The operation of valet parking and a full-service garage create additional responsibility for the hotel. In order that the safety and security of its guests and employees are ensured, there are certain areas that must not be overlooked. Employees that will be driving guests' cars must be careful, especially when busy, to take the time to locate all of the car's controls before driving off. Guests' cars should be inspected for damage before they are driven away. When damage is found, a full description should be written on the guest parking ticket and shown to the guest. Guests should be requested to remove any valuables or belongings that they have left in the car. After the guest's car is parked, the keys will be removed and taken to a secure location in the garage office along with the hotel's half of the parking ticket. Caution must be exercised when a guest returns to pick up his or her car. The procedure must require the guest to submit his or her portion of the parking ticket to the attendant, who must then carefully match it to the portion of the parking ticket attached to the keys. Parking attendants must never leave a car with the keys in it unattended for any length of time. In addition, they must exercise caution not to leave cars parked in the fire lane.

Safety Deposit Boxes

Safety deposit boxes are not just a service being provided to the guests of the hotel. In many states, hotels are required to provide a safety deposit box for guests to store their valuables. If a hotel does not comply, it may be liable for a loss of the guests' possessions. When a guest chooses to use a safety deposit box, the hotel must, for its own sake, follow some simple yet important procedures.

Every three months the hotel's controller should inspect the safety deposit boxes to ensure that they are functioning properly and that all of the keys are accounted for. In addition to guests of the hotel using the safety deposit boxes, cashiers and tenants who rent store space in the hotel may keep their banks there as well. When a guest of the hotel wishes to use a safety deposit box, the employee handling the boxes—usually a cashier or front desk clerk—must be very cautious in handling the matter. The employee will enter the guest's name, address, room number, and safety deposit box number on the safety deposit box form (see Exhibit 10-4). Next, the guest must sign the form before the box can be issued. The clerk will open the box and remove the inner tin box. At that point, the guest is free to place his valuables into the tin box. Employees must never place the items in the box or even touch them. The clerk will then put the tin box back into the safety deposit box and lock it in front of the guest. When this is completed, the clerk will remove the key and give it to the guest. The guest must be told at this point that this is the only key that will open the box. If the key is

89- № 9059   SAFE DEPOSIT BOX RECORD

BOX NO.	DATE
RM. NO.	**CLERK**

NAME ....

LAST   FIRST   INITIAL

HOME ADDRESS ....

STREET

....

CITY   STATE   ZIP

The undersigned agrees to remove the contents of the above numbered safe deposit box at or before the time of departure and all contents remaining therein thereafter shall be deemed abandoned. In the event the key to the box is not returned before departure, the undersigned agrees to pay a charge of $75.00.

AUTHORIZED SIGNATURE

....

....

CONCORD RESORT HOTEL   KIAMESHA LAKE, N.Y.

3/7/89

Exhibit 10-4   Safety Deposit Box Record   *Source:* Courtesy of the Concord Resort Hotel.

lost, the hotel must call a locksmith to drill out the lock to open it. The guest is responsible for the charge of the locksmith and a new lock installation. The record the guest signs when taking out the box has these stipulations on it. After the guest leaves, the clerk will file the record by alphabetical order in a file used for this purpose. A record of the transaction, including the number of the safe deposit box, should be placed in the guest's folio.

When a guest returns to the desk to gain access to the safety deposit box, the clerk must have the guest write his signature on the original record used. This signature will then be compared with the original one. If there is a discrepancy between the two signatures, a manager should be called. When the signatures agree, the clerk will take the key from the guest and open the box. The guest will then be given the inner box in order to remove his possessions. After this, the clerk will file the safety deposit box record in a closed file.

In most states, a hotel must provide its guests with safety deposit boxes if it is going to limit its liability with the guest. Therefore, if there are no safety deposit boxes available for a guest to use, he or she should be offered the hotel safe. The procedure would be to have the guest place his valuables in an envelope and sign it, attesting to the fact that it was sealed in front of him. If the guest does not want to handle the situation this way, he may be offered the suggestion of using a bank or jeweler. When the guest does not wish to accept any of these alternatives, the hotel may have to refuse to provide the guest with a room.

DISCUSSION QUESTIONS

1. It has been said that being a hotel front desk clerk or a cashier at a fast food restaurant are among the most dangerous occupations in the United States in terms of the possibility of robberies resulting in physical attacks. What are the legal implications to the hotel from this? Should the hotel redesign the front desk in order to provide more protection for the staff?

2. Hotels are responsible for the actions taken by their employees. How can we be more confident that our employees will be acting properly toward our guests?

3. Design a fire emergency plan for a high-rise hotel.

4. Locks can cost as much as $450 per door (for the computerized variety), while old fashioned key locks can cost as little as $15. Is the added cost justified?

STUDY QUESTIONS

1. What are the three types of fires hotels may be faced with? Describe them.

2. What are the three things a fire needs?

3. What is the first thing a telephone operator should do in a medical emergency?

4. Should an employee try to resist an armed robber?

5. In a power failure, should candles be handed out?

6. When was the first electronic lock available?

7. Hotels have at least _____ levels of keys for guest rooms and other rooms. What do they open?

8. Where should a guest keep his or her valuables?

APPENDIX

Guidelines on What to Say, What Not to Say, and Why— During a Crisis*

When a crisis arises at a hotel—for instance, a fire, a rape, or even a terrorist threat—communications, inside and out, assume an overwhelming importance. When members of the news media descend on the scene, a hotel's whole future is at stake. Blundering, ill-prepared, panic-stricken responses to reporters' questions can virtually destroy a hotel, at least for a time.

* Reprinted with permission of *Lodging Magazine*, "Crisis Communications," June 1987, pp. 64–67.

Properly handled, communications can help deflect liability suits, preserve the hotel's (and the general manager's) reputation and future, and provide an atmosphere of calm in which wise decisions can be made, and life and property protected.

In a dead-serious effort to provide AH&MA members with basic guidelines on how to handle communications in and after a crisis, AH&MA's Communications Committee has so far developed: a crisis communications manual (salesto-date, about 800 copies), a video tape dramatizing communications in four imaginary crises, and the framework for a seminar based on the tape, scheduled for the Association's annual convention this month.

The following article is derived from both the manual and the script for the tape, which covers a fire, a rape, a pool accident and a hostage situation.

The advice in the manual and video tape comes from the communications executives of five leading hotel chains. Another participant in the manual was Cindy Swartz of AIRCOA.

What is a crisis? A crisis in a hotel can be as dramatically obvious as a fire, and as deceivingly subtle as a slowly incubating food-borne disease. A crisis can be defined as any event or situation that could harm a property's viability and reputation.

Communications in any crisis should be based on certain axiomatic concepts. Among them:

- Every lodging establishment, from a small roadside motel to a center-city tower, should be ready with a prepared crisis communication plan. A plan can provide a coherent way for management to tell its side of a crisis story, and present the hotel's image as professional, caring and concerned.

- If management does not tell the hotel's side of the story, no one else will. An audience with the press in the heat of a crisis may be the only opportunity to explain the steps taken to guard against such a crisis, and to show the operator's efforts to protect guests, employees and the community.

- Providing information and cooperating with the press gives management some control over the way the crisis is reported. Failure to talk to the press forces reporters to seek information from sources that have no reason to protect the hotel's interests. Silence may even imply that the hotel operator has something to hide, thus encouraging an aggressive reporter to find out what that is.

Truthfulness is mandatory. One lie, misrepresentation or intentional failure to disclose relevant information will destroy the hotel operator's credibility before the press, the public, the guests and the employees.

- In addition to providing information to the press, it is highly important to inform guests and employees. Making them aware of efforts to resolve the crisis—and providing them with instructions on a regular basis—assuages feelings of helplessness, frustration and despair, and could insure their cooperation when it is most needed.

- Whatever the nature or cause of the crisis, management must publicly express concern for the victims for any inconvenience, loss or harm caused by the crisis. Failure to do so can result in news coverage that focuses on the hotel's culpability and lack of compassion.

- Designating a single spokesman to communicate with the press in time of crisis—and instructing all employees to refer all questions to this spokesman—is essential. It is the only way to ensure that facts are reported accurately and consistently, with no speculation by employees as to what occurred.

What should a spokesman (who should work from a prepared statement wherever possible) say—or not say—in press interviews?

- Do not speculate; relate the facts only; don't allow yourself to be led off the track.

- Avoid speaking in jargon. Present information in a straightforward, understandable way.

- Don't suggest possible causes of accidents or assign blame. Stress instead that efforts are being concentrated on aiding the victims. Offer assurances that the situation will be investigated thoroughly.

- Do express management's concern for the safety of guests and employees—and concern for victims—before stating concern for the property.

- Do take the opportunity to state the hotel's safety record and safety features, and any precautions that had been taken to prevent the crisis.

- Never answer a question with "no comment"; always give the reason for not answering.

- Never attempt to estimate the monetary extent of damage in the midst of a crisis. Indicate that this will be estimated following a thorough investigation.

Once the crisis is over, management must act immediately and fast to protect the hotel's reputation, and to get the message out that business is proceeding as usual. A prepared statement by the general manager for the press should stress:

The successful implementation of the emergency action plan, complimenting the hotel's employees for their courage and efficiency in carrying the plan through.

The hotel's policy in employee training for crisis management, specifying regular reviews and inspections.

The fire safety devices in the hotel (for example, sprinkler system, smoke or other alarms, public address systems), if the crisis was a fire.

Appreciation to employees and guests for their cooperation and understanding; also, of course, after a fire crisis, to the fire department, and after any type of crisis, to any such agency (fire, police, etc.) involved.

After a fire, it is recommended that the general manager's press briefing include a statement by the fire department chief, covering the details of the fire itself.

Hotel operators should use every tool at their disposal to spread the "all's well" message—anything to build traffic back to the property. These might include (where appropriate): a direct mail campaign to preferred customers, a special discount, or a "fam" tour for travel agents and/or the press.

Additional specifics on how to handle crisis communications are contained in the crisis communications manual and video tape, both available from AH&MA's Communications Department. Cost of the manual alone is $5.00; cost of the tape, $299.00, including a free manual.

On the tape, members of the Communications Committee introduce and comment on each of the four case studies (fire, rape, pool accident, hostage threat), but professional actors fill the roles of reporters and general managers, providing a dramatic as well as instructive experience.

To illustrate how the advice contained in the foregoing story is conveyed on the tape, excerpts from one section of the script—covering a fire crisis—are presented here.

Communications in a Fire Crisis: Two Scenarios

Scenario A

The Scene: The fire alarm is going off in your property. It's 8:09 p.m. You (the general manager) are having a pleasant dinner at home when you receive a phone call from the hotel operator telling you the hotel's on fire, people are being evacuated, she thinks some guests are trapped in rooms, the fire department is on their way and what should she do? It's 8:12. You hang up and are out your door and on your way. You arrive, the fire engines are just unloading hoses; firefighters are beginning to enter the hotel. Guests are everywhere, and a reporter approaches you with camera in hand. . . .

Reporter: "Good evening. I understand you're the general manager. Is anybody hurt or killed? How many guests are staying in your hotel?"

General Manager: I can't talk to you now! Can't you see that my hotel is on fire? . . . People could be dying and I'm standing out here talking to you. . . . This is a 200 million dollar property going up in flames and you want to know how many guests are staying with us . . . who the hell cares!

Narrator: Now let's see how it appears on the evening news.

TV Newscaster: Good evening and welcome to the 9 o'clock evening news with Clark Kent and Lois Lane. Our top story tonight is a fire at the world famous Bounty Hotel in downtown Beverly Hills. As guests fled for their lives out of the flaming building, firefighers attempted to bring the raging blaze under control. It's still not known how many persons are left in the hotel as management did not know how many guests were registered, forcing firemen to check every room in order to be certain that no one is left to burn in the ashes of what was once a great hotel.

Narrator: Now, I think you know what was wrong. What should have happened that didn't?

Comment: Let's review what happened. First of all, no one met the reporter or the GM so that the GM was "caught" so to speak. Secondly, the GM appeared to be out of control, and showed no concern for guest safety. There was clearly no emergency action plan or team; the property was unprepared as witnessed by the total lack of organization of the evacuation of the guests, and the employees. Further, the GM made no attempt to satisfy the needs of the reporter. This was an opportunity for the GM to state his case, show sympathy for the victims, highlight the hotel's safety record and instead he literally tarnished his own reputation because he was *totally* unprepared!

Scenario B

The scene: Here we see the general manager arriving at the property and he is met by the assistant manager who briefs him as to what has happened so far.

Assistant Manager: Thank God you're here! But don't worry, everything's under control. The hotel has been evacuated, the alarm system went off like clock work, it appears that it started in Room 1565 and the smoke kicked off the alarm. The hotel operator followed procedures to a tee and called the Fire Department, then the hotel fire brigade, me and you as well as security, right down the line to every department head. We immediately put our emergency procedures in to effect, emptying the public areas first and then asking people to remain in their rooms until notified except for the 15th floor which we evacuated. The P.A. system worked perfectly and we instructed all guests to wait for instructions from the hotel staff and the Fire Department. The staff have been terrific. Everyone immediately assumed their emergency action team positions. We set up a command post in Room 1400. It seems as though the fire was contained to the one room, but I can't really tell. I don't think anyone is injured.

As far as press is concerned, all calls are being switched over to our command post and Linda is logging them. Also, there's a guy here from KTVU Channel 2 News who just arrived and would like to talk to you. I've told you everything there is to know so far. I'll be in the command post, Room 1400, if you need me. We've set up Fontaine as the press and information room.

Now here is the reporter. Barry Kendall, this is Brad Host, our General Manager.

Reporter: "I am pleased to meet you. Is anybody hurt or killed? How many guests are staying in your hotel?"

General Manager: All of the guests are safe to the best of our knowledge. As you can see the Fire Department just arrived and is currently conducting a sweep of the floor to make sure it's contained, but we feel confident that our guests are safe.

Reporter: What do you think caused the fire?

General Manager: I don't have that information yet. As I said, it appears to be contained to one guest room but it's impossible for me to know the cause.

Reporter: How much damage do you think has been incurred?

General Manager: Again, I don't have that information yet. My first priority is making sure my guests are safe and that the fire is out. Then I'll worry about the physical damage to the property. As soon as I have more information I will be happy to share it with you. We have set up a command post in the Fontaine Room and you're welcome to go there to await further news.

Reporter: Thank you. I'll file my story and wait for more information at the Fontaine Room.

Narrator: Now let's see this version of the 9 o'clock news.

Newscaster: Good evening. I'm Clark Kent and this is Lois Lane with the 9 o'clock news. Our top story tonight is the fire at Bounty Hotel in downtown Beverly Hills. According to General Manager Brad Host there are no reported injuries and the Fire Department has the fire under control. The cause of the fire is still unknown, but it appears to have been started in a guest room.

Reporter: How much damage do you think has been incurred?

General Manager: I don't have that information yet. My first priority is making sure everyone is safe and that the fire is out. Then I will worry about the physical damage to the property. As soon as I have more information I will be happy to share it with you.

Comment: Well! Quite a difference. What is it that made the difference? Preparation. The staff knew exactly where to go, what to do. There was an emergency action plan to follow and they followed it. An important lesson. When people are in a panic, they will take instruction. They are looking for direction. You need to provide a calm, efficient system for your guests and employees to remove themselves from a scene of danger to one of safety.

The preparation allowed the General Manager to be briefed, to appear calm and in control, because he had confidence in his emergency action plan.

So let's review the plan. Each staff person was pre-assigned a responsibility.

By the time the general manager arrived, the guests had been informed, the staff had taken the responsibility assigned to them and the safety of the guests and employees was ensured. A press and information room and a field command post had been set up. When interviewed, the general manager appeared calm, controlled, self-assured, offering the public an image of a concerned manager who put the safety of his charges first and foremost. It is this concern for guest safety that must come across in every interview so that the public associates you with the victims and not with the cause. You will gain the sympathy of the public if you follow these basic steps and you will ensure the safety and gain the confidence of your guests and employees. It's up to you to present yourself in the best possible light.

A well prepared emergency action team response to a crisis will impress guests and reporters alike. Even if you don't have the opportunity to express your concern for the safety of your guests and employees on the air, the manner in which the crisis is handled cannot fail to impress your audience.

Once the fire is out, we would recommend a press briefing with the chief of the Fire Department to bring everyone up to date. Remember to inform your employees and guests as well, though in a separate location if possible. This press briefing is your opportunity to take credit for how well your plan worked.

Let the authorities cover the details of the fire itself. Also, be sure and have your general counsel review your prepared statement whenever possible.

Question: What are some of the things that should be included in a prepared statement for the general manager?

First, highlight the preparations and planning—the implementation of the emergency action plan and training of staff in crisis management; stress the hotel's commitment to safety, the hotel's policy of staff training and constant review in drills and inspections. Cover the fire safety devices in the hotel; for example, sprinkler, alarm, public address systems, pointing out the dollar value of the system and how well it worked, compliment employees and guests on their full cooperation and understanding. And of course, don't forget to compliment the Fire Department for their swift response. Finally, be sure to state that everything is back to normal and business is continuing as usual.

KEY PRINCIPLES TO REMEMBER

1. You must have an emergency action plan;
2. The plan should include clear instructions to all staff as to what to do in the event of an emergency on the property;
3. Whenever possible, prepare a statement and make your remarks to the press clear and concise without speculation;
4. Always express concern for public safety before company profits;
5. Leave the facts of the crisis to the authorities;
6. Be sure and talk about your safety record and the dollar value investment made in any safety devices;
7. When the crisis is over, let the media know it's business as usual.

CHAPTER 11

Training in the Front Office

CHAPTER OBJECTIVES

After reading this chapter you will understand:

- Why training is such an important task.
- What employee learning needs are and how to satisfy those needs.
- Various training methods and their uses.
- How to plan for effective training.
- Who trains and how to train the trainer.
- The value of positive reinforcement in maintaining well-motivated staff.
- How to build a winning team.

INTRODUCTION

Today's guest is no longer willing to accept mediocre service from the hotel industry, as was the case, perhaps, in the past. This new emphasis on quality service, along with the addition of new technology, has created a tremendous burden on those who manage hotels. With the high cost of labor and the shortage of qualified workers, the response from management must include a focus on the training function. Nowhere is this need for training more evident than in the front office area of the hotel. The demands placed on front office employees in the areas of technology, guest relations, and the multitude of tasks that must be accomplished by these workers is evidence of this need. A front office manager must, in addition to dealing with the above tasks, be able to deal with issues such as stress management, motivation, communication, time management, and leadership—for her- or himself as well as for his or her employees. Thus, the focus of this chapter will be on all areas of training that are relevant to the role of a front office manager, especially within the context of this new, more demanding environment.

When turnover of employees in the hotel industry is analyzed, it is evident that most terminations take place during the first three months of employment. When exit interviews are conducted with these employees, it is found that many of these short-term employees say they never felt as if they had become part of the operation. Such employees do not feel that they were introduced to the procedures that need to be followed in the hotel, nor do they feel that there was enough training given on the various tasks they were required to perform. Most of these employees state that they were interviewed, hired, and put to work without an adequate orientation program. In most cases, they were tossed into a job and told to follow an experienced worker around to learn what their new job entailed. The outcome of this type of indoctrination program is a high turnover rate. The employee leaves, and the manager is faced with the same problem of finding a qualified worker. Despite the information obtained from exiting employees, however, when a new worker is hired, it is often the case that the same ill-fated procedure is followed again, leaving the hotel with a slim chance of retaining this new worker.

It is important to realize that new employees are usually very intent on satisfying the manager by doing the best job they can. Employees gain a sense of accomplishment by performing their job correctly. When an employee does not know how to perform a job, feelings of stress-producing frustration for the already anxious new employee are usually the result. These feelings will grow if proper training is not provided. This does not mean that all properly trained employees will be satisfied with their jobs. However, proper training is the first step in the attempt to accomplish a high level of satisfaction. What correct training will ensure is that the employee knows what to do and how to do it in the best way possible.

Training can be defined as the process that is used in the acquisition of skills and knowledge needed to perform activities. Training programs are designed to give employees the opportunity to learn the skills and gain the knowledge required to function in their jobs.

The training process can be broken down into four major steps. First, determination must be made about what the employees need to learn. Second, objectives must be set that will state the change expected to occur with the new employees. Third, the training program must be designed with consideration of the costs involved, time allowed, and objectives. Fourth, a viable method of evaluation must be established in order to indicate if the desired level of learning has taken place.

Learning Needs

In order for a training program to be successful, it must be accepted by the employees. That is, it must take into consideration their needs and expectations and, at the least, match them. Employees naturally want to feel that their needs are being met.

Learning needs can be determined through a variety of methods. Employees may be asked on their own to be involved in a training program. For example, a front desk clerk might desire to be trained as a night auditor in order to better understand the guest accounting cycle, which may have to be explained to guests. In a case such as this, the employee is very motivated to learn, and with the required ability, would make an excellent candidate for a training program. Guest complaints are another good indicator of the areas where training is needed. For this reason, a log book should be kept on all guest complaints and reviewed for possible indicators of training needs. Direct observation by the front office manager can also uncover areas requiring training. These observations will yield two different types of training needs: first, training needs that deal with interpersonal communications skills utilized with guests and fellow workers; and second, training needs that involve the carrying out of specific tasks that make up a job. For example, a manager might observe a desk clerk that loses his patience when confronted by a guest who is unhappy with the room he or she has been given, or a cashier who accepts an expired credit card for payment of a guest account. Both of these incidents represent observations that indicate a possible need for one of the forms of training mentioned previously.

Change in the front office area represents a need for training. When employees are given a new job, or have an additional task added to their current job, this change requires some type of training. In addition, when procedures are diversified or a new piece of equipment is added (such as a computerized front office system), new training programs must be developed and implemented.

Records and reports prepared in the hotel will often reveal the areas where training may be necessary. For example, absenteeism information may indicate where employees are experiencing frustrations or boredom. If these problems are caught in time, training programs may aid in the retention of these employees. An accident report is another source of information and can bring to management's attention the need for training in order to prevent similar accidents in the future. A bellperson that injures his back, for instance, may signal the need for training or retraining this type of employee in safe lifting and carrying procedures.

The job application of a new employee should be carefully reviewed by the supervisor responsible for assigning the trainee to a training program. An application may contain the information needed for initially assessing the abilities of the new employee and his or her past learning achievements.

Financial reports can also bring to light areas in which training programs may be needed. Payroll figures running over budgeted amounts, or a reduction in productivity evidenced by more working hours being used than required, can be evidence of a training deficit in these areas. All of these learning/training need indicators, however, are very limited in their analysis of a specific need. Caution must be exercised when one encounters any of these indicators to be sure that the need one is addressing is truly that—a training need. Training is costly and time consuming. Careful analysis needs to be done to ensure that neither financial resources nor management's time is wasted.

Training Objectives

A training objective indicates exactly what the employee should know and be able to do at the successful completion of the training. Establishing training objectives is not as easy as it may at first seem. This is because measuring certain types of learning can be difficult. If a front desk clerk is trained how to check in a guest, it is relatively simple to observe the trainee in action to determine if learning has taken place. However, if a manager is trying to measure the degree to which the employee has gained a "feel" for the guest service philosophy of the hotel after an orientation session, it becomes more difficult to determine if the objective has been achieved.

When setting an objective, one must first place the main focus on the behavior to be exhibited after the training has taken place. Second, some standard or test must be developed to evaluate whether the training has been successful. For example, if a front desk clerk is being trained to cancel a guest's reservation, the objective would read as follows: "Upon successful completion of this training module, the trainee will be able to cancel a guest's reservation using the computer system." In this objective, the new behavior is the ability to cancel a reservation using the computer. A simple evaluation would be to allow the trainee an opportunity to attempt this cancellation procedure without any assistance. The formulating of some objectives may seem simple and unnecessary, but if they are not used, training may not always achieve its original intention.

Training Methods

To get the maximum return for the amount of time and money invested in training, management must be sure that the proper method of instruction is being utilized. There is not one correct method of instruction to be used in all situations or with all employees. Thus, the following section will discuss three types of training methods: telling, showing, and doing. Before using one of these methods, the trainer must know when one method would be more effective than another. When trying to improve the trainee's knowledge, the "telling" method is best. When attempting to change a person's attitude, role playing, using both the "telling" and "doing" methods provide the best experience, along with the use of videos. Methods that are effective in the area of skill improvement include demonstrations, case studies, role playing, and problem-solving groups—the "doing" methods.

The "Telling" Method

The "telling" method, which includes lectures, readings, discussions, and tests, is usually best employed when the goal is to improve the trainee's knowledge. The most commonly used telling method is the lecture. The lecture method of instruction is preferred when many people have to be taught something in a short period of time. In order to be effective in covering a large amount of material in a short time, the trainer must be well prepared. The trainer must plan what to tell the employees, tell it to them, and then review what they have been told. To improve on the lecture method, trainers should keep the following points of advice in mind: First, think about the audience. Make sure that the presentation is not too complicated to confuse them or too simple to bore them. Second, always practice what is going to be presented. If possible, have someone view a practice presentation and have this person make comments that will improve its delivery. Third, during the lecture, use notes only to provide organization to the presentation; never read the lecture word for word to the trainees, for this would result in a loss of their attention. Fourth, throughout the presentation, maintain eye contact with the trainees. This keeps their attention and draws them into the subject. Vary the tone of speech and volume during the presentation; a monotone presentation will surely put the group to sleep.

The "Showing" Method

Demonstrations, including those on video as well as in person, can also be highly effective in training employees. These demonstrations can be classified as the "showing" method of instruction. The video tape presentation, for example, is useful when a new employee is being introduced to a job. A video can be shown that deals with carrying out the tasks involved in the job. Videos are especially effective in the area of guest relations training. Through the video, an employee can observe the incorrect way and then the correct way of dealing with a guest.

The demonstration is another variation of the showing method. Through demonstration, the trainee is shown how to perform a specific task. When preparing a demonstration, the trainer must be certain that the location is large enough and set up so that all involved can see what is being demonstrated. (This is particularly important when demonstrating on a computer. The monitor is difficult to view when it is moved too far from the trainee.) The trainer must have a plan worked out that follows a step-by-step, timed format in conducting the demonstration, so that nothing will be left out or rushed. Objectives should be set for the learning that is going to take place. The trainer must remember to keep the objectives in line with the trainee's previous learning and future needs. The trainees must be made aware of the importance of what they are about to learn and how it is to benefit them in their job. As the steps in completing a task are being demonstrated, the trainees should be told why it is important that it be done in this fashion. The trainer should ask the trainees questions to determine if they have grasped the content of the demonstration. After the demonstration is completed, the trainees should be allowed to try the task on their own, following the same procedures just learned.

The "Doing" Method

The third method is the "doing" method, which is really a combination of the telling and showing methods. It involves the trainer and trainees working at the same time on accomplishing the task. The best known and most widely used doing method is Job Instruction Training, more commonly referred to as JIT. JIT works mainly because it follows a logical flow and is based on learning theory principles. For JIT to work, there has to be a commitment on the part of management to utilize it as the main method of instruction. Also employees must be selected to act as trainers. These trainers must be completely familiar with the JIT method of instruction from both a setting up and instructional standpoint.

Three steps must be completed prior to setting up the JIT training plan. They are the job description, the task analysis, and the task detailing. A job description indicates what the employee will be doing in the job and addresses the conditions that exist for the job. The job description should be specific in describing the main areas that compare the job of the employee. The next step is to conduct a task analysis that results in a task listing. A task is made up of a logical grouping of steps that, when followed, result in the successful completion of a desired activity. For example, a task that partially constitutes the job of a front desk clerk is the checking of guests into the hotel. In order to complete this task, certain steps must be followed. When all of the tasks performed by one person are put together, we have what we call a *job*. The listing of these tasks is referred to as the *task listing* and is where management must turn its attention to see what it must train its employees to do. By conducting a task analysis, management may discover that certain tasks do not need to be performed or that there is an easier way to complete them. When a task analysis is being done, the employees who are currently in that job should be consulted for their input.

Task Detailing

After a task analysis has been completed, the next step is to take the task listing for the job and prepare a task detailing for each task on the task listing. A *task detailing* indicates what the employee does in carrying out the task. This follows a step-by-step approach and expands in detail exactly what is involved in completing the task. Every step in the procedure should be listed in order of its occurrence. The level of difficulty in performing the step in the task detailing should also be described. When an employee is able to carry out the step in the task, it should be checked off to indicate this.

Training Plan

After the task detailings are completed for each task in the task listing, a training plan is developed for each task detailing. Job Instruction Training (JIT) is conducted by using the training plans along with the four-step method of training. A training plan is also called a *job breakdown*. This training plan indicates which task is being trained, the frequency with which the task is performed and when, the equipment that is needed to carry out the task, the steps (procedure) followed in carrying out the task, and, where needed, an explanation of how to complete each step in the task. The sequencing of the steps is based on what experience has shown to be the best setup. By having the explanation of how to do each step in the training plan, the trainer is assisted in how to teach the task. Also, trainees can be given a copy of the training plan to read on their own to review the steps and reinforce the learning. The training plans are put to use through the four-step method of instruction. The four steps are:

1. Get the employee ready for training.
2. Demonstrate the task to the trainee.
3. Have the employee attempt and practice the task.
4. Reinforce and coach the trainee.

The first step involves getting employees ready for the training. Encourage trainees to relax by letting them know that there are no stupid questions and that making a mistake now is all right—that is what training is for. Explain to the trainees what their jobs involve and what will be covered in this first training session. Remember not to just tell the trainees what to do; it is very important that the trainer explain why this job is important to the success of the hotel. This is also the stage at which the trainer should emphasize why the task must be completed *as it is being taught*.

Demonstration of the task must be taken as slowly as needed for the trainee to absorb the steps in the task. This is the "show and tell" portion of the training process. Dialogue between the trainer and trainee should be going on throughout the entire demonstration phase. The trainer must remember to be patient during this part of training. A trainer may have checked in thousands of guests and may feel confident of being able to perform the task automatically, but the trainee has only recently attempted doing these tasks. Thus, a trainee should not be overloaded with information before he or she is given a chance to try out a newly learned skill.

The next step is the attempting and practicing of the task by the trainee. After the trainer has demonstrated the procedure and allowed an opportunity for questions, the trainee is ready to try it on his or her own. As the employee is going through the steps, the trainee should be asked to explain aloud to the trainer what he or she is doing and, if appropriate, why it is being done in that particular way. Positive reinforcement should be utilized at this point. Comments like "You're doing a good job—keep going!" make the employee feel good about his or her ability to learn and encourage the learning of the other tasks. As the employee is going through the task, the trainer may find it helpful to ask the trainee questions about what he or she is doing and why. After the trainee has completed the task once, the trainer should review the whole procedure once again, and then allow the trainee several chances at practice before allowing the trainee to do it alone. It is never safe to assume that the trainee has learned the task because he or she gets it correct the first time. The trainee may just be copying the trainer and not really understanding why he or she is doing it.

The last step is to reinforce the training and to coach the trainee along in his new job. Once the trainee has learned the tasks required to start the job, he or she can be given less supervision over a period of time. As stated previously, the employee should never be taught a task and then turned loose on his or her own. The chance of failure is increased if this is done and the blow to the trainee's self-confidence at this early stage of entry into the job could be devastating to the employee's emerging professional confidence. The employee should repeatedly be reassured that any time he or she has questions, he or she should not hesitate to come to the trainer with them. Completion of training does not mean that the employee is expected to know everything there is to know about the job. The supervisor should also remember that even though the training is over, the employee needs frequent assessment of his or her performance on the job. It is only through this feedback that the employee can be sure that he or she is achieving the expectations of the supervisor.

The Trainer

The procedures covered in this section on training require a great deal of time and commitment on the part of management. One of the most important elements in the training process—the trainer—has yet to be expanded upon. A person who is going to serve as a trainer must possess several attributes. First, the trainer should be someone who knows the job, but not necessarily the one who is the most proficient at it. The person selected as trainer should want to be involved in training because of the enjoyment that teaching brings. To train someone means, as we have seen above, to go through the process step-by-step, explaining throughout each stage. This requires a great deal of patience on the part of the trainer. While it is easy for an experienced employee to complete a task very quickly, a trainee has to have it explained step-by-step. Thus, if any requirement stands out as being the most important qualification for a trainer, patience is it. A patient, caring trainer will not cure all of the labor problems on the front desk, but he or she can contribute greatly to a well-planned and well-executed training program that can move a hotel's front desk operation one step closer to excellence.

GUEST SERVICE TRAINING

In the first section of this chapter, the importance of training in the front office area was discussed. In this next chapter segment, the focus will be on the importance of guest service training and the procedures by which this training may be delivered in the front office.

Hotels, it must be remembered, provide different work environments than other types of businesses. What other business, for example, calls its customers "guests"? This characteristic alone tends to focus more attention on quality service than in other types of businesses. In fact, as emphasized throughout this text, earned revenue in hotels is not from the sale of products, but, instead, from the sale of services. Thus, hotels are challenged in ways that other types of businesses are not. Since the actual rooms sold by a given hotel are really not much different from those of its competitors, the differentiation for guests when it comes to choosing a hotel will, in many cases, be based on the quality of service received.

There are four major principles of good service that need to be applied in the front office area: (1) immediate recognition, (2) mind set, (3) guest-oriented procedures, and (4) constant assistance. Providing immediate recognition means that as soon as a guest approaches the front desk and is seen by one of the staff, he or she should be recognized. Even if the guest cannot be given assistance at once, he or she will, during this recognition stage, be told by the clerk that someone will be right with him or her. An employee should never be talking with other employees about anything unrelated to the hotel business when a guest is at or near the front desk area. This is coherent with the principle of mind set. (*Mind set* refers to the attitude that the front desk staff has toward its guests.) All employees should be more than willing to go out of their way to satisfy the requirements of the guests. Even when clerks are extremely busy, they must not give the impression that they are trying to rush the guest away from the front desk area. Employees must remember that if it were not for the guests, there would be no hotel to employ them. Bearing in mind the volume of business, the manager will schedule the staff with guest service in mind. Front office and desk managers must also be willing to jump in and assist when needed to expedite the flow of services to guests. By helping out whenever needed, they are proving, to their employees, their own commitment to guest service.

Guest-oriented procedures are not always the standard in the hotel business. That is, a particular procedure may be causing the guests some dissatisfaction. In such a case, the employees should be encouraged by management to report any of these procedures so that exceptions can be made where needed to accommodate certain guest's needs. A common example of this in many hotels deals with guests that arrive who claim to have a reservation but none can be found. Some clerks push the guest through a grueling process of questions and answers in a search for the reservation. If a hotel has rooms available during the time that the guest wants to stay, and the rate is acceptable, the guest should be registered into the hotel and roomed. The search can be continued after the tired guest is taken care of, without the frustration and embarrassment of such a search in the presence of the guest.

Constant assistance is the fourth principle of good service. After the guest has checked into the hotel, the job of guest service has just begun for the front office staff. Front desk clerks must understand that checking the guest into the hotel is the beginning of many services that will be provided to the guest. The next step is to be sure that the guest is escorted to his or her room and not left standing around unassisted. Additional service includes giving directions, telling the time of day, suggesting restaurants, and many, many more helpful behaviors.

Excellence in Hospitality

For a hotel to achieve excellence in hospitality, many guest relations skills must be learned by the employees who will be delivering the services. Eleven basic skills of hospitality will serve as a beginning to achieving this excellence. These skills are smiling, greeting, conversing, using proper telephone etiquette, providing assistance, giving attention, providing positive endings, following through, maintaining a positive attitude, making positive decisions, and keeping a sense of humor.

Smiling

Smiling when dealing with guests helps to create a friendly atmosphere. The positive consequences of smiling are many. When employees smile, they feel better themselves. Guests that are greeted by a smile will, in most cases, find difficulty in responding negatively. By smiling, the clerks are showing the guests that they are glad they chose this hotel for their stay. A smile says, "We're glad you're here!"

Greeting

Greeting a guest includes smiling as well as eye contact. The front desk clerk should ask the guest if he or she can be of assistance. Employees should not expect the guests to take the initiative—they may not. Courtesy should always be the norm. For example, if the guest's name is not known, 'Sir" or "Madame" is the appropriate address. Some hotels have the doorperson call to the front desk with the guest's name so when the guest approaches the desk, he or she can be properly greeted.

Conversing

A guest's name should be used as many times in the conversation as possible. As discussed previously, people love to hear their name; it is a very positive form of recognition. At the same time, employees must remember that guests are not their friends. Respect as well as hospitality must be shown.

Telephone Etiquette

The telephone should be answered as quickly as possible, certainly by the third ring. No one likes to be put on hold, but when this is necessary, the guest should be thanked for waiting. Remember that a guest waiting on the phone does not know that the employee is busy. If a guest is put on hold on the phone abruptly, he or she will interpret this as a sign of rudeness.

Assistance

When the guest arrives at the hotel and during the course of his or her stay, the guest should know that the employees are there to assist with his or her needs. The principle is really very simple: Whenever an employee speaks with a guest, the employee should end the conversation with the statement, "Please call on me if I can be of any further assistance."

Attention

Providing attention to the guest is enhanced by the little extras in guest interactions. For instance, when guests return to the hotel at the end of the day, they should be welcomed back. It is these little things that make the guest feel at home. When guests are around, they should not be ignored. Employees must remember to chat with the guests, not their co-workers.

Positive Endings

Upon departure from the establishment, guests should be thanked for staying at the hotel and told how much they are wanted back again. Statements such as "Please stay with us again" and "Have a nice trip home" or "Enjoy the rest of your vacation" help to ensure that the guest will depart with a smile.

Follow-Through

The initial follow-through comes after check in. After the guest is roomed, the front desk can call the room to see if everything is satisfactory. During the guest's stay, a follow-up call should be made after any problems are reported to ensure that the guest has been pleased with the service.

Positive Attitude

Having a positive attitude means that the employee has the desire to consistently provide excellent service to the guests. It is the manager's responsibility to create the kind of atmosphere that satisfies the guests' needs.

Positive Decisions

"Think before speaking or acting" is a rule that every person—especially those in the service business—should follow. This is particularly true when one is working in a high-volume customer-contact position like the front office of a hotel. Employees must be taught to be objective when making decisions. This includes keeping their emotions under control at all times.

Humor

Humor is the eleventh skill needed to achieve excellence in hospitality. When appropriate, employees should always be able to laugh at themselves and the things that go wrong (maintaining, of course, a demeanor of respect toward guests at all times). Managers can keep up the spirits of their staff by adding humor to situations that warrant it. In other words, the little problems of today must not be blown out of proportion, but rather, held in proper perspective.

GUEST COMPLAINTS

Even in the fine hotels of the world where training has been taken to heart as one very important way of achieving excellence in hospitality, complaints still occur. There are a variety of reasons why guests complain and what they complain about. Two pitfalls to avoid initially in the complaint process are the immediate placing of blame and the attempt to revise hotel policies. Assessing blame and revising policy, if appropriate, can be done later. In the meantime, it is helpful to remember the old saying that the guest is always right. Neither should employees be concerned with who is right early in the complaint stage, unless of course this is critical to dealing with the problem or complaint at the moment. The main objective in handling guest complaints in the initial stage is to satisfy the guest. Anything else is secondary.

There may not be an easy answer to solving guest complaints, but there are some basic rules that can be followed. By following these rules, the employees and management will stand a better than average chance of turning that complaining guest into a permanent repeat guest for the hotel. The following represent a few basic ideas for handling guest complaints:

> Don't ever argue with a guest who is complaining; assume he or she is correct, because the guest may be right.
>
> Always listen with undivided attention to what the guest is complaining about; remember the guest feels he or she is right.
>
> Try to put yourself in the guest's place; how would you feel? Be objective and understanding.

Never raise your voice or yell at the guest; remember, if you are pleasant, you may be able to turn the guest around.

Be objective and get all of the facts; try to weed out the subjective statements the guest may be making.

Show the guest you are concerned about the situation and that you are not taking it lightly.

When the guest is correct, tell him or her that you and the hotel will go to work on correcting the situation at once.

If the guest is wrong and the complaint is in regard to a policy of the hotel that you know must be followed, be pleasant but explain the policy and the need for it. An example of this is the check-out time policy.

When the guest is very loud or if you feel the situation is of a private nature, move the guest to a location that is out of the hearing range of other guests.

A front office employee should be supported by the supervisor. If the guest's complaint cannot be resolved by the employee, the supervisor should step in and attempt to resolve it.

In the case of an accident or theft, employees should never accept responsibility on behalf of the hotel. A manager is the only person who should handle these matters.

Employees should always be polite, however, this does not mean they have to suffer abuse from guests. In cases where a guest becomes abusive to an employee, a manager should be called at once to deal with the issues.

Six Steps in Handling Guest Complaints

In addition to the above ideas, it has been found that in dealing with complaints, there are certain steps to follow. When these six steps are taken, the chances of a complaint being satisfactorily resolved is improved. These steps are addressing the guest, giving attention, determining the solution options, finding answers, taking action, and checking up.

Addressing the Guest

When a guest comes forward with a complaint, the employee receiving it should address the guest with his or her full attention. The guest must be shown, right from the start, that he or she is important to the hotel and that the complaint is of concern to the hotel as well. An employee that has to deal with a guest who is making a complaint must be ready for the emotional state of the guest. That is, it should be recognized that the guest may have been bothered by this problem for a long time or that the incident has possibly occurred more than once. So that when the guest finally decides to lodge the complaint, he or she may be extremely emotional in the way chosen to confront the employee.

Attention

The next step involves paying attention to what the guest is saying. The employee should listen to the guest and not try to speak while the guest is talking. The best approach is for the employee to keep a pleasant expression and to nod in agreement. At this point, the guest wants to talk and he or she should be allowed to. The employee should never argue with the guest about what is being said. Also, what the guest is saying and the way he or she is saying it should not be taken personally. Employees must remain objective when dealing with guests, particularly at this point. It is important that the employee understand that the guest feels what he or she is saying is correct. Even if the guest is wrong, let the guest speak—he or she is still the guest.

Determination

Now it is time to determine exactly what the problem is. The guest has had time to vent to a more normal emotional state. At this point, the employee should focus on the facts of the problem and deal with the problem, not the personality. The employee can focus his or her questions on clarifying the problem and repeating to the guest in his or her own words what the problem is, always including who, what, where, and when in this analysis. Hopefully, when the guest hears the problem as stated by the employee, it will lose some of its magnitude.

Answers

At this point, the guest is ready to hear some answers to the problem he or she has brought forward. The employee should indicate that the guest's feelings are understandable and that the employee would feel the same way if he or she were in the guest's position. At this point, the employee might offer a solution to the problem. If the guest is not happy with that solution, an alternative one can be suggested. If several suggestions are refused, the employee should let the guest know that he or she wants to please the guest and to do everything possible to make his or her stay a pleasant one. By this point, the guest will usually have overcome his or her highly emotional state and will be able to make a decision.

Action

Action should be taken immediately after the complaint is discussed. When the guest sees that the employee is taking action to solve the problem, he or she will feel vindicated. For example, if the solution means housekeeping has to be called, a note should not be made to call later. The call should be made while the guest is still there. If the employee cannot solve the problem, a manager should be brought in at once to resolve it. The idea here is to make the guest feel that his or her problem is so important that anyone needed will be called in to solve it. This is service, and it should be flaunted, not covered up. Also, a guest should always be thanked for bringing the problem forward. In many cases, the guest has helped to correct a problem that many guests may have previously experienced, but most guests check out without saying a word, never to return again.

Check-up

After the problem is resolved, the guest should be contacted to ensure that he or she is satisfied with the resolution. This is just one more way of showing the guest that the problem has received attention and the hotel wants to make sure he or she is satisfied.

When guest complaints are handled in this manner, a bad situation can be turned around into a positive experience. Through a problem resolution process such as this, the hotel may gain a loyal customer and very positive word-of-mouth advertising.

MANAGING STRESS

The hotel business is considered, by many, to be a "people" business. This is so because of the high degree of contact a hotel's employees have with its guests. Along with this high degree of guest contact, comes a great number of stress-producing occasions. Thus, managing stress is part of a manager's job. He or she must manage personal stress and, more important, help reduce the stress his or her employees feel from their work. In this section, we will look at what stress is and how it can be dealt with in the front office.

Stress has often been given a negative connotation, but it is not necessarily bad. Stress, by itself, may be a positive or a negative thing. Stress is needed to put a little life into life. The complete absence of stress is death.

Dr. Hans Selye, in his book *Stress Without Distress,* says that "stress is the nonspecific responses of the body to any demand made upon it." This is a very broad definition of stress. Every person has a different ability to deal with stressful situations. What may cause one person to be depressed may not affect another at all. It is incumbent upon managers to try to determine, during the selection process, which employee will be able to deal with the type of stress experienced in the front office of a hotel. One of the best ways to do this is to give the applicant a realistic picture of what it is like to work in the hotel. A manager never does her- or himself or the applicant a favor by only talking about the positive aspects of the job. If a hiree is not well-suited to dealing with the type of stress that will be encountered, the consequences will be negative. That is, when the employee cannot handle the stress well, it is classified as negative stress.

In cases of negative stress, the body's physical reaction will be a negative one that may cause damage to the body if experienced for a prolonged period of time. When the stressful event occurs, the body has an instinctive response of "fight or flight." By this, we mean that the person *stays to fight* the stressful situation or *runs away to avoid* any conflict. Many times a manager may wonder why a person quits. One possible reason for his or her quitting may be that his or her reaction to the stress was flight. Other than trying to hire the right people, the manager must do more to help his employees deal with the stress of guest service.

Management can help the situation by not being the cause of the stress. When a manager behaves in a condescending manner with his or her employees, this causes stress. Managers who are not willing to discuss things with their people, who have a "take-it-or-leave-it" attitude, put stress on their employees. A manager that is erratic in his or her behavior, one day friendly, the next day unpleasant, confuses his or her employees. They do not know what to expect as a reaction from the manager or how to approach him or her at any given time.

With today's emphasis on customer service, the manager must remember to deal effectively with the employees. For it is only when the employees are relaxed, that they will be able to provide excellent service to the guests.

Although it may seem improbable, some hotels are run by people who claim to be leading experts in customer service and yet they do not follow simple patterns to reduce stress and obtain better customer service. One does not obtain quality customer service from employees by yelling at them and demanding it. The only result of such management style is a group of very stressed workers who behave the way the manager wants when he or she is there, and then change the minute the manager leaves.

A manager who wants his or her employees to be free of stress might try the following: Talk to the employees. Tell them what changes are planned way ahead of their implementation. Let them know how these changes will affect them. Listen to all employees. Let them know that their ideas are respected. Always be honest with them. If a manager is caught in a lie, the employees will never know what to believe in the future. When it is really busy on the front desk, jump in and give them a hand. This makes the manager seem more approachable in the future.

Employees must know what is expected of them in their job. If a good training program is set up as was indicated at the beginning of this chapter, the employees will not feel a great deal of stress from not knowing what to do or how to do it. Managers must be willing to deal with any problem that arises. One such problem is conflict between employees. Many managers don't do anything, hoping it will go away. This creates stress for the managers and the employees. Upper management should be aware that changing managers frequently is stressful for the employees. Employees must report to one supervisor, and it should be clearly indicated who this person is.

Managers must never let their tempers get the better of them. If an employee needs to be disciplined, it should be done in a calm manner, away from other employees and guests. The intention of discipline should be to ensure that the negative behavior does not occur again. After the disciplining, the employee should feel badly about what he has done wrong, but confident that he will do a good job in the future.

If enough employees are not scheduled for work, the overload can cause stress for the workers. When this occurs for an extended period of time, the workers can burn out. By *burning out*, we mean that state of exhaustion and stress that occurs from overworking for a prolonged period of time.

Limiting the stress that is caused by co-workers is also the responsibility of management. A lack of teamwork can cause stress for workers. Later in this chapter, we will deal with team building techniques. Many hotel managers feel competition between employees is positive. It may be, but when this competition causes conflict, lack of cooperation, and back stabbing, it is definitely a source of stress that should be eliminated. Managers should be aware of the amount of stress that each of their employees is able to withstand. When a guest is producing more than this limit for an employee, it is the responsibility of the manager to step in and take "the heat." If employees know they have the support of management in times of trouble, they will feel much better about facing those negative situations. Managers cannot stop their employees from experiencing stress; however, they can help reduce it through the information provided here.

Decision Making

The way that a manager makes decisions can have a large impact on how employees accept those decisions and view the manager's effectiveness as a leader. With this in mind, it is to the advantage of all managers to develop a method for making decisions that will meet with the acceptance of the employees. For it is not always the decision that the employees complain about, but the method that was used in reaching it. With an increased emphasis on employee involvement in decision making, a manager will benefit by having a procedure to utilize when faced with making decisions. This section will discuss an approach to decision making that is modeled after the work of Victor Vroom, a leading researcher in the area of leadership and decision making.

When faced with making a decision, a manager can choose to allow participation or be autocratic in the style he or she uses. The idea behind the model we will discuss is that the manager will not choose one style and stay with it, but will choose the style that is most appropriate for the situation. By making the correct choice, the manager will improve his or her leadership effectiveness with employees.

1. When the decision is important and subordinates possess relevant information lacked by the leader, an autocratic decision (AI, AII) is not appropriate because an important decision would be made without all of the relevant, available information.
2. When decision quality is important and subordinates do not share the leader's concern for task goals, a group decision (GII) is not appropriate because these procedures would give too much influence over an important decision to uncooperative or even hostile people.
3. When decision quality is important, the decision problem is unstructured, and the leader does not possess the necessary information and expertise to make a good decision, then the decision should be made by interaction among the people who have the relevant information (CII, GII).
4. When decision acceptance is important and subordinates are unlikely to accept an autocratic decision, then an autocratic decision (AI, AII) is not appropriate because the decision may not be implemented effectively.
5. When decision acceptance is important and subordinates are likely to disagree among themselves about the best solution to an important problem, autocratic procedures (AI, AII) and individual consultation (CI) are not appropriate because they do not provide the opportunity to resolve differences through discussion and negotiation among subordinates and between the subordinates and the leader.
6. When decision quality is not important but acceptance is critical and unlikely to result from an autocratic decision, the only appropriate procedure is a group decision (GII), because acceptance is maximized without risking quality.
7. When decision acceptance is important and not likely to result from an autocratic decision, and subordinates share the leader's task objectives, subordinates should be given equal partnership in the decision process (GII), because acceptance is maximized without risking quality.

Exhibit 11-1 Decision-Making Questions *Source:* Reprinted by permission of Prentice Hall. Adapted from *Leadership in Organizations,* by Gary Yukl, © 1994 by Prentice-Hall, Inc.

When using the decision-making model, the manager must ask questions with regard to the problem. As a result of answering these questions, the manager will be given one or more ways to proceed with the decision-making process. The seven questions to be used in the process are displayed in Exhibit 11-1. Some of the more important points to keep in mind when using the model are the following: When the decision has to be made, is there a certain level of knowledge or experience that is going to be needed by the decision maker? The time factor is another. In many cases, decisions have to be made in a very short period of time, limiting the procedures that can be used. Also, the employee's reaction to the procedure has to be given serious consideration. Are the employees going to be supportive of a decision to which they did not have a chance to contribute?

After asking the seven questions, decision procedures will be indicated that can be used in making a decision. These choices are listed and defined in Exhibit 11-2. When a decision affects a group of employees, there are five choices from which to choose. An example of how this process can be utilized will help to clarify it.

A-I.   You solve the problem or make the decision yourself, using information available to you at the time.

A-II.   You obtain the necessary information from your subordinates, then decide the solution to the problem yourself. You may or may not tell your subordinates what the problem is in getting the information from them. The role played by your subordinates in making the decision is clearly one of providing necessary information to you, rather than generating or evaluating alternative solutions.

C-I.   You share the problem with the relevant subordinates individually, getting their ideas and suggestions, without bringing them together as a group. Then you make the decision, which may or may not reflect your subordinates' influence.

C-II.   You share the problem with your subordinates as a group, obtaining their collective ideas and suggestions. Then you make the decision, which may or may not reflect your subordinates' influence.

G-II.   You share the problem with your subordinates as a group. Together you generate and evaluate alternatives and attempt to reach agreement (consensus) on a solution. Your role is much like that of chairman. You do not try to influence the group to adopt "your" solution, and you are willing to accept and implement any solution which has the support of the entire group.

Exhibit 11-2   Decision-Making Styles   *Source:* Reprinted by permission of Prentice Hall. Adapted from *Leadership in Organizations,* by Gary Yukl, © 1994 by Prentice-Hall, Inc.

In this example, we will look at a front office manager who has been given the task of selecting uniforms for the desk clerks by the general manager of the hotel. If she or he uses the A-I procedure, he or she will select the uniforms based upon the information the manager has without consulting the clerks. The A-II procedure would differ from this in that the manager is asking questions of the clerks, but may not be telling them why the questions are being asked. In this case, the questions will be directed toward finding out the colors they like or if they like wearing jackets. These questions are not asked to find out what the opinions of the clerks are. When using the C-I procedure, the manager will inform the employees of the decision that has to be made by meeting with them on an individual basis. In this meeting, the manager will tell them that a choice will have to be made for uniforms for them to wear at the front desk. Then the manager will ask for their opinions and show them possible styles and colors that can be chosen. After meeting with the employees, the manager will make a decision and inform them of it. C-II is similar to C-I—the major difference is that the manager meets with the clerks and they discuss their ideas as a group. In this case, the manager may bring samples of the uniforms to show to the group in order to get their opinions. The last procedure is the G-II. When using the G-II approach, the manager will meet with the clerks and explain to them the decision that has to be made. Next, he or she will let them make the decision and whatever the clerks decide is the choice the manager will go with. At first glance, G-II may seem to be giving up complete control to the clerks. Many managers have a problem dealing with the idea of giving up control. However, complete control does not have to be given up. In our example regarding the uniforms, the front office manager could have first selected three different uniforms that he or she felt would fit nicely within the requirements of the hotel. Then, when the manager met with the group of clerks in the G-II procedure, he or she would give them the ability to select whatever they wanted from that group. By giving only the information he or she wants to give, and by limiting the choice of uniform, both the manager and the clerks will be satisfied.

Our intention in introducing this model is not to say that a manager should carry the model around with him, pulling it out when making decisions. What a manager should be aware of is that employees want a voice in the affairs of the hotel. A manager can give the employees a chance to be involved in different situations requiring decision making without giving up control of the front office. Through this method of involvement, better decisions will be made, the employees will be more willing to accept the decisions, and they will view the manager as a better leader.

Team Building

Coaches of sports' teams have known about "it" for decades, and they have known that with it they can do the best possible job. The "it" we are talking about is the synergistic relationship that can be brought about when a group of people work together as a team. Synergism exists where the whole is greater than the sum of the independent parts. By this we mean that the efforts put forth when a group of employees functions as a team enables them to achieve much greater results than when those employees are not functioning as a team. When employees in the front office work as a team, the number of mistakes will be reduced significantly and the quality of guest service will improve greatly. It is the responsibility of the front office manager to see that his or her employees function as a team.

To build a team, the manager must create an environment where there is an atmosphere of trust and respect. For it is only in an environment such as this that a team can be built. In the front office, employees working as a team produce many benefits to themselves and the hotel. When employees are working as a team, their ability to handle problems and come up with creative solutions will improve. Front office employees that are part of a team will be able to provide faster service to the guests of the hotel. The motivational level of employees is much higher when they are functioning as a team. Employees working as a team are like a boulder rolling down a hill—they just keep going faster and faster with more determination. When employees are a team, they come up with better decisions and ones that they will agree on after discussion. Then, when these decisions need their support, they will give it. We are not advocating what some people might call "team think." *Team think* exists when the members of a team agree on things all of the time. This is negative for many reasons. One of the main reasons is that new ideas and creativity will suffer in the long run. When a true team spirit exists, the employees will discuss things until a decision is reached. Not all of the employees will be pleased with the decision, but because they had the opportunity to discuss it and give their point of view, they will support the final decision.

William G. Dyer, in his book *Team Building: Issues and Alternatives*, lists eleven problems that are indicators of a need for team building.

- Loss of production or unit output.
- Increase in grievances or complaints within the staff.
- Conflicts or hostility among staff members.
- Confusion about assignments, missed signals, and unclear relationships.
- Decisions misunderstood or not carried through properly.
- Apathy and general lack of involvement on the part of staff members.
- Routine actions in response to complex problems instead of initiation, imagination, and innovation.
- Ineffective staff meetings, low participation, and minimally effective decisions.
- High dependence on, or negative reactions to, the manager.
- Complaints from users or customers about the quality of services.
- Cost increases that are unchecked and unaccounted for.

One of a biggest problems in the front office that team building can improve upon is in the area of poor communication between employees. The team-building process consists of six steps that must be followed in developing a team. The six steps are identifying the problem, collecting data, discussing data, planning improvement, putting plans into action, and providing evaluation.

The identification of the problem usually starts by the locating of a situation that is similar to one or more of the indicators mentioned above. It is important throughout the early stages that the employees be informed that the team building is for their benefit rather than to punish them in any way.

Collecting the data can be accomplished by having a meeting with the employees where they are free to express their frustrations. This technique has two major problems associated with it. First, the employees may not express their true feelings for fear of retaliation on the part of management. Second, meetings such as this may get emotionally charged, causing interpersonal conflict among the employees. To prevent this, the discussion should be limited to the facts and not deal with employee personalities. A second method of collecting data is to carry out a survey and let the employees express their feelings this way. The third technique is the most costly of the three, but may yield the best results. That is to hire a third-party consultant to come in and conduct the team building process. This person would come in and initially conduct the data-gathering process through interviews and surveys.

The third step in team building is to bring the employees together to begin discussing the data gathered. Every piece of information that was collected should be presented to the group for discussion. During the discussion, all of the employees should be encouraged to contribute their ideas. If this happens, then all parties involved in the final decision will feel that they have added something to its creation.

In step four, a plan is laid out for improving the situation so that the end product is a positive one. This change process is accomplished by the setting of objectives for the different items needing consideration. For instance, the front desks of many hotels have problems working with the housekeeping departments to accommodate guests that arrive before the scheduled check-in time. While many hotels adhere to their check-in time, a guest-oriented property will do everything it can to "room" a guest upon arrival. Both the front desk and housekeeping must work together to meet this situation. This situation is an excellent example of how two areas in the rooms division, using the team building process, can get together and work on the resolution to a problem.

As a result of step four of the change planning phase, a plan will be developed that meets with the satisfaction of the newly built team. Step five is where the plan developed in step four is put into action. All employees in the affected departments must be informed about the new plan that is being put into play. In our example, the front desk could arrange to notify housekeeping as to what type of rooms are needed first so that housekeeping can make these rooms up first.

The sixth and last step is that of evaluation. Any plan that is put into play is only as good as the time spent on evaluating its effectiveness. When the team puts together the plan for overcoming the problem, it must also include the evaluation mechanism. This evaluation mechanism will be used throughout the action phase to keep the team on task. When the team itself develops the evaluation tool, it will be more supportive of its usage and the resulting information.

The front office manager and his or her assistants must remember that any team is only as good as its coach. It is the responsibility of the manager to function as a coach throughout the process. *Coaching* refers to the technique used by managers to reinforce positive behavior so that it is repeated, and to reprimand negative behavior so it is not repeated. When a manager sees an employee doing something correctly or handling a difficult guest very well, he or she should let the employee know. This small act of recognition is what employees want and need from their supervisors. On the other hand, when a manager finds an employee has done something wrong, he or she must also take action. A three-step approach may be used in this correction phase. First, the manager must be sure that the employee knows that what has happened is a deviation from the set standards. Second, the manager has to confirm that the employee understands that proper behavior or technique and how to perform it. Third, the manager must leave the employee feeling good about her- or himself. This last step allows the employee to retain his or her self-respect and not develop hostilities toward the manager or the team.

Conflict Management

Conflict between the employees, employee and guest, and employee and supervisor are a fact of life in a business that has so much stress associated with it. It is the manager's job to keep the conflict to a minimum through proper conflict management techniques. This section will deal with a method for locating conflict and with methods to resolve and reduce conflict.

The first step is to determine where conflict is "hiding." By *hiding*, we are referring to the situation where employees don't communicate or where they are masking the real problem with an "I don't care" attitude. A manager who communicates well with his or her employees will find it much easier to locate conflict. The next step is when the employee lets out his or her hostile emotions on a co-worker, guest, or manager. At this point, the manager must be willing to listen to the employee and, through an atmosphere of trust, get the employee to talk about what is really bothering him or her. Managers must be able to take an objective position and not take what is being said personally. In the third step, the manager must focus on and reinforce the team effort that is needed in the front office for it to achieve its goals. Step four is where the manager works with the employee to develop a plan for resolving the conflict. It is important that the employee come up with the solution and that it is not imposed by the manager or the employee. If it is imposed by the manager, there may be a lack of commitment on the part of the employee to pursue the solution.

The last step is for the manager to monitor the situation. The manager has to first see if the employee stays with his or her plan to eliminate the conflict from the work place. Next, the manager must keep his or her eyes open to this type of conflict recurring in others or in other areas.

DISCUSSION QUESTIONS

1. Discuss why you think people today are less willing to accept poor service than they were years ago.
2. Most terminated employees say that they never felt as if they had become a part of the operation. How can this problem be avoided?
3. Describe the four-step process in training.
4. Describe the three training methods mentioned in the text and tell us why trainers say that no one training method is correct.
5. What is the four-step method of instruction? Describe the steps.
6. What are the basic guest relations skills mentioned in the text? Do you believe that these skills are important? Why?
7. While too much stress is obviously bad for an employee's health, as well as his or her job performance, it can be argued that *some* stress is important. Why?

STUDY QUESTIONS

1. When during the employee's employment are they most likely to be terminated?
2. What is the definition of training?
3. How can guests directly determine training needs?
4. How might a training objective be written for training a clerk to cancel a guest reservation?
5. What are the three methods of training?
6. What does *task* mean?
7. A *training plan* is also called:
8. List the four steps in the four-step method of instruction.
9. What are the four principles of good service?
10. What are the steps outlined in the text for handling guest complaints?

CHAPTER **12**

Budgeting in the Rooms Department

CHAPTER OBJECTIVES

After reading this chapter you will understand:

- The importance of budgeting as a way to achieve profitability.
- What types of financial information are contained in the budget.
- How to create a budget.
- The advantages and disadvantages of budgeting.
- Various forms of ratio analysis and their uses.

INTRODUCTION

The ultimate financial goals of a good manager are to:

1. Maximize revenues
2. Minimize expenses
3. Minimize investment

When revenue is maximized and expenses are minimized profit is maximized. Furthermore, it is more efficient to generate a profit of $100,000, for example, with an investment of $900,000 than it is to generate this same profit with an investment of $1 million. Although the president of an organization bears the ultimate responsibility for achieving these goals, it is impossible for one person to control directly an entire organization. He or she must therefore organize the business enterprise into departments and subdepartments to delegate to subordinates the responsibility and authority for achieving the above goals on a smaller scale within each of their own areas. These departments and subdepartments should be structured so that managers are responsible for groups of related activities for which they can reasonably be held responsible. When subdivisions are created along such logical lines within an organization, they can be called *responsibility centers*. Responsibility centers fall into four categories: (1) revenue centers, (2) cost centers, (3) profit centers, and (4) investment centers. The president can then delegate to these responsibility centers a manager who will assume a portion of the overall responsibility.

Experience has proven that the best way to achieve management goals is for different levels of a business organization to use the following procedures in each responsibility center:

1. Prepare a plan that defines the goal managers want their organization, division, or department to achieve and to specify how this goal is to be achieved (called the *planning* procedure).
2. Exercise a leadership role in translating the plan into action (called the *leadership* procedure).
3. Establish procedures for verifying whether or not, and to what extent, the planned goal was achieved (called the *control* procedure).

BUDGETING

Budgeting is the process of preparing the plan mentioned in procedure 1 above. Budgeting is sometimes called *profit planning*, which is a better name because it avoids the connotation that budgeting implies skimping on costs and expenditures. Accountants are often seen as purse string–closers. However, that is a lopsided view of accountants and accounting. Nowhere are the growth-producing benefits of good accounting more visible than in the area of budgeting. A well-prepared budget plan provides the framework, not for penny-pinching, but for solid reasonable growth that is more likely to succeed because a budget exists. This usually involves an increase, not a decrease, in expenditures to help a business realize its planned-for sales growth. Because it is planned for in advance on a logical basis, such an increase in expenses will minimize the increase in expenses required to achieve stated budget goals. Managing a business's growth without a budget is like driving from Miami, Florida, to Tulsa, Oklahoma, with a compass, instead of using a road map. More precisely a budget (1) states the goals of a business organization, and (2) defines how they will be achieved.

Sometimes budgeting is confused with forecasting or projecting. This is a mistake because forecasting is a "what-if" function. It projects what future results will be *if* a specific assumption is true; for example, what will rooms department income be if my payroll increases by $5,000 per month? A budget, on the other hand, states the goals of an organization and specifies how they are to be achieved. For example, if our goal is to increase room sales by 20 percent, the budget would project a 20 percent increase in sales and the increase in expenses that would accompany this planned increase in sales, and it would indicate whether we wish to increase sales by advertising more on television or in newspapers, or by paying higher travel agency commissions. If our hotel is running a 90 percent occupancy, the budget might also need to include additional funds for a feasibility study to determine if the construction of more rooms is justified.

The structure of a budget is extremely important because as road maps can be confusing or inadequate, so also a budget can be unclear or inadequate. This can occur when there is either too much detail in the budget for the particular level of management for which it is prepared, or because there is not enough detail. Whether a budget is or is not sufficiently detailed depends on the particular style of top management. For instance, some company presidents might like to receive a budget that shows maid salaries in a particular wing of a hotel. Usually, however, this would be too much detail for that particular level of management. On the other hand, a budget for the rooms department that did not include this amount of detail would not permit the rooms department manager to effectively control payroll expense in his or her department.

Although the budget itself is only a plan, it helps management exercise its leadership role by creating clear and specific goals for the organization. Furthermore, a budget that is prepared on a monthly basis helps management become aware if budget goals are not being met, and it allows management to take remedial leadership action where necessary. A budget plan also helps management determine what type of action is needed by indicating where it is that goals are not being met.

There are three basic categories of budgets:

1. Budgeted income statements.
2. Budgeted cash flows.
3. Budgeted balance sheets.

Budgets used to plan for maximizing sales, minimizing costs, and maximizing profits fall into the income statement budget category. Budgets used to minimize investment fall into the cash flow budget category, because it is necessary to know how much cash is available for investment, what the planned capital expenditures are, and what financing will be needed. This information is available from the cash flow budget for operations, the capital budget, and the financing budget, all three of which are cash flow budgets. Budgeted balance sheets show the impact on the asset, liability, and equity accounts produced by the transactions recorded on both the income statement and cash flow budgets.

This chapter will discuss the various types of income statement and cash flow budgets from the point of view of the rooms department. It will not deal with budgeted balance sheets because investment center analysis takes place at higher management levels. Since the rooms department is a profit center, the rooms department manager does not bear full responsibility for major asset acquisitions and financing decisions, although the manager should have a participatory role in this decision-making process. This chapter will explain how income statement and cash flow budgets can help the rooms department manager define financial goals, better exercise a leadership role, and evaluate the extent to which these goals are being achieved in the department.

THE UNIFORM SYSTEM OF ACCOUNTS AND RESPONSIBILITY CENTERS

Before proceeding to discuss the budgeted income statement and budgeted cash flow, it is necessary to review the structure of the hospitality industry hotel income statement. The industry has adopted what is known as the Uniform System of Accounts for Hotels. This is a format for organizing the accounts of a hotel according to the responsibility center accounting concept mentioned earlier in the chapter. The format enables top managers to evaluate the performance of lower-level managers by showing the results of operations of individual responsibility centers independently of the results of the organization as a whole. Since responsibility centers are structured around the three ultimate management financial goals mentioned at the beginning of this chapter, there can be up to four types of responsibility centers. They are (1) revenue centers, whose managers are responsible for maximizing revenues; (2) cost centers, whose managers are responsible for minimizing costs without curtailing services; (3) profit centers, whose managers are responsible for maximizing profits (that is, maximizing revenues and minimizing costs); and (4) investment centers, whose managers are responsible for maximizing profits and minimizing investment.

A summary hotel income statement such as the one shown in Exhibit 12-1 enables us to evaluate the performance of the hotel as a whole, but it gives very little information concerning the performance of individual hotel departments. In contrast, the hotel long-form income statement shown in Exhibit 12-2, prepared according to the Uniform Systems of Accounts, does enable us to evaluate the performance of each department in the hotel. Additionally, the Uniform System of Accounts for Hotels provides for detailed departmental schedules that effect a further breakdown of the departmental information contained in the

EXHIBIT 12-1
HOTEL INCOME STATEMENT

Statement of Income
for the Year Ended December 31, 2000

Revenues	
Rooms	$2,961,000
Food and Beverage	1,050,675
Telephone	189,605
Garage and Parking	13,737
Guest Laundry	15,882
Rentals and Other Income	68,103
Total Revenues	$4,299,002
Costs and Expenses	
Rooms	778,743
Food and Beverage	905,682
Telephone	180,577
Garage and Parking	9,616
Guest Laundry	9,529
Administrative & General	395,508
Marketing	177,979
Energy Costs	287,990
Property Operation & Maintenance	255,361
Rent, Taxes & Insurance	219,448
Interest Expense	231,775
Depreciation & Amortization	346,973
Total Costs and Expenses	$3,799,181
Income Before Income Taxes	499,821
Income Taxes	169,940
Net Income	$ 329,881

long-form income statement. The schedule for the hotel rooms department (a departmental income statement) prepared according to the Uniform System of Accounts is shown in Exhibit 12-3. A list of rooms department accounts, the types of expenses that should be recorded in each account, and a sample account number structure are presented in the appendix at the end of this chapter.

A good responsibility accounting system is built upon the following two elements. *First*, there must be a chart of accounts that enables management to segregate accounts not only according to their revenue and expense category, but also by department. This is accomplished by inserting a code in the account number indicating the department where the account belongs. *Second*, the manager of each department must be able to control the activity for which he or she is responsible. To control these activities managers must have a sufficiently de-

EXHIBIT 12-2
LONG-FORM INCOME STATEMENT

Departmental Statement of Income for the Year Ended December 31, 2000	Net Revenues	Cost of Sales	Payroll and Related Expenses	Other Expenses	Income (Loss)
Operating Departments					
Rooms	$2,961,000		$532,980	$245,763	$2,182,257
Food and Beverage	1,050,675	$325,709	441,284	138,689	144,993
Telephone	189,605	54,173	108,346	18,058	9,028
Garage and Parking	13,737		8,242	1,374	4,121
Guest Laundry	15,882		7,941	1,588	6,353
Rentals and Other Income	68,103				68,103
Total Operating Departments	$4,299,002	$379,882	$1,098,793	$405,472	$2,414,855
Undistributed Operating Expenses					
Administrative & General			214,950	180,558	
Marketing			100,597	77,382	
Energy Costs			163,319	124,671	
Property Operation & Maintenance			139,288	116,073	
Total Undistributed Operating Expenses			618,154	498,684	1,116,838
Income Before Fixed Charges	$4,299,002	$379,882	$1,716,947	$904,156	$1,298,017
Rent, Taxes & Insurance				219,448	
Interest Expense				231,775	
Depreciation & Amortization				346,973	798,196
Income Before Income Taxes					499,821
Income Taxes					169,940
Net Income					$ 329,881

tailed breakdown of account categories so that they may know precisely what each revenue and expense is. The Uniform System of Accounts provides such a listing of account categories that is sufficiently detailed and can be given a department code. In the appendix at the end of this chapter the reader can observe the degree of detail in the rooms department account categories. A possible account numbering system is also shown, where the account prefix "01" identifies these accounts as all belonging to the rooms department. If they belonged to the food department another prefix, such as "02," might be used.

But this is not enough, in and of itself, to constitute a good responsibility accounting system. Additionally, each manager must be given the authority, not just the responsibility, to control his or her department. A rooms department manager who does not have authority to hire and fire maids, for instance, cannot be held responsible for the departmental income of the rooms department. De-

EXHIBIT 12-3
ROOMS DEPARTMENT SCHEDULE
FOR THE YEAR ENDED DECEMBER 31, 2000

Revenue	
Transient-Regular	$1,591,000
Transient-Group	1,143,653
Permanent	226,000
Other Rooms Revenue	32,854
Total Revenue	2,993,507
Allowances	32,507
Net Revenue	2,961,000
Expenses	
Salaries and Wages	453,461
Employee Benefits	79,519
Total Payroll & Related Expenses	532,980
Other Expenses	
Commissions	28,562
Contract Cleaning	14,029
Guest Transportation	10,530
Laundry and Dry Cleaning	54,376
Linen	23,994
Operating Supplies	48,725
Reservations	39,263
Uniforms	9,044
Other	17,240
Total Other Expenses	245,763
Total Expenses	778,743
Departmental Income	$2,182,257

partment managers' performances should not be evaluated on the basis of accounts that are not under their control.

In summary, a responsibility accounting system enhances the chances of success of the budgeting process because it permits the structuring of budget goals on a department-by-department basis and then enables the subsequent evaluation of the progress each department is making in achieving their budget goals.

The Budgeted Income Statement

This chapter deals with a profit center: the rooms department. Thus, we will be concerned with planning to maximize revenues and minimize expenses. The budgeted income statement is easy to visualize for anyone who understands basic accounting because it appears as being identical to a historical income statement. The difference is that amounts in a budgeted income statement represent future management revenue and expense goals rather than historical revenue and expense amounts already achieved. A sample rooms department schedule containing a budgeted departmental income schedule is presented in Exhibit 12-4 for comparison with the actual historical income schedule shown in Exhibit 12-3.

The budgeted income statement should always be prepared first because it specifies the desired sales goals. Sales goals are the basis for planning or budgeting expenses and for planning capital expenditures (expenditures for assets, that will benefit the rooms department in future accounting periods), such as increas-

EXHIBIT 12-4
BUDGETED DEPARTMENTAL INCOME STATEMENT

Budgeted Rooms Department Schedule
Fixed Budget
for the Year Ended December 31, 2000

Revenue	
Transient-Regular	$1,523,974
Transient-Group	1,049,526
Permanent	200,000
Other Rooms Revenue	30,491
Total Revenue	$2,803,991
Allowances	31,771
Net Revenue	$2,772,220
Expenses	
Salaries and Wages	$ 424,468
Employee Benefits	71,329
Total Payroll & Related Expenses	$ 495,797
Other Expenses	
Commissions	$ 27,372
Contract Cleaning	13,883
Guest Transportation	9,240
Laundry and Dry Cleaning	52,336
Linen	21,692
Operating Supplies	46,125
Reservations	38,369
Uniforms	8,922
Other	17,001
Total Other Expenses	$ 234,940
Total Expenses	730,737
Departmental Income	$2,041,483

ing supplies inventory, refurbishing all or parts of the rooms department, or even expanding the hotel. Of equal importance is that budgeted sales and expenses are the basis for the cash flow budget, which will be dealt with in the following section.

Before proceeding to the next section, notice that the rooms department schedule shown in Exhibit 12-3 does not include any of the *fixed charges* that appear at the bottom of the long-form hotel income statement in Exhibit 12-2. This is because these fixed charges are the result of upper management decisions and are beyond the control of the rooms manager. It would be unfair to the rooms manager if his or her performance were evaluated on the basis of these noncontrollable expenses. The same applies to the *undistributed operating expenses* shown on the long-form income statement.

Budgeted Cash Flows

Although the budgeted income statement schedule should be prepared first, the cash flow budgets are the most helpful in planning the day-to-day operations of a business. In order to understand why this is so, we must first understand the difference between the cash flow budget and the budgeted income statement. Budgeted income statements are prepared on the basis of *accrual accounting*. They are composed of revenues and expenses. Revenues are recorded when a service is rendered, not when the hotel receives payment for it, and expenses are recorded when an asset or service is consumed, not when it is paid for. The amount of cash that a hotel receives on a given day and the amount of revenue earned will not be the same because some sales of services may be credit sales, for which the hotel receives no cash in the current accounting period. Likewise, some expenses recorded on the current rooms income statement are not paid for in the current accounting period and therefore do not represent an outflow of cash.

The main goal of cash budgets is to enable managers, such as the rooms department manager, to plan expected total cash receipts and cash expenditures, as well as indicate the net cash flow difference between receipts and expenditures. This is useful knowledge because if a net outflow condition is expected to exist, the rooms department manager must inform the finance department personnel so that they may anticipate the required additional financing needs, rather than being caught by surprise. The cash budget will also tell the manager how long to expect this condition to last, useful knowledge when deciding the best source for these funds. Lines of credit for indefinite periods of time are the most expensive way to obtain financing. Rather than have excess amounts of cash on call at a bank through a high-interest line of credit, it is better to know a company's approximate cash needs and borrow specific amounts for specific periods of time at lower interest rates.

On the other hand, if the cash budget indicates that the rooms department will be generating cash, knowing how much and when it will be available enables management to make better plans for using it since it can be taken into account when preparing the nonoperating budgets: the financing budget or capital expenditure budget. If business is cyclical, as is typical in the hotel industry, the rooms department may face a cash surplus during part of the year and a net cash outflow during the remainder of the year. Knowing how long the surplus is expected to last helps management determine the best way to invest the excess funds on a temporary basis. The interest rate of a nine-month certificate of deposit may not be much greater than that of a six-month certificate of deposit, but when applied to hundreds of thousands or even millions of dollars, this small differential can become significant, especially in view of the slim profit margins some hotel chains survive on.

One must never forget that cash is the lifeblood of a business. A business can't survive and a rooms department can't be managed successfully without cash any more than a person can survive without blood. The cash flow budgets measure how much of this life-giving cash will or will not be available in the department.

Types of Cash Flow Budgets

Cash flow budgets can be presented in several ways, depending on how wide a scope is covered. Some examples of cash flow budgets are named below. The master budget is usually prepared on an organizationwide basis and includes all the departments' departmental budgets. The cash flow portion of the master budget can be divided into two sections, the operating and nonoperating budgets. The nonoperating budget can, in its turn, be divided into the capital expenditure budget and the financing budget. As its name implies, the hybrid budget is a composite of the other budgets.

1. Master budget
   (a) Operating cash flow budget
   (b) Nonoperating cash flow budget
       (1) Capital expenditure budget
       (2) Financing budget
2. Hybrid budget

A master budget is the most comprehensive budget. It includes income statement budgets, operating and nonoperating cash flow budgets, and budgeted balance sheets for all departments in an organization.

A nonoperating cash flow budget indicates the cash receipts and expenditures a company can expect from cash sources and cash uses other than its repetitive daily operations. The nonoperating sources and uses of cash are mostly those which affect the noncurrent balance sheet accounts. It is important for managers to be aware of these sources and uses since they help to understand capital expenditure budgets, in which rooms managers participate. These non-operating sources and uses are listed below:

NONOPERATING SOURCES

1. Sale of assets
2. Borrowing
3. Sale of shares in the company

NONOPERATING USES

1. Purchase of assets
2. Repayment of debt
3. Purchase of treasury stock
4. Payment of dividends

These nonoperating sources and uses can be reclassified and transformed into a *capital expenditure budget* or a *financing budget.*

A capital expenditure budget involves planning expenditures for noncurrent assets such as the purchase of furniture, improvements, or expansions to a property. In contrast to expenditures for expenses, which benefit a business in the current period, capital expenditures benefit an enterprise in future periods. Each department presents its capital expenditure needs to the general manager. The general manager may have the authority to decide concerning capital expenditures up to a certain amount, $10,000 for example. Capital expenditure requests greater than this amount would then be referred to regional, divisional, or corporate offices, which must then establish a method of selecting from these requests those which will generate a satisfactory return on investment. Though rooms department managers are not likely to be responsible for the preparation of a nonoperating budget, they are likely to be involved with a capital expenditure budget since they need to participate in budgeting for the purchase of furniture, for making improvements, and for building expansions.

A financing budget prepares and lists the sources of funds required to meet potential operating budget deficits as well as the expenditure needs arising from the capital expenditure budget. The possible nonoperating cash sources included in the financing budget are (1) the sale of unutilized or underutilized assets, (2) borrowing, or (3) the sale of more ownership equity (shares of stock in the case of a corporation). A financing budget can also show uses of cash for such nonoperating transactions as (4) the payment of debt, (5) the purchase of treasury stock, and (6) the payment of dividends.

The hybrid cash budget is used mostly in small businesses where there is insufficient activity to warrant all the formal procedures required to prepare several individual budgets. Usually a hybrid budget includes operating activities, capital expenditures, and financing activities together.

OTHER DIMENSIONS OF INCOME STATEMENT AND CASH FLOW BUDGETS

There are several other aspects of budgets that need to be reviewed before proceeding to the budgeting process itself. A budget can be prepared for an individual department, such as the rooms department. This is called a departmental budget, and this is the type we will be concerned with in this chapter. Or budgets can cover the entire organization, including all three budget categories. As stated earlier, these are called master budgets.

Budgets also cover different periods of time. They can be prepared to cover daily, weekly, monthly, quarterly, semiannual, or annual periods. A staffing guide is an example of a daily budget. Of the more time-encompassing budgets, a monthly budget for the next year (sometimes called the *tactical budget*) and annual budgets for the next five years (sometimes called *strategic budgets*) are sufficient. Exhibit 12-5 presents a six-month monthly budgeted income statement for the "Look-Ahead Hotel." Exhibit 12-6 presents a six-month monthly operating cash budget for the same company, and Exhibit 12-7 shows a comprehensive cash budget for the company, including both operating and nonoperating cash budgets. Since cash budgets use cash basis, as opposed to accrual basis accounting, the generally accepted accounting principals (GAAP), which govern accrual accounting, do not apply. It is therefore more important to list the assumptions concerning the periods in which revenues will be collected and expenses paid. These assumptions are listed below each budget in each of the budget illustrations.

Finally, budgets differ according to how they are prepared. The three most commonly used types of budgets in this regard are the following:

1. Fixed budget
2. Flexible budget
3. Zero-base budget

Fixed Budgets

In the case of the fixed budget, all amounts, both revenues and expenses, receipts and expenditures, are planned for and included in their respective budgets in terms of fixed dollar amounts. The budgeted income statement shown in Exhibit 12-4 was prepared on the fixed budget principal. The disadvantage in preparing budgets this way is that if sales exceed the planned amount, then most likely so will expenses. This, in turn, would generate a series of unfavorable dif-

EXHIBIT 12-5
SIX-MONTH MONTHLY BUDGETED INCOME STATEMENT

Look-Ahead Hotel
Budgeted Monthly Statement of Income
for the Six Months Ended December 31, 2001

Revenues	July	August	September	October	November	December
Rooms	$259,772	$278,427	$297,879	$317,446	$337,128	$375,710
Food and Beverage	64,524	69,157	73,989	78,849	83,738	93,321
Telephone	11,644	12,480	13,352	14,229	15,111	16,841
Garage and Parking	844	904	967	1,031	1,095	1,220
Guest Laundry	975	1,045	1,118	1,192	1,266	1,411
Rentals and Other Income	4,182	4,483	4,797	5,111	5,428	6,049
Total Revenues	$341,941	$366,496	$392,102	$417,858	$443,766	$494,552
Costs and Expenses						
Rooms	$ 68,525	$ 73,446	$ 78,577	$ 83,739	$ 88,931	$ 99,108
Food and Beverage	79,695	85,418	91,386	97,389	103,427	115,263
Telephone	15,890	17,031	18,221	19,418	20,621	22,981
Garage and Parking	846	907	970	1,034	1,098	1,224
Guest Laundry	839	899	962	1,025	1,088	1,213
Administrative & General	34,802	37,302	39,908	42,529	45,166	50,335
Marketing	15,661	16,786	17,958	19,138	20,325	22,651
Energy Costs	25,342	27,161	29,059	30,968	32,888	36,652
Property Operation & Maintenance	22,470	24,084	25,767	27,459	29,162	32,499
Rent, Taxes & Insurance	19,310	19,310	19,310	19,310	19,310	19,310
Interest Expense	20,395	20,395	20,395	20,395	20,395	20,395
Depreciation & Amortization	30,531	30,531	30,531	30,531	30,531	30,531
Total Costs and Expenses	$334,306	353,270	373,044	392,935	$412,842	$452,163
Income Before Income Taxes	7,635	13,226	19,058	24,923	30,924	42,389
Income Taxes	2,596	4,496	6,480	8,473	10,480	14,412
Net Income	$ 5,039	$ 8,730	$ 12,578	$ 16,450	$ 20,444	$ 27,977

ferences between the planned-for expense amount and the achieved amount. If viewed without consideration to the increase in sales, these excess expenses would create a negative impression concerning the rooms department manager's ability to minimize expenses.

Flexible Budgets

In a flexible budget this problem does not exist because planned-for expenses are related to revenues on a percentage basis whenever appropriate. In order to understand a flexible budget we must briefly review the meaning of variable, semivariable, and fixed expenses. A *variable expense* is one that changes in the same direction and same percentage amount as sales. It varies in direct proportion to sales. "Guest supplies" expense, a subcategory of operating supplies, is an example of this type of expense. A *fixed expense* is an expense that does not vary in response to sales over the short term (about one year). As explained earlier, the rooms department has no expense categories that are 100 percent fixed. A *semivariable expense* is one that is partially variable and partially fixed. For instance, in the rooms department, the manager's salary and any office personnel would constitute the fixed portion, or element, of the rooms payroll expense category. The maids, which must be increased when more rooms are occupied, constitute the variable element of rooms payroll.

EXHIBIT 12-6
SIX-MONTH MONTHLY OPERATING CASH BUDGET

Look-Ahead Hotel
Budgeted Monthly Operating Cash Flow
for the Six Months Ended December 31, 2001

Receipts		July	August	September	October	November	December
Collections:							
---- Cash Sales (60%)	1	$202,655	$217,208	$232,382	$247,648	$263,002	$293,102
---- 31–60 Days (30%)	2		101,328	108,604	116,192	123,824	131,501
---- 61–90 Days (10%)	3			33,776	36,201	38,731	41,275
Rentals and Other Income		4,182	4,483	4,797	5,111	5,428	6,049
Total Operating Receipts		$206,837	$323,018	$379,559	$405,152	$430,985	$471,927
Expenditures							
Rooms		$ 68,525	$ 73,446	$ 78,577	$ 83,739	$ 88,931	$ 99,108
Cost of Food and Beverage							
---- Paid Cash (60%)	4	47,817	51,251	54,832	58,434	62,056	69,158
---- 31–60 Days (40%)	5		31,878	34,167	36,554	38,955	41,371
Telephone	6		15,890	17,031	18,221	19,418	20,621
Garage and Parking		846	907	970	1,034	1,098	1,224
Guest Laundry		839	899	962	1,025	1,088	1,213
Administrative & General		34,802	37,302	39,908	42,529	45,166	50,335
Marketing		15,661	16,786	17,958	19,138	20,325	22,651
Energy Costs		25,342	27,161	29,059	30,968	32,888	36,652
Property Operation & Maintenance		22,470	24,084	25,767	27,459	29,162	32,499
Rent & Insurance		12,310	12,310	12,310	12,310	12,310	12,310
Property Taxes	7					42,000	
Interest Expense		20,395	20,395	20,395	20,395	20,395	20,395
Income Taxes	8			13,572			33,366
Total Operating Disbursements		$249,007	$312,308	$345,508	$351,806	$413,792	$440,903
Net Monthly Operating Cash Flow		($42,170)	$10,710	$34,051	$53,346	$17,193	$31,024

EXHIBIT 12-6 *(continued)*

Facts and Assumptions

The above cash flow is based on the following facts and assumptions:

(A) The hotel will open for business on July 1, 2001.

(B) 60% of sales are cash sales, 30% are credit sales to be collected 31–60 days after the sale is made, and 10% of sales will be collected 61–90 days after sale is made.

(C) Rentals and other income will be collected monthly.

(D) 60% of food and beverage will be paid for cash and 40% will be paid for in 31–60 days after purchase.

(E) Telephone expenses will be paid for in the month after they are incurred.

(F) Property taxes will be paid in November.

(G) Income taxes will be paid quarterly.

(H) Depreciation being a non-cash expense is not deducted from the cash flow.

Explanation of Operating Cash Flow

An explanation of the differences between the above budgeted cash flow and the budgeted income statement shown in Exhibit 12-5 is given below. Lines that are numbered contain amounts that are different from the budgeted income statement.

(1) This line contains 60% of non-rental sales—equivalent to the cash sales of this hotel—for each month.

(2) This line contains 30% of monthly non-rental sales—equivalent to credit sales that are collected 31–60 days after they are made.

(3) This line contains 10% of monthly non-rental sales—equivalent to credit sales that are collected 61–90 days after they are made.

Note: Receipts per this cash flow can be reconciled with sales on the budgeted income statements as follows:

July – Cash Sales	$202,655 ----) appears in July column of cash flow
July – 31 to 60 Day Credit Sales	$101,328 ----) appears in August column of cash flow
July – 61 to 90 Day Credit Sales	$33,776 ----) appears in September column of cash flow
July – Rentals and Other Income	$4,182 ----) appears in July column of cash flow

Total sales in July per budgeted income statement $341,941

(4) This line contains 60% of food and beverage purchases – the amount of purchases made on a cash basis.

(5) This line contains 40% of the cost of food and beverages – equivalent to the food and beverages purchased on credit.

Note: Disbursements per this cash flow can be reconciled with food and beverage expense on the budgeted income statements as follows:

July – Cash Purchases	$47,817
July – 31 to 60 Day Credit Purchases	$31,878
Total food and beverage purchases in July per budgeted income statement	$79,695

(6) Since telephone expenses are paid for in the month after they are incurred, there is no entry on this line for July and the telephone expenses that appear on the July budgeted income statement are listed on this cash budget in August.

(7) Property taxes are all paid in November—the total of the rent and insurance plus the property taxes line on this cash budget equals the total of the rent, taxes, and insurance line on the budgeted income statements.

(8) Income taxes are paid quarterly and therefore July, August, and September income taxes all appear on this cash flow in September.

Depreciation: There is no expenditure for depreciation because it is a non-cash expense.

A flexible budget income statement for the rooms department might contain the following revenue and sample expense estimates at the beginning of the month when the budget was prepared:

	Fixed Element	Variable Element
Total Revenue $10,000		
Payroll		
Manager's Salary	$3,000	—
Maids' salaries (10 percent of sales) —		$1,000
Guest amenities (5 percent of sales) —		$500

EXHIBIT 12-7
BUDGETED MONTHLY MASTER CASH FLOW

Look-Ahead Hotel
Budgeted Monthly Master Cash Flow
for the Six Months Ended December 31, 2001

	July	August	September	October	November	December
Monthly Operating Cash Flow	($42,170)	$10,710	$34,051	$53,346	$17,193	$ 31,024
Non-Operating Receipts						
Sale of Assets	-0-	-0-	-0-	-0-	-0-	0
Sale of Stock	1,300,000	-0-	-0-	-0-	-0-	-0-
Loans Obtained						
Working Capital Loan	42,170	-0-	-0-	-0-	-0-	-0-
Building Purchase Loan	1,500,000	-0-	-0-	-0-	-0-	-0-
Equipment Purchase Loan	500,000	-0-	-0-	-0-	-0-	-0-
Unanticipated Expenditures	24,000	-0-	-0-	-0-	-0-	-0-
Total Non-Operating Receipts	$3,324,000	$10,710	$34,051	$53,346	$17,193	$ 31,024
Non-Operating Expenditures						
Purchase of Assets						
Building	$2,500,000	-0-	-0-	-0-	-0-	-0-
Equipment	800,000	-0-	-0-	-0-	-0-	-0-
Purchase of Treasury Stock	-0-	-0-	-0-	-0-	-0-	-0-
Repayment of Loans						
Working Capital Loan	-0-	3,514	3,514	3,514	3,514	3,514
Building Purchase Loan	-0-	4,167	4,167	4,167	4,167	4,167
Equipment Purchase Loan	-0-	4,167	4,167	4,167	4,167	4,167
Unanticipated Expenditures Loan	-0-	2,000	2,000	2,000	2,000	2,000
Payment of Dividends	-0-	-0-	-0-	-0-	-0-	-0-
	$3,300,000	$13,848	$13,848	$13,848	$13,848	$ 13,848
Net Total Monthly Cash Flow	24,000	(3,137)	20,203	39,498	(3,345)	17,176
Cumulative Cash Available	$ 24,000	$20,863	$41,066	$80,564	$83,909	$101,085

EXHIBIT 12-7 *(continued)*

Facts and Assumptions

(A) It is assumed that there are no pre-opening expenses (as stated in Exhibit 12-6).

(B) Interest expense is included as an operating expense deduction in Exhibit 12-6.

(C) The working capital loan and the unanticipated expenditures loan will be repaid in monthly installments over 12 months.

(D) The building purchase loan will be repaid in monthly installments over 30 years.

(E) The equipment purchase loan will be repaid in monthly installments over 10 years.

(F) The purchase of the building and equipment was only partially financed with loans. The balance was financed through the sale of stock in the company.

Explanation of Master Cash Flow

The master cash flow begins with the net operating cash flow from the bottom line of Exhibit 12-6 and then includes all the sources and uses of cash that are not related to the actual operations of the company in the form of revenues and expenses.

It indicates the overall monthly cash flow of the company, as well as its cumulative cash balance at the end of each month. Separating the cash flow budgets this way enables the company to determine how much cash the company is using or generating in its normal operations and how much it is using in its non-operating transactions.

All the non-operating transactions can be grouped into seven categories. These are:

Non-Operating Sources	Non-Operating Uses
(1) Sale of Assets	(4) Purchase of Assets
(2) Sale of Stock	(5) Purchase of Treasury Stock
(3) Obtaining Loans	(6) Repayment of Loans
	(7) Payment of Dividends

These transaction categories are all listed in the above master budget even though no transactions occurred in some of the categories.

It is evident that the rooms payroll consists of two types of expenses—fixed and variable. It is, therefore, called a semivariable expense. Guest amenities varies entirely in direct proportion to sales. It is therefore called a variable expense. In preparing a flexible budget, the fixed and variable elements of all semivariable expenses are estimated separately, as was done above. At the end of the month, assuming sales were actually $12,000, instead of the $10,000 estimated, then the partial flexible budget would appear as follows:

	Budgeted	Actual
Sales	$10,000	$12,000
Payroll		
Manager's Salary	3,000	3,000
Maids' salaries (10 percent of sales)	1,000	1,300
Guest amenities (5 percent of sales)	500	600

The flexible budget indicates that even though the rooms manager spent $600 on guest amenities, instead of the $500 budgeted for the $10,000 total revenue estimate, this did not create an unfavorable budget variance. When the actual revenue exceeded budgeted revenue by $2,000, the flexible budget automatically adjusted because the cost of guest amenities was expressed as a percent of revenue. In the case of payroll expense, however, it is evident that the manager overspent on maid salaries and was right on plan with his own salary. He overspent on maids' salaries because 10 percent of the actual revenue of $12,000 is $1,200, but the actual expense was $1,300, which is $100 greater than it should be for the higher actual revenue.

Had this been a fixed budget, the guest amenities budget amount would have remained at $500, though sales exceeded expectations, and it would have appeared that the manager had also overspent for guest supplies. Although a flexible budget takes some extra effort to prepare, it has the advantage of forcing rooms department managers to think about their expenses in greater depth. They must make an effort to identify the variable and fixed elements of their semivariable expenses. This exercise gives managers a much better feel for the operation of their department and its profit-earning potential. In exchange for this extra effort, the manager is rewarded with a budget that presents more reasonable spending targets than a fixed budget—targets which are less likely to produce unfavorable budget variances when actual total revenue exceeds budgeted total revenue.

For the sake of comparison the Fixed Budget Rooms Department Income Schedule shown in Exhibit 12-4 is shown as a flexible budget in Exhibit 12-10.

Zero-Base Budgeting

In the case of both fixed and flexible budgets, spending limits, however they are determined, are carried over as acceptable lower limits in subsequent budgets. Only increases above these previously established lower limits need be justified. This often leads to what is called "spending to budget." If a department manager has controlled expenses particularly well during the year and has some excess cash, he or she may be tempted to spend this cash in frivolous expenditures, such as for an overly elaborate office party, in order to keep this minimum expenditure floor for the subsequent budget year.

The zero-base budget avoids this problem by reducing every budgeted amount to zero at the beginning of a new budget year. This forces managers to justify all budgeted amounts annually. The disadvantage of zero-base budgeting is that it takes an enormous amount of time and effort to prepare what are, in essence, new business plans every year. To reduce this workload a modified zero-base budgeting system is sometimes used. In such a case the zero-base amounts are reduced to some percentage (such as 70 percent) of the prior year amounts, and managers only need to justify increases above this 70 percent floor.

Zero-base budgeting gives rise to the following types of questions concerning the employees in the rooms department: Why is this job being performed in this way? By this employee? In this place? At this time?

The essence of zero-base budgeting is that no budget amount is beyond question. Because all the operations of a department must be reanalyzed and justified annually, zero-base budgeting requires more time and effort than the preparation of standard budgets. Therefore, the additional cost of preparing a zero-base budget may not always be justified.

General Considerations

If a budget is to be the effective growth-promoting tool that it can be, it must be properly prepared. This means not only that it must contain reasonable goals, but equally as important, that the definition of these goals must be arrived at through the proper procedures. As stated in the introduction to this chapter, good management not only requires that a plan be established, but also that managers exercise leadership in achieving the plan. They must then establish procedures to control how the planned goals are achieved. When properly prepared, the budget serves as a rallying point for the organization and later as a milestone for the organization to use to measure accomplishment. The key to the success of a budget as a motivator is the participation of all who will be affected by the budget. They must have a part both in defining the goals and, later, in reviewing and evaluating the degree of success achieved.

Of equal importance when preparing budgets is the realization that the numbers included in these budgets are nothing but a figment of some collective or individual imagination. It is therefore advisable to prepare three budgets. One budget should include amounts for the most likely scenario. The other two budgets should be (1) an optimistic budget, based on exceeding the most likely goals; and (2) a pessimistic budget, which would assume a worst-case scenario. One possible basis for preparing this pessimistic budget might be to project sales based on management's doing nothing to encourage growth.

Having a range of budgets helps management prepare contingency plans, should the most likely budget be undershot or exceeded. The rooms manager should be able to anticipate whom and how many employees to lay off or hire, to prepare training teams in case they are needed, to prepare for increases or decreases in supplies purchases, and to prepare to take all the other steps that might be required if the most likely scenario is not realized.

ADVANTAGES AND DISADVANTAGES OF BUDGETING

There are many advantages to having a financial road map, so to speak, in the form of budgets. Some of them follow:

1. The budget serves as a game plan for the entire organization. The members of the organization feel that higher management knows where the organization is going; they enjoy the security of knowing there is a comprehensive plan and that there is a leader. They also know what the leader expects of them, and how they are expected to achieve their designated goals. This creates a highly motivating atmosphere to work in.

2. The budget process when properly executed brings together managers at the same as well as at different levels of an organization, thereby increasing communication within the organization. For instance, though the rooms department manager is not directly responsible for major capital expenditure decisions in the rooms department, he or she should be part of the budget committee where these decisions are made. Since his or her cooperation is essential to the proper utilization of these facilities, decisions regarding changes in decor, furniture, or layout should take the rooms department manager's opinion into account. Likewise, the budget for cleaning and guest supplies should be prepared by the housekeeper together with the rooms department manager in order to make the housekeeper and maids feel they are an important part of the hotel. A disgruntled or alienated housekeeper will communicate these feelings to the maids, who in turn will communicate such feelings to the guests. Maids, front desk clerks, and concierges are the persons guests come in contact with. They don't meet the owner, who may be a warm and charming person. Disgruntled maids, front desk clerks, and concierges make terrible "goodwill" ambassadors for a hotel.

3. The preparation of a budget forces those preparing it to consider alternative courses of action. How should I spend the money to increase room sales? Is it better spent in using advertising to bring in more first-time guests, or should I improve the decor, furniture, and service in the rooms department to be sure I keep my current customers?

4. Those preparing the budget must look back at previous years' experience to avoid past mistakes. Perhaps guests complained about the amenities from a certain supplier. Will we change suppliers, even though they were the cheapest supplier?

5. Since they provide what the budget committee considers an optimum relationship between revenues, expenses, and investments, budgets serve as a basis against which to compare and evaluate actual results. If the personnel affected by the budget were part of the budget committee, then the evaluation process is the even healthier one of self-evaluation.

6. Budgets help identify the problem that is impeding the organization from achieving its goals. Analyzing the variances between budgeted and actual results may locate discrepancies in the hours worked, the hourly pay, the average room rate, the types of rooms sold, and so forth. This may indicate the source of a problem.

7. The budget provides a range of expected activity, between the most optimistic and pessimistic scenarios. This enables management to be prepared for either of these eventualities.

8. A budget forces management to consider the total impact of particular budget decisions. If a 30 percent increase in room sales is planned for, then the rooms department not only needs a larger operating budget, but perhaps the hotel may need more rooms. It is harder to overlook a particular aspect of a business when you have its entire operation laid out in budget format.

9. Finally, a budget makes managers and employees focus on future events that may be forthcoming outside of the organization, such as pending minimum wage legislation.

Some of the disadvantages of budgeting are the following:

1. It takes time, money, and hard work to prepare a budget. Studies indicate that the typical committee meeting costs approximately $1,000 per hour, and for every hour spent in the meeting there are many hours of preparation.

2. Budgets are, in fact, based on mere suppositions. Though a good budget is consistent with past trends, there is the danger that an excessively optimistic budget may serve to demotivate management and employees, rather than motivate them.

3. Budget amounts are based on confidential statistics such as percentage of room occupancy, variable cost per room, types of rooms sold, maids per occupied room, and so forth. Making these statistics generally available to an entire committee may expose the organization to leakage of such confidential data, which may assist competitors in planning their advertising campaigns or in otherwise benefiting from the hotel's experience.

4. A budget that is not prepared with total participation, or with the appropriate built-in rewards for spending under budget, may produce the opposite effect of that desired. It may polarize management and employees against the organization, resulting in spending to budget or over budget.

5. Budgets tend to make an organization rigid and inflexible.

On balance, the advantages of budgeting seem to far outweigh the disadvantages. This is especially true in medium- to large-size organizations, where budgets help to understand and deal with the complexity of these organizations, while bringing employees together with management in a spirit of cooperation. Some of the disadvantages, such as the rigidity they foster within an organization, can be overcome by proper management communication and motivation of lower managers and employees.

THE BUDGETING PROCESS

There are four steps in the budgeting process, often called the budgeting cycle:

1. Defining objectives and goals.
2. Preparing the plan to achieve the goals.
3. Analyzing differences between planned and actual performance.
4. Making necessary modifications and/or improvements, either within the operations of the business organization, or to the budget and budget process.

Defining Goals

As you may have suspected from the reading to this point, the budget process is not simply an accounting procedure that involves putting numbers to paper. It is not a method of using numbers to deny expenditures or keeping managers from overspending. Budgeting is a way of organizing management's and the employees' thoughts concerning an organization—concerning its goals and concerning how to achieve these goals. Therefore, the most successful budgeting processes generate an information flow from both the very pinnacle of the corporate structure, the board of directors, downward, and from the very bottom of the organization, the lowest level of employees, upward. Before an organization can respond, the board of directors must determine and communicate to the organization and the public what a particular organization's objectives are. This information must be transmitted downward to the lowest levels of the organization. Without this clear challenge an organization cannot respond, nor will it have guidelines along which to respond.

Once these objectives have been stated, then the second flow of information can begin, the flow of information from the bottom of the organization upward. This is the "response" to top management's challenge. This is the part of the budgeting process we are more familiar with. Through it, in the process of putting budget amounts to paper, subordinates tell top management how they feel their departments can respond to the challenge, that is, what goals they can achieve. An organization where the first flow of information, the statement of objectives, does not begin with top management is like a ship without a rudder. An organization where the actual budget is imposed from the top down is not a cooperative effort with all the motivating factors this implies, but rather a totalitarian organization, whose employees may become disgruntled and try to sabotage the budget goals. Employees with feelings of participation, belonging, and high morale are especially important in a service industry such as the hotel industry, where most employees are in constant contact with customers and can mold a customer's opinion regarding the organization. One of the objectives of all hospitality organizations should always be to maintain an atmosphere where employees feel appreciated.

Objectives

Objectives differ from goals in that they represent a more philosophical and general statement concerning what the corporation stands for. Therefore, the organization's goals must be set within the context of its objectives. A corporation's objectives must take into account (1) the financial aspects of the company, (2) the company's impact on society, (3) its impact on its employees, and (4) its impact on the owners. Except when a monopoly exists the company will enhance its financial position most when it best serves its customers. Customer interests, therefore, should not be considered a separate potential objective. For instance, a hotel corporation might have as its objectives to maximize financial growth while maintaining its historic dividend policy. It may state that it wants to do this while creating a friendly yet stimulating working environment for its employees, an environment that will give them the maximum opportunity to grow. It may also wish to make it an objective to create hotels that blend in with and beautify their environment.

Goals

Once its objectives have been made clear, the organization can proceed to focus on its goals within the context of these objectives. If it is a business organization, its ultimate financial goals are those stated at the beginning of this chapter: (1) to maximize sales, (2) to minimize expenses, and (3) to minimize investment. These ultimate financial goals must be considered within the broader context of the hospitality industry and so some intermediate, more specific, objectives may have to be created. Some intermediate objectives might be (1) to enter the all-suite hotel market, (2) to obtain a 30 percent market share in the southeastern United States, (3) to have a 10 percent overall profit margin, and (4) to attain an overall annual sales growth rate of 20 percent. These intermediate objectives can be further broken down into specific objectives for each hotel within a chain. Thus one hotel will be targeted for conversion to suites, whereas another will continue to target the middle market. It may be desired to increase market share in the Southeast to 30 percent mostly by adding new hotels and increasing the existing hotels' sales only by 7 percent annually. Hotels in the Northeast region may be targeted for a 20 percent growth rate in sales. Organizationwide goals need to be translated into hotel-specific goals.

It is only after the objectives and goals of a business organization have been thus established that a given hotel's management can begin to prepare the profit plan, or budget. Because it is so intimately connected with, and should reflect the broad objectives and goals of the organization, it is essential that management not allow the budget process to become disconnected from this "big picture" viewpoint. But that is exactly what will happen if management ignores the behavioral aspects of budgeting and sees it merely as an accounting exercise of projecting numbers on paper.

Behavioral Aspects of Budgeting

If top management has done its job properly, for example, the hotel managers will have had meetings with regional or divisional managers, who will have informed them of next year's objectives and goals for the entire organization and for their individual hotels orally and in writing. There they will have presented any objections to their hotel's assigned goals. Once they understand these goals and feel they are reasonable, hotel managers will return to their properties and present to their department managers the overall organization's objectives and goals along with the specific goals for their hotel. Sometimes these meetings may be complemented with regional or organizationwide convocations or conventions where the overall objectives and goals are presented, thereby adding emotional impact and vitality to the budget process. Companies that do this tend to understand the full scope of budgeting and give due importance to the behavioral impact of budgeting. Department managers then meet with their subordinates, the housekeepers and front office managers in the case of the rooms department, to prepare their departmental budget. These budgets are then sent back up the organization to top management.

The behavioral aspects of budgeting have been mentioned frequently because they are crucial to converting a budget from a cost-control scheme into a truly growth-stimulating profit plan. A budget imposed from the top down may not count on the full support of the organization's employees. No matter how reasonable the budget goals, employees may try to prove these goals unreasonable if they were not a part of the decision leading to these goals. On the other hand, when they are truly a part of the budget process, employees are more likely to make it a matter of pride to achieve budget goals. Furthermore, when it comes time to measure the success of the organization, fully involved employees are more likely to accept with a sense of personal responsibility those areas where goals were not met, rather than ridiculing the goals for having been set unreasonably high by their superiors. It is better to set goals that are slightly unreasonable by consensus, than to set more reasonable goals by a unilateral top-down decision. Care must be taken that the consensus achieved in the budget committees is not only apparent, but also real. If an upper management's spokesperson dominates the committee, the consequences can be similar to those of an imposed budget. Resistance to budget goals may also arise when budgets seem to be intended to "pressure" lower management to perform, or when they favor other departments, or when they are too inflexible.

Besides outright resistance to a particular budget, other problems may reduce the effectiveness of the budgeting process. There is a natural tendency to understate sales, overstate expenses, and overstate cash needs in order to look good when budget goals are exceeded or to be sure a department doesn't run out of cash. This is known as "padding the budget" or *budgetary slack*. These problems can greatly reduce the motivating power of the budget process. To avoid these problems top management must exercise its leadership role from the start by explaining the need for such a process. Then management must convince middle managers to identify with the organization's objectives and goals. Leadership also means selecting the right type of budget (fixed, flexible, or zero base), establishing proper incentives to meet or exceed budget goals, and, most important of all, keeping open channels of communication with subordinates.

If it is informed and in constant communication with subordinates, management is more likely to become aware of and avoid such problems as "padding the budget." An employee whose boss loosens the purse strings when presented with a reasonable need will not be as prone to pad the budget as an employee whose boss adheres inflexibly to budgetary restrictions. Constant communication can serve to bring employee focus back to the goals of the organization when they become distracted. That a plan as formal as a budget exists helps top management and subordinates adhere to a specific frame of reference, thereby adding consistency to management's leadership and providing specific topics of discussion. When all of these leadership functions have been properly exercised by upper management in developing a budget, the budget goals will tend to be seen as fair.

Preparing the Budget Plan

As explained earlier, the rooms department is a profit center, thus the rooms department manager is responsible for maximizing sales and minimizing expenses. This means that the rooms department manager will only be responsible for preparing a budgeted income statement and a budgeted operating cash flow. A nonoperating budget, which includes the financing and capital expenditures budgets and budgeted balance sheet, will not usually be required of rooms department managers.

Since sales are the basis for calculating expenses and cash needs, budgets should be prepared in the following order:

1. Sales budgets
2. Expense budgets
3. Operating cash flows

Because of the complexity of the budgeting process, most organizations develop a *budget manual* to help managers and employees prepare their budgets. A brief overview of the format and usefulness of this manual will be presented later. Here, we will explain the various ways of projecting sales, expenses, and operating cash flows.

Developing the Sales Plan

The five-year annual or *strategic sales plan* should be prepared first. The first year of this strategic sales plan should then be prepared on a detailed monthly basis. This monthly budget is the *tactical sales plan* because it helps managers make day-to-day tactical decisions. The process for preparing the sales plan is different for a new business than for an established business, since the latter's past experience serves as a basis for its future plan. Also, before beginning to prepare the sales plan, the rooms department manager must be informed of the company's overall objectives and goals, which he or she should take into account in preparing the plan. He or she must also be provided with specific parameters within which to structure the sales plan. The rooms department manager must be told what markets the hotel is trying to reach, what strategies it will use to reach them, what pricing philosophy to use, and what the hotel's competitive position is. The rooms department manager must also be told what financial resources can be made available by the organization to the hotel and to the rooms department.

For an established business a sales budget plan is the same as a sales projection, with the difference that a budget plan is backed up by management judgment, planned strategies, and committed resources. When projecting sales, an estimate of reasonably attainable growth should be made while taking two sets of factors into account:

1. Demand for outputs (the demand for rooms in the case of rooms department) as reflected by the following factors:
   (a) Long-term growth achieved in previous years
   (b) The current growth trend
   (c) Management decisions affecting growth trend
   (d) The state of the economy
   — Recessionary or growing
   — Inflationary
   (e) Strength of demand and expected growth in demand
   (f) Competition that can be expected within the next five years
   (g) Room rate structure
2. Supply of inputs (internal company bottlenecks that may place limits on speed and amount of sales growth):
   (a) Will all of our current employees continue to work?
   (b) Can we expect our current employees to do more work?
   (c) How quickly can new employees be hired?
   (d) How quickly can they be trained?
   (e) How easily can we obtain needed supplies?
   (f) Do we need to rehabilitate unused rooms or add new?
   (g) Do we need to make the facilities more efficient to enable our current employees to perform more work?
   (h) Can we expect the organization to obtain for our department the money necessary to hire more employees, buy more supplies, and expand or improve our facilities?

In evaluating the overall impact of the above factors, an estimate of their individual impact should be made. The chart shown in Exhibit 12-8 presents an example of how this might be done. A more sophisticated approach might include assigning probabilities of occurrence to each of the projected changes in sales growth (known as the use of *fuzzy logic*). This same analytic approach can be applied to the estimated changes in the inputs needed to generate the projected sales.

The logic behind a sales budget can best be summarized with the question: What sales growth can we reasonably expect to generate with the resources we have, or can expect to obtain, given the environment we will be working in? The answer is, at best, a guess, for which accuracy increases with experience. But it is a guess that must be made, because it is better to guess and then build logical expense and cash flow relationships around this sales guess, than it is to leave sales, expenses, and cash needs all to happenstance. Established businesses can use sophisticated statistical techniques, such as regression analysis and exponential smoothing, for projecting past experience into the future. It is beyond the scope of this chapter to explain these techniques and generally, at the rooms de-

EXHIBIT 12-8
IMPACT ON SALES GROWTH OF CERTAIN PERTINENT FACTORS
EXPRESSED AS AN ANNUAL PERCENTAGE

	Increase	Decrease
(a) Long-term growth trend		
– Management feels the current (recent) growth trend represents eventual future growth better than the long-term growth trend.	0%	0%
(b) Current growth trend	7.0%	
(c) Management decisions affecting growth		
– Management has decided to withdraw from the northeast market.		2.0%
(d) Economy entering a recession		1.0%
(e) Expected growth in demand		
– Company has introduced a new concept in hotel rooms.	1.0%	
(f) Competition expected within next five years.		1.0%
– There is currently overbuilding		1.0%
(g) Room rate structure		
– Room rate strata restructured to partially compensate for overbuilding.	0.5%	
	8.5%	5.0%
Factors tending to increase sales		8.5%
less: Factors tending to decrease sales		5.0%
Expected net annual growth in sales =		3.5%

partment management level, the additional accuracy gained by using them does not warrant the extra work. A logical interpretation of past trends, and good judgment in determining how these trends may be modified in the future are the best tools for preparing sales budget projections. For example, let's look at the breakdown of sales accounts that appears in the rooms department income schedule prepared according to the Uniform System of Accounts for Hotels and shown in Exhibit 12-3.

In the Transient-Regular category, we may count on recurring sales from corporations, such as airlines, for lodging their employees. In the Transient-Group category we can count on a certain number of conventions that were sold in prior years. In the Permanent category we can count on guests who use the hotel as a year-round residence. These three sales categories provide a more solid basis for making projections than mere "guesstimating." Also, the techniques for estimating sales used by new enterprises, explained below, are helpful in testing the reasonableness of sales projections made on the basis of general good judgment as applied to past experience in an established business.

In the case of a new business, the sales guess cannot be made with the benefit of past experience. In this case, it is best to break down room sales into its components and try to determine reasonable expectations for each component. This procedure is based on the following two relationships:

$$\text{sales} = \text{room nights sold} \times \text{average room rate}$$
$$\text{room nights sold} = \text{days open} \times \text{occupancy percentage} \times \text{available rooms}$$

The marketing department should help the rooms department manager determine what a logical average room rate should be. This decision should take into account whether emphasis will be given to selling more rooms at a lower rate or selling less rooms at a higher rate. In other words some thought and study should be given to determination of the elasticity of demand for the hotel's rooms. Demand characteristics will depend on the competitiveness of the market. In a more competitive market, higher dollar sales are achieved by selling more rooms at a lower price. In a more monopolistic market, higher dollar sales are achieved by maximizing room rates without much concern for the impact this will have on the occupancy percentage.

At any rate, once the average rate has been determined, the *DeVeau formula*, explained in Chapter 4 of this book, can be used to translate this average room rate into rates for individual room categories. This, in turn, enables a manager to evaluate whether or not an overall average rate is reasonable in view of what the individual room category rates will have to be to achieve it. The days a hotel will be open and the available rooms are known factors. Thus, the remaining factor in predicting a hotel's dollar sales is to predict an occupancy percentage within the context of the targeted average room rate.

The above relationships can also be used to test sales projections for an existing hotel. When sales are projected on the basis of nonquantitative judgments applied to past trends, it is easier to get out of touch with reality. Breaking down a general sales estimate into its components (room rates, days open, percentage occupancy, and number of rooms) helps to evaluate the reasonableness of a projection. In Exhibit 12-9 a hotel's year 2001 estimated sales are shown in comparison with 1999 and 2000 actual sales. A 20 percent increase in sales is budgeted between the years 2000 and 2001. However, breaking this sales estimate down into its components makes us realize that in order to achieve this apparently reasonable sales plan, it will be necessary to do one of, or a combination of, the following:

1. Increase the average room rate to $88.
2. Increase the occupancy percentage to 66 percent.
3. Be open 300 days per year.
4. Achieve some combination of the above three goals.

This helps to pinpoint exactly what management's goals should be with regard to each of these three components of sales if the hotel wishes to achieve the bud-

EXHIBIT 12-9
PROJECTING ROOM SALES BY ESTIMATING SALES COMPONENTS FOR A
148-ROOM HOTEL

	Actual Sales		Projected Sales
Year	1999	2000	2001
	$1,309,055	$1,492,266	$1,790,800

Actual Percentage Increase	Projected Percentage Increase
1999–2000	2000–2001
$\dfrac{\$1,492,266 - \$1,309,055}{\$1,309,055} = .14$	$\dfrac{\$1,790,800 - \$1,492,266}{\$1,492,266} = .20$

Rooms Sales Components Achieved in 2000 to Generate $1,492,266 Sales

Average Room Rate	×	% Occupancy	×	Days Open	×	Available Rooms	=	Dollar Sales
$73.33	×	55%	×	250	×	148	=	$1,492,266

Alternative Sales Component Combinations Required to Achieve
Projected 2001 Sales

Alt. #	Average Room Rate	×	% Occupancy	×	Days Open	×	Available Rooms	=	Dollar Sales
(1)	$88.00	×	55%	×	250	×	148	=	$1,790,800
(2)	$73.33	×	66%	×	250	×	148	=	$1,790,719
(3)	$73.33	×	55%	×	300	×	148	=	$1,790,719

geted dollar sales amount. It also helps to determine whether they are in fact reasonable goals in the market in which the hotel is operating and with the resources that the hotel has available.

Projecting Expenses

Once sales have been projected, expenses must be matched to them. As explained earlier, there are three types of expenses:

1. Variable—which change in direct proportion to sales
2. Semivariable—which change in the same direction as sales, but not in the same proportion
3. Fixed—which do not change over the short run

In an earlier section of this chapter, when we thought about the expense categories in the rooms department income schedule shown in Exhibit 12-3, we came to the conclusion that they all fall into the semivariable category. If we review the Uniform System of Accounts listed in the appendix at the end of this chapter, we see that certain expense subcategories included in each of the major expense categories shown in Exhibit 12-3 can be considered to be truly variable expenses and not semivariable. An example of this is guest supplies expense, which is a subcategory of operating supplies. These are, however, the exceptions.

Most rooms expenses, to a greater or lesser degree, have both a variable and a fixed element in them. In projecting these expenses, therefore, they must be hypothetically divided into two amounts. The fixed element of each account must be projected first and then the variable element. In the case of Salaries and Wages category, the salaries of all the year-round permanent personnel would be considered the "fixed" element of the Salaries and Wages expense category. The salaries of part-time help and any additional maids that might be needed would be considered the "variable" element. An established hotel rooms department, with past experience, might express the variable portion of wages as a percentage of sales, demonstrated earlier in this chapter. But the best procedure is to have the housekeeper prepare a staffing guide based on sales projections. Once the budget sales and expense estimates have been made, they can be presented either in a fixed budget or flexible budget format, described earlier in this chapter. A sample of a *flexible budget rooms department income schedule* is shown in Exhibit 12-10 and a *fixed budget rooms department income schedule* is shown in Exhibit 12-4.

When prepared as a fixed budget, specific dollar amounts will be included in the budget. When prepared on a flexible budget basis, the variable element of rooms department expenses will be expressed as a percent of sales, and the fixed element will be expressed as a specific dollar amount. Depending upon whether this is a zero-based budget or a standard budget, the rooms department manager would have to back up these budget estimates with a business plan justifying 100 percent of all the expenses (zero-based budget), or one that merely justifies the increase in expenses over last year's budget (standard budget).

EXHIBIT 12-10
FLEXIBLE BUDGET

Budgeted Rooms Department Schedule
Flexible Budget
For the Year Ended December 31, 2000

Revenue	Fixed Element	Variable Element	Total Budgeted
Transient-Regular	---	54.3502%	$1,523,974
Transient-Group	---	37.4297%	1,049,526
Permanent	---	7.1327%	200,000
Other Rooms Revenue	---	1.0874%	30,491
Total Revenue	---	100.0000%	$2,803,991
Allowances	---	1.1331%	31,771
Net Revenue		98.8669%	$2,772,220
Expenses			
Salaries and Wages	$350,000	2.6558%	424,468
Employee Benefits	50,100	0.7571%	71,329
Total Payroll & Related Expenses	$400,100	3.4129%	$495,797
Other Expenses			
Commissions	---	0.9762%	27,372
Contract Cleaning	2,000	0.4238%	13,883
Guest Transportation	---	0.3295%	9,240
Laundry and Dry Cleaning	8,312	1.5700%	52,336
Linen	6,540	0.5404%	21,692
Operating Supplies	15,271	1.1004%	46,125
Reservations	---	1.3684%	38,369
Uniforms	7,239	0.0600%	8,922
Other	9,427	0.2701%	17,001
Total Other Expenses	$48,789	6.6388%	$234,940
Total Expenses			730,737
Departmental Income			$2,041,483

Explanation of Fixed and Variable Elements

The fixed element is the part of each expense category that remains constant as sales increase. For example, in salaries and wages, the managers' salaries are fixed. Cleaning personnel, on the other hand, are part of the variable element because they increase as sales increase.

Preparing the Operating Cash Flow Budget

As previously explained, the rooms department income schedule is prepared according to accrual basis accounting concepts. More specifically, it is based on the *realization concept* and the *matching concept*. These two concepts define the difference between revenues and expenses, used in preparing the income schedule, and receipts and expenditures, used in preparing the cash flow budgets. The *realization concept* states that revenue is generated when a service is rendered, not when payment is received. The *matching concept* states that an expense should be recorded when it is incurred, not when it is paid for.

Since the operating cash budget is prepared under cash basis accounting, the accrual basis terms, such as revenues and expenses (which are tied to the rendering of services and incurring expenses), have no place in preparing the operating cash budget, except as a starting point for estimating cash receipts and expenditures. Only terms such as *receipts* and *expenditures* or their equivalents can be used when preparing cash basis budgets. Over the long run both the income schedule and operating cash budget will tell the same story concerning a company's operating results. Over the short run, however, the operating cash budget gives a rooms department manager a clear picture of what the department's cash inflows and cash outflows are expected to be, which the budgeted income schedule is not designed to do.

In order to prepare an operating cash budget, estimates of when actual payments on sales will be received need to be made. Likewise, estimates of the dates when expenses will be paid are necessary. After these estimates have been made, it is possible to translate a budgeted income schedule, such as the one in Exhibit 12-5, into the operating cash budget shown in Exhibit 12-6. For example, the budgeted income schedule shown in Exhibit 12-5 indicates total July revenue is $341,941. But the operating cash budget in Exhibit 12-6 shows that of this amount only $202,655 and $4,182 are actually collected in July and appear in the July column of the operating cash budget. The balance of the $341,941 is collected as follows: $101,328 in August and $33,776 in September. These latter two amounts, therefore, appear in the August and September columns of the operating cash budget. The same type of staggered reporting occurs when including certain expenses on the operating cash budget if they are not paid in the same month that they were incurred. For example, the cost of food and beverage sales appears as $79,695 in the July column of the budgeted income schedule. On the operating cash budget, however, $47,817 of this total is included in the July column and $31,878 appears in the August column, corresponding to the months in which these expenses were actually paid. Cash budgets, therefore, are based on receipts and expenditures, not on accrual accounting concepts such as revenue and expense. The footnote numbers in the exhibit refer the reader to notes explaining how individual amounts were obtained. Depreciation and amortization do not appear on the cash budget because they are non-cash expenses.

Evaluating Results

As stated repeatedly in this chapter, a budget is a plan for growth that should unite and motivate an organization in a common effort. We have seen how management exercises its management function by communicating objectives and goals downward to the organization, and how the organization responds by communicating upward to management, in the form of the budget plan, the goals that it considers reasonable and the means of achieving them. The third step in the budget process is to look back and evaluate how successfully these goals were met. This should be done on an interim basis, monthly or quarterly, through performance reports, and annually through the annual budget analysis.

The following techniques are available to help management evaluate performance:

1. Comparative Analysis
2. Vertical Analysis
3. Variance Analysis
    (a) Simple dollar variance analysis
    (b) Percentage variance analysis
    (c) Compound dollar variance analysis
4. Ratio Analysis

Comparative Statement Analysis

Comparative statement analysis, as the name implies, involves comparing the actual rooms departmental income schedule on a monthly, annual, or any periodic basis with the budgeted departmental income schedule. This is done by placing them side-by-side and scanning the budgeted and actual statements while trying to detect any outstanding differences between budgeted and actual amounts. In Exhibit 12-5 we can see the monthly budgeted income statements arranged in contiguous vertical columns ready for scanning. For a comparative analysis the actual income statements would be placed below the budgeted so that they could be readily compared with the budget. Through a comparative analysis the major differences between actual and budgeted amounts can be detected. It is difficult to detect minor, however, yet significant differences. Other, more sensitive, methods of analysis are needed for this purpose. These methods—vertical analysis, variance analysis, and ratio analysis—will be discussed next.

Vertical Analysis

Vertical analysis, one of the techniques of common-size statement analysis, allows for more sensitive detection of changes in account balances. It is one of the common-size analysis techniques because it relates individual revenue and expense amounts to total revenues on a percentage basis, thereby allowing comparisons between actual and budgeted amounts as if they were a common size. By relating account balances to revenue, small percentage changes between actual and budgeted amounts can be detected, and also the relative importance of large deviations from budgeted amounts can be evaluated.

To perform a vertical analysis, actual and budgeted revenue and expense accounts are expressed as a percent of total revenue. This is accomplished by dividing each revenue and expense account by total revenue. Vertical analysis enables a manager to evaluate and to compare with the budget the actual percentage of revenue generated by the various revenue accounts and the percentage of total revenue spent on the various expense accounts. Revenue accounts whose percentage of total revenue is increasing indicate good management performance, and expense accounts whose percentage of total revenue is decreasing also indicate good performance.

Exhibit 12-11 shows a vertical analysis, which compares the actual rooms department income schedule shown in Exhibit 12-3 with the fixed budget rooms department income schedule shown in Exhibit 12-4. Because account amounts are related to total revenue, it is possible to appreciate deviations from budgeted

EXHIBIT 12-11
VERTICAL ANALYSIS

Vertical Analysis of Rooms Department Schedules
Actual vs. Budgeted for the Year Ended December 31, 2000

Revenue	Budgeted	%	Actual	%
Transient-Regular	1,523,974	54.97%	$1,591,000	53.73%
Transient-Group	1,049,526	37.86%	1,143,653	38.62%
Permanent	200,000	7.21%	226,000	7.63%
Other Rooms Revenue	30,491	1.10%	32,854	1.11%
Total Revenue	2,803,991	101.15%	2,993,507	101.10%
Allowances	31,771	1.15%	32,507	1.10%
Net Revenue	2,772,220	100.00%	2,961,000	100.00%
Expenses				
Salaries and Wages	424,468	15.31%	453,461	15.31%
Employee Benefits	71,329	2.57%	79,519	2.69%
Total Payroll & Related Expenses	495,797	17.88%	532,980	18.00%
Other Expenses				
Commissions	27,372	0.99%	28,562	0.96%
Contract Cleaning	13,883	0.50%	14,029	0.47%
Guest Transportation	9,240	0.33%	10,530	0.36%
Laundry and Dry Cleaning	52,336	1.89%	54,376	1.84%
Linen	21,692	0.78%	23,994	0.81%
Operating Supplies	46,125	1.66%	48,725	1.65%
Reservations	38,369	1.38%	39,263	1.33%
Uniforms	8,922	0.32%	9,044	0.31%
Other	17,001	0.61%	17,240	0.58%
Total Other Expenses	234,940	8.47%	245,763	8.30%
Total Expenses	730,737	26.36%	778,743	26.30%
Departmental Income	$2,041,483	73.64%	$2,182,257	73.70%

percentages as well as to appreciate their importance with regard to revenue of dollar deviations from budgeted amounts.

Simple Dollar and Percent Variance Analysis

There are three types of variance analysis: (1) simple dollar variance analysis, (2) percent variance analysis, and (3) compound dollar variance analysis. Simple dollar variances are the differences between budgeted and actual revenue and expense amounts. An evaluation of the dollar amount of these differences helps determine how far off-budget the actual results were. In Exhibit 12-12 is shown a simple dollar variance analysis of the actual and budgeted rooms department income schedules from Exhibits 12-3 and 12-4.

A percent variance analysis goes one step further by dividing these dollar variances by their respective budget amounts. This enables us to determine by what percent the actual amounts exceeded or were short of budgeted amounts. In Exhibit 12-12 there is also a column indicating the percentage variation between the above-mentioned actual and budgeted rooms department schedule amounts. The report in Exhibit 12-12 is one of several possible *performance reports* that can be used in the rooms department.

Compound Dollar Variance Analysis

To understand compound variance analysis it is necessary to review the makeup of dollar sales and expense amounts. Sales and expenses are the result of two components: (1) unit price or unit cost, and (2) unit volume. For example, if actual room sales fall short of budgeted room sales, it is either because the actual average room rate was lower than the budgeted average room rate or because less rooms were sold, or some combination of these two factors. The same can be said of actual cost deviations from budget. By analyzing variances it is possible to determine to what extent each component has contributed to any deviation from budget. We will see how this is done through the following example. Let us begin by analyzing the following sales variance:

	Actual	Budgeted	Variance
Room sales	$100,000	$110,000	($10,000)
Variable labor cost	$2200	$2250	($50)
Rooms sold	1000	1200	(200)
Hours worked	550	600	(50)

First the actual and budgeted average room rates must be calculated:

	Actual	Budgeted
Average Room Rates	$100.00	$91.67

EXHIBIT 12-12
SIMPLE VARIANCE ANALYSIS

Simple Dollar Variance and Percent Variance Analysis
Actual vs. Budgeted for the Year Ended December 31, 2000

Revenue	Budgeted	Actual	Variance	Percent Variance
Transient-Regular	1,523,974	$1,591,000	$67,026	4.40%
Transient-Group	1,049,526	1,143,653	94,127	8.97%
Permanent	200,000	226,000	26,000	13.00%
Other Rooms Revenue	30,491	32,854	2,363	7.75%
Total Revenue	2,803,991	2,993,507	189,516	6.76%
Allowances	31,771	32,507	736	2.32%
Net Revenue	2,772,220	2,961,000	188,780	6.81%
Expenses				
Salaries and Wages	424,468	453,461	28,993	6.83%
Employee Benefits	71,329	79,519	8,190	11.48%
Total Payroll & Related Expenses	495,797	532,980	37,183	7.50%
Other Expenses				
Commissions	27,372	28,562	1,190	4.35%
Contract Cleaning	13,883	14,029	146	1.05%
Guest Transportation	9,240	10,530	1,290	13.96%
Laundry and Dry Cleaning	52,336	54,376	2,040	3.90%
Linen	21,692	23,994	2,302	10.61%
Operating Supplies	46,125	48,725	2,600	5.64%
Reservations	38,369	39,263	894	2.33%
Uniforms	8,922	9,044	122	1.37%
Other	17,001	17,240	239	1.41%
Total Other Expenses	234,940	245,763	10,823	4.61%
Total Expenses	730,737	778,743	48,006	6.57%
Departmental Income	$2,041,483	$2,182,257	140,774	6.90%

Next, the differences between actual and budgeted average room rates and actual and budgeted unit sales are calculated.

	Average Rate	Unit Sales
Budgeted	$91.67	1200
Actual	100.00	1000
Differences	$ 8.33	200

These differences indicate that rooms were sold at a higher average rate than budgeted, but that 200 less rooms were sold than budgeted. The extent to which each of these factors is responsible for the $10,000 unfavorable variance in sales is ascertained by calculating what are called (1) the unit price variance, and (2) the unit volume variance. This is done below:

Unit price variance $8.33 × 1000 = $8330 Favorable
Unit volume variance   200   × $91.67 = ($18,334) Unfavorable
Net variance   ($10,004) Unfavorable

These calculations indicate that the $100 average room rate, higher than budgeted, causes a favorable unit price variance of $8330. But the fact that 200 less rooms than budgeted were sold creates an unfavorable unit volume variance of $18,334. The net variance of $10,004 is not exactly equal to the $10,000 variance in sales originally calculated because of rounding. If exact amounts are desired, four decimal places should be used in these calculations.

The same procedure can be applied to the analysis of cost variances. As in the case of sales variance analysis, the actual and budgeted hourly wage must first be calculated:

HOURLY WAGES

Actual	Budgeted
$4.00	$3.75

Next, the differences between actual and budgeted hourly wage and actual and budgeted hours worked are calculated.

	Hourly Wage	Hours Worked
Budgeted	$3.75	600
Actual	$4.00	550
Differences	$.25	50

These differences indicate that the hourly wage paid was $.25 higher than budgeted, but that 50 less hours were worked than budgeted. The extent to which each of these factors is responsible for the $50 favorable variance in labor cost is ascertained by calculating what are called (1) the unit cost variance, and (2) the unit volume variance. This is done below.

Unit cost variance $.25 × 550 = $137.50 Unfavorable
Unit volume variance   50 × $3.75 = $187.50 Favorable
Net variance $ 50.00 Favorable

These calculations indicate that the $4.00 hourly wage, higher than budgeted, causes an unfavorable unit cost variance of $137.50. But the fact that 50 less hours were worked than budgeted creates a favorable unit volume variance of $187.50. The net result is that $50 less than budgeted was spent on variable labor expense. However, this is not such good news because, if the wage rate had been kept at the budgeted $3.75 per hour, then the favorable variance would have been $137.50 ($2,200 − [$3.75 × 550 hours]).

The general rule for calculating unit sales or cost variance and unit volume variance is that the unit sales price or cost difference is multiplied by the actual volume to calculate the unit price or cost variance, and the unit volume difference is multiplied by the budgeted unit sales price or unit cost (whichever applies) to calculate the unit volume variance. When analyzing results, an actual revenue higher than budgeted revenue is obviously favorable, and an actual expense higher than the budgeted amount is unfavorable.

Something that is difficult to accept is that when actual volume is lower than budgeted volume it creates a favorable cost volume variance. To help accept this, it should be remembered that an unfavorable sales variance is created when volume drops, and this usually offsets the favorable cost volume variance.

Operating Ratio Analysis

The final technique for analyzing differences between actual and budgeted amounts to be dealt with here is called *operating ratio analysis*. Operating ratios measure the relationship between revenues and expenses and units of input and units of output. Thus they help to pinpoint areas where better management might enable the attainment of budget goals.

Some typical ratios that might be used in the rooms department are the following:

$$1. \text{ Average room rate} = \frac{\text{Rooms revenue}}{\text{Total occupied rooms}}$$

$$2. \text{ Guest occupancy} = \frac{\text{Guest occupied rooms}}{\text{Available rooms}}$$

In addition to the overall average room rate, average rates may be calculated for transient regular guests, transient groups, and permanent guests. Also, percentage occupancy may be calculated for transient regular guests, transient groups, permanent guests, and temporary house use. Changes in percentage occupancy from higher-rate room categories to lower-rate categories might explain why actual sales fell short of budgeted sales. A high temporary house use occupancy percentage might also be causing lost sales in moments of peak sales activity. Some other ratios to look at are the following:

$$\text{Guests per occupied room} = \frac{\text{Total guests}}{\text{Number of guest occupied rooms}}$$

$$\text{Multiple occupancy percentage} = \frac{\text{Rooms with multiple guests}}{\text{Number of guest-occupied rooms}}$$

A high number of guests per occupied room or a high multiple occupancy percentage might also be causing sales to fall short of budget, because multiple guests in one room pay much less than on a single-occupancy basis.

Some operating ratios for controlling costs might be the following:

$$\text{Occupied rooms per maid} = \frac{\text{Occupied rooms}}{\text{Number of maids}}$$

$$\text{Occupied rooms per front desk clerk} = \frac{\text{Occupied rooms}}{\text{Number of front desk clerks}}$$

As these ratios decline they indicate decreasing efficiency in labor utilization, which might cause payroll expense to exceed budgeted amounts.

The previous examples are the most commonly used operating ratios for analyzing actual versus budgeted management performance in the rooms department. However, other ratios may, and should be, created when a particular situation requires it.

Performance Reports and Management by Exception

To determine how well budget goals are being met and how well they are exercising their control function, management should establish a system of periodic performance reports, either on a monthly or quarterly basis, in addition to the year-end budget analysis. These reports should employ the techniques discussed above to analyze management performance. With this feedback managers can take corrective action where necessary. In some instances a manager may decide that budget goals were unrealistic and may decide to correct remaining portions of the current budget. But, because the various departmental budgets are so intertwined, this can be a cumbersome and awkward procedure, so it might be better to wait for next year's budget period to make corrections. Managers can also use this feedback to further stimulate employees to meet budget goals and/or to take measures that will help the different departments to meet their goals. Perhaps more training is necessary, perhaps a small modification (such as the relocation of the linen storage from a central location to the points of use) might help, or perhaps establishing better controls over guest amenities is what is needed.

To be effective a performance report must be simple and straightforward. Accounting information that is unintelligible to management is useless. Exhibit 12-13 presents a performance report that might be utilized in the rooms department. This report enables the rooms department manager to see his actual performance results for the current month and for the year-to-date. Managers might compare each month's report to those of previous months. A vertical analysis, percent variance analysis, or operating ratio analysis might also be attached to the report to give management a deeper understanding of what is causing variances.

To facilitate the review of monthly performance reports and the year-end budget analysis, management should predetermine what amount of variance will be considered acceptable for each account. Thus management need devote

EXHIBIT 12-13
PERFORMANCE REPORT

Sample Performance Report
Actual vs. Budgeted for the Month and Year Ended December 31, 2000

	Current Month			Year-to-Date		
Revenue	Budgeted	Actual	Variance	Budgeted	Actual	Variance
Transient-Regular	$1,523,974	$1,591,000	$ 67,026	$18,104,811	$18,758,606	$ 653,795
Transient-Group	1,049,526	1,143,653	94,127	12,216,483	12,822,523	606,040
Permanent	200,000	226,000	26,000	2,256,000	2,287,120	31,120
Other Rooms Revenue	30,491	32,854	2,363	353,086	410,018	56,932
Total Revenue	$2,803,991	$2,993,507	$189,516	$32,930,380	$34,278,267	$1,347,887
Allowances	31,771	32,507	736	372,102	401,461	29,359
Net Revenue	$2,772,220	$2,961,000	$188,780	$32,558,278	$33,876,806	$1,318,528
Expenses						
Salaries and Wages	$ 424,468	$ 453,461	$ 28,993	$ 5,068,148	$ 5,280,179	$ 212,031
Employee Benefits	71,329	79,519	8,190	847,816	962,856	115,040
Total Payroll and Related Expenses	$ 495,797	$ 532,980	$ 37,183	$ 5,915,964	$ 6,243,035	$ 327,071
Other Expenses						
Commissions	27,372	28,562	1,190	$ 317,953	$ 322,999	5,046
Contract Cleaning	13,883	14,029	146	$ 162,930	$ 157,186	(5,744)
Guest Transportation	9,240	10,530	1,290	$ 104,172	$ 125,728	21,556
Laundry and Dry Cleaning	52,336	54,376	2,040	$ 613,273	$ 625,444	12,171
Linen	21,692	23,994	2,302	$ 256,659	$ 293,035	36,376
Operating Supplies	46,125	48,725	2,600	$ 551,009	$ 571,617	20,608
Reservations	38,369	39,263	894	$ 449,148	$ 467,784	18,636
Uniforms	8,922	9,044	122	$ 103,103	$ 107,716	4,613
Other	17,001	17,240	239	$ 197,790	$ 210,886	13,096
Total Other Expenses	$ 234,940	$ 245,763	$ 10,823	$ 2,756,036	$ 2,882,395	$ 126,359
Total Expenses	$ 730,737	$ 778,743	$ 48,006	$ 8,672,000	$ 9,125,430	$ 453,430
Departmental Income	$2,041,483	$2,182,257	$140,774	$23,886,278	$24,751,376	$ 865,098

time only to those accounts that have exceeded these tolerances either monthly or year-to-date. This method of looking only at accounts that are being managed exceptionally well or exceptionally poorly is called "management by exception." It saves a considerable amount of time by calling management's attention only to those accounts that need it.

The Budget Manual

Another time-saving tool is the use of a budget manual to prepare the budget. It reduces wasted time in preparing the budget by focusing management's atten-

EXHIBIT 12-14
PERFORMANCE REPORT

	Current Month				Same Month Last Year			
			—Variance—				—Variance—	
Revenue	Budgeted	Actual	Dollar	%	Budgeted	Actual	Dollar	%
Transient-Regular	$1,523,974	$1,591,000	$67,026	4.40%	$1,493,495	$1,543,270	$49,775	3.33%
Transient-Group	1,049,526	1,143,653	94,127	8.97%	986,554	1,105,912	119,358	12.10%
Permanent	200,000	226,000	26,000	13.00%	176,000	189,840	13,840	7.86%
Other Rooms Revenue	30,491	32,854	2,363	7.75%	28,357	30,226	1,869	6.59%
Total Revenue	$2,803,991	$2,993,507	$189,516	6.76%	$2,684,406	$2,869,248	$184,842	6.89%
Allowances	31,771	32,507	736	2.32%	31,008	32,117	1,108	3.5%
Net Revenue	$2,772,220	$2,961,000	$188,780	6.81%	$2,653,397	$2,837,131	$183,734	6.92%
Expenses								
Salaries and Wages	$424,468	$453,461	$28,993	6.83%	$420,223	$453,008	$32,785	7.80%
Employee Benefits	71,329	79,519	8,190	11.48%	69,974	78,326	8,352	11.9%
Total Payroll &								
Related Expenses	$495,797	$532,980	$37,183	7.50%	$490,197	$531,334	$41,137	8.39%
Other Expenses								
Commissions	27,372	28,562	1,190	4.35%	25,620	28,505	2,885	11.26%
Contract Cleaning	13,883	14,029	146	1.05%	13,272	14,015	743	5.60%
Guest Transportation	9,240	10,530	1,290	13.96%	8,122	10,425	2,303	28.35%
Laundry and Dry Cleaning	52,336	54,376	2,040	3.90%	49,876	53,832	3,956	7.93%
Linen	21,692	23,994	2,302	10.61%	21,085	23,538	2,453	11.64%
Operating Supplies	46,125	48,725	2,600	5.64%	45,710	47,751	2,041	4.46%
Reservations	38,369	39,263	894	2.33%	36,489	38,831	2,342	6.42%
Uniforms	8,922	9,044	122	1.37%	8,262	8,746	484	5.86%
Other	17,001	17,240	239	1.41%	15,964	17,050	1,086	6.18%
Total Other Expenses	$234,940	$245,763	$10,823	4.61%	$224,400	$242,693	$18,293	8.15%
Total Expenses	$730,737	$778,743	$48,006	6.57%	$714,597	$774,027	$59,430	8.32%
Departmental Income	$2,041,483	$2,182,257	$140,774	6.90%	$1,938,800	$2,063,104	$124,304	6.41%
Rooms Sold	11,100	11,400	300	2.70%	10,650	10,950	300	2.82%
Percentage Occupancy	74%	76%	2%	—	71%	73%	2%	—
Average Room Rate	$137	$140	$3	1.65%	$140	$141	$1	0.50%

tion on the goals, procedures, and timing of the budget process. A budget manual should include the following:

1. Overall company objectives and specific goals of this particular budget.
2. An explanation of the budget process hierarchy.

- Who establishes company goals
- Divisional budget committee

| | Year-to-Date | | | Vertical Analysis of —-Actual Amounts—- Same Month | | |
| | | —-Variance—- | | Current | Last | Year- |
Budgeted	Actual	Dollar	%	Month	Year	to-Date
$18,104,811	$18,758,606	$653,795	3.61%	53.73%	54.40%	55.37%
12,216,483	12,822,523	606,040	4.96%	38.62%	38.98%	37.85%
2,256,000	2,287,120	31,120	1.38%	7.63%	6.69%	6.75%
353,086	410,018	56,932	16.12%	1.11%	1.07%	1.21%
$32,930,380	$34,278,267	$1,347,887	4.09%	101.10%	101.13%	101.19%
372,102	401,461	29,359	7.89%	1.10%	1.13%	1.19%
$32,558,278	$33,876,806	$1,318,528	4.05%	100.00%	100.00%	100.00%
$5,068,148	$5,280,179	$212,031	4.18%	15.31%	15.97%	15.59%
847,816	926,856	115,040	13.57%	2.69%	2.76%	2.84%
$5,915,964	$6,243,035	$327,071	5.53%	18.00%	18.73%	18.43%
$317,953	$322,999	5,046	1.59%	0.96%	1.00%	0.95%
$162,930	$157,186	(5,744)	−3.53%	0.47%	0.49%	0.46%
$104,172	$125,728	21,556	20.69%	0.36%	0.37%	0.37%
$613,273	$625,444	12,171	1.98%	1.84%	1.90%	1.85%
$256,659	$293,035	36,376	14.17%	0.81%	0.83%	0.87%
$551,009	$571,617	20,608	3.74%	1.65%	1.68%	1.69%
$449,148	$467,784	18,636	4.15%	1.33%	1.37%	1.38%
$103,103	$107,716	4,613	4.47%	0.31%	0.31%	0.32%
$197,790	$210,886	13,096	6.62%	0.58%	0.60%	0.62%
$2,756,037	$2,882,395	126,359	4.58%	8.30%	8.55%	8.51%
$8,672,001	$9,125,430	453,430	5.23%	26.30%	27.28%	26.94%
$23,886,277	$24,751,376	865,098	3.62%	73.70%	72.72%	73.06%
133,225	135,780	2,555	1.92%			
73%	74%	1%	—			
$136	$138	$2	1.47%			

- Hotel budget committee
- Departmental budget committees

3. A calendar of due dates for budgets.
4. Instructions concerning who receives budget schedules.
5. Instructions explaining the format, and how and by whom portions of the budget should be prepared. (Budget amounts, actual results, and variances and analyses.)
6. Format, content, and distribution of performance reports.

7. Evaluation and remedial action procedures for variances (both favorable and unfavorable).
8. Year-end budget review and modification procedures.

A well-prepared budget manual highlights the budget's function as a stimulator of communication among the members of a hotel organization. It gives the rooms department manager an appreciation for what other members of the hotel organization are contributing to the budget process. It indicates where particular questions are likely to be answered, and where the information the rooms department generates is going to be used and by whom it will be used. It inspires confidence in the budget process by demonstrating to the hotel organization how the budget works its way up from the bottom of the organization toward the top and how intertwined the various parts of the budget are. Furthermore, it presents the budget planning process for all to see, so that constructive suggestions may be made for improving the process in the future if appropriate.

Electronic Spreadsheets and Budgeting

As should be evident by now, preparing a budget is not a simple process. Although it involves much more than a numerical plan, such a plan is at the heart of the budget and is the most time-consuming part of the budget process. It involves making numerous estimates, calculations, and changes in these estimates. Electronic spreadsheets are specifically designed to handle just these types of numerical manipulations. The use of electronic spreadsheets is commonly called "number crunching." Because different cells in an electronic spreadsheet can be related to each other, it is possible to change one number and have all the numbers related to it change almost instantaneously. This eliminates the constant erasures and tedious manual recalculations that once plagued the budget process. This facility, coupled with the low cost of microcomputers, renders the old manual spreadsheet as completely outdated. Some outstanding electronic spreadsheet programs are Lotus 1-2-3, Microsoft Excel, and Quattro Pro. The performance report shown in Exhibit 12-14 is a conservative example of the type of report an electronic spreadsheet is capable of making. It has been set up to automatically perform percent variance and certain operating ratio analyses of the actual and budgeted data entered into the performance report shown in Exhibit 12-13.

Another advantage of using a preprogrammed electronic spreadsheet for preparing the budget is its "what-if" capacity. Assumptions concerning percentage occupancy or multiple occupancy or average room rate can be changed and their impact on budgeted sales can be instantly seen. With such speed it is possible not only to prepare budgets for the most likely pessimistic and optimistic scenarios, but also for a broad range of possible sales plans. This enables management to understand the implications of, and react much more quickly to, unexpected situations.

DISCUSSION QUESTIONS

1. Why is budgeting often confused with forecasting or projecting?
2. What does the Uniform System of Accounts for Hotels allow top managers to do?
3. What is a key element of responsibility accounting?
4. Compare the three budget preparation methods. How are revenues expressed in the budgets? How are expenses expressed? What are the advantages and disadvantages of each?
5. Discuss the advantages and disadvantages of budgeting.

STUDY QUESTIONS

1. What are the ultimate financial goals for managers?
2. What are the three categories of budgets?
3. What are the elements of a good responsibility accounting system?
4. Where do the fixed charges show up on the budgeted income statement for the rooms department?
5. What is the main goal of cash budgets?
6. In which budget would one place the sale of assets?
7. What is another term for budgetary slack?
8. How does a new hotel establish an amount for budgeted room sales?
9. What are the ways we analyze actual operating results?
10. When we review only those accounts where there is a substantial variance between the budget and the actual results, we are using what management technique?

PROBLEMS

1. Which operation is more efficient? Why?

	Operation A	Operation B
Revenues	$8,000,000	$5,000,000
Expenses	$6,750,000	$3,895,000
Investment	$1,000,000	$800,000

2. (A) From the following data and for the months of January, February, and March, the New Hotel Company has asked you to prepare a:
    (1) budgeted income statement,
    (2) budgeted operating cash flow,
    (3) budgeted non-operating cash flow.
   (B) If a cumulative cash deficit appears in any month, list five measures you might take to eliminate this deficit.

Note: This company has an initial cash balance of $4,000 as of December 31 of the preceding year.

Sales

January:	$130,000
February:	$134,000
March:	$137,000

Sales collection percentages

Collected in month of sale:	70%
Collected later than 30 days after sale:	20%
Collected later than 60 days after sale:	10%

Expenses

Cost of sales

January:	$39,000
February:	$40,200
March:	$41,100

Payments for replacement inventory

Paid for in month of purchase:	70%
Paid for later than 30 days after purchase:	20%
Paid for later than 60 days after purchase:	10%

Payroll expense

$17,000 per month, paid monthly.

Rent expense for storage space elsewhere.

Prepaid three months' rent of $6,000 ($2,000 per month) on January 1.

Other operating expenses

Other operating expenses of $60,000 per month are paid as follows:

— 80% Cash

— 20% the month after they are incurred.

Depreciation expense

$10,000 per month.

Income tax rate is: 40%

It is company policy to pay income taxes for each quarter during the third month of the quarter (March in this problem).

		Date
Investing activities		
Purchased extra inventory to increase par stock.	$10,000	January
Made improvements in hotel restaurant	$60,000	March
Financing activities		
Sold additional common stock	$45,000	February
Borrowed from bank	$5,000	January
Borrowed from bank	$60,000	March

---

3. From the following data make a sales projection for next year for the ABC Hotel. These percentage increases are incremental. In other words, the 5% sales increase due to

room expansion should be added to, or subtracted from, any percentage changes produced by other factors.

	Annual Percentage Impact
(a) Long-term annual growth rate	8.00%
(b) Annual growth in previous three years.	3.00%
(c) Management plans a 25% increase in hotel rooms	5.00%
(d) Economy is recovering from a recession	1.00%
(e) The city where hotel is located is a historic site celebrating a centenary anniversary with numerous events of national interest planned throughout the year.	4.00%
(f) Most local hotels increased their number of rooms for this centenary celebration and occupancy is expected to decrease, even after lowering room rates as planned in (g) below.	−2.00%
(g) Hotel is restructuring its room rates towards the lower end in order to partially offset expected decrease in occupancy percentage. (If room rates were not decreased, it is expected that occupancy percentage in (f) above would decline by 5% instead of 2%.)	−1.00%

4. Use the following information to budget the expenses of the Growth Hotel for 2020, 2021 and 2022. You are in September of 2019 and you expect sales for 2019 to be $1,000,000.

   (a)   Expected annual growth in sales: 10%

   (b)   Expenses for the year 2019:

	Fixed Element	Percent Variable
Salaries and wages	$500,000	5.00%
Commissions	-0-	0.90%
Laundry and dry cleaning	$20,000	1.50%
Linen	$7,000	0.75%
Operating supplies	$10,000	1.40%
Reservations	$32,000	0.30%
Uniforms	$15,000	0.10%
Other	$22,000	0.20%

5. Prepare a fixed budget and a flexible budget for May based on the actual income statements for March and April shown below. Assume the revenue will increase by the same percent between April and May that it increased between March and April. Also for those expenses which increased between March and April, assume the growth trend will continue between April and May. It is your decision as to how you will budget expenses that decreased between March and April.

	March	April
Sales	$224,000	$226,240
Salaries and Wages	31,360	31,000
Commissions	7,400	7,450
Contract Cleaning	800	780
Guest Transportation	300	250
Laundry and Dry Cleaning	3,000	3,400
Linen	2,300	2,320
Operating Supplies	3,600	3,638
Reservations	5,500	5,535
Uniforms	400	435
Other	1,100	1,000
Departmental Income	$168,240	$170,432

Discussion Questions:

(a) Do you think the budgeted departmental income for May obtained using the above methods is reasonable? Explain why or why not.

(b) Which budget do you prefer, the fixed budget or the flexible budget? Explain why you prefer the budget prepared this way.

(c) Which budget do you think is the more accurate?

(d) Do you think it is wise to make budget projections based on month-to-month changes? Why or why not?

(e) Is there any additional information you would like to have in order to make your flexible budget more accurate?

6. Your hotel has budgeted sales of $4,455,000 for next year, a 20% increase over this year's sales. It can achieve this sales growth by making one of the following changes, or some combination of these changes:

(1) increasing its average room rate to $79.

(2) increasing its occupancy percentage to 90%.

(3) increasing the days it is open to 360 days.

(4) increasing the available rooms to 300 rooms.

The hotel's sales of $3,712,500 are currently being generated as follows:

Average Rate		Occupancy Percent		Days Open		Available Rooms		Sales
$66	×	75%	×	300	×	250	=	$3,712,500

Additional information:

(a) You have determined, based on past experience, that demand for your hotel rooms is quite elastic. Specifically, you have found that a 10% drop in average room rate will produce a 20% increase in occupancy percentage.

(b) The hotel currently closes during two months of the year because these months were so slow that it did not make sense to remain open. But you now believe that these two months have the potential to generate as much business as the other months of the year.

(c) It would cost $1,000,000 to build the 50 room addition. The hotel's variable cost per occupied room is $25. The additional fixed costs would be $400,000. The hotel currently generates a 12% average annual return on its total assets.

The calculation of the desired 20% growth in sales based on each of the changes (1) through (4) listed above is presented below:

Average Rate		Occupancy Percent		Days Open		Available Rooms		Sales
$79	×	75%	×	300	×	250	=	$4,443,750
$66	×	90%	×	300	×	250	=	$4,455,000
$66	×	75%	×	360	×	250	=	$4,455,000
$66	×	75%	×	300	×	300	=	$4,455,000

Question:

What change, or changes, would you make to achieve the budgeted sales goal? Explain at length, and with as much detail as possible, why you chose this change or changes. You may make more than one of the above changes on a partial basis in order to achieve the budgeted sales goal.

APPENDIX FOR CHAPTER 12

Account Number	Account Name	Revenues or Expenses Included in Each Account
Revenues and revenue-related accounts:		
01-401	Transient-regular	These first three revenue categories are self-explanatory.
01-405	Transient-group	
01-410	Permanent	
01-415	Other rooms revenue	Rooms rented for parties, conferences, and other non-resident purposes.
01-490	Allowances	Records special discounts and allowances.
Expenses:		
01-601	Salaries and wages	In addition to salaries and wages this account includes: vacation pay, bonus, and severance pay.
01-603	Employee benefits	Includes payroll taxes, health and other insurance, pensions, and employee meals.
01-606	Commissions	Includes commissions to agents for bringing business to the hotel.
01-609	Contract cleaning	Includes cleaning, exterminating, and disinfecting expenses contracted for outside the hotel.
01-612	Guest transportation	Includes expenses related to transporting guests to and from the hotel.
01-615	Laundry & dry cleaning	Includes cost of laundering and cleaning items that are billed by outside contractors and are directly related to the rooms department, including drapes, carpets and other room-related items. When a hotel has its own laundry, a portion of the cost is allocated to this account.
01-618	Linen	Includes rental (or expired cost, if owned) of all towels, bed linens used in guest rooms as well as such items used in other areas of the rooms department.
01-621	Operating supplies	Includes cleaning supplies, guest supplies, and office supplies.
01-624	Reservations	Includes all expenses related to any reservation service the hotel may have.
01-627	Uniforms	Includes the rental (or expired cost, if owned) of uniforms and uniform-related expenses, such as mending.
01-630	Other	Includes any item that does not fall under any other expense category.

Index